Pioneers and Plodders

The American
Entrepreneurial Spirit

Other Books by Robert C. Baron

Author or Contributing Author
Colorado Rockies: The Inaugural Season
Concepts of Digital Logic and Computers
Digital Logic and Computer Operations
Footsteps on the Sands of Time
Hudson: The Story of a River
Microelektronics 1, 2, and 3
Micropower Electronics
Twentieth Century America: Key Events in History
Twentieth Century America: One Hundred Influential People
What Was It Like Orville: Observations on the Early Space Program

Editor, with Contributed Essay
America: One Land, One People
The Best American Novels of the Twentieth Century Still Readable Today
Colorado: A Liquid History and Tavern Guide to the Highest State
The Fulcrum Reader
The Garden and Farm Books of Thomas Jefferson
Jefferson the Man: In His Own Words
The Mountains of California
Of Discovery and Destiny
Soul of America: Documenting the American Past, 1492–1974
Thomas Hornsby Ferril and the American West
Thoreau's World and Ours: A Natural Legacy

Pioneers and Plodders

The American
Entrepreneurial Spirit

Robert C. Baron

Fulcrum Publishing
Golden, Colorado

Text copyright © 2004 Robert C. Baron

Library of Congress Cataloging-in-Publication Data

Baron, Robert C.
    Pioneers and plodders : the American entrepreneurial spirit / by Robert C. Baron.
       p. cm.
    Includes bibliographical references and index.
    ISBN 1-55591-518-3 (hard cover : alk. paper)
    1. Entrepreneurship—United States—History. 2. Business enterprises—United States—History. 3. Businesspeople—United States. I. Title.
    HB615.B367 2004
    338'.04'0973—dc22

2004013716

Printed in the United States of America
0 9 8 7 6 5 4 3 2 1

Editorial: Alison Auch, Faith Marcovecchio
Design: Patty Maher

Fulcrum Publishing
16100 Table Mountain Parkway, Suite 300
Golden, Colorado 80403
(800) 992-2908 • (303) 277-1623
www.fulcrum-books.com

To Charlotte, Kay, Leo, and Marietta Baron,
and to all the entrepreneurs
who took the long view

There are always two kinds of people in the world—those who pioneer and those who plod. The plodders always attack the pioneers. They say that the pioneers have gobbled up all the opportunity, when, as a plain matter of fact, the plodders would have nowhere to plod had not the pioneers first cleared the way.

Think about your work in the world. Did you make your place or did someone make it for you? Did you start the work you are in or did someone else? Have you ever found or made an opportunity for yourself or are you the beneficiary of opportunity, which others have found or made?

—Henry Ford, Today and Tomorrow

Entrepreneur:
A person who organizes, operates, and assumes the risk of a business venture.

Contents

Preface

The genesis of this book occurred thirty years ago when, on a visit to Goodspeed's Book Shop in Boston, I found a 1904 annual report from American Telephone and Telegraph. I wondered how this company, started in Boston a few years earlier, had grown to become the largest company in the world. Then I began to watch as new companies were founded and industries developed in the fields of computers, semiconductors, space electronics, networks, medical electronics, and other areas. I knew many of the founders of these companies and knew of others from a distance. Ultimately, I had to wonder, what causes some companies to grow and some leaders to have a strong influence on the development of American business? At the same time, why do some companies, having established themselves, then disappear without a trace?

Over the years, I read and talked to others about these questions. *Pioneers and Plodders* is the result of this study. This is a book about business in America. But it is also a book about people, for business ultimately is people. People, not numbers—no matter what the bankers, financiers, or lawyers think. People, not machinery, factories, or computers—no matter what the manufacturers or technocrats claim. People as individuals, as groups working to move together in a direction, to develop and manufacture a product and satisfy a need, people as customers, as suppliers, as marketing, sales, and service. And people as leaders.

A friend once described an accountant as someone who counts the mice while the elephants gallop by. And certainly, a focus on the details of numbers not only misses the big picture, it usually misses the little things that make up an enterprise. The ability to have vision, to provide leadership in achieving that vision, the ability to select, motivate, and work with people—these are the essence of business leadership. For that matter, they are the essence of leadership in government, education, the military, sports, and other human endeavors.

I start with an assumption, which I want to get on the table immediately. I believe that individuals can and do make a difference, that good leadership leads companies and that bad leadership destroys them. I believe that the stories of most companies and industries can be examined through the eyes of a limited number of people who provide vision, leadership, and enthusiasm and build something of value.

I also believe that the entrepreneur is essential to the formation and growth of business. I worked for one of the entrepreneurs described in this book and have competed for years against another. From the 1950s on, I knew and talked to the people who started and built companies in communications, computers, electronics, semiconductors, and space equipment. To the business leaders I have been fortunate enough to know personally, as well as those I've read about, I owe a special debt of gratitude.

There are many ways to evaluate the past, just as there are the present. The lawyer looks at laws, the politician looks at elections, and the general looks at battles. The filter, or vantage point, that this book uses is to look backward in terms of jobs, technology, economic progress, and the development of new industries. And this is not just one view of the past, it may be the best. People need jobs and income. Those who are struggling for existence, for food, for shelter, for clothing are, except in rare cases, unlikely to think of elections, of laws, of education, of the past, of the arts. Jobs impart every aspect of political, professional, and personal life.

This book will therefore move backward to the seventeenth century and travel through to the twentieth century. Along the way, it will reveal some fascinating people and explore some important business developments. Technology and its applications are at the heart of American history, its politics, its society. This is the story of the entrepreneurs who developed technology and created the companies, the industries, and jobs and are of interest. How did they do it and what can they teach us today?

Acknowledgments

Many people have assisted me with this book and the research leading to it by providing their own examples and suggestions and, in some cases by reviewing and commenting on portions of the text. The interpretations, opinions, and mistakes contained herein are ultimately my responsibility.

I would especially like to thank Paul Bothwell, David Boyd, Sid Davidson, Bjoern Doerner, Carol Grossman, Ted Elliott, Ed Hampson, Kirk Kirchoff, Colin Knight, Jay Last, Drew Littell, Hal Miller, Bill Osgood, Sam Scinta, and Alan Watts. I would also like to thank my editors, Alison Auch and Faith Marcovecchio, and the book designer, Patty Maher. The writings on business history from the Newcomen Society of the United States as well as the authors of the books quoted in the text and bibliography have been of great value. I would also like to thank the staffs at the American Antiquarian Society, the Auraria Library, the Boston Public Library, the Denver Public Library, the Harvard Business School Library, and the Massachusetts Historical Society.

CHAPTER 1

Technology, Growth, and Employment

I do not know what I may appear to the world; but to myself I
seem to have been like a boy playing on the seashore, and
diverting myself now and then in finding a smoother pebble or a
prettier shell than ordinary, whilst the great ocean of truth lay all
undiscovered before me.
                                              —Sir Isaac Newton

For the things we have to learn before we can do them, we learn
by doing them.
                                              —Aristotle

Employment in the United States

The history of the United States is more than a history of its wars. Few people came
to this country to fight, although many people fought and many died in America's
wars. The history of the United States is more than a history of its presidents, sena-
tors, governors, and other elected officials. Few people came to this country to vote,
although millions of immigrants voted and did so proudly, as soon as they were able.
Most people came to the United States for a better economic life for themselves and
their families. They immigrated not just for freedom but also for bread. They came
here and continue to come to earn a living. America was created in our ancestors'
search for a better life for themselves and for their children and their descendants.

During the seventeenth, eighteenth, and early nineteenth centuries,
employment generally implied agriculture. But beginning in the middle of the
nineteenth century, the United States, like England, moved from an agrarian
society to an industrialized one. Most employment was created in industry, in
manufacturing, and in service jobs. The history of the United States is in fact a
history of employment, of jobs created and filled, of new companies, technologies, and industries. It is the story of employment and how companies and
industries are created that this book attempts to tell.

1

There has been significant growth in population and employment during the last two centuries. In 1830, the population of the United States was 12.8 million. By 2000, the population had increased to 281 million and is now more than three and a half times what it was at the turn of the twentieth century.[1] In the last century and a half, more than 60 million men, women, and children immigrated to the United States—27.5 million in the 50-year period between 1880 and 1930. These people came to the United States to build a better life.

Often, attention is focused on unemployment, but it is employment that should receive the attention. Throughout its history, the United States has been a country where jobs have been created, with more than 90 million jobs added in the twentieth century. In the last 100 years, the number of jobs created exceeded the total population of the United States in 1900.[2] The products and services produced by these workers affected how people have lived, where they have resided, and their health and standard of living. Employment has made the United States the promised land, as much today as yesterday.

Jobs affect which towns and regions grow and which shrink; which families and areas can afford to educate their children and which cannot; whether these children, once educated, are able to reside near their homes or whether they must migrate long distances in search of employment; whether families over time can improve themselves economically or whether they remain at the same economic and educational level; and whether towns, regions, and the entire country are strong economically, politically, industrially, and militarily. In 1890, less than 4 percent of Americans over the age of seventeen had graduated from high school; by 2000, the figure was more than 81 percent, and 95 percent of those aged fourteen to seventeen were in high school.[3] More than 15 million Americans were enrolled in college. The growth in the number of college and university graduates is also related to the employment and financial situation of their parents and the future opportunities possible for these graduates.

In a very real sense, then, the history of America is a history of employment, of jobs created and filled, of new industries and opportunities. Patterns of employment have changed; industries have been created, have expanded, and have then declined. In 1800, more than 70 percent of jobs were in agriculture. Through 1870, more than half the country's employment was in agriculture. In 1910, more than 32 million people worked on farms. By the end of the twentieth century, that number was fewer than 4 million. Other industries, such as textiles, steel, and railroads, have grown and then lost employment. But during the twentieth century, the total number of jobs has increased and is now more than 132 million.[4]

How are jobs created? Why do industries grow or shrink? What does the past tell us about the present, and what does it hint of the future? And looking behind the statistics and charts, what does it all mean for our country, for our communities and regions, for ourselves and our families?

The Permanence of Change

Companies, like people, are born, grow, age, and die. Every company was once a start-up, and every company, at some time, will close its doors and go out of business. And industries, which are the accumulation of many companies and many people, also are born, grow, age, and die. In the birth and growth phases, jobs are created, businesses grow, and financial benefits accumulate to be shared among employees, management, owners, and government in various ways and amounts. During the declining years, businesses shrink, jobs are lost, financial resources are used up, and the major concern becomes one of survival. These growth and decline phases are not always a function of age. As is true of people, some companies continue to grow and develop for very many decades, while others coast and become lazy, sick, and worn-out at an early age.

An examination of the Fortune directory of the 500 largest industrial companies or the Forbes list of leading companies over several decades shows a large number of companies that ceased to exist either through bankruptcy, merger, or complete change of business. During the same period, many new organizations were founded, grew, and became significant factors in the marketplace.

A reading of the annual report of one such young company indicates the energy of youth:

> *The development of the business during the past year exceeds that of any preceding year and this applies not only to an increase in the number of subscribers ... but to the development and extension of services. ... Present indications point to even larger growth in the business in the coming year ... as improved equipment and more intelligent methods of construction, maintenance and operation are put into use. A spirit of loyalty and devotion to the work pervades our entire organization throughout the country.*[5]

Although this quote could have been taken from any high technology company in California's Silicon Valley or along Massachusetts's Route 128, it was actually taken from the 1904 *Annual Report* of the American Telephone and Telegraph company (AT&T). In that year, AT&T had revenues of $18.5 million, operating profits of $11.3 million (60.8 percent of revenue), and paid dividends of $9.8 million (52.8 percent of revenue).

Another quote from the same report reads:

In some places in the country, particularly where there has been the demoralizing effect of unintelligent competition, the rates at the present time are too low. The service rendered is worth substantially more than users pay for it, and the net return to the operating companies in these particular localities is inadequate.[6]

In every young boy, there is the outline of the man. The character of a company may also be established early.

It is possible to look back on every successful company and discover the circumstances of its founding and how it grew. It is also possible to look at many established companies that have stopped growing and speculate on their prospects for a future life and independent existence. Companies are organisms that can grow or shrink, succeed or fail, live or die.

Jobs are not created automatically. Companies and industries grow, and jobs are created because individuals provide leadership and learn how to bring success to their companies and their industries. Jobs disappear and industries die because other people, in positions of responsibility, fail to provide this leadership. A winning business provides greater opportunities for all. Much has been written about the relationship between management and labor, but it is often overlooked that, with a decline in the business, there will be less to divide—a shrinking pie, with management, employees, and stockholders all obtaining less.

The creation of jobs and leadership in American business has a major impact on every aspect of American life. A successful and growing company influences not only its employees and shareholders, it affects suppliers, customers, and the community.

Can one person make a difference in the establishment and direction of a business? Andrew Carnegie believed so and expressed his opinion that someone trained within an industry could establish a new business or win a partnership in one that exists. He believed that experience was the foundation of growth and that the self-made person had an advantage.

I select the best known industrial establishments in each department, many of them the most extensive works of their kind and of worldwide reputation: Baldwin Works, for locomotives; Sellers & Co., Bement and Dougherty, for mechanical tools; Disston's Works, for saws; works of Mssrs. Dobson, and of Thomas Dolan, Philadelphia and Gary, of Baltimore, textile fabrics; Fairbanks, for scales; Studebakers, for wagons, who count their wagons by the acre; Pullman, of Chicago; Allison, of Philadelphia, for cars; Washburn and Moen, and Cleveland Rolling Mills, steel wire; Bartlett, iron founder, Baltimore; Sloanes, also Higgins, carpets; Westinghouse, electrical apparatus;

Peter Henderson & Co. and Landreth and Co., seeds; Harper Brothers, publishers; Peter Babbitt, for Babbitt's metal; Otis Works, Cleveland, boiler steel; the Remington's Works and Colt's Works, Hartford, firearms; Singer company, Howe, Grover, sewing machines; McCormick Works of Chicago, Balls of Canton and Walter A. Woods, for agricultural implements; steamship building, Roach, Cramp, Neafie, on the Atlantic; Scott upon the Pacific; Parkhurst, Wheeler, Kirby, McDugall, Craig, Coffinberry, Wallace, the leading officials of shipbuilding on our great lakes; horseshoes, Burdens; Atterbury Works, for glass; Groetzingers, tanning; Ames Works, for shovels; Steinway, Chickering and Knabe, pianos. Every one of these great works was founded and managed by mechanics, men who served their apprenticeship.[7]

At that time, at least, leaders were trained within companies. No one believed that management could be taught except by participating in the business, or that education was a substitute for business experience, or that a good manager could manage any kind of business. Then, as well as in a number of cases throughout the twentieth century, the character and success of a business and its founder were interdependent.

It is also worth noting how many of these businesses, which were leading companies at the turn of the last century, are no longer in existence. More recent examples of leading companies that have disappeared from the scene or no longer influence their marketplace are also numerous. Some names that come to mind include American Gulf and West Indies Lines, American Cotton Oil, American Woolen, Atlantic Sugar, Atwater Kent, Baldwin Locomotive, Bethlehem Steel, Central Leather, Chicago Gas, Cuba Cane Sugar, Curtis Publishing, Dumont, Firestone, Great Atlantic and Pacific Teas, International Match, International Mercantile Marine, Kaiser Motors, Maxwell Motors, Midvale Steel, Montgomery Ward, New York Central, Prairie Oil and Gas, Studebaker, Texas Corporation, U.S. Leather, Warner Brothers, Willys-Overland, Woolworth, and United Shoe Machinery.

There are three major reasons for the existence of a business: (1) service to customers by offering new products or older products with better features at lower cost, (2) the creation of jobs by growing a business, and (3) return on investment to the shareholders. In each of these areas, new businesses and developing companies often outperform more established operations.

So older companies can disappear, and new companies be born and become significant. What can be learned about the birth, growth, decline, and death of a company, and how does it relate to leadership?

High Technology and Transformation

It has often been said that large companies dominate most industries. Although this may be true in some established industries, it is almost never true for new industries or new technologies. Every industry was once young and, during its youth, was strongly influenced by new companies and a few very creative people, for example, Otto Mergenthaler and the Linotype typesetter, John Deere and the steel plow, Cyrus McCormick and the reaper, Alexander Graham Bell and the telephone, Henry Ford and the automobile, Glenn Curtis and Donald Douglas and the airplane, Chester Carlson and xerography, Edwin Land and instant photography, Pat Haggerty and Bob Noyce and transistors, and Ken Olsen and Steve Jobs and the minicomputer and personal computer. Each of their companies was young when new technological directions and industries were being established. Individuals make an essential difference in the birth and growth of enterprises by providing leadership at a time of opportunity and change.

History is also full of examples of older companies that could not cope with change—iron foundries that could not convert to Bessemer steel, buggy manufacturers that ignored the horseless carriage, and railroads that could not deal with changing passenger and freight requirements. But how prevalent is the inability to deal with change?

Generally, a change in technology results in a change in competition, even though established companies have substantial financial resources, a qualified technical staff, and good management. In 1955, vacuum tubes were used for all electronic switching and amplification in radios, television sets, and other products. The leading vacuum tube manufacturers were General Electric, Philco, Radio Corporation of America, Raytheon, Sylvania, and Westinghouse. Within a dozen years, the transistor had replaced vacuum tubes in most electronic applications. The dominant transistor companies were Fairchild, Motorola, National Semiconductor, Signetics, and Texas Instruments. Not one of the vacuum tube manufacturers, all very large and strong companies with excellent marketing and strong financing, became a significant factor in the transistor industry. As integrated circuits and then microprocessors impacted transistors, new competitors joined the market.

In 1960, the list of major computer companies included Bendix, Burroughs, Control Data, General Electric, Honeywell, IBM, National Cash Register, Philco, RCA, Remington Rand, Royal McBee, and UNIVAC. Some of these companies did not continue as factors in the large computer market, none were factors in the minicomputer market, and only one was a factor in the personal computer market. Instead, newer companies, including Amdahl, Apple Computer, Commodore, Compaq Computer, Computer Control, Data General, Datapoint, Dell, Digital Equipment, Hewlett-Packard, Microsoft, Prime

Computer, Seagate, Sun Microsystems, Tandem Computers, Tandy, Toshiba, and Wang Laboratories, were founded and grew into large companies.

A similar trend can be observed in many other industries in which technological changes have occurred. Core memories were superseded by semiconductor memories; no manufacturer made the transition. Mechanical calculators were replaced by electronic calculators, and competition changed. When analog watches were impacted by digital watches, when typewriters were replaced by word processors, or when movie studios were affected by television, the competitive character in each of these industries changed. No railroad is in the airline or trucking business, few gas producers became pipeline companies, and television producers and networks are suffering a similar fate as new approaches to cable and satellite television and home entertainment develop. A change in technology transforms the competitive environment.

Almost every industry was at one time considered high technology—the manufacture of textiles, steel, automobiles, glass, clocks, shoes, sewing machines, typewriters, radios, refrigerators, machine tools, tires, railroads, plastics, farm machinery, electrical equipment, elevators, and washing machines. When each industry was young, substantial new companies were established, and older companies, with older technology and great financial resources, were replaced. These established companies were unable, for a variety of both internal and external reasons, to apply these resources to a new technology or a new market. As industrial changes occur and companies age and die, resources are shifted to new industries capable of generating more jobs and often higher wages for their people.

The process of birth, growth, decline, and death continues today. It is worthwhile to study and understand the process of change, whether one is interested from a historical viewpoint or is evaluating one's career or investments.

Jobs and Companies

Where are the jobs in the United States? Despite the impression that large companies dominate the country and the world, most jobs are not found in the larger companies. There are more than 22 million businesses in America, and most are small companies. Each year, somewhere between 500,000 and 600,000 new companies are established, and more than 90 percent of them continue in business for a while, although in time, many go out of business. Small companies account for a major share of the employment and sales in the United States. If one were to add the employment figures in the 1997 *Fortune* magazine list of the 500 largest industrial companies, the 100 largest service companies, the 100 largest banks, the 50 largest retailing companies, the 50 largest utilities, the 50 largest financial companies, the 50 largest savings and loans, the 50 largest insurance companies, and the 50 largest transportation companies, the total number of employees for these 1,000 large United States companies would come to about 20 million people and account for less than 20 percent of American jobs. If one expands the list to evaluate the next level of very large companies, the total still does not include the majority of working Americans. More than half of the jobs in America are in companies with fewer than 500 employees.[8]

Small companies are to a large extent the strength of the economy and provide most jobs. The success and continued existence of the small company is highly dependent on its leadership and the entire company working together. Most entrepreneurs start their companies with few employees. Some of these new companies then become larger, and a very few grow to become significantly large organizations. Despite statements made by businesspeople and financial advisers that there is an economy of scale in business and that new companies cannot compete—something that this author believes a review of business history shows to be incorrect—some start-ups do grow into large and very successful organizations, and established companies disappear.

It is difficult to predict which new companies will grow into the industry successes, whether evaluating the first automobile companies of the 1890s and 1900s or the computer companies of the 1960s, 1970s, and 1980s. It depends on leadership. One individual can make a difference in the establishment and direction of a business when it is founded, and often, as it grows into a large enterprise. Recent examples that come to mind include An Wang, Bob Noyce, Ken Olsen, Steve Jobs, Michael Dell, and Bill Gates.

Companies, like babies, are born each year, and this is independent of whether being an entrepreneur is fashionable and whether little or a great deal of money is available for new ideas. Each year, for the last half century, about half a million new companies have been started. Perhaps 10 percent fail in the first year. In time, many of them go out of business, just as many people die each year. But from 1990 to 2000, the number of business births exceeded the number of business deaths by an average of 60,000 each year.[9]

To expand from one employee to ten, to satisfy a local need, to establish relationships with customers and vendors, to provide a payroll for many employees, these leaders and their companies are the successes of the business world. A small percentage of these new companies reach 250 employees and annual sales of more than $10 million. A few, a very few, go on to become substantial companies with annual sales of more than $100 million. The author's research indicates that the number is in the order of two to ten per year, which means that, since World War II, no more than 500 companies have reached that size. No more than 10 of the 500,000 companies started each year become very large.

Table 1.1 lists 108 companies founded in the last 50 years, with 20 or more selected from each decade. Each of these companies started with a few people, and each became a major corporation. Together, these companies had peak revenues of more than $1.1 trillion and had total employment of more than 5.2 million employees. The revenue of these companies is greater than the 2000 gross national product of the Scandinavian countries of Denmark, Finland, Norway, and Sweden, plus Switzerland, Ireland, and the Czech Republic combined. These companies, which did not exist fifty years ago, have added more jobs than the entire population of thirty-five states.

Small does not necessarily mean always small, nor does large always mean growing, secure, or stable. Large and established companies often decline in employment, and some go out of business regardless of the economy. Some business executives earn large salaries and bonuses for laying off thousands of employees based, in many cases, on what was a failure of executive leadership. In each of the ten years of the 1980s, according to surveys by the American Management Association, roughly one-third of American companies cut their payrolls. Taken together, the Fortune 500 companies eliminated 3.2 million jobs in the 1980s.[10] In the 1990s, employment declined in a number of large companies, including Dow Chemical, DuPont, Eastman Kodak, General Mills, General Motors, LTV, Minnesota Mining, Philip Morris, United Technologies, and Xerox, whereas others, including Digital Equipment, Firestone, Montgomery Ward, and Mobil, ceased to exist as independent companies. But new companies and small companies created additional jobs, and total employment kept increasing. Each decade, companies, like babies, have been born, while some companies, like some adults, have died.

The Rise and Fall of American Industries and Technologies

This book opens with a short history of the first two and a half centuries of American business. It then focuses on four technologies and industries that have impacted American life and created significant employment opportunities and are now in various stages of the aging process. In discussing these industries—steel, automobiles, electronics, and computers—an attempt is made to describe not only what happened, but how it happened. Each industry is examined by itself and through the life of one individual who provided significant leadership in the establishment, direction, and growth of the industry during its formative years.

These industries were selected for two reasons. First, each is very large, with annual revenues in the hundreds of billions of dollars, and each has provided many millions of jobs. These industries have created not only manufacturing jobs, but also have made possible significant new service industries. For example, the development of the motor vehicle not only resulted in significant manufacturing jobs at General Motors, Ford, Chrysler, and American Motors and for their suppliers in the steel, tire, glass, and plastics industries, but it also created jobs in new service industries, including automobile dealers, gasoline service stations, fast-food restaurants, motels, shopping centers, road construction, insurance, long-distance trucking, taxicabs, and buses, that would not have been possible without the widespread availability of the automobile.

Second, each of the four industries described has had a profound effect on the development of the United States and the world. Steel became the basic building block in most late nineteenth- and early twentieth-century manufacturing, including railroads, ships, automobiles, machinery, weapons, and farm implements. The automobile changed America in major ways and affected where people lived, worked, shopped, and vacationed. Electronics became the building block of the twentieth century and, through the development of telephones, radio, and television, changed what people saw and heard, how they communicated, and what they knew and believed. Advances in semiconductor electronics also made possible advances in other industries, including computers and communications. Computers are having a major effect on recordkeeping and productivity, on business and education, and on the availability of information and calculating power to people everywhere. If knowledge is power, then the computer is the tool to provide that power to people anywhere in the world.

The lives of four business leaders are examined in an attempt to evaluate the leadership process. Although they have been outstanding leaders, they are also representative of other entrepreneurs who helped to build these industries. These four men—Andrew Carnegie, Henry Ford, David Sarnoff, and Kenneth Olsen—have much to teach us. Their experiences are reviewed and some of their ideas on management are quoted. In many respects, those who have created companies and industries have had a greater influence on this country than the politicians, generals, educators, artists, writers, and scholars.

These and other leaders recognize that things take time. To build companies and industries, one has to have a vision of where one wants the company to go and the ability and patience to lead it there. The executive who is concerned with the daily stock price or the quarterly earnings is unlikely to build anything of lasting value. The good business leader recognizes that short-term ups and downs, problems, and challenges are the heart of business. And success in business, as in life, is not measured daily or quarterly.

Businesspeople, like politicians, are dependent on the economic, social, and cultural environment in which they live. But, as with all leaders, they are eventually measured by what they do with these resources. The creation of jobs has largely been the effect of good leadership. The decline and destruction of established companies has largely been the result of poor leadership.

Entrepreneurs control the use of market, technology, and economic factors in all stages of business. Therefore, growth or decline is largely the long shadow of management. The availability of capital, land, and resources is secondary. Examples of this idea will be given throughout the book, but the reader has only to think of New England in the nineteenth and early twentieth centuries or Japan in the late twentieth century to realize that business success is more dependent on good management than on the availability of resources. Good leadership is essential and will be addressed throughout this story.

Why do some business leaders build major enterprises? What are the characteristics of successful entrepreneurs? Why do some companies disappear through acquisition or bankruptcy? How important is leadership and how is it identified? These are some questions for the reader to keep in mind.

In summary, this book examines four industries from a historical viewpoint and four business leaders from a biographical viewpoint. To understand an industry, one should read both the history of the industry and of the individual leader. For example, it is impossible to understand the automobile industry without knowing about Henry Ford.

In chapter 11, certain observations are made about the nature of change, growth, and performance in technology, in business and on an individual level. The chapter also addresses the issue of leadership and some of the factors encouraging and inhibiting it. For those readers who wish to explore an industry further, an extensive bibliography is included, listing a number of references about the history of each industry and its leaders.

Table 1.1. Examples of start-ups that became large companies

New Companies of the 1950s

Automatic Data Processing	Consolidated Freightways	McDonalds	Roadway Express
Burger King	Control Data	Medtronic	Ryder Systems
Coastal	Digital Equipment	Millipore	Thermo Electron
Computer Control	Fairchild	National Semiconductor	Tosco
Computer Sciences	Maxxam	Nucor	Wang Labs

New Companies of the 1960s

Advanced Micro Devices	Data General	Intel	Storage Technology
American International	Comshare	The Limited	Teledyne
Analog Devices	Electronic Data Systems	MCI	TJX
Applied Materials	The Gap	Nike	Tyco
Comcast	HCA	Science Applications	Wal-Mart
Cyprus Minerals	Humana	SCI Systems	Waste Management

New Companies of the 1970s

Amdahl	Cardinal Health	Louisiana-Pacific	Southwest Airlines
American Management	Computer Associates	Micron Technology	Starbucks
Apple Computer	EMC	Prime Computer	Tech Data
AutoZone	Federal Express	Reebok	Toys "R" Us
3C Com	Genetech	Seagate Technology	Turner Broadcasting
Cablevision	Health Management	Solectron	Western Digital

New Companies of the 1980s

Adobe Systems	Cisco Systems	Home Depot	PeopleSoft
America Online	Compaq	LSI Logic	Perot Systems
Amgen	Cypress Semiconductor	Maxtor	PETsMART
Auto Nation	Dell Computer	Microsoft	Staples
Blockbuster	Electronic Arts	Office Depot	Sun Microsystems
Charles Schwab	Gateway	Oracle Systems	Tandem Computers

New Companies of the 1990s

Abgenix	CIENA Corporation	Google	Overture
Amazon.com	EarthLink	Juniper Networks	Palm
Broadcom	eBay	Level 3 Communications	Qwest
Caremark	Frontier Airlines	Openware	Yahoo!

Two Hundred Years of American Business

As the world grows more and more complex, and as its complex-
ities come to conceal an increasing number of pitfalls which can
drop the whole human race straight down into the starless dark
if they are not noticed in time, it becomes more and more
important for men to understand their own history, to see how
former trials were met, to learn how some of these pitfalls
develop, and to get the knowledge they must have if they are to
make their way through the perplexing and ominous twentieth
century. Above all things, they need to know the story of their
own past, and if they don't get it from the historian they won't
get it from anybody—not, at least, in a form that will be of any
use to them.

—Bruce Catton

From the first European settlements in the early seventeenth century, America was principally an agrarian society. Yet through the years up to 1860, changes occurred that led to the rapid industrialization of the United States in the nineteenth century, increasing in speed and extent during and after the Civil War. It is this story that this chapter will tell.

The Colonial Period

The exploration and settlement of the New World has often been described in terms of religion—the Catholics in New Spain and New France, and the Pilgrims, Puritans, Baptists, Anglicans, Calvinists, Unitarians, Quakers, and Catholics in the English colonies, all seeking religious freedom. Yet a case can be made that the first colonizing expeditions in America were business ventures that made profits by sending settlers to the New World to set up trade and bring riches back to Europe.

The Spanish explored Florida, Mexico, and the American Southwest, looking for the gold and silver they had found in South America. They did not find large amounts of riches, but they did leave a permanent cultural imprint, with settlements in Mexico, the Caribbean, Florida, and Santa Fe in the seventeenth and eighteenth centuries, and the establishment of printing presses and universities in the New World—a century before the English.

New France was first administered by companies of merchants holding royal charters. It was not until 1664 that French North America passed under the direct supervision of the Crown to be administered by court favorites as well as businessmen. The Hudson's Bay Company, with substantial financial backing, moved settlers to North America. French explorers, priests, and traders looking for fish, furs, and other valuable resources established trading posts and explored the land at both ends of the Mississippi. In 1621, the Dutch granted a charter to the Dutch West India Company, a private business, to trade and colonize the land along the Hudson River, which eventually became New Amsterdam. Delaware was settled by the Swedish New South Company in 1638. The English kings James I, Charles I, and Charles II awarded large land tracts in the colonies to favorite individuals and charter companies to establish colonies in America and bring back wealth to the English shareholders. The kings paid little attention to these settlements, whereas English merchant capitalists, through joint stock companies, invested in colonizing projects and increasing trade.

In 1584 and 1585, Sir Walter Raleigh sponsored two trips to America and attempted a settlement at Roanoke, Virginia, to seek new worlds for gold, for praise, and for glory. An American colony might make England a self-sustaining nation.[1] He named the new land Virginia in honor of Queen Elizabeth I, the virgin queen. In 1609, the Virginia Company, located in London, received total responsibility for government in their settlements and in 1619, with the export of tobacco from the New World, began to earn some returns on its investments. The Plymouth Company started the first settlements in Maine and Massachusetts in the early seventeenth century. Maryland was settled in 1632 on land granted to Lord Baltimore, who managed the colony as a sovereign territory. The king granted a charter to a group of investors for the Carolinas; Georgia trustees sent James Oglethorpe to establish Savannah; and the Puritans received a charter to settle the Massachusetts Bay Colony. In 1681, William Penn received the land that became Pennsylvania because the king, Charles II, owed money to Penn's father, Admiral Sir William Penn. While some of these settlements started as trading centers, they grew from that original purpose.

These chartered companies enabled sponsors to spread risks and rewards among many investors. Profits for some of the settlements were divided between stockholders in England and the planters in the colonies who supplied and controlled labor. The shareholders for most of these real estate development ventures were typically London merchant capitalists, and stockholder meetings were held in England. The Board of Trade and the Privy Council were major groups concerned with colonial matters, with members of Parliament, minor officials, and clerks controlling the laws and regulations for the colonies.

Because most of the seventeenth-century settlements were privately sponsored, they were widely scattered along the eastern seaboard and had only vague land grants. And since various proprietors and chartered companies controlled the colonial land, power gradually shifted from England to the New World. Generally, settlers came to the New World to obtain land for farms and to advance economically; opportunities for owning land were much more restricted in England. It is accurate to state that the colonies were started as business ventures, and most of the colonists came to improve their lot in life.

The population in colonial America grew fast. By 1650, 50,000 English immigrants had settled in the New World; by 1700, 250,000; by 1750, 1,170,000; and in 1775, at the onset of the Revolutionary War, about 2,500,000 people had settled in America. Most of these people were farmers, and cities were small. In 1700, Boston was the largest city with 6,700 people; New York and Philadelphia were next with 4,900 and 4,700 people, respectively.[2] These cities collected agricultural and other colonial products for export and shipped British goods to farmers, with the merchants often being the source of credit. In 1790, when the first federal census was conducted, less than 3 percent of the population lived in towns of more than 10,000 people. New York, the largest city, had 33,000 people, Philadelphia about 28,000, Boston 18,000, and Charleston, the largest city in the South, had just 16,000 residents. Salem, Massachusetts, was the seventh largest city, with 7,921 residents. Many eighteenth-century immigrants were from Germany, Ireland, and Scotland and had little loyalty to England. They and the other colonists wanted more independence from English control.

Fish were abundant in the North American oceans, lakes, and streams. Beginning in the sixteenth century, the English and French made money by catching large amounts of fish off the Atlantic shore. By 1675, more than 600 colonial vessels were fishing for cod. By 1700, a large proportion of Boston's population of 12,000 earned their livelihood from the sea. The New England fishing industry at the end of the colonial period was the colonies' largest business with more than $1 million in exports annually.

Although some of the New England settlers earned their living from the sea, three-quarters of the economic activity occurring in America prior to the Revolutionary War took place in agriculture. In the seventeenth and eighteenth centuries, agriculture remained largely a manual operation, employing techniques and tools differing little from those of medieval Europe. The farmer relied on his family for labor, and therefore farms were small. The principle differences between European and American agriculture lay in America's abundance of land and scarcity of labor. In Europe, limitations on the availability of new land dictated conservative farming methods such as crop rotation, careful tilling of the soil, and the use of manure. In America, with seemingly unlimited land resources, these conservation procedures were extravagant and unnecessary. Fields were cleared and then abandoned when productivity declined.

The first settlers had to focus on cultivating the soil and feeding their families. Hence, the first industries related to subsistence: agriculture, carpentry for home building, the blacksmith, the wheelwright, the gristmill and the sawmill, and the preparation of clothing. But the colonists needed other items in order to survive. In 1644, John Winthrop Jr. petitioned the Massachusetts General Court:

> *Humbly sheweth that wheareas these plantacions much abounding with rockie hills the nurceries of mynes and minearalls may probablie conteyne not only the most necessarie mynes of iron ... but alsoe with mynes of lead, tynne, Copper and other metalls noe lesse profitable to the Countrye.*[3]

Winthrop asked for a monopoly operation, free of taxes, to extract the minerals for stamping mills and refineries. Furthermore, colonial authorities encouraged through subsidies the immigration of craftspeople and mechanics, building of dams and mills, local manufacturing of many items, including leather tanneries, and the production of iron, glass, yarn, and clothing. Winthrop soon established the Hammersmith ironworks on the Saugus River in Massachusetts, which flows from the swamps into Massachusetts Bay.

Farming was a difficult occupation. The northern farmers were able to grow the Indian crops of corn, beans, squash, and pumpkin; in addition, they brought from England the turnip, the onion, the parsnip, and the cabbage. They also began to raise imported swine and cattle to add to the deer, turkeys, and migrating fowl they could get hunting and the fish and clams they could get from the lakes and rivers. They grew grass and hay to feed the livestock. Later, farmers added sheep, goats, horses, and poultry, and apple, pear, and quince trees to complement the wild berries and grapes they found. They also grew the English grains of wheat, rye, and barley in their fields.

A farmer's wife had to make the most of her family's belongings. She spun the thread from wool or flax (linen), dyed it, and wove it into cloth; made the clothing, soap, and candles; preserved meats, fruits, and vegetables; churned butter; and made beer. Wood was made into buildings and furniture, leather was tanned, nails were made from wood or bog iron. The remoteness of villages made for self-reliance—a need for farmers to build and repair items on their own.

Surplus crops and natural resources were shipped to England. In 1676, Edward Randolph, the English customs collector for New England, sent a list of exports to the Commission for Trade and Plantations. He listed cod, mackerel, fat herring, furs, bar iron, cattle, hogs, horses, sheep, wheat, rye, barley, oats, flax, corn, peas, potatoes, flour, lumber, and all things necessary for shipping—pine for masts, pitch, tar, and hemp. Northern colonies shipped grain, flour, meat and fish, furs, pig iron, ship timbers, and lumber; and southern colonies shipped rice, tobacco, sugar, silk, and indigo to England and the West Indies, and as early as 1644 were bringing back from the Indies peppers, oranges, and limes, and from England, fruits, wine, iron, wool, and luxury goods.

In America, with poor transportation except along the Atlantic seaboard, farmers had trouble getting their surplus crops to domestic and overseas markets. Moreover, agriculture remained largely marginal throughout some of the country, providing little more than subsistence. In the southern colonies, staple crops such as tobacco, sugar, and rice were produced for export. Most of the profits generated by these commercial crops were expended in personal consumption rather than contributing to capital accumulation. And for colonists, money and credit were rare or nonexistent, except from British lenders or local merchants.

Starting in the seventeenth century, the Europeans established a relationship with the colonies in which the New World would supply raw materials and in return would receive manufactured goods. New England had a plentiful supply of the timber, wine, and fish that were needed in England. Trade was controlled from Europe, and there was an outflow of wealth from this hemisphere. But the colonists wanted to control their own affairs.

The colonies developed their own institutions, including local assemblies to control their financial and political destiny. However, in the late seventeenth and early eighteenth centuries, England began an attempt to regulate the colonies. A colonial office was organized, and royal governors were sent to North America. England's economic control of the colonies was established through a series of laws called the Acts of Trade Navigation. Trade had to be in ships owned by Britain and with crews of British subjects. Some products could only be shipped within the British Empire, including tobacco, indigo, rice, molasses, sugar, and furs. This gave the raw materials to England, which might in turn ship them, at great profit, to other places. Most goods from Europe had to be shipped through a British port, giving the English a monopoly on shipping to the colonies. The colonies were forbidden to trade directly with France, Spain, and the Dutch and French West Indies. Finally, the colonies were forbidden to export certain products anywhere since these were British monopolies. Examples included, at times, fur hats, finished iron and steel products, and woolen goods.[4] The Woolen Act of 1699 prohibited the export of woolen cloth beyond a colony's borders. That same year, Parliament forbade the export from America of wool yarn, cloth, and paper. The colonies could send pig iron but could not have rolling mills. The British Law of 1750 read: "No mill or other engine for slitting or rolling of iron shall be erected in His Majesty's Colonies of America." Clearly, England wanted the colonies to be dependent.

From the beginning, there were exceptions, as the colonists attempted to achieve financial and political independence. New Englanders in particular were involved in trade and manufacturing because for many it was the only way they could survive and prosper. Commerce and trade provided the greatest opportunities for innovation and experimentation in the pre-Revolutionary period. Colonial ships took goods to Great Britain, to the West Indies, to Newfoundland, and between the colonies. British policy was that the colonies only be sources of raw materials to be shipped home to England in English and colonial ships. But the colonists ignored English laws, including the Molasses Act of 1733, and increased trade with the French West Indies and other non-British areas.

In the eighteenth century, Britain imported from America wood for ships, since much of the British forests had been cut down. Shipbuilding was started early in the colonies because of the abundant forests with tall, straight white pines that could be used for masts, the closeness of the sea to the forests, and the cheap labor in the colonies. The related industries—sail-loft making, block making, rope-walk production, masonry, painting, rigging, sail making, smithing, instrument making, and carpentry—provided employment to many. There were shipyards all along the Atlantic coast. By 1670, a total of 730 ships had been built in Massachusetts. In 1676, a Massachusetts report listed the ships owned and built in Massachusetts, with 30 of them over 100 tons and 200 between 50 and 100 tons. By 1760, the colonies were producing a total of 300 to 400 vessels a year, selling them in the colonies, to England, and to the West Indian colonies. The main building centers were Boston, Charleston, Salem, Ipswich, Salisbury, Massachusetts and Portsmouth, New Hampshire. Over the next quarter century, Newbury, Scituate, and Plymouth, Massachusetts; Taunton, Rhode Island; and Kennebec, Maine, joined as centers of shipbuilding. The sale of colonial ships to British customers provided American merchants an important source of income to pay for their imports.[5]

Some manufacturing did take place in the American colonies before the Revolution. These industries were mainly restricted to consumer goods produced for local markets, however, and were practiced largely by a few skilled craftspeople located in the larger urban centers of New York, Boston, Charleston, and, particularly, Philadelphia. American craftsmen included hatmakers, pewterers, printers, candle makers, tanners, sawyers, carpenters, shoemakers, and smiths. Some worked in the larger towns, some in the villages. The artisan techniques employed in the production of furniture, shoes, clothing, carriages, and metalware allowed little scope for innovation or experimentation. As in Europe, these skills remained the property of a closed class of artisans and were transmitted through apprenticeships. But apprentices were hard to find and to keep. Ben Franklin's story of running away from his service as a printer's apprentice to his brother and fleeing to Philadelphia was not uncommon.

Under these circumstances, it is easy to see that tradition rather than experimentation would predominate, with small shops and industries subject to localized demand. Limited goods were available on the farms and in the smaller towns, and there were major transportation problems involved in reaching these markets. But colonial authorities tried to encourage local manufacturing in order to lessen their dependence on Britain.

With a shortage of labor in the early colonial days, people had to do many things for themselves. Tradespeople had to be jacks of all trades. The printer became papermaker, binder, writer, ink maker, bookseller, and in some cases, postmaster. He also was often a public printer, printing all the government documents; the printer of the only local newspaper; and the source of all news and gossip. A carpenter was frequently a cooper and cabinetmaker.

America had two major advantages over England: a plentiful supply of raw materials and a great supply of energy—initially waterpower and then coal. America's disadvantages during the eighteenth century were a limited supply of labor, a limited local market, poor transportation—except along the seacoast—and inadequate capital to finance business expansion. Throughout the first century of its settlement, the American colonies traded mainly with England or outside North America rather than with one another.

The country provided virtually unlimited space for agricultural expansion, and hence from New York south, only limited interest was found in promoting trade. The region most involved in commerce was New England, an area of rough climate, rocky soils, and only marginal agriculture. Limited by harsh land and weather, New Englanders sought their opportunities on the sea. By the middle of the seventeenth century, they were already exploring trade openings as far afield as the Azores and Africa; by the middle of the eighteenth century, they dominated trade in several Caribbean and Atlantic ports. In addition, unlike their plantation counterparts in the South, New England merchants had little inclination toward conspicuous consumption. Most profits were plowed back into commerce, and businesses grew as they were passed from generation to generation. Furthermore, the very nature of trade demanded the development of versatility and business acumen. In the days of sail, individual shipmasters had to be given wide scope in purchasing and selling decisions; credit systems extended from Salem to Suriname; and new business techniques like "the Italian method of bookkeeping" (i.e., double-entry bookkeeping) were adopted to keep closer account of profits and losses. Given this tradition of commercial adventurism and willingness to experiment and take risks, it should not be a surprise to find that New England would lead America's industrial revolution in the decades following its political revolution.

East Coast rivers don't go very far into the interior; the Charles and Merrimack Rivers run only a few miles west. Furthermore, The Hudson and the Connecticut run north and south. Thus trade had to be by sea. With trade by sea, there was a need for large ships and navies to protect shipping, and British domination of the seas was essential to protecting colonial ships.

As noted earlier, early trade was controlled by Britain and often conducted on British ships. By 1771, the colonies were importing $4 million, mostly manufactured goods, and exporting $1.3 million, mostly raw materials.[6] The Revolutionary War changed the nature of trade between America and Britain and was a watershed in America's economic growth. It both affected trading patterns and increased the need for locally manufactured goods.

American Independence

At the time of the Revolutionary War, Britain had the strongest navy and one of the best armies in the world. During the war, the Americans could not match the British in the manufacture of guns, ships, cannons, bullets, clothing, and the other necessities of modern warfare. Americans were dominant only in total labor supply, and even there the British often had the military advantage. So without dominance on either side, the war dragged on from 1775 until 1784.

The Revolutionary War meant economic as well as political independence for the United States. To a large extent, though, economic independence was achieved with a great deal more reluctance. The Declaration of Independence in 1776 suddenly cut off America from English sources for basic manufactured goods. As noted previously, manufacturing was limited in both the kinds of goods America was capable of producing and in its ability to reach wide markets. Even for simple but essential items like iron nails, Americans had relied almost exclusively on English imports (although Thomas Jefferson had a small nail-making machine installed at Monticello). Thus, revolt against English authority necessitated the development of some basic manufacturing industries in the new nation. In addition, American commerce, although independently developed, had been largely tied to British or British-controlled markets. Continuing attachment to these older markets created a centrifugal tendency that for a time threatened to detach New England from the rest of the nation. This situation was probably the reason Rhode Island failed to send delegates to the constitutional convention of 1787, and why secession was first proposed at the Hartford Convention of 1814–1815.

The ending of the Revolutionary War created opportunities for American trade and economic growth. Restrictions against manufacturing were removed;

the colonists could buy and sell where they wanted. Moreover, some people amassed personal fortunes during the war, allowing them to contribute greatly to postwar expansion. For example, George Cabot of Massachusetts, who began his career as a privateer, became a leader in America's China trade after becoming wealthy during the war. This trade was part of the rapid diversification of New England commerce seeking new markets abroad to replace those lost as a result of war and independence from Britain. After the Revolutionary War, American vessels found their old ports of call closed to them, and they needed to find new trading partners. In February 1784, *The Empress of China* left New York for a trip around Cape Horn to Canton, China, carrying a cargo of ginseng, with which it made very large profits. Tea, silk, chinaware, and other products were brought back home. Much of the China trade was centered in the small town of Salem, Massachusetts. By 1784, New England ships had carried the American flag to places as far away as India, China, and Saint Petersburg. So prevalent were New Englanders in the expansion of American trade that in many markets New England became synonymous with the United States. Native Americans of the northwest coast supplying otter skins to Massachusetts merchants used the name "Boston" to refer to the nation as a whole, and merchants of the South Pacific thought of Salem as a country unto itself.

According to the census of 1790, farmers made up about 90 percent of the labor force.[7] George Washington was a farmer, and Thomas Jefferson believed that "those who labour in the earth are the chosen people of God."[8] But Alexander Hamilton believed in industry, banking, and commerce. As secretary of the treasury under President Washington, he had written the *Report on the Subject of Manufactures* in 1791 and had rejected the notion that the country could grow based only on agriculture. Hamilton encouraged manufacturing, expansion of trade, protection of America's young industries through tariffs, and American technological innovation. He also helped create the First Bank of the United States, which was based on the Bank of England.

Hamilton in a letter referred to

the boundless extent of territory we possess, the wholesome temperament of our climate, the luxuriance and fertility of our soil, the variety of our products, the rapidity of the growth of our population, the industry of our countrymen, and the commodiousness of our ports.[9]

Hamilton believed that the inventive genius of the American people would make the country prosper and be independent of Great Britain. In his *Report of Manufactures*, he wrote that invention-driven manufacturing industries in the North linked to agricultural suppliers in the South would make the country economically strong and independent.

Hamilton's Reports were not discrete projects. They formed a coherent design. Settling America's debts would fortify its credits; credit would allow manufactures to develop; a diverse and flourishing economy would generate the revenue that would ensure the debt's proper funding.[10]

Independence contributed in another way to American economic growth. After the conclusion of the Revolutionary War, both the national and state governments found themselves burdened with extensive public debts. Following the proposals of Alexander Hamilton, all public debts were now assumed by the national government. They reached $45 million in 1811, increased during the war of 1812, and then were completely eliminated by 1835. The United States became one of the first nations in history to pay off accumulated war debts, establishing a reputation for creditworthiness that attracted foreign capital investment in the early years of economic expansion. Moreover, Hamilton significantly increased the sale of securities, including federal and state government bonds and stocks in banks and insurance companies. In 1790, there were three state banks; by 1800 there were twenty-nine; by 1829 there were 329.[11]

Commerce continued to expand, with American shipping handling 124,000 tons in 1784 and rising to 981,000 tons after the Revolution. During the War of 1812, however, exports declined from $61 million in 1811 to $7 million in 1814, and imports dropped from $53 million to $13 million. After the war, conditions improved. Exports climbed to $93 million by 1818; imports soared to $147 million by 1816, providing additional goods but, for a time, glutting the market and hurting the new manufacturing firms.

Although short of capital, the young United States was still one of the most developed countries, with a relatively educated populace who had a strong interest in technology, a desire to push to new lands, an eagerness to exploit natural resources, and a flourishing ocean commerce. And the population kept on growing. Between 1800 and 1850, the population of the United States grew from 5.3 million to 23.2 million, and the proportion living west of the Alleghenies increased from 27 percent to 45 percent.

The country invested much of the capital it did have into infrastructure development. And of the $188 million provided by the national government for canal construction, about 30 percent was raised through loans from British banks—one cannot overemphasize the importance of these British investments to the growth of the American economy. The United States had to be interconnected and the subject of transportation will be discussed shortly. Prior to the expansion of canal construction beginning in the 1800s, midwestern farmers faced transportation costs that virtually prohibited their contact with eastern markets. By the 1840s, the development of direct transportation routes made possible the expansion of commercial farming in the states of the Old Northwest territory, raising per capita incomes and leading to the growth of a national market for commodities and labor.

In a very real sense, then, the Revolutionary War was a watershed in America's economic development. Independence led to the development of new external and internal markets for American goods. These new markets in turn created new conditions and new needs that would lead to a dramatic diversification of the American economy and the creation of an entirely new system of manufacturing.

With the Revolution and the embargoes during the War of 1812, America was forced to be more self-sufficient. Eventually, population increased and national markets began to develop. But transportation was still a problem until the opening of the canals in the first half of the nineteenth century and the development of the railroads in the mid- to latter years of the nineteenth century. Capital remained a problem until very late in the nineteenth century, despite the opening of international trade, and most businesses were small and sold their products to a local market.

Trade, Raw Materials, and Early Manufacturing

The industrial revolution started in England in the eighteenth century. It was characterized by four major innovations: (1) the use of waterpower and the coal-based steam engine, (2) the development of power-driven machines to replace human beings for spinning thread and weaving cloth (3) the bringing together of large numbers of workers in a factory production system, and (4) the use of furnaces for making iron ore into finished products. (The latter will be discussed in the next chapter.)

The industrial revolution changed the way first England and then the United States produced goods, and it decreased the costs of production. In England and America the manufacture of cloth was for centuries primarily a cottage industry, with a spinning wheel and a loom in the farmhouse. A farmer's wife had to make most of her textiles, spin the thread from wool or flax, dye the thread, and weave it into cloth to make clothing. As the need for textiles increased and production expanded, most of the work continued to be done in the home and was usually combined with farming. A farmer might have several looms in his house, and the entire family might work on the material together, carding (disentangling and cleaning fibers), spinning (making threads or yarn), and weaving (combing individual yarn into fabric). In addition, the material was usually dyed or bleached for color. Starting in the mid-seventeenth century, however, technical innovation in Great Britain started to change traditional textile manufacture.

A major innovation was the steam engine, which was first successfully developed in England by Thomas Newcomen and patented in 1705. His engines were initially used to pump water from the Cornish tin mines. They also were widely used to pump water and increase the supply of drinking water. Then, in 1769, James Watt developed a different design for the steam engine, one that increased performance. The steam engine enabled machine power to be substituted for animal and human power and provided an almost unlimited supply of energy, first in mines and then in cotton mills.

A number of innovations in the textile industry also occurred at this time. In 1764, James Hargreaves invented a machine that enabled a spinster to spin ten threads at a time instead of just one. He named it the spinning jenny after his wife. Later improvements allowed up to eighty threads to be spun simultaneously. Then Richard Arkwright in 1769 invented a spinning frame that was driven by waterpower to produce fine yarns; Samuel Crompton invented the spinning mule that could spin finer and more regular yarns; and Joseph Jacquard, a silk weaver in France, developed a way of instructing the loom in the patterns to be woven. Edmund Cartwright developed a power loom, and in 1802, William Horrocks patented an improved power loom. By 1850, there were 250,000 power looms in Britain.

Four materials were used in the making of cloth. The Romans had introduced flax (linen) to England, and the woolen industry dates back to the Middle Ages and used wool from local animals. Silk was also used for making cloth. Cotton was first imported into England in the seventeenth century. Imports of raw cotton from the West Indies and the American colonies in 1751 reached 3.8 million pounds. By 1790, they had reached 31.5 million pounds. Wool dominated for most of the eighteenth century, representing one-third of British exports in 1770, but cotton became the dominant material in the nineteenth century. The woolen trade was supported by the landed interests, whereas the newer industrialists supported cotton. With the rising of the industrial revolution, new economic forces began to control the English government.

Traditionally, wool was put into households where it was spun into yarn and then the yarn returned to weavers. Cotton would be cleaned and then spun into yarn or thread. When yarn availability was no longer a limitation, the individual weavers could not keep up with the supply. Arkwright's water frame had a capacity of several hundred spindles and demanded more power—waterpower from the streams and rivers and then steam engines. Eventually, specialized mills that integrated spinning and weaving machinery in a single building were opened, employing hundreds of workers.

Britain was poised for industrialization. Capital, backed by a sound banking system, was available. Internal and international transportation was improved, and the government was supportive of business. Soon came the large woolen textile mills in Derbyshire, Nottingham, Somerset, Worcester, and Yorkshire, and the cotton mills of northern England. The towns of Liverpool, Manchester, Birmingham, Bristol, and Norwich grew with the textile industry.

This change affected not only the manufacture of cloth, it also induced workers to leave the farms and move into the cities. Moreover, it brought demands for even better transportation systems, for social and educational services, and resulted in the accumulation of capital, enabling additional business expansion in England.

British trade increased significantly with the development of the factory system, and Britain had a goal to supply the world with a majority of its textiles and it succeeded. Britain became the strongest power economically in the world. The United States became the major source for Britain's yarn and the leading market for the British cloth and iron industries.

Cotton was grown in the New World before Europeans settled there. In the eighteenth century, Southern upland cotton was so poor in quality that colonists only used it for homespun clothing. Cotton was too expensive for large-scale manufacturing since large amounts of labor were necessary to hand-separate cotton from its seeds. In 1793, Eli Whitney invented the cotton gin, a machine that could remove the seeds from cotton balls, and the cotton gin substantially increased worker productivity. Whitney was unable to collect royalties from his patent and made little money from his invention, but it made the South wealthy, with cotton crops doubling every decade for forty years to supply the mills of England and New England. Production soared from 2 million pounds in 1791 to a billion pounds in 1860. By 1840, the United States was producing more than 60 percent of the world's cotton, and cotton accounted for more than half of American exports. By 1856, the United States was supplying 87 percent of the world's cotton.[12]

Samuel Slater was born in 1768 in Derbyshire, England. He worked in England for Jedediah Strutt, the partner of Richard Arkwright, inventor of the water-powered spinning machine. Employed by Strutt for eight years, Slater grew in responsibility and became superintendent of Strutt's mill. He developed a complete understanding of Arkwright's machine and memorized how the English machines were assembled. Soon Slater knew how to build as well as operate a textile mill. In 1786, he had completed his indenture and, three years later, decided to go to the United States, obtain additional financing, and start a yarn factory of his own. However, Parliament had passed laws forbidding the export of any textile, glass, clock, or other manufacturing equipment; plans for them; or the emigration of their skilled artisans to countries outside the empire for continuing their trade. Nevertheless, Slater slipped through and went to the United States.

When his ship docked in New York in November 1789, Slater heard about Moses Brown, a wealthy Quaker merchant from Providence who wanted to duplicate the English system of textile production. Slater contacted Brown about an opportunity to copy the cotton textile mill where he had worked in Derbyshire, England, and along with William Almy (Brown's son-in-law) they formed the firm of Almy, Brown and Slater.

On December 20, 1790, Samuel Slater introduced the first successful American cotton-spinning mill on the Blackstone River in Pawtucket, Rhode Island, in what may have been America's first factory. He hired entire families, including children, to work in the mill. He developed mill villages, in which employees lived, worked, and shopped. They attended company schools and churches. By the third year, he had thirty employees, many of them children. Young children, some only four to ten years old, were hired to work in the mills, and their wages went to their family. Later, Slater constructed additional mills in Massachusetts, Connecticut, New Hampshire, and Rhode Island. Life in the mills was difficult, with long hours, air filled with fibers that caused respiratory diseases, cold in winter, hot in summer, and danger from the machines.

Eli Whitney and the Connecticut Valley Inventors

Although Eli Whitney is traditionally credited with the invention of the Uniformity System, as described below, he was only one of several New England manufacturers to begin employing this system at about the same time. In 1798, Whitney received a contract from the U.S. War Department to produce muskets—one that promised to deliver one thousand muskets in only twenty-eight months. This was an extraordinary contract, which Whitney assured the government he could fulfill with his new manufacturing process. Whitney also invented some of the first machine tools, including milling machines, and he expanded the system of interchangeable manufacturing parts. Furthermore, he hired and trained the workers required in his factory.

If manufacturing complex goods was broken down into a number of simple operations, production could be accomplished without resort to any skilled labor. Instead, complete tasks could be performed by machines operated by unskilled laborers, who could turn out greater quantities of more uniform goods than an equivalent number of craftspeople. Moreover, uniformly made machined parts would be interchangeable, so that if one part of the whole were to fail it could be easily replaced with an equivalent part on hand rather than a part that was handcrafted to fit the specific finished product.

This concept seems so obvious, and has become so commonplace, that one can only wonder that it had not been hit upon earlier. In fact, it had. In the 1780s, the Frenchman Honore Blanc had employed a system of interchangeable parts in the manufacture of muskets. Interest in Blanc's process had faded, however, with the advent of war with England, creating a high demand for weapons the French government felt could be more comfortably met by tried-and-true artisan methods.

By January 1801, Whitney had received advance payments totaling $10,000, the final delivery date of the contract had passed, and yet he had failed to deliver a single musket to the War Department. Under pressure to produce evidence of good faith, he put on a demonstration that has become famous in the annals of American business. In the presence of President John Adams, Vice President Jefferson, and several cabinet members, Whitney disassembled ten musket locks, spreading their parts out on a table. He then asked the men present to choose parts at random and reassemble the ten locks, thus proving that he had developed a new procedure of manufacturing with interchangeable parts. So impressed were those present that the government not only granted Whitney an extension on the contract, but advanced him a further $15,000 prior to the delivery of the first stand of arms.

Until the 1960s, this demonstration stood as unquestioned proof of Whitney's invention of the Uniformity System. By that time, however, various researchers had noticed that Whitney's muskets, including those delivered under the 1798 contract, were "not even approximately interchangeable."[13] Furthermore, individual lock components carried special identifying marks, indicating that they were not standardized parts. Other manufacturers and craftspeople, notably Simeon North, John H. Hall, Oliver Evans, Thomas Blanchard, Samuel Colt, and Eli Terry, probably deserve greater credit for the development of the Uniformity System of mass production.

Notwithstanding this, Whitney still deserves some credit for advancing American industry. First, although he may not have been so clearly the developer of standardized manufacturing techniques as was formerly believed, he continued to speak out as the greatest advocate of the system during his lifetime and should be honored for furthering its acceptance. Second, Whitney was very cost conscious—one might even say penny-pinching. He was the first manufacturer to apply truly modern cost accounting techniques, adding depreciation, insurance, and interest costs into the production process. For this contribution, all modern manufacturers should be grateful.

Development of the American System of Manufacturing

As noted, independence had cut the United States off from its former sources of basic manufactured goods. Although the simplest of these goods could be provided by local workshops, a demand for more complex commodities would eventually necessitate the emergence of larger-scale manufacturing capabilities.

In Europe, large-scale manufacturing had relied on the availability of skilled labor in combination with a large pool of cheap unskilled labor. In America, however, there were shortages of both skilled and unskilled labor owing to the large amounts of available low-cost land. Because of this labor shortage, wages in the United States, particularly for unskilled labor, averaged much higher than in Europe. If Americans were to be able to compete with Europeans in the American market and provide their own manufacturing capability, then the country's higher priced labor had to be made more productive. Before the turn of the nineteenth century, a number of American businesspeople had hit upon a method for increasing productivity. The essential innovations in American manufacturing during this time derive directly from this shortage of unskilled labor and the desire to hold down wage costs by replacing human skills with machine skills.

The American System of Manufacturing might be more precisely dubbed the "New England System" since the experiments that created it were all tried for the first time in manufacturing facilities in Massachusetts, Rhode Island, and Connecticut with the use of interchangeable parts. The second component of the American System was the Lowell system of factory organization. In 1790, an English immigrant named Samuel Slater had established America's first cotton-spinning facility on the Blackstone River near Providence, Rhode Island. Although this marked the introduction of new technology to the continent, Slater's spinning factory operated along the lines of English textile enterprises, performing only one of the processes in the manufacturing of cloth. Not until 1814 did Francis Cabot Lowell truly revolutionize the manufacturing process. Lowell, a Boston aristocrat and graduate of Harvard class of 1793, had been involved in trade. In 1810, he traveled to Britain, supposedly on a vacation. While there he visited several cotton mills with his friend Nathan Appleton, a Boston financier. Lowell, an imaginative and well-connected businessman, then formulated plans to open his own cotton mill.

In 1814, the world's first factory to convert raw cotton into cloth by power machinery was erected in Waltham, Massachusetts, by the Boston Manufacturing Company under the leadership of Francis Cabot Lowell. In order to eliminate problems of timing, shipping, coordination, and quality control, Lowell put all processes in the manufacture of cloth under one roof. Simply put, raw cotton came into the factory and finished cloth left. Employing this simple strategy, Lowell and the Boston Company merchants were able to produce miles of cloth every year. Capitalized at $600,000, a very large sum at the time, the mill initially employed more than 300 workers, mostly young women recruited from neighboring farms. The women were paid good wages, lived in supervised boardinghouses with good food, and had many self-improvement programs, including a literary magazine. Most women worked in the factory for a few years and then returned home.

A quest for greater waterpower brought the company north to the Merrimack River where the town of Lowell was established in 1822. By 1826, Lowell's business, now called the Merrimack Company, was making 2 million yards of cotton per year. Within a short time, the town of Lowell was the textile-manufacturing center of the country. By 1850, the population had grown to 32,000 people tending 300,000 spindles and 9,000 looms. The factory was organized by department, with cost accounting introduced and production and selling managed in detail.

An adequate supply of waterpower, workers who were willing to leave the farms for better-paying factory jobs, and the availability of capital from an existing merchant class enabled New England to become the center of the textile industry for more than a century. Textile factories grew throughout the region, such as Amoskeag, founded in New Hampshire in 1810, the Ipswich mills in Massachusetts in 1818, the York Manufacturing Company of Maine in 1831, and numerous other mills throughout the area.

Furthermore, after 1815, it was possible to maintain in the United States a diversified cotton and woolen industry employing only domestic raw material. Introduction of saxony sheep and improvement of merino and other breeds increased the quality of the wool.

These two concepts of manufacturing, the Whitney Uniformity System, which broke down the manufacturing system into a number of easily replicated steps, and the Lowell system, which brought all manufacturing together under one roof, served as the basis for the rapid industrial expansion in the nineteenth century. Together these two innovations in manufacturing would become hallmarks of American industrial production. Mass production of finished goods within one facility would allow American industry to rapidly catch up to, and soon surpass, the leading nations of Europe. Moreover, these techniques, based not on the application of craftspeople's skill, but rather on know-how and ingenuity, could be applied to the production of nearly any commodity. By the second half of the nineteenth century, American industry would be producing everything from sausages to steel rails, from cameras to combines, using methods pioneered by experimental entrepreneurs such as Eli Whitney, Simeon North, Francis Cabot Lowell, and Eli Terry. The American System of Manufacturing also led to the industrialization of New England with larger organizations, economies of scale, and the decline of cottage industries.

Some Nineteenth-Century Growth Industries

The development of American business can be examined by looking at the history of several major industries, including machine tools, guns, sewing machines, clocks, agricultural implements, and shipbuilding. In each of these industries, the United States went from a position of copying English and European products to a position of technological and manufacturing leadership, and in some cases became a significant marketing force. America began to build a position of worldwide leadership that it would hold for the next century.

Unlike the Mississippi, the Missouri, and the Ohio, which became rivers of exploration and commerce, the rivers of New England only travel short distances.

But in the eighteenth and nineteenth centuries, they became the rivers of industry. The Charles meanders around eastern Massachusetts but never gets more than twenty miles from Boston. The Blackstone goes but a short distance from its origin in central Massachusetts before it empties into the bay in Rhode Island. The Merrimack flows from its base in New Hampshire into Massachusetts, a trip significantly less than 100 miles. The longest of the New England rivers, the Connecticut, flows from near the Canadian border at Bloomfield, Vermont, to empty into Long Island Sound near Saybrook, Connecticut. Along the banks of these rivers, the industries of New England grew. These rivers provided waterpower, ways of getting finished products to the sea, and a source of labor among those who did not want to work on farms anymore and were looking for better opportunities. Moreover, the distances between these New England business centers are short, and many inventors influenced one another.

The essence of economic growth and development, as Joseph Schumpeter pointed out, is entrepreneurship.[14] Entrepreneurs may or may not be innovators, but they are always experimenters; they are individuals able to recognize new opportunities and willing to take the risks necessary to develop those opportunities. In examining the basis of America's dramatic industrial expansion beginning in the nineteenth century, it is worthwhile, therefore, to seek out what in the American economy was new and different from traditional techniques, particularly European traditions, and who the entrepreneurs were who promoted these technical and economic experiments.

Once, most items were made of wood—barrels, baskets, wagons, carts, wheels, rakes, plows, hoes, looms, fences, clocks, shovels, hammers, axes, saws, and other tools. Specialized woodworking machinery—saws, planes, and machines for shaping, boring, and mortising—were valuable in a country with a vast abundance of forest products. But in the nineteenth century, America went from a wood-based to a metal-based economy. And to create and work metal, a machine-tool industry was necessary. The next chapter will discuss iron and steel. To use metals, tools are needed to work the metal and for interchangeable parts, the metalworking must be precise.

By the end of the nineteenth century, iron and other metals were used for a variety of new purposes, including making nails, screws, cutlery, clocks, iron pipes and tubes, hand tools, stoves, drills, wrenches, pumps, sewing machines, muskets, rifles and cannons, carriages, locomotives, bridges and rails, lathes, molding machines, wire, locks, waterwheels, roads, printing presses, skyscrapers, elevators, looms, carding machines, spoolers, shearing machines, knitting machines, shoe-making machines, paper-manufacturing machines, musical instruments, scales, and ships. Although many of these technologies had employed metal before the nineteenth century, the amount used and the number of products made increased significantly. The metalworking industry made modern industry possible.

A machine tool is a power-operated metalworking machine, having one or more tools used for removing metal accurately in the form of chips. Machine tools are the basis for all modern industrial production. A craftsperson could work wood by hand by using a hammer and chisel, but no machinist's hand was strong or steady enough to hold a scraping tool against a piece of iron for more than a few minutes. Machines had to be made to hold and cut metal. There are many individuals and companies that developed this technology and built the lathe, the plane, milling machines, and the cutting tools, measuring tools, and fixtures that allow metal to be worked to specific tolerances. And many of the inventors and innovators in American industry, including Eli Whitney, developed their own tools.

Some major names worthy of mention here include Thomas Blanchard of Worcester, Massachusetts; Joseph R. Brown and Lucien Sharpe of Providence, Rhode Island; David Wilkinson of Pawtucket, Rhode Island; Frances Pratt and Amos Whitney, who joined forces in 1860 to start a precision machine tool company; the Ames Manufacturing Company of Chicopee Falls, Massachusetts; Robbins and Lawrence of Windsor, Vermont; the Norton Company of Worcester; Gage, Warner, and Whitney of Nashua, New Hampshire; and many others. Most of the nineteenth-century businesses could not have developed without two things: the availability of metal and the ability to work it to increased tolerances.

One of the major industries in the nineteenth century was the manufacture of weapons—rifles, pistols, and cannons. The availability of firearms enabled the West to be settled, the buffalo and other game to be hunted more efficiently, and gave the country the firepower to make the Civil War deadlier than all prior American wars taken together.

Colonists used the rifle, with powder and shot. The Pennsylvania and Kentucky rifle makers lengthened the barrels and narrowed the bore to make the rifle more accurate for long-distance hunting. John Hall in 1813 proposed that the rifle be loaded at the breech rather than at the barrel. He also manufactured the locks by machinery using interchangeable parts and made them at Springfield in the 1820s. Another early manufacturer was Thomas Blanchard of Worcester, who developed a copying machine for turning the stocks of rifles, using a model to key the machine.

Samuel Colt was born in Connecticut in 1814. He devised a six-barreled rotating barrel and then modified the design so that all bullets exited through a single barrel. He obtained a patent for the revolver in 1835, and the first major sales of his five-shot revolvers were to westerners, including the Texas Rangers who used them to fight Indians. A thousand of these revolvers were used in the Mexican War. Ranger Captain Samuel Walker wanted a heavier gun, a .44 caliber six-shooter, so Colt designed the Walker gun, which found an even larger market. Colt started a large factory in Hartford, Connecticut, to make 5,000 revolvers per year and hired Eliza Root to run it. Colt adopted the concept of interchangeable parts, with 80 percent of gun making done by machine. Root, a mechanical genius, invented many belt-driven machines for turning, boring, and barreling gunstocks, and making cartridges. In 1851, Colt exhibited 500 of his guns in London at the first World's Fair. He received many orders and soon opened a branch factory in England on the banks of the Thames. Firearms continued to improve, American guns were sold widely in Europe, and with better armaments being manufactured in the North, they became a major factor in the Union's victory in the American Civil War.

In the eighteenth century, clocks were made one at a time. In 1793, Eli Terry of East Windsor, Connecticut, the father of the clock-making industry, started his own business and began to make wooden clocks by the hundreds. He traveled around the countryside by wagon and sold his thirty-hour clock to farmers and merchants. In order to increase his clock production to the thousands, Terry adopted the technique of using interchangeable and standardized parts. He then assigned one villager to each workstation to make one part. Skilled mechanics improved the machine that made the most precise parts, and Terry started mass production using brass and steel to make 1,000 clocks in his factory in Plymouth, Connecticut.

In 1808, Eli Terry began to make 4,000 identical clocks simultaneously. In 1814, he patented his thirty-day, weight-driven shelf clock that sold for $15. His factory became the training ground for many future leaders, including Seth Thomas, Silas Hoadley, and Chauncey Jerome. In 1837, Jerome started a new factory in Bristol, Connecticut, and built 40,000 brass movements. Jerome shipped his excess production to England where his clocks sold at much lower prices than the standard English clocks. English dealers began to import them in large quantities. These clocks—many driven by the steel and brass works of the new machine age—were eventually built in the hundreds of thousands and sold around the world.

In 1849, Aaron Dennison of Boston and Edward Howard of Roxbury formed the American Waltham Watch Company. Earlier, Dennison had visited the Springfield Armory where he saw how modern manufacturing techniques were being applied to weapons. By 1854, the Waltham Watch Company was able to make five watches per day, and by 1880, 425 watches per day. Costs came down, and an increasing number of Americans could now afford a watch.

In 1790, an Englishman named Thomas Saint patented the first sewing machine. Four Americans, John Adams Dodge (1826), Walter Hunt (1832), Elias Howe (1845), and Isaac Singer (1851), also developed the sewing machine. The sewing machine, unlike most inventions, led to decentralization because it allowed people to work at home. It also was one of the first laborsaving devices for the housewife. In the years between 1860 and 1869, 1.5 million sewing machines were sold, and in the ensuing ten-year period, another 4.8 million.[15] In the year 1860, 116,000 sewing machines were manufactured, with 3,000 salespeople going door to door to sell them. This implied not only efficiency of manufacturing but also significant developments in sales and marketing.

Wagons were turned out by hand until 1830, after which they were mass-produced. The new Concord Coach could carry ten passengers plus a driver at speeds up to eight miles per hour. A wagon produced in the Conestoga Valley of Pennsylvania became the most versatile method of moving goods westward for almost a century. Modern manufacturing techniques (i.e., mass production) were also applied to tanning leather; making shoes, paper, and clothing; building textile and other machinery; and hundreds of other products.

The Americans in the colonies had built ships for the British Empire since the seventeenth century. Starting in the nineteenth century, Americans began to build the best ships in the world for themselves. The country needed a variety of sloops, schooners, and other ships for worldwide trade, for fishing, and for whaling. Until the railroad system was built across the country, most transpiration was by ship—the steamships along the rivers and waterways of America, with California and the Oregon territory reached by ships sailing around Cape Horn.

One of America's most important figures was Nathaniel Bowditch. Raised in Salem, Massachusetts, Bowditch went to sea in 1795 when he was twenty-two and retired a wealthy man eight years later. He taught himself math, navigation, surveying, and even Latin so he could read scientific books. At the time, navigation was a crude science at best, and captains found their way by dead reckoning. Latitudes (north and south) were fairly simple to gauge, but longitudes (east and west) were difficult to estimate in the days before chronometers (accurate shipborne clocks). Then, in 1802, the first edition of Bowditch's the *New American Practical Navigator* was published. In his book, Bowditch included a new method of calculating longitude by using a sextant to measure the angular distances from the moon to certain fixed stars. He also included navigational aids, tides, and astronomical tables. The *New American Practical Navigator* ultimately went through sixty editions and became the standard for navigation.

The ability of American shipbuilders to build faster boats with large carrying capacities that were manned by smaller crews enabled America to trade at an increasing rate. Traders, merchants, and whalers from Salem, Marblehead, Nantucket, and other coastal regions visited all the oceans of the world. Fishermen left the northeast ports and went to the Grand Banks off the coast of Newfoundland, returning with their holds full of fish.

But it is perhaps with the building of the clipper ships that Americans reached their peak. Clipper ships were high-speed sailing vessels built for the

China, East Indies, and California trade. John Griffiths built the first true clipper ship, the *Rainbow,* which was launched in January 1845 for the China trade. It sailed to China in ninety-two days and home in eighty-eight. The names of the clipper ship designers, including Isaac Webb, David Brown, William Webb, and Henry Eckford, and their designs are known to all who love American sailing ships. Donald and Lauchlan McKay designed and built many ships, including the *Ocean Monarch,* the *Daniel Webster,* the *Stag-Hound,* and the *Flying Cloud,* perhaps the most beautiful and the fastest of the clipper ships.

In the 1840s, there was heavy passenger traffic from the East Coast to the California goldfields, and for decades trade increased from the United States to points around the world, especially Asia. By the middle of the nineteenth century, the American sailing ship was dominating the race for speed on the world's oceans.

Transportation

In the seventeenth and early eighteenth centuries, colonial settlements were within a few miles of the Atlantic coast. Trade and communication were by sea. But with the Revolution, and especially with the Louisiana Purchase in 1803, the United States moved westward. How were these new settlements to be reached and how was trade to be accomplished?

Although the colonies had seemingly unlimited land to the west, people needed a way to get themselves as well as supplies there. The Allegheny Mountains slowed westward migration, and without safe, efficient ways of transporting goods, westerners needed a high degree of self-sufficiency to survive. Many of those who moved west settled near the Ohio and Mississippi Rivers and their tributaries so that agricultural products could be floated downstream by raft or boat. If more people were to move west, there had to be better ways of getting supplies to them and getting their farm products out.

The years between 1770 and 1860 saw major changes in transportation. In addition to ocean trade, there were three other major developments during the eighteenth and early nineteenth centuries: the development of roads and turnpikes, the building of canals—especially the Erie Canal—and the start of the railroad system.

Improved transportation increased trade, lowered distribution costs, and helped create a national market. Westerners became producers and consumers of goods, with grain and lumber sent from the West, and leather, textiles, wagons, tools, and other products sent from the East.

The first innovation in transportation came with the development of turnpikes and toll bridges between 1776 and 1830. In 1790, the first private turnpike was built. In 1808, the federal government authorized the construction of the Cumberland Road from Baltimore to the Mississippi. The War of 1812 heightened the need for roads as problems with transporting troops and supplies to the Canadian border became apparent. This growth in turnpikes resulted in a network that by 1820 had connected all of the major eastern cities. Turnpikes were often privately financed, with the tolls paying the investors and financing improvements. In New York alone, there were 900 miles of toll roads by 1807. However, these roads did not really solve the problem of transporting large amounts of goods and raw materials. Roads were still few and in bad condition, and freight could only be moved by horse and ox-drawn wagons. Roads were usually compacted dirt and were not kept in good condition. During summer, the roads were muddy, and during the winter, snow-covered. Only in spring and fall were they passable, and even then mud could impede movement.

Thomas Newcomen and James Watt invented the steam engine, and at first, it was used in factories and mines. But with the invention and production of the steamboat by Oliver Evans, John Fitch, John Stevens, and Robert Fulton, the steam engine was applied to transportation. Oliver Evans had developed an automated flour mill, received the third patent given by the new government in 1790, designed a high-pressure steam engine in 1804, and developed a steam-driven boat that went down the Schuylkill River. The boat was an amphibian, and Evans drove it onto land and into the city center. On August 26, 1791, Nathan Reede of Warren, Massachusetts, received a patent signed by Thomas Jefferson and George Washington for a land carriage—"a simple method of moving land carriages by means of steam." Samuel Morey of Fairlee, Vermont; William Henry of Lancaster, Pennsylvania; James Rumsey of Virginia; and John Fitch of Connecticut all built and operated steam-driven vessels before 1790. Rumsey probably deserves the credit for the first; in 1786 he designed a mechanically driven boat. On August 26, 1791, Fitch was granted a patent for the steamboat, but it was John Stevens and Robert Fulton who commercialized the vessel.

Robert Fulton, born in Pennsylvania, was a painter who went to London to study with Benjamin West. While there, he turned his attention to engineering and designed and patented a method of raising boats in a canal without using locks. He continued to work as a painter and an inventor in London and Paris. In 1806, he returned to the United States and completed the design of the Clermont, a steam-driven ship. He demonstrated the steamboat with a trip upriver on the Hudson from New York to Albany in 1807. Two years later, he put a successor on Lake Champlain. He received a twenty-year monopoly on New York waters and a similar exclusive on the waters of the lower Mississippi. In 1814, Fulton and Edward Livingston began to offer regular steamboat service between New Orleans and Natchez. Fulton steamboats for the Hudson along with ferries connected Manhattan with New Jersey and Long Island. After 1830, the entire East Coast became alive with steamboats, some complete with luxurious dining and sleeping quarters. By 1848, steamships were running between the East Coast and California.

It was easy for river traffic to go downstream from the Ohio and Missouri River basins down the Mississippi to New Orleans on rafts and keelboats. However, getting goods upstream was very difficult, if not impossible, and often the crew walked home and then built another boat for the next load south. Steamboat building continued in the United States because the Hudson and the Mississippi were ideally suited for steamboat travel. Robert Livingston, a signer of the Declaration of Independence, started the Mississippi Steamboat Company in 1809 and built the *New Orleans* in 1812. By 1820, there were sixty steamboats on western rivers, with many traveling the lower Mississippi. Steamboats were largely responsible for the growth of Mississippi River commerce as well as travel on the Great Lakes. The steam engine solved the problem of getting upstream, growing from 17 boats handling 3,290 tons of freight in 1817 to 727 boats handling 170,000 tons in 1855.

In the twenty years after 1814, annual steamboat arrivals in New Orleans increased from 20 to 1,200. By 1838, the United States had at least 800 steam engines in boats, 350 in locomotives, and almost 1,900 in mills and plants.

Canals were another major innovation during this period. The major East Coast rivers flow north and south and do not connect together. Canals were designed in part to overcome this geographical obstacle. Several canals were started in the 1790s, including the Santee Canal in South Carolina to connect the Santee River to the Cooper River and then into Charleston Harbor, the Middlesex Canal in Massachusetts to connect the Merrimack River to the Concord River, and the Schuylkill Canal near Philadelphia.

In the 1780s, it was proposed that a canal be dug across New York from Albany westward that would connect the Hudson River to the Great Lakes and the West. Then, in 1800, Gouverneur Morris advocated a waterway to link the Hudson River and Lake Erie, and a route was laid out in 1809. New York mayor DeWitt Clinton and John Stevens pushed the idea, and in 1817, the New York legislature authorized construction of the Erie Canal with DeWitt Clinton as the project's chairman. Parts of the canal were opened in 1820, and the canal was finished by 1825 when boats could go from New York City to Buffalo and then onward to the Great Lakes. The Erie Canal, 363 miles long, was 4 feet deep and 42 feet wide at the top. In 1826, the Erie Canal took in $700,000 in tolls. Ultimately, the canal reduced the cost of shipping one ton of goods from Albany to Buffalo from $100 to $15 and cut travel time between Albany and Buffalo from twenty days to ten, with passengers able to travel a mile and a half per hour for a cent and a half per mile. A flood of immigrants began their journey west by canal, and New York City soon became the commercial metropolis of the country.

By 1840, when the era of large canal building ended, many canals had been built, including from Portsmouth on the Ohio River to Cleveland, and from Cincinnati to Lake Erie. Later canals were constructed, although at a slower rate, including the Chesapeake and Ohio Canal; the Wabash and Erie Canal in Indiana, which allowed shipments south to the Ohio and then on to New Orleans, or north to the Great Lakes and via the Erie Canal to New York City; a canal system partway from Philadelphia to Pittsburgh; and a canal from Lake Michigan at Chicago to the Illinois River. Canals were supported by state governments and in some instances by the federal government. Occasionally, the federal government granted right-of-way to the canal builders, a forerunner of railroad-expansion financing.

In 1830, there were 1,277 miles of canal in the United States; by 1840, there were 3,326, and by 1850, 3,698 miles. Canals do, however, have problems as a method of transportation. Floods and droughts affect them. Canals can freeze in winter and become impassable when water is low. Furthermore, they only function on level ground. In the end, many canal companies failed because revenue never met costs.

In 1826, John Stevens demonstrated the feasibility of steam locomotion on a circular track in Hoboken, New Jersey, and the era of railroads in America officially began. In the next few years, steam-driven rail transit began to claim the transportation world from canals and turnpikes. Railroads improved the national transportation system. The railroad industry became the first large national business with improvements in technology, finance, marketing, and management. Railroads were cheaper to build than canals and could go almost anywhere. And, unlike canals, there was no winter-freeze period. Unlike roads, trains could supply their own power. In 1828, work began on a railroad that would stretch between Baltimore and Ohio. In 1830, there were 73 railroad miles in operation in the United States; in 1840, there were 3,328 miles; in 1850, the number grew to 9,021; and by 1860, there were 30,600 railroad miles in the United States.

In the early days, most railroads were in the Northeast, with the Boston and Lowell Railroad, the Boston Worcester, and a variety of lines in New York and Pennsylvania. In 1840, New England had 2,083 miles of track, whereas the Old Northwest had only 89 miles. But, as will be described in chapter 3, railroad technology developed alongside the steel industry, and the railroads began to move across the land. The national rail network grew from 35,000 miles in 1865 to 93,000 miles in 1880.

In the 1850s, the government began to send out survey teams to plan a transcontinental railroad that would reach the new state of California. Because of differences between the North and the South about the desired route, the railroad was not built until after the Civil War.

Railroad technology was instrumental in developing travel and trade within America. It provided the opportunity for mass manufacturing combined with mass distribution.

Finance, Agriculture, and the Industrialization of America

In colonial America, there were no banks because the British would not allow them. There was relatively little money—only some Spanish, English, Dutch, and French coins; paper money issued by colonial governments; and notes backed by some commodity. Credit was from England or local merchants who supplied credit and money to their customers. Barter was the most common method of exchange, with farmers trading crops or furs for manufactured goods.

Encouraged by Alexander Hamilton, America developed a banking system after the Revolution (see discussion earlier in this chapter). These banks accepted deposits and made short-term loans, payable on demand. But as the country grew, the need for money and credit increased. By 1811, there were 117 banks chartered by the states, each authorized to issue its own banknotes.

Philadelphia, New York, and to a lesser extent, Boston, became the financial centers of the new country because of their proximity and business ties to Europe. There was an increase in tradable securities, federal bonds, state bonds, stock in banks, insurance on cargoes, and funding of wholesalers and retailers who were buying imported and local manufactured goods and products.

Alexander Hamilton had founded New York's first bank, the Bank of New York, in 1784. By 1792, the Stock Exchange office, the first place for traders to meet, was founded on Wall Street, and New York was quickly becoming the center for security trading. As noted earlier, New York became the undisputed center of American finance with the building of the Erie Canal, which opened up the riches of the interior through the Hudson River.

Business needs capital to expand, and the combination of banks and investors enabled the country to grow throughout the early nineteenth century. But it is interesting to note how much of America's growth was financed from Britain and Europe. The growth of Wall Street and the financing of American business expansion is well documented in John Steele Gordon's book *The Great Game*.[16]

Related to the quest for capital are a number of other factors. Money is only available in the long run if there are profits from investments and savings from consumers. Furthermore, the investor has to have some guarantee that he will be paid back, which in turn necessitates improvements in accounting and other business control systems, knowledge of how to manage larger enterprises, and advances in management. Improved banking practices were developed so that the bank would know the risk of various loans, could price them accordingly, had sufficient reserves to pay the depositors when they needed their money, and could accumulate capital so that future investments would be possible.

Early in the nineteenth century, America's national debt was shrinking, as was the securities market. Eventually, however, the canals and railroads required great amounts of capital, and the New York Stock Exchange grew. There were a variety of investment alternatives in the mid-nineteenth century—roads, canals, railroads, land and goods that became available as the country expanded westward, new industries and technologies, existing business expansion, increased trade around the world, various needs of the central and state governments, and many others. In many ways, these are the same alternatives available today.

What is different, however, is the role of the government. Throughout the nineteenth century, the federal government played a relatively small role in setting national economic priorities. Income came predominantly from two sources: tariffs on imported goods and the selling of western land. There were no corporate or individual income taxes and few sales taxes, and the government was minimally engaged in setting standards or writing laws regarding corporate or investor behavior. Government involvement (described in future chapters) in worker and consumer safety, child labor, financial reporting, and many other areas did not come onto the scene until the twentieth century.

In order to understand the growth of American business and its cities, an examination of food production and large-scale agriculture is in order here. In colonial days, most people lived on farms and most agricultural processes were not significantly different from those practiced in Elizabethan England. But from the beginning, American ingenuity was applied to making agricultural work more efficient and farmers' lives easier and more rewarding.

The first plows were made of wood, and a great deal of manual or animal effort was needed to draw them. In 1788, Thomas Jefferson studied the plow and its cutting edge and invented a moldboard plow for the soils of Virginia, which won an award from the Society of Agriculture in Paris.[17] In general, science was applied to agriculture early. Thomas Jefferson and George Washington exchanged numerous letters on land preparation, fertilization, and crop rotation.

In the colonial era, grain elevators were small operations consisting of a single pair of millstones. Men had to carry grain to the top of the gravity system and then carry the finished flour into storage silos. In the 1780s, Oliver Evans designed and patented a series of interconnected machines that, using steam power, handled the entire milling process, from receiving the grain from a wagon to storing the superfine flour ready for packing. He wrote a manual called *The Young Mill-Wright and Miller's Guide,* which was published in fifteen editions between 1790 and 1860, and his mill was copied in thousands of mills around the country.

In 1819, Jethro Wood introduced a cast-iron moldboard plow that was suited to the rocky soils of the East. In 1837, John Deere followed with a steel moldboard plow suited for turning over the rich, moist soil of the midwestern plains—a soil so thick that farmers called it a mixture of tar, mud, and molasses. By 1858, Deere was manufacturing 13,000 saw-steel plows for the western prairies.

The use of animal power and better plows, the use of the cultivator to replace the hand-operated hoe in the fields, and the reaper, which solved the problem of the need for large amounts of labor during planting and harvest season, together increased agricultural output significantly.

Midwestern agriculture grew quickly. In 1838, the shipment of wheat from Chicago was only seventy-eight bushels. Ten years later, it was more than 2 million bushels. Wheat is easy to sow and to grow; reaping, in the nation's early days, was another matter. A man had to go through a field swinging a scythe in backbreaking labor, and a farmer would only grow as much wheat as he and his family could harvest by hand. With the reaper, horsepower was substituted for manpower. Things changed when, in 1831, Cyrus McCormick, a young Virginia mechanic, introduced a horse-drawn reaper that could cut through six acres of oats in one day. Jerome Case began to manufacture threshing machines that efficiently separated wheat from chaff. In 1841, McCormick only sold two machines, but in 1852, he sold 1,000 reapers, and in 1857, 23,000.

New threshing machines, corn huskers, and other farm machinery continued to be developed. Simplicity of design meant that a farmer could repair his equipment without having to send it back to the factory. Farmers could now produce more food and feed more city dwellers, and these mechanical advances solved the labor problem in farming. By the end of the nineteenth century, giant combines pulled by large teams of horses worked the wheat fields of the Midwest. McCormick and John Deere increased western food production, enabling more men to leave the farm and go to the city or, in the 1860s, to the Civil War. Ninety percent of the American population was involved in agriculture in the seventeenth and eighteenth centuries. Eighty percent of the people lived on farms, which made up half the nation's wealth. Today, less than 2 percent of the U.S. population is engaged in agriculture. Today most people live in cities and suburbs. Technological improvements in agriculture enabled the feeding of America and allowed the vast migration to the cities.

As the nation grew geographically, it became difficult to keep it unified from an information standpoint. But, as will be discussed in chapter 7, advances in the understanding of electricity by Samuel F. B. Morse, Thomas Alva Edison, and Alexander Graham Bell improved communication. In the first industrial revolution, which lasted from the mid-eighteenth to the mid-nineteenth century, steam engines powered by coal had begun to replace human and animal energy. In a second revolution in the last half of the nineteenth century, transportation and communication were rapidly altered by railroad, telegraph, telephone, radio, automobile, truck, and airplane. In addition, mass marketing was added to mass production.

Samuel F. B. Morse was born in 1791 in Charleston, Massachusetts, the son of a geographer and the grandson of a Princeton University president. In 1832, he devised a system of interrupting electrical signals and sending coded messages on wires over a long distance. With the help of Joseph Henry, a leading scientist and future president of the Smithsonian Institution, and Alfred Vail, a young scientist, Morse demonstrated the telegraph system in New York in 1837. In 1844, with the support of a congressional appropriation, Morse built a demonstration line between Baltimore and Washington. At a telegraph key in the U.S. Supreme Court chambers, he sent the first message: "What hath God wrought!"

By 1850, telegraph lines went across the country to Philadelphia, Newark, New York City, Buffalo, Boston, Cincinnati, Cleveland, Detroit, and Chicago. America could now communicate quickly across long distances. Several competing companies offering telegraph lines developed, and one, led by Cyrus Field, built lines to Newfoundland in Canada and then in 1866 across the Atlantic Ocean to London. Telegraph lines reached Missouri by 1859, and three years later they reached San Francisco. A national communication system was built, with 200,000 miles of telegraph lines in service by 1870.

Railroads and other businesses needed the telegraph to run their operations. For several decades, many young men learned Morse code and worked as telegraph operators. Two leaders discussed in future chapters, Andrew Carnegie and David Sarnoff, started their careers working as telegraph operators.

As the country grew, local newspapers were started, and every newspaper needed a telegraph line to discover what was happening in the outside world. The Associated Press was formed in 1848, using its own wire to gather important national and world news. By 1860, there were 3,000 newspapers in America. The country was united through the telegraph.

American science and technology developed throughout the nineteenth century, going from a group of tinkerers and a few scientists being aware of the latest scientific knowledge in Great Britain to significant original work in science and technology. The first patent issued in America went to Joseph Jenks in 1646 for a water-powered sawmill. During the nineteenth century, innovation had increased considerably and thousands of patents were issued for some of the major advances in American technology.

At the beginning of the nineteenth century, America was primarily a farming and trading country, with many of its products manufactured in England. By the end of the nineteenth century, America was the most powerful industrial country in the world, producing more steel than the next two most industrialized countries combined—Great Britain and Germany. Someone who lived through the entire century would have witnessed the invention of the bicycle, the sewing machine, the match, the fountain pen, the adding machine, the plow, the reaper, canned food, the telegraph, the telephone, the typewriter, the cash register, photography, the phonograph, amusement centers, motion pictures, the electric transformer, the alternating current motor, and central power stations as oil and electricity provided power and light. They would have seen the nation creating canals and then a national railroad system, the Brooklyn

Bridge, streetcars, oil wells, kerosene manufacture, electric batteries, vulcanized rubber, steam engines, and the automobile.

In 1800, the population of the United States was slightly more than 5 million people, most of whom lived in a narrow band within 100 miles of the Atlantic Ocean. The center of population in 1800 was twenty-three miles west of Baltimore, Maryland. The land area of the United States was 865 thousand square miles. It grew to 1,749 thousand square miles by 1820 with the Louisiana Purchase and the acquisition of Florida, and by 1900 it had increased to 3,547 thousand square miles with the addition of the West, the Southwest, and the territories of Alaska and Hawaii.[18]

Population growth was even greater. From 3.9 million people in 1790, the number reached 9.6 million in 1820, 17 million in 1840, and 31.4 million in 1860. Part of that increase was due to immigration—4.9 million in the three decades between 1830 and 1860.[19] These people came from countries around the world, including Germany, Italy, Ireland, Austria-Hungary, Canada, Russia, England, and Mexico. Americans spread west across North America, first over the Appalachian Mountains, then, after Thomas Jefferson purchased the Louisiana territory from the French, across the Mississippi, the Great Plains, and then on to the Pacific Ocean.

These people, both native-born and immigrants, staffed the factories, mines, and building projects and provided the service labor for the country. Whereas labor shortages had been common in colonial days, the increasing population and the accelerating rate of immigration provided the labor that enabled the American economy to grow in the years leading up to the Civil War.

But these people were not only producers, they were consumers. Between 1790 and 1860, the American population grew at a rate of nearly 3 percent a year—a rate more than twice that of any European country. Rapid population growth through immigration resulted in a very high rate of new household formation and therefore a rapid growth in the demand for household goods. Because of advances in agriculture, Americans spent less on food and more on other things than did Europeans; they were the consumers of many of the products listed previously. More Americans lived in frame houses with furniture, stoves, carpets, china, glassware, clocks, and watches; rode in carriages; and performed their work with improved machinery. People had left their homes and villages in Europe and come to North America in search of a better living. And during the nineteenth century, they found it. The value of manufacturing products exceeded $1 billion in 1850, with most of them consumed by American workers.

There is one other facet of the population that should be stressed. Enough Americans were interested in their own and their children's education, in voting, in reading newspapers, magazines, and books, and in the music, art, and culture of America—that education, literature, and the arts grew. Many immigrants had left a situation in which their position in society was fixed; in America they believed they could grow economically and that their children would have a better life than they themselves had had.

During the nineteenth century, the federal government had a very limited role. It allowed substantial immigration because business leaders wanted low-cost labor. The government had no role whatsoever in consumer protection, child and adult labor protection, worker safety, environmental considerations, or any of the social issues that has characterized the twentieth century. These were business issues to be settled by business.

The government did, however, actively participate in setting tariffs. Tariffs can raise money for the government or protect domestic industries from lower-priced foreign competition, and custom duties were a major source of revenue before the Civil War. Hamilton, in his *Report on Manufactures,* recommended a program of tariffs to help American industry. The North, as a manufacturing region, was for high tariffs; the South, as a producer of raw materials, was for low tariffs. This was an issue that had kept Congress occupied since the Revolution. Tariff rates in the nineteenth century ranged from 5 percent in the early days to as much as 50 percent in 1890.

Some Factors in the Environment for Success

In the eight decades between the end of the Revolution in 1783 and the beginning of the Civil War in 1861, the United States had built the basis for becoming the greatest industrial power in the world. Blessed with extensive land and great national resources, the country's population of workers and consumers increased dramatically. The population that had been 50,000 in 1650 and 3.9 million in the first national census of 1790 stood at 31.4 million in 1860—more than an eightfold increase since independence.[20] The abundance of potential wealth in industrial jobs and in owning land that was open at low cost to most individuals attracted yet more immigration.

The American people were not only producers, they were consumers. And there were merchants and a distribution system to support them. Manufacturing costs were low and getting lower. Each decade American workers could afford more.

Transportation was improving. Canals, roads, rivers, and the developing railroads could move raw materials and goods to factories and consumers around the country. Remote settlements were being linked to the national market. And American sailing ships could bring American manufactured goods around the world.

The availability of banks, a capital market, and the finance supplied from Europe allowed businesses to expand. There was no limit to what American ingenuity could do. America had become the foremost industrial country in the world. Agriculture, raw materials, and factories had made this country nearly self-sustaining.

Businesses and industries developed with new technology, and this technology and industry had many effects, not all of them immediately apparent. They affected not only specific products, but how Americans could live.

The innovative Yankee entrepreneurs had built the technology, products, and manufacturing capability to make America one of the world's leaders in textiles, metalworking, guns, railroads, shipping, and most of the basics of a modern state. The physically distributed population could be fed by a smaller farm population and supplied with clothing, shelter, and requirements of nineteenth-century living.

Low-cost power, the availability of qualified workers, a large and growing national market, improved transportation systems for both domestic and foreign markets, sources of finance to support business expansion, a "can-do" attitude among business leaders, and a government friendly to business—taken together, they provided the environment for the rapid expansion of business after the Civil War.

And during the Civil War, the North's advantages in manufacturing goods from weapons to textiles and shoes, its strong transportation and communication systems, its large pool of manpower, its available capital, and its business leadership provided the factors that guaranteed its success in the coming war.

By the beginning of the Civil War, the stage had been set for rapid American industrialization. Labor was plentiful and the labor force could be fed by fewer farmers. There was a national market, and transportation was being improved to serve this market. American technology was the best, or second best, in the world in many areas. There was a strong feeling that Americans could do anything they set their minds to do. Management techniques were being improved. Only the lack of adequate capital was holding back the expansion of business, and that capital was being obtained from England and other European countries. America was poised for a move into the twentieth century.

The next chapter will describe one industry that served as the foundation for the twentieth century—iron and steel, a high-technology industry in which all American know-how was brought to bear. And by 1900, the country was united by almost 200,000 miles of railroad, more than 200,000 miles of telegraph lines, and more than 1 million miles of telephone service.[21] That year, there were 11.2 million tons of steel, 1.7 million tons of rails, and 4,192 automobiles manufactured in this country. The United States had become the number-one economic power in the world.

CHAPTER 3

Steel
The Basic Material (1860–2000)

Good sense, which only is the gift of Heaven,
And though no science, fairly worth the seven
—Alexander Pope

Vision is the art of seeing things invisible.
—Jonathan Swift

Although the textile industry and railroads can be considered the first important industries in the United States during the eighteenth and nineteenth
centuries, by the end of the nineteenth century, steel had become king. After the
Revolutionary War, the country moved from a dependency on wood as the basic
material to a society based on its ability to manufacture and work metals. Iron
and steel became the foundation for industrialization in America. Industries that
developed and grew based on the availability of low-cost iron and steel ranged
from railroads, textile machinery, and bridge building in the nineteenth century
to automobiles, office buildings, and superhighways in the twentieth century.
For a very long time, more than 40 percent of all jobs in the United States were
either involved in the manufacture of steel or relied directly or indirectly in its
use. Many American families have parents, grandparents, great-grandparents, or
other relatives who immigrated to this country and earned their living in the
steel industry, the mills, or the mines; or in the railroads and barges that brought
the raw materials together and the finished product to market; or in any one of
a number of industries dependent on steel, including shipbuilding, automobile
manufacture and service, mechanical and electrical machinery, railroad building,
airplane building, appliance manufacture, heavy industry, modern agriculture,
and construction.

Throughout the last six centuries, technical progress, especially progress in the
development of weapons, tools, and machinery, has been related to the ability to

make iron and steel of known characteristics and at low cost. The development of the iron and steel industry during the last 200 years can be viewed as one of the most important technological developments and the main industrial foundation of contemporary civilization. When the age of steel arrived during the late nineteenth and early twentieth centuries, it had a profound impact on the industrialization of the United Kingdom, France, Germany, and the United States, and later Japan, Russia, and Korea. Industrial, military, and economic power were closely related to steelmaking capability. The iron and steel industry is the first great modern American industry and the parent of many other modern industries. It can also serve as an example of both good and bad management, and of growth, age, and decline. Where did the industry come from? How did it grow? And why is it in so much trouble today?

The Iron Age

Beginning about 4000 B.C., humans began to learn how to work metals. They discovered that certain rocks could be melted by fire to yield a superior material. A metal tool was significantly more durable than one made of stone. Smelting, or melting metal and then separating it from its nonmetallic elements, was first applied to copper. By 3000 B.C., bronze was being made by melting copper and tin together in a furnace. During these early centuries, humans learned how to hammer metals into particular shapes and also to cast them by pouring molten metal into a clay mold where they would harden. There developed an early relationship between the coppersmith and the potter who made the molds. Copper and bronze were widely used for weapons, tools, bowls, jars, jewelry, ornamental artwork, and a variety of household applications. The use of copper and bronze gradually spread from its origin in the Middle East to the more remote areas of Europe and Asia.

The use of iron may have originated several thousand years ago when humans discovered meteorites, which are largely iron, and used pieces to make sharp points for spears and arrows. In many ancient languages, iron was called the "sky metal." But the material was rare until around 1600 B.C., when iron smelting began. Iron was introduced into Syria around 1400 B.C. and into Palestine shortly thereafter. The Iron Age is generally described as having begun around the eighth century B.C. when iron metallurgy was introduced to Europe. The Phoenicians, Greeks, Egyptians, Syrians, Romans, Chinese, and Indians were all familiar with the use of iron. The Romans used iron in weapons and machinery and established ironworks in Spain, Gaul, and Britain. The uses of iron, however, were specialized and the material expensive. From 800 B.C. until the Middle Ages, both iron and bronze were widely used, depending on the particular application. Iron is a very common metallic element that occurs abundantly in nature, always in combination with other elements. Like silicon, the building block of much of the late-twentieth-century technology, iron must be heated and purified at elevated temperatures to be of great use. It took humans more than 3,000 years to completely understand this process.

Over the centuries, humans learned how to melt, purify, and work iron. The making of iron and steel was an art to which countless people contributed. Making iron from iron ore is dependent on the temperature of the furnace, but for centuries there was no way to accurately measure furnace temperatures. Only the color of the flame could be used as an approximate indicator of heat. Making iron is dependent on the chemical composition of the ore, but for a long time there was no science of chemistry with which to identify the elements affecting the properties of the metal. The process was varied according to what seemed to work. Making iron is dependent on the ore's metallurgical characteristics, and yet, until the late nineteenth century, there was no science of metallurgy. And so the evolution of the iron industry is similar to the evolution of cooking, in which a cook, centuries ago using a wood stove, would combine just enough of this ingredient, and not too much of that ingredient, and cook until done. Without the ability to measure the characteristics, purity, and amounts of ingredients or the temperature of the oven, both the cook and the iron maker relied on experience and judgment. And both had variable results.

Eventually, the science of iron making and steelmaking developed. Sulfur and carbon were identified as critical elements in the manufacture of the metal. Other elements, including nickel, manganese, cobalt, and tungsten, were isolated and their influences on the chemical and physical properties of steel were determined.

Iron combines readily with oxygen, which explains why iron rusts in the atmosphere and why iron ores are oxides of iron. Iron is also found in combination with a variety of other materials, including sulfur, silicon, manganese, and phosphorous. Therefore, the objective of iron smelting was to eliminate the oxygen and separate the iron from other materials. When iron is heated in the presence of an abundant supply of carbon, such as charcoal, various reactions take place. These reactions depend on the temperature of the furnace, the length of time the materials are heated, the amount of carbon present, the other ingredients in the ore, and whether and when oxygen is in contact with the iron. They also depend on adding the proper flux, such as limestone, to separate the impurities from the metal to form a slag and take away the waste matter in the ore.

As iron ore is heated and the temperature exceeds 2,100 degrees Fahrenheit, a spongy mass of relatively pure iron is mixed with slag, the vitreous mass of residue produced during the process. A smith could then lift the lump of iron and hammer it on an anvil to drive out the cinders and unify the iron. The smith would heat the iron whenever it cooled too much. This relatively pure iron, with less than two-tenths of 1 percent carbon, is called wrought iron. The amount of carbon in wrought iron is just enough to make it tough and malleable. In the early days of iron making, iron was heated in a furnace or hearth until it was hot enough to be forged or shaped by a hammer. If the iron was heated beyond this point—to temperatures in excess of 2,400 degrees Fahrenheit—the iron ore began to melt. It absorbed between 2 and 4.5 percent carbon and became hard and brittle. This form of iron is called cast iron.

Molten iron could be poured directly into a mold, which meant that the furnace and the place where the metal was to be cast had to be in close proximity. Often, smaller amounts were needed for casting and the molten iron was stored in a reservoir. In the early eighteenth century, the process was modified so that the molten iron could be run from the furnace into a sand trough and then flowed into a number of smaller side troughs where it was allowed to cool. The troughs resembled a sow suckling a litter of pigs, and this crude cast iron is still known as pig iron. When a small amount of iron was needed, a pig would be remelted in a separate, smaller furnace. Thus, a foundry could exist a distance from a blast furnace and have the pig iron shipped to it.

In the 2,000 years during which humans learned how to make and use iron, the main motivations were military, as people moved from making spear and arrow points to making swords, suits of armor for knights, cannons, and guns. Foundries in England have been casting iron cannons since about 1543. Beginning in approximately A.D. 1400, the major emphasis was on designing better furnaces and on gaining a more complete knowledge of how to use and make iron. Because the manufacture of iron was expensive, for centuries wood remained the principal material for making farm implements, ships, machinery, tools, and many items of daily living. As the cost of iron was reduced, iron replaced bronze and began to be used for plows, looms, wagons, hay forks, horseshoes, nails, bolts, hinges, pots and pans, tin plates and cans, iron wire for carding wool, small machines, tools for industry and agriculture, and the thousands of other applications in modern life. The change from a society based on wood to one based on metal took place from the sixteenth to the mid-nineteenth century.

For millennia, iron making was essentially a small-scale local affair that used local materials. Iron ore was put into a furnace, typically fueled by charcoal, and then heated to a high temperature. Eventually, blast furnaces were developed in which air was driven by bellows in order to intensify the combustion; iron furnaces were dug into hillsides, with walls of clay or stone, and natural drafts on the hillside were often used to provide oxygen to the flame. The final properties of smelted iron depended on the temperature achieved, the amount of time the ore was at that temperature, the type of furnace, the specific impurities in the iron ore, the carbon content of the finished material, whether the material was heat treated, and how the iron was worked after it was made.

As the iron-making process developed, people discovered that using coal to smelt iron made more sense than using wood. Far less coal than wood is needed, and coal is easier to transport. The major industrialized countries of the nineteenth century—Germany, England, and the United States—had large stores of both iron and coal. Hence, charcoal, which requires burning large amounts of wood, was eventually replaced by coal as wood supplies dwindled. Higher temperature furnaces were designed. Blacksmiths could forge the finished material to achieve certain standard properties and shapes, or they could extrude the iron and roll it into the desired shape.

There are three major forms of iron. All come from the same iron ore and fuel, and all are more than 95 percent pure iron. The difference lies in the amount of carbon each absorbs and ultimately retains—a function of the furnace design and the processing procedures. The three forms of iron are

1. Cast iron or pig iron, which is easily melted and cast to shape, relatively soft, and easily machined, but is also quite brittle. It has a very high carbon content.
2. Wrought iron, which is forgeable when hot, ductile when cold. Wrought iron can be forged, rolled, and shaped in various ways, but it cannot be hardened and does not retain an edge.
3. Steel, which has a relatively low melting point, is capable of being forged at a red heat, is relatively soft when cooled slowly, but is extremely hard when quenched in water.

Steel was made in the ancient world. India had a very fine steel called *wootz.* The Persians also made steel, as did the ancient Greeks. Spain became a leading producer of steel in the West. Eventually, the process for making steel spread throughout Europe and then to Japan, the United States, and wherever iron was made. By the nineteenth century, Sheffield, England, had become a center for the manufacture of steel.

For centuries, steel was made by placing iron ore in clay crucibles that were sealed with clay to keep out any air and then heated for many hours at an extremely high temperature. The iron in the crucible melted and absorbed enough carbon to become steel. Steel was also made by the cementation process, which involved piling alternate layers of charcoal and iron ore, covering the mixture with layers of fine sand, and keeping the mixture red-hot for several days. The carbon in the charcoal diffused into the iron, forming a surface layer of steel that was hammered off. The layers of steel were fused or hammered together to form layered laminated steel. Steel production was not only very slow, it was very expensive to manufacture by either the crucible or cementation process. Therefore, although stronger than iron and less material-intensive, steel was used only in limited applications until the middle of the nineteenth century. Although steel was known more than 2,000 ago, the famous steel sword of Damascus and Toledo steel being outstanding examples of this technology, steel was a relatively rare and expensive material until the middle of the nineteenth century.

Eventually, people learned to make better iron and steel. For example, the wire industry started when humans learned how to form wire by drawing iron through a die. By 1720, mills for rolling flat iron sheets were common in Europe. Wrought iron, with so little carbon, was soft and so weapons and tools made from it could not maintain a cutting edge. Iron makers then learned to add carbon to the metal. They learned how to make certain kinds of iron hard by rapidly quenching—that is, cooling—the hot iron by immersing it in water or other liquid. They learned how to eliminate brittleness by heating the quenched iron to relatively low temperatures. Iron subjected to rapid cooling becomes a different material. The iron, however, must have carbon in the range of 0.3 percent to 1.5 percent for rapid cooling to have a major effect. For centuries, however, humans had no method of measuring carbon content, or even of knowing the major effects carbon and sulfur had in iron making. When molten iron was treated with oxygen, by adding either rich oxides or air to the furnace with the iron, the carbon, which made cast iron brittle, would be burned out in the puddling furnace and steel would be made. A puddling furnace is one in which a molten bath of pig iron is stirred or agitated in an oxidizing atmosphere. But this was a slow and expensive process, which required skilled labor to make.

Iron Making in North America

There is no documented use of iron by the Indians in the New World. As soon as the British visited North America, however, they sought iron. In 1585, Sir Richard Grenville, sent by his cousin Sir Walter Raleigh, made the first recorded discovery of iron ore in America on Roanoke Island, off the coast of North Carolina. Captain John Smith wrote about the production of iron implements by a Virginia blacksmith named James Rand in 1609. An iron-making furnace was started in Falling Creek, near Richmond, Virginia, in 1621, but the attempt was unsuccessful owing to Indian hostilities. James Winthrop Jr., with backing from England, established a company for the development of ironworks in New England less than two decades after the founding of Boston, and in 1643, the Massachusetts General Court gave him a twenty-one year monopoly on iron making. Within two years, a furnace was put into operation, and over the next five years, the ironworks on the Saugus River in Lynn was established. This operation, "the birthplace of the U.S. iron and steel industry," operated only in the spring, summer, and fall months, weather permitting, and produced from five to eight tons of cast and wrought iron per week. Another facility was established at Braintree,

Massachusetts, and for the next century, Massachusetts retained the lead for colonial production of iron. By 1700, ironworks had also been established in Connecticut, Delaware, Maryland, New Jersey, New York, Pennsylvania, Rhode Island, and Virginia. Forests were available for charcoal making, iron ore had been discovered in widespread locations, shells and limestone were plentiful, waterpower was readily available, and there was a sufficient labor supply.

The manufacture of steel was not common in the United States in the early eighteenth century, although at least four steel furnaces were in operation in the colonies by 1750. However, the production of iron continued to increase and eventually the center of iron production shifted to Pennsylvania, particularly the Pittsburgh area, because of its waterways and available raw materials. By 1775, the colonies had surpassed England in both number of blast furnaces and operational forges. Cannonballs were made for the Revolutionary army and iron implements for farming and industry. By 1810, the total annual production of iron in the United States was more than 53,000 tons, with almost half produced in Pennsylvania.

In the years between 1780 and 1880, there were significant improvements in iron production. There were general increases in the scale of blast furnaces and in the puddling process for making wrought iron. There were studies made of the mechanical properties of iron in an attempt to understand its strength. This study of tensile and fatigue strength was essential to civil engineers engaged in bridge building, ordnance engineers responsible for gun performance, and for most of the developing engineering professions. The science of metallurgy still lay ahead, but the manufacture of iron was evolving into a science.

In the mid- to late nineteenth century, the shift from using charcoal to anthracite coal and then to coke was made in iron production, partially because of the decrease in available wood, and partially for economic reasons. Iron plantations had been established in Pennsylvania, each consisting of an iron mine, a large surrounding forest to supply the charcoal for fuel, and waterpower to operate the machinery and provide the blast. A large blast furnace could use up a full acre of timber in one day's operation. A quarter acre of hardwood timber would produce enough timber to make one ton of pig iron. Pit coal, or metallurgical anthracite coal, was used as fuel for a period of time, but it was eventually replaced by coke. Coke is what is left of coal after the gasses and tars—the hydrocarbons—have been removed. Coke was cheap, abundant, and of a fibrous nature, which could support the load in the tall furnaces necessary for an economical scale of production. Because it could be used in very large furnaces and producing units, coke eventually led to the industrial giants that took over the iron and steel industry as well as the large iron-making centers. In 1850, the transition from charcoal to anthracite coal to coke started, and by 1870, the transition was largely complete.

During the nineteenth century, America went from an agrarian society to an industrialized one, from a country bordering the Atlantic to one spreading across the continent, from a nation of primarily British immigrants to a nation of immigrants from many countries—a true melting pot—and from a nation of 23 million in 1850 to a nation of nearly 92 million in 1910. More than 25 million people immigrated to the United States in this sixty-year period. Jobs were created, the nation changed, and the foundation for the twentieth century's progress, opportunities, and problems was established. Railroads and bridges were built, farm production was increased, machinery was developed, productivity was improved, and the manufacturing, financial, transportation, and agricultural base for the country's industrial, economic, and military dominance throughout the twentieth century was established.

The iron and steel industry was at the heart of much of this change. In 1810, the iron production in United States was 53 thousand tons. In 1900, the U.S. iron and steel industry produced more than 11 million tons, and by 1970, annual production had climbed to 135 million tons. What enabled the country to increase its industrial iron and steel production so much? How did it handle this industrial revolution? And what changed in the last decades of the twentieth century?

Early progress was the result of a number of simultaneous events. Markets for iron and steel developed quickly as the country expanded geographically, built a national railroad system, modernized its navy, constructed bridges and buildings, and developed new machinery and new products, including the automobile and the telephone. Technological developments allowed steel to be built to predetermined characteristics at an increasing rate and at lower costs. New management techniques were developed that allowed work in the mills to be organized and supervised differently. Immigration provided new workers for the jobs that were created. Earnings became sufficient to attract new sources of capital. New energy sources were developed. Abundant raw materials were found for conversion into iron and steel. Improved transportation allowed business to obtain supplies and customers on a national basis. Inventors, entrepreneurs, and investors were attracted to this new industry. Social attitudes favored rapid expansion of business. Government policies and actions were strongly in favor of American business, believing that the economic, industrial, and military strength of the United States were of major national importance.

The Age of Steel: The Early Years (1860–1900)

Steel does not exist in nature. Steelmaking is a refining process whereby certain elements present in pig iron, such as carbon and sulfur, are reduced. Steel contains less than 1 percent carbon, which makes it less brittle and more malleable than the parent metal. It is also stronger than iron so less material can be used for a given application.

For millennia, iron making and steelmaking were local and rudimentary affairs, carried out in the country in small blast furnaces. Castings, wrought iron, and finished iron were the products of other independent manufacturers. Early iron and steel were used by local blacksmiths in forging implements for agriculture, wagon making, use in mills, and other applications. Then, after 1850, the industry began to change in response to the needs of new manufacturers producing finished iron goods and new machinery. One of the first integrated plants in which steel and steel products were made was the Trenton Iron Works established in the 1840s. Three large companies appeared in the 1850s: Jones and Laughlin, Cambra Iron Works, and Bethlehem Iron Company. All sought to make wrought-iron rails, but, despite high tariffs, most American supplies were still being imported from England. The railroads began requiring large amounts of iron and steel for their construction, and at the time that American railroads were reaching their peak, British manufacturers dominated the market by offering rails made of the finest Bessemer steel (see below). Steel was also required for industrial tools, for wagon wheels, for gun barrels, for bridges, and for many other aspects of industrialization.

As late as 1810, the entire country produced only 917 tons of steel, with Pennsylvania's share being 531 tons, or more than half. Even in 1831, steel production was only 1,600 tons, an amount that was said then to equal the whole amount imported. But this steel was made chiefly by cementation; crucible steel was to come later. From 1831 until as late as 1860, little progress was made in developing the manufacture of steel; the total product in Pennsylvania in 1850 was only 6,000 tons. In 1840, Isaac Jones and William Coleman began steel manufacture in Pittsburgh. In 1853, Singer, Nimick & Co. successfully produced grades of cast steel for saws, machinery, and for kindred purposes. Hussey, Wells & Co. in 1860 made top quality crucible steel out of American iron. Steel was first used in America as a building material in the construction of a bridge over the Ohio River near Steubenville and the Eads Bridge over the Mississippi River at Saint Louis in 1874. However, not until the 1890s did steel supplant iron as the primary structural material.

For more than three centuries, iron had been the dominant building material worldwide. Beginning in the 1840s, a number of men in Great Britain, the United States, Germany, France, and other countries addressed the problem of making low-cost, high-quality steel. Working independently at first, and then sometimes in cooperation, men such as Sir Henry Bessemer, James Nasmyth, George Parry, Sidney Gilchrist Thomas, and Robert Mushet of Great Britain, and William Kelly and Joseph Gilbert Martien of the United States developed the pneumatic process of making steel from molten iron. Kelly developed the process first but lacked the scientific and business background for large-scale implementation. In 1847, Henry Bessemer in England had perfected a pneumatic method of producing steel: air blown through molten metal. Bessemer realized that iron required a sudden infusion of oxygen to become finished steel and discovered that an air blast would burn off the excess carbon in the pig iron. He was eventually successful, but for a long time suffered repeated failures because he lacked a method of measuring the carbon content of steel. The pneumatic process was followed shortly by the invention of an open-hearth furnace in 1856 by William Siemens, a German working in France and Great Britain, and Emile and Pierre Martin of France. Many workers and managers in iron plants experimented with and developed these methods.

The Kelly-Bessemer process, developed in the 1850s, consists of oxidizing carbon, silicon, phosphorus, and other impurities in molten pig iron by passing a blast of cold air through the bath of molten iron. A Bessemer converter is a large open pear-shaped refractory-lined steel vessel, which holds five to fifty tons of pig iron as well as limestone and coal. The bottom of the converter contains a large number of holes, and a blast of air is blown through the molten iron from nozzles in the bottom in order to oxidize the carbon, sulfur, manganese, and other ingredients. Flames and sparks rush out as the oxygen burns the impurities, and after about fifteen minutes, the flames die out. After oxidation is complete, the converter is tilted and the molten slag is poured out, and then the molten steel is poured into ingot molds.

Using the Bessemer process, steel could be made up to a thousand times faster than with the old crucible process. By 1864, the first U.S. steel plant using the Bessemer process was operational in Wynadotte, Michigan, and the following year in Troy, New York, at the works of Winslow, Griswold, and Holley. Andrew Carnegie, with engineering help from Alexander Lyman Holley, took the Bessemer process and made it into an entire system for making steel. Certain alloys, including tungsten, chromium, titanium, and nickel, were added to the process to make specialty steels with different properties.

The Siemens-Martin process, developed in the 1860s, uses a regenerative furnace and converts iron to steel in an open hearth where steel is exposed directly to the flames. The open-hearth process is based on the fact that hot air will make the flames burn with a greater heat than will cold air. Pig iron, together in some cases with a certain amount of scrap iron, is placed in a brick-lined furnace with coke and limestone. Preheated gas and air are burned in the hearth, and the hot gases are led through a brick-lined heating chamber, which is heated to red-hot temperatures by the passage of these gases. Air for combustion is then forced through the hot chambers, taking up some of the heat and raising the temperature of the flames. The limestone melts and mixes with the impurities in the ore and coke to form slag. Samples of the steel can be taken out with a long-handled ladle, poured into a mold, and allowed to cool.

As the science of metallurgy developed, steelmakers learned to analyze the steel through spectrum analysis to determine the percentage of each ingredient in the steel and then modify the process as required. When the process is complete, with the slag floating on top of the molten steel tapped off and cooled, the molten steel is poured, flowing through channels to the place where it is used. In 1868, a New Jersey iron maker, Abram S. Hewitt, introduced the open-hearth process in the United States, and in 1870, installed a small open-hearth furnace at the Bay State Works in South Boston.

These two processes, the Bessemer converter and the open-hearth furnace, ushered in the Age of Steel. These processes enabled steel to be made in great quantities and in ever-larger dimensions. The steel can be formed into ingots and rolled into semifinished products or cast into forms by continuous castings. The semifinished products could then be rolled, forged (hammered), or extruded (shaped by forcing through a die) into finished steel products. The blast-furnace process has to run twenty-four hours per day, seven days per week for efficient operation. With the developments of the huge plants based on these processes, the annual output of steel in the United States increased from 6,000 tons in 1858 to 11 million tons in 1900. By the 1890s, steel had replaced iron as the primary structural material, and within a decade, the United States led the world in the production of iron and steel.

Table 3.1 shows both the growth of steel output over the course of a century and the type of steelmaking process used. The Bessemer converter, because of its earlier introduction, was the leading process during the nineteenth century, accounting for more than 85 percent of steel produced between 1875 and 1890. However, by 1910, because of its greater capacity and higher quality steel, the open furnace became the leading process for making steel, accounting for the vast majority of steel made in the United States during the first sixty years of the twentieth century. These two processes, together with the electric arc furnace and the basic oxygen furnace introduced in the twentieth century, became the bases for the great increase in steel manufacture.

Table 3.1 Raw steel produced in the United States
(total and type of facility)

Year	Thousand Tons Steel Produced	Type of Facility (%)			
		Bessemer	Open Crucible Hearth	Electric	Basic Oxygen
1860	13		100%		
1865	15		100%		
1870	77	54%	3%	43%	
1875	437	86%	2%	12%	
1880	1,397	86%	8%	6%	
1885	1,917	89%	8%	3%	
1890	4,779	86%	12%	2%	
1895	6,785	81%	18%	1%	
1900	11,227	68%	32%		
1905	21,880	56%	44%		
1910	28,330	37%	62%		1%
1915	35,180	26%	73%		1%
1920	46,183	21%	78%		1%
1925	49,795	15%	84%		1%
1930	44,591	13%	86%		1%
1935	38,184	8%	90%		2%
1940	66,893	6%	92%		2%
1945	79,702	6%	90%		4%
1950	96,836	5%	89%		6%
1955	117,036	3%	90%		7%
1960	99,382	1%	87%	8%	4%
1965	131,462		72%	11%	17%
1970	135,514		37%	16%	47%
1975	116,600		19%	19%	62%
1980	111,800		12%	28%	60%

Source: Data from American Iron and Steel Institute.[1]

Following the Civil War, the United States built a national railroad system. Railroad trackage, which was 9,000 miles in 1850 and 30,000 miles in 1860, reached 93,000 miles in 1880 and 193,000 miles in 1900.[2] In order to expand track mileage and allow trains to run faster, the railroads needed a metal stronger than wrought iron to absorb the shock of passing wheels. Iron rails were too soft, wore down on one side, and had to be turned frequently. Iron rails also broke or cracked and had to be continually inspected to prevent accidents. Gradually, the use of steel rails became widespread and replaced the iron rails in service. Steel was also used for the manufacture of locomotives and railroad cars, providing stronger and lighter trains, increasing the carrying capacity of trains by a factor of ten, reducing car weights, increasing locomotive power, and decreasing transportation costs. The expansion of the railroad system was only possible because of advances in steel manufacture.

For more than twenty years, the majority of steel produced in the United States was used by the railroads. But steel was equally dependent on the railroads. The steel industry needed the railroads to haul the millions of tons of materials required in manufacture—90 percent of steelmaking involves moving raw materials and large amounts of finished and semifinished materials from place to place. Fleets of boats were used to carry ore and networks of railroads to carry coal, limestone, and ore to mills and finished products to nationwide markets.

The expansion of railroads made possible the hauling of the large amounts of material required for modern steelmaking. Railroads and steelmaking were highly interdependent, each needing the other to succeed.

In 1845, one of the richest and largest bodies of iron ore was discovered in the Lake Superior region. The ranges were more than 50 percent iron. The canal around the rapids at Sault Ste. Marie on the Saint Mary's River between Lake Superior and Lake Huron and a railroad in upper Michigan enabled ore to be shipped from Minnesota and Michigan directly to ports on the lower Great Lakes and then by railroad to mills in Pennsylvania, Ohio, and New York. Fleets of boats were used to carry ore, and networks of railroads were used to carry raw materials to mills and finished products to markets. By the 1870s, the mines in the Upper Peninsula of Michigan were furnishing half the country's iron ore supply. By the 1890s, the extensive Mesabi Range in Minnesota was in operation, and open-pit mining became economically feasible. Another rich source of iron ore was discovered around Birmingham, Alabama. These large sources of iron ore from the Lake Superior region, and the bituminous coal from the northern part of the Appalachian Plain transported long distances by ship and railroad, required significant sources of investment capital and led to the concentration of the country's iron-making capacity in the Great Lakes basin, especially western Pennsylvania, eastern Ohio, Indiana, Illinois, and Buffalo, New York.

During the 1870s, most steel produced went into rails. In the next decades, as the national railroad network neared completion, structural steel for the new urban construction became a major market. Andrew Carnegie's decision to use the open-hearth Homestead Works for structural steel rather than rails was a major development as the nation rebuilt and expanded its cities.

In 1882, the U.S. government made a decision to modernize the navy. By eventually replacing its entire fleet of wooden ships with a fleet made using steel, the navy would become stronger, foreign trade could be expanded and protected, and a more active foreign policy could be promoted. For decades, the power of cannon shells had been increasing. Wooden vessels were no longer strong enough to withstand them, and cast-iron plates for ships were becoming much too heavy. Cast iron was appropriate as a plate for use on land where weight is not an issue, but by 1876, it required nearly twenty-two inches of iron to blunt the heaviest cannon shell fired at a ship. The government looked for steel plating for naval vessels to provide greater protection while lightening the vessel. At the same time, repairs to older ships were to be limited and newer steel ships constructed. The commitment to an American steel navy between 1885 and 1915 enabled the steel industry to diversify its markets. Military contracts were very important to firms like Bethlehem, Carnegie, and Midvale Steel.

Advances in steelmaking also were important in other industries as tools were developed for manufacturing and agriculture. Heavy steel equipment was used in the design of large electric power plants. Rolling replaced forging as a principal method of working steel into a variety of shapes. Improvements were made in the production of wire for bridges, telephone and telegraph lines, steel bars, nails, pipes and tubes, sheet metal, tin-plated steel, and structural steel. In 1900, 300 pounds of steel were produced for every person in the United States, and the steel industry was well diversified.

Steel manufacturing companies selling to varied markets, including machinery and agricultural companies, the government, and contractors, needed a larger sales force than companies selling only to the railroads. In response to this and other changes, companies began to develop new management structures. Entrepreneurs organized companies financially and administratively in new ways to utilize workers, raw materials, and machines efficiently. Furthermore, there developed raw material and energy sources: coal, iron ore, waterpower, and a growing supply of labor. According to the census of 1880, there were more than 2,000 independent steel mills in the country. The smaller manufacturers performed a single function: buying raw materials from another supplier and selling their products through brokers. The government refrained from any negative interference with business, erected protective tariff barriers against foreign competition in order to encourage growth of the domestic steel industry, and turned over public resources for private exploitation by steel companies and railroads.

During these years, the role of Andrew Carnegie and Carnegie Steel increased. In 1872, Carnegie built the Edgar Thompson Steel Works, the leading Bessemer facility in the country. The plant continued to make money in good times and bad while rivals went bankrupt. Carnegie bought up steel mills during the Panic of 1873 and in the several recessions that occurred in the last two decades of the nineteenth century. When good times returned, he had some of the most advanced plants in the world. Carnegie continued to buy out competition, lowered his cost of production, reinvested profits in the business, replacing old plants with new and building everything with the most modern equipment. He purchased iron ore mines in the Mesabi Range, railroad lines, coke and limestone furnaces, and Great Lake ore ships.

Carnegie wanted to become an integrated supplier, controlling steel from the mine to the market, so he shifted back toward sources of supply. By the

1890s, he had obtained control of the coke and coal sources, although not all of the required iron ore. He then moved forward toward the finished product. Carnegie Steel made and sold raw and semifinished steel and heavy products such as rails, structural steel, and armor plate. It did not, however, make lighter products such as steel tubes, wire, and sheets.

During the 1890s, a number of mergers and consolidations occurred in the steel industry. John W. ("Bet a Million") Gates formed the American Steel and Wire Company to make bridge cabling, fencing, telegraph and telephone lines, and other wire products. With the backing of J. P. Morgan, Gates bought out many existing wire manufacturers. Federal Steel was also formed by a merger of several steel companies and became second in size only to Carnegie Steel. Judge Elbert Gary became president of the new firm with Morgan's backing. Morgan also owned a significant position in the National Tube Company. In Chicago, the Moore brothers and other financiers merged a number of small mills into four interrelated companies: the National Steel, American Tin Plate, American Steel Hoop, and American Sheet Steel companies.

In 1900, Andrew Carnegie developed plans to make steel tubing by a new process, threatening the investment Morgan had made in the National Tube Company. It was becoming obvious that some steel manufacturers were moving toward finished products whereas other manufacturers were contemplating building steelmaking facilities to supply more of their own steel requirements. In December, Charles M. Schwab, the president of Carnegie Steel, gave a speech at a private dinner about the future of the steel industry in which he stressed the benefits of large-scale integrated steel manufacture. He believed that great economies would be achieved by having one mill make one product and make that product continuously. Based on that speech and Judge Gary's strong support, Morgan decided to buy out Carnegie.

In 1900, the American steel industry was led by eight major companies: Carnegie Steel, Federal Steel, National Tube Company, American Steel and Wire, National Steel, American Tin Plate, American Steel Hoop, and American Sheet Steel. United States Steel Corporation was formed from these and other organizations, including American Bridge, Shelby Steel Tube, and Lorraine Steel Company, and was incorporated on February 25, 1901. It had an initial capitalization of $1.1 billion, making it the largest corporation in the world. Judge Gary of Federal Steel was appointed chief executive officer and Charles Schwab, at thirty-nine years of age, was appointed president. When formed, United States Steel Corporation controlled almost two-thirds of the nation's steel production.

The consolidation for a time dominated the market. U.S. Steel owned almost half the coke ovens in the country, 112 steamships, and 1,000 miles of railroad. It produced 50 percent of the country's pig iron, 68 percent of the steel rails, 60 percent of the structural steel, steel plates, bars, wire and wire rods, and nearly all its tin plates, barbed wire, and woven-wire fence. It also built 85 to 90 percent of the country's bridges. Its ratio of heavy and finished steel kept falling, for it could not bar the entry of new and more progressive firms. Nevertheless, it was the kingpin in steel and the price leader for a number of years.

World Domination (1901–1950)

By the turn of the century, the American steel industry was beginning to dominate the world in terms of quality, quantity, and cost of iron and steel products. Leading the American steel industry was the United States Steel Corporation. Andrew Carnegie had retired from the steel industry, and, as mentioned earlier, his protégé, Charles Schwab, was president of U.S. Steel. The next fifty years were the golden age of steel; production was increased, new markets were developed, and steel served as the foundation for the U.S. military strength in both World War I and World War II. It was a time of growth, but also a time of change.

Surviving changes in customers and markets, new technologies, and two world wars separated by the Great Depression, the steel industry and its leaders had reasons to be satisfied. No matter that labor was exploited to the point that unionization, after a series of sometimes violent battles, finally entered the industry. No matter that investments in new technologies and new plants slowed down. No matter that the consolidation of the industry in 1901 resulted in a dominant supplier that immediately started to lose market share to its competitors. No matter that few new firms entered the marketplace for a long period of time. No matter that the strength of the steel industry, which contributed to the defeat of Germany and Japan, also led to the revitalization of the steel industries of these very countries—using more modern and efficient technologies than the United States. For the first half of the twentieth century, the American steel industry was prosperous. And like some prosperous middle-aged individuals, the industry did little either to prepare for its old age or try to recapture the energy and success of its youth. For about fifty years, steel was an aging king.

During the early days of the steel industry, railroads had been the major customer with their great demands for rails, locomotives, axles, and wheels. But then the market began to diversify. Industries such as petroleum, construction, bridge building, shipbuilding, agricultural implements, machinery, and chemicals began to require increasing amounts of steel. Steel began to be produced for plates, rods, slabs, bars, girders, structural shapes, tubing and piping, sheets, bolts, nuts, rivets, and tin plate. By 1900, more than 1 million tons of steel wire were produced for use in a variety of applications, including bridge cables, fencing, and telegraph and telephone lines.

During the first three decades of the twentieth century, the automobile industry developed (see chapter 5). Fewer than 5,000 automobiles were registered in 1900, but before long, the industry expanded. There were more than 9 million automobiles registered in 1920 and more than 26.7 million registered in 1930, with each new automobile requiring many hundreds of pounds of steel. The electrical industry also developed during the twentieth century (see chapter 7). Electrical power increased in the early twentieth century, and the nation built new electrical power capacity and a nationwide power distribution system. Steel was required for turbine generators, wiring, electrical machinery, pumps, and appliances. Furthermore, the military demand for steel increased for guns, ships, tanks, and planes. The commercial aircraft industry developed in the 1930s and began to require specialty steels. Railroads also demanded more steel as track mileage and freight traffic increased significantly during the late nineteenth and early twentieth centuries. Massive building projects such as the Empire State Building required more than 50,000 tons of steel; the Golden Gate Bridge required more than 107,000 tons. In addition, each year more than 700,000 tons of steel were used for nails and 3 million tons for tin cans.

Steel production, which was 77,000 tons in 1870, increased to more than 11 million tons in 1900, 46 million tons in 1920, and almost 97 million tons in 1950. In fact, a person born in 1870 would have witnessed tremendous change if he or she lived for eighty years. Population increased from fewer than 40 million to more than 150 million people, average human life expectancy increased by 50 percent from about forty years to more than sixty-five years, and average weekly wages rose significantly. Beyond the quantitative figures, the way in which people lived their lives changed markedly owing to the expansion of the national railroad system, the development and wide distribution of the automobile, and the building of a national highway system—all of which changed living patterns and minimized physical isolation. Furthermore, people were connected as never before through the development of new communication systems, including the telegraph, the telephone, the radio, and movies. The electrification of America provided electrical lights, washing machines, refrigerators, and vacuum cleaners. The development of more productive farming equipment enabled more people to live in the cities. Throughout this revolution, steel played a key part, as the use of steel increased between 1870 and 1960 from fewer than four pounds per person per year to almost 1,200 pounds per person per year.

It is worth noting that the steel industry did not create any of these markets, it only took advantage of them. The demand for steel increased because entrepreneurs created new steel-consuming industries. The steel industry, of course, benefited from these changes and expanded production. Although steel was often referred to as "king steel," the "king" was very much influenced by a variety of factors outside his control—and perhaps took his title too seriously.

Steel from the beginning had a major problem—a difficulty in adjusting supply to demand. The steel industry involved constructing plants with very large capacities. These plants called for a high, steady rate of continuous production. When demand was high relative to industry capacity, prices increased and new capacity was established with the retained earnings. When capacity exceeded demand, prices dropped, and overextended suppliers were driven into merging or closing down facilities. Within a year or two (e.g., the years 1906 to 1908), the industry could drop from 90 percent capacity to 40 percent capacity. Very early on, steel acquired the reputation as a prince-or-pauper industry. Changes in demand quickly resulted in a scarcity or a significant oversupply. For the nearly four decades prior to World War II, U.S. Steel averaged operating at 70.8 percent of capacity. But in eight of these years it operated at over 90 percent of capacity, and in five other years, it operated below 40 percent of capacity. The swings could be extreme. In 1920, U.S. Steel operated at 86.2 percent capacity; in 1921, 48.3 percent capacity; in 1922, 70.9 percent capacity; in 1923, 89.1 percent capacity; and in 1924, the company operated at 72.2 percent capacity. Revenues, earnings, and employment swung wildly through the years. In fact, there are many parallels between the steel and the semiconductor industries.

Within three years of United States Steel Corporation's formation, Charles Schwab had left as president and director. His departure has been variously credited to a number of factors: disagreement with other senior management, many of whom had backgrounds in law and finance and not in steel manufacturing; ill health; the fact that he couldn't be his own man; and also, more interestingly, newspapers that had widely publicized his gambling at Monte Carlo, which resulted in Schwab losing the confidence of Morgan and others. His resignation certainly was related to the way that United States Steel had been set up, with power shared between the entire Board of Directors, the Finance Committee, the Executive Committee, and senior management. No one person had undisputed authority. Schwab's departure could have been for a variety of reasons—many not unfamiliar to any entrepreneur whose business has been acquired. Charles Schwab went on to purchase Bethlehem Steel and built it into the nation's second largest steel producer. And for the next quarter century, Judge Elbert Gary ran U.S. Steel.

Judge Gary was one of the more interesting figures in the long history of the steel industry. A gentleman, a good businessman, an honest, ethical, and considerate person, a progressive and yet very conservative leader, he was admired, respected, and honored by colleagues, competitors, and customers alike. His vision had led to the formation of American Steel and Wire Company, Federal Steel Corporation, and subsequently the United States Steel Corporation. Until his death in 1927, he was chairman of the board of U.S. Steel. As Irving S. Olds, a subsequent board chairman, said in his paper, *Half a Century of United States Steel*:

Judge Gary was firmly of the opinion that the steel requirements of a rapidly developing country could be best served by the formation of a large, stable, integrated steel company, with operations extending all the way from mining through the manufacture and distribution of the finished steel products. ... The Judge also wanted a company which could be capable of conducting a regular and extensive steel import business.[3]

Judge Gary believed in providing full information about the company and was one of the first businesspeople to supply an annual report and quarterly earnings statements to the stockholders. He was very open with the press, stating, "I believe thoroughly in publicity. ... The surest and wisest of all regulations is public opinion."[4]

From the beginning, U.S. Steel attempted to centralize its planning, management, and control. The 1902 *Annual Report* states:

Diversified management has been dispensed with as far as possible, and the several companies have endeavored to adopt similar methods as far as suited their respective businesses. The effort also is made by the different companies to regulate their manufacture of various products so that the fullest advantage can be taken of the economical production of any special article and its cheapest distribution to the consumer. ... Methods of accounting are being made uniform as rapidly as possible so that comparisons can readily be made. In this way, the best result attained by any of the companies is taken as the standard and the other companies endeavor to conform thereto.[5]

Centralization of management policies and manufacturing planning, rapid dissemination of an improved manufacturing process discovered in one plant throughout the entire corporation, and common accounting and financial control were the corporation's management philosophies, guiding it for the next half century. Irving Olds in 1947 wrote:

Judge Gary was a firm believer in rewarding initiative and ability on the part of employees within the organization by promotions to positions of greater responsibility. Ninety per cent of the executives of the Steel Corporation were men who rose from the ranks.[6]

So the centralization philosophy was reinforced by people who had been trained in this philosophy. There were few outsiders to challenge the way things were done.

Judge Gary disagreed with certain management techniques that Andrew Carnegie had developed at Carnegie Steel and that Charles Schwab believed in and applied at Bethlehem Steel. For example, Carnegie had established a bonus system for production workers and had offered partnerships to successful young managers and superintendents. Gary stressed standards rather than competition for the workers, focused on security rather than risk taking, and offered promotions to good managers but not ownership in the company. Carnegie had expanded plant capacity whenever funds were available; Gary instead believed that the industry capacity should be stabilized before any new expansion took place. While still at U.S. Steel, Schwab was requested by Judge Gary to close down small, older plants rather than build new ones.

United States Steel built its business by integrating backward and forward. It gained control of its sources of supply—iron ore, coal coke, and limestone; it built sales of by-products like portland cement; it acquired and expanded transportation companies; and it sold not only steel ingots and castings, but also rolled, forged, and welded finished steel products. The 1926 *Annual Report* lists more than ten pages of manufacturing plants; iron ore, coke, gas and oil, and limestone properties; and steamships and railroads. The 1937 *Annual Report* lists eighty-eight different categories of product. The industry had come a long way from its early dependence on railroads for its markets.

Under Judge Gary's leadership, United States Steel grew. From a revenue of $560 million in 1902, the company reached $745 million in 1912, $1,774 million in the war year of 1918, $1,092 million in 1922, and $1,310 million in the last year of Gary's life, 1927. Even with this growth, however, there were difficult years. Revenue was down from the prior year nine times between 1903 and 1928, and operating earnings were down in twelve of its twenty-six years of leadership.

United States Steel had been well financed, with more than $1.1 billion of capitalization, much of it in bonds and preferred stock. Perhaps it was too well capitalized. Each year from 1902 to 1931, preferred stock dividends were $25.2 million—except in the first two years, when they were more than $30 million. Andrew Carnegie had insisted on having his portion of the sale of Carnegie Steel paid in 5 percent, fifty-year gold bonds, and the company had significant debt. Interest and other costs of debt were between $25 million and $32 million a year every year between 1902 and 1928. Common stockholders had a variable payout in the thirty-nine years prior to World War II—more than $40 million in each of seven years, between $20 million and $40 million in sixteen years, less than $20 million in seven years, and nothing at all in nine years. In the company's first thirty-nine years, annual earnings exceeded $50 million in only nine years, in twelve years retained earnings were between $25 million and $50 million, and in the remaining years less money was retained in the business than the $25 million that was committed to the holders of preferred stock. In fact, in nine years between 1914 and 1938, the company had a negative figure for annual retained earnings; that is, the company spent and distributed to stockholders more than it earned. In the thirty-nine-year period, the amount of earnings retained in the business was less than one-third the amount paid in dividends and interest. In the cumulative years from 1902 through 1940, U.S. Steel had revenues in excess of $38 billion. During that time, it paid out 7.3 percent of revenue as preferred and common stock dividends and in interest. During that same thirty-nine-year period, the company invested 5.6 percent of revenue in all capital expenditures to replace obsolete and worn-out equipment, build new facilities, reduce costs, and provide for the future.[7]

United States Steel may have been established with too much debt and too much preferred stock. Either U.S. Steel proves that companies, like individuals, can borrow too much capital if they do not grow significantly, make more profits, and increase market share, or, based on the company's actual performance, such a large amount of capital should not have been required, a subject demonstrated almost a century later in the communication and dot-com industries. Andrew Carnegie had sold out at a very good price and had taken his money in debt, not in common stock. He and his partners had been well rewarded.

Judge Gary believed in stabilizing prices in the industry, since, in his view, the wild fluctuations in steel prices during the 1890s had hurt the industry. He stated: "Most of us would rather have the price of our tailor or grocer substantially uniform, assuming they are fair and reasonable year in and year out, than to have prices very low in times of panic and depression, and then in other times very high and unreasonable."[8] He believed that the consumers benefited from price stability. Judge Gary also said: "I think we have used our influence in keeping the prices of many steel commodities from increasing while the demand was greater than the supply."[9]

Although not directly fixing prices, U.S. Steel did strongly influence them. For years, the corporation produced a price book and only infrequently deviated from those prices. In bad times, this produced a price umbrella, which enabled higher-cost producers to survive. In good times, it enabled some companies to increase market share by cutting prices. It also enabled U.S. Steel to meet its high payout obligations to its bond and preferred stockholders even in bad times. While production might decrease, prices did not collapse as they had done in the 1880s and 1890s. Therefore, the company had better earnings.

U.S. Steel had been established to dominate the steel industry, but it did not accomplish this objective. Judge Gary himself had no intention of exercising a monopoly or restraining trade. In fact, from the moment of its formation, the company began to lose market share. Sued by the federal government in 1911 for antitrust practices, partially because of price-fixing charges and partly because it was too large, United States Steel Corporation ultimately was absolved of all monopoly charges. The court's unanimous decision in 1915 was that the corporation was not to be dissolved, for it was not a monopoly in restraint of trade. In its decision the court stated:

The views of its competitors are the best gauge. It may be accepted as fact where no competitor complains and more so, where they unite in testifying that the business conduct of the Steel Corporation has been fair, we can rest assured that there has been neither monopoly nor restraint.

The decision was appealed to the Supreme Court, which, in 1920, upheld the verdict, based to a large extent on the favorable testimony of competitors. As part of its defense, the corporation pointed out that, at the time of its founding in 1901, it made and sold almost two-thirds of the country's steel, but that market share had quickly decreased. In its twenty-fifth annual report in 1926, the company stated that in 1901 it represented 65 percent of the country's output, but by 1925, it represented 45 percent. Despite the fact that this was an effective defense against antitrust charges, it might not have been a good direction for either the stockholders or the employees—although it may have been good for the country.

While with Carnegie Steel, Charles Schwab had been involved in the mergers of three organizations: United States Steel, International Nickel, and American Steel Foundries. In 1901, while president of U.S. Steel, Schwab purchased Bethlehem Steel for $7.5 million. He then sold it, at the same price, to J. P. Morgan, who offered it for sale to U.S. Steel. The company turned it down, and Schwab repurchased Bethlehem and sold it to United States Shipbuilding Company, which was being formed from eight ship construction companies. However, within one year, United States Shipbuilding had failed and was in receivership. Schwab had been a major factor in both the formation of the company and in its foreclosure. The company traced its history back to the establishment of the Saucona Iron Company in 1857. In 1861, the name was changed to Bethlehem Iron Company, and, for the next quarter century, the company's major product was iron rails. In 1885, the company began to make heavy forgings for the navy—hollow forgings for guns and solid forgings for the shafts of ships and for engines. In 1886, Bethlehem became the first company to open a plant to make armor plate, receiving a $4 million contract from the U.S. Navy. For the next twenty years, the company's major business was in the manufacture of nickel alloy steel and face-hardened armor plate, guns, and forgings for military contracts. This technology to make heavy forgings was later important as large power plants were established throughout the country.

As noted earlier, in 1903, Charles Schwab resigned as president of United States Steel and became president of Bethlehem Steel. The company purchased all the properties of U.S. Shipbuilding and was recapitalized in December 1904. Schwab had left the presidency of the largest steel company in the world to take over one of the smallest. In 1905, its first year of operation, Bethlehem Steel and subsidiary companies had revenues of $14.5 million. The same year, U.S. Steel had revenues of $585 million, more than forty times greater than Bethlehem.

Within a few years, Schwab had begun to build Bethlehem Steel into the second largest steel company in America. Charles Schwab evaluated the people in the company and identified Eugene Grace as the best manager within the organization. In 1908, he appointed the thirty-two-year-old Grace as general manager of Bethlehem Steel. From then on, Grace supervised production, operations, and management; Schwab was concerned with finance, and together with Archibald Johnston, focused on the company's sales.

Schwab decided to manufacture commercial steel and deemphasize government business. He expanded the core business and sold off facilities that did not fit his plans, including the Bath Iron Works and the Eastern Shipbuilding Corporation. He started purchasing smaller companies and properties, and then began to acquire larger ones. His acquisitions included the Tofo Iron Mines in Chile, the Fore River Shipbuilding Company in Quincy, Massachusetts, and the Pennsylvania Steel Company. At times, he was able to borrow the money to purchase a company and then repay the debt out of the first few years' earnings.

Bethlehem Steel made no dividend payments from 1907 to 1913. Instead, Schwab preferred to plow back earnings for business expansion and improvement. He believed strongly in using the newest and best technology. Bethlehem had few significant investments in old or obsolete equipment and could evaluate each new application in terms of the lowest cost and highest quality manufacturing process. In 1905, Schwab announced his intention to make Bethlehem the greatest steel plant in the world. Under Andrew Carnegie, Schwab had learned three lessons: (1) Use the earnings for the modernization of the business, not for dividends. The payout to Carnegie's partners was when the business was sold as U.S. Steel. (2) Secure sources of raw materials long before the materials are needed. (3) Expand the business in times of depression when costs of labor and raw materials are lower. Then, in good times, as the industry expands, the capacity is in place to increase market share. Carnegie had built his business following that advice. Today, a century later, several semiconductor manufacturers followed that same advice during the 1982 and other recessions and the subsequent industry expansions.

Schwab did not, however, have access to the sources of capital that Carnegie had. He used all the sources he could, including personal guarantees on loans to businesses; advances from customers; deferred and partial payments to vendors, contractors, and railroads; notes to suppliers; the use of stock dividends in lieu of cash dividends; and significant increases in long-term debt. He was able to use his reputation and friendships to finance the growth of the business. He also was driven by his own need to see the company grow and increase its market share. In 1907, his associates tried to discourage him from building a new plant to manufacture a new form of structural steel—the Grey beam, invented by Henry Grey. U.S. Steel and other manufacturers were not in favor of the technology, but Schwab believed in it. Although he had to sell $5 million in bonds during a period of difficult economic conditions in America, he decided to proceed. To an associate, Schwab said: "I've thought the whole thing over, and if we are going to bust, we'll go bust big."[10] Although it took time to persuade customers to change to a new method of construction, the Grey, or Bethlehem, beam eventually took over the major share of the structural steel business from the riveted beam.

Under Schwab's leadership, Bethlehem Steel started to expand its market share. In 1905, the company was 2.5 percent of the size of U.S. Steel. Over the next fifteen years, Bethlehem's annual capacity for pig iron and steel ingots increased more than thirteen times. By 1926, Bethlehem had increased market share and was more than 20 percent of the industry leader's size. The company eventually became a significant competitor, growing to almost 60 percent of the size of U.S. Steel. Its earnings also increased—from 3 percent of U.S. Steel's earnings in 1905 to 15 percent of their earnings in 1926. Employment, too, increased significantly, from 9,461 employees in 1904 to 15,600 employees in 1914 and more than 60,000 employees in 1925.[11] While volume increases contributed to increased profits, so did cost reduction and increased efficiency. Control of the source supply, new technologies, and the bonus system all contributed to a reduction in costs.

Charles Schwab's leadership style was more like that of Andrew Carnegie than of Judge Gary. Whereas U.S. Steel was highly centralized, Bethlehem was much more decentralized. Schwab cared far more about what was achieved than how it was achieved, and he gave his department managers a great deal of latitude in managing their operations. Like Carnegie, Schwab was a strong believer in bonus plans. He established a bonus system for machinists based on each individual's output, another system for foremen, superintendents, and managers, and a third for the sales force based on the profitability of orders, not on sales volume. Once, when a foreman questioned Schwab's production goal for a blast furnace, Schwab told him that when the furnace achieved the desired efficiency, Schwab would pay off the mortgage on the man's house. The foreman drove his workers to achieve the goal, and his mortgage was paid. The lesson was widely publicized throughout the company. Schwab eventually established a bonus system that rewarded all employees who improved their efficiency. U.S. Steel had a bonus system, established in 1905, that was based on the progress of the entire company, not the performance of the individual. The bonus was not paid in cash but in shares of preferred stock of the company, which would be forfeited if the employee left the company for any reason. In contrast, Bethlehem's bonuses were immediate and personal.

Perhaps the biggest difference between the leaders of U.S. Steel and Bethlehem Steel was in their philosophy regarding prices. Judge Gary did not like price competition, believing it was unprofitable, immoral, and that it upset business stability. He established fixed prices for products and widely published them.

Judge Gary believed that price stability, in good times and bad, was beneficial to everyone in the industry, and he was willing to lose a portion of some orders to smaller firms in order to maintain the fixed prices. Charles Schwab, on the other hand, was a salesman who would give volume discounts or do whatever was required to get the order. He also knew the costs in his mills and what could be delivered and was able to both increase market share and total profitability.

Other firms, aware of U.S. Steel's prices, were able to cut their own prices to enter new businesses, knowing the prices they would have to meet. If U.S. Steel had cut prices during the early recessions in the industry, smaller firms such as Bethlehem Steel might not have been able to survive. Instead, aggressive smaller firms were able to enter product and market competition with the larger companies. Finally, in 1909, Judge Gary was forced to modify his price stabilization policy in order to reduce the competition from smaller firms.

Throughout the years of World War I and afterward, steel production increased. But in 1921, steel was in a decline. During that year, rumors began to circulate about the possible merger of seven steel companies: Midvale Steel and Ordnance Company, Lackawanna Steel, Youngstown Sheet and Tube Company, Republic Iron and Steel Company, Inland Steel, Sheet and Tube Company of America, and Brier Hill Steel Company. Together, these seven companies produced 20 percent of the country's steel and would be a significant competitor for U.S. Steel, which produced 45 percent, and Bethlehem, which produced 6 percent. In May 1922, Eugene Grace, president of Bethlehem Steel, announced that his company had acquired the properties of the Lackawanna Steel Company for a small cash payment and Bethlehem stock. The Department of Justice approved the merger. Bethlehem now controlled 9.7 percent of the nation's production and was clearly a significant competitor.

After the temporary setback in 1921, the steel industry began to expand. Production in the last half of the 1920s was more than 20 percent higher than in the last half of the prior decade. The 1920s were boom times for the steel industry. By the early 1920s, the steel industry had assumed its long-term character with seven major competitors. During the next forty years, only the market share and sizes of the competitors changed.

The depression hit the steel industry as hard as it did the rest of America. Production dropped precipitously, and by 1932, steel production was less than one-quarter what it had been in 1929. Although production climbed from these depths gradually through 1937, it decreased again in 1938. In the years 1930 through 1938, steel production was less than it had been in the years 1920 through 1928. Revenues decreased even faster than production. Revenue for U.S. Steel was down 39 percent in the period from 1920 through 1928. In both 1932 and 1933, corporate revenue was below that of 1902, the company's first full year of operation. Other companies did not fare much better. Only with the arrival of World War II did the steel industry and the country begin to recover economically.

During the depression, the major issue was survival. Common stock dividends were eliminated, preferred dividends and interest were cut as much as possible, capital expenditures for new plants and equipment were minimized, and labor forces were cut way back. During the decade 1931 to 1940, both U.S. Steel and Bethlehem Steel invested less in capital expenditures than they had in the decades 1911 to 1920 or 1921 to 1930. During the depression, U.S. Steel attempted to dispose of obsolete and marginal plants and modernize others. Capital investments usually had been made in the steel industry when profits were high and money was available, not when increased capacity should be brought on-line or when technological advances made possible better or lower-cost production. Innovation was not adopted rapidly especially during the depression. Several years typically passed between knowledge of a new process and its widespread use. Due to price inflexibility in the steel industry, obsolete equipment could continue to be operated profitably for a long time. Thus, the advent of World War II and its increased demand for steel production found the industry with aging facilities.

In the 1930s, United States Steel ran at an average production capacity of 45.7 percent, with five years below 40 percent, including the 1932 record low of 17.7 percent of full capacity. Employment followed this decline. Whereas the company had between 220,000 and 260,000 employees in the eight years before the depression, people were quickly cut from the payroll or put on a part-time basis. The company's 1932 *Annual Report* shows the company's workforce with 18,938 full-time employees and 139,094 part-time employee. In 1933, the company showed 172,577 part-time employees, working an average of 30 hours per week and making 60 cents per hour.

Not surprisingly, the 1930s were the years during which the industry finally became unionized. The iron and steel industry had always been a difficult place to work—dust and heat contributed to illness among workers and the machinery and processes contributed to accidents and deaths. Hours were long—a twelve-hour day was typical—and the plant usually was operational seven days a week, closed only on Christmas and the Fourth of July. A twelve-hour day meant that only two shifts of workers were required instead of the third shift needed with an eight-hour workday. In the early part of the twentieth century, most steelworkers were employed for fifty-four to seventy-two hours per week, with some working even more hours. Carnegie had introduced the eight-hour workday in the Edgar Thompson plant in 1872, but its use had not become widespread. After the Homestead strike in 1892—a deadly conflict at Carnegie's Homestead, Pennsylvania, plant between hired guards and striking members of the Amalgamated Association—Carnegie reintroduced the twelve-hour shift. In order to change from a day shift to a night shift, every other week employees worked a double shift—twenty-four hours straight—and then twenty-four hours off in alternate weeks when the other team worked a double shift. Twenty-four hours straight in a steel mill challenged all but the strongest workers. Attempts were made to change to an eight-hour day, but U.S. Steel fought them through the 1910s. The advent of World War I and the increased demand for steel resulted in the industry continuing the twelve-hour days, seven days a week. Only in 1923 did the eight-hour day become an industry standard.

Workers had tried to organize into unions before the 1930s. In 1842, workers in Pennsylvania called an unsuccessful strike to protest wage reductions. Between 1880 and 1890, nearly all the iron mills in Allegheny County, Pennsylvania, were unionized; nevertheless, unionism was not widespread. The Homestead strike had been one of a number of battles that the Amalgamated Association had lost. In 1901, with the merger of several companies into U.S. Steel, the Amalgamated Association struck several subsidiaries in an attempt to increase power, but lost. In 1909, American Sheet and Tube Plate, a U.S. Steel subsidiary, notified the union that it would hereafter operate on a nonunion basis. The workers struck, but, fourteen months later, the strike collapsed and with it unionization in the steel industry. Wages went up during World War I, although not as fast as prices, but after the war they fell. In 1919, there was another unsuccessful union organization drive, but once again a national strike collapsed, and the union was not recognized.

There were many reasons for those early union failures. There were always more workers than jobs, and the companies frequently brought in new workers—European immigrants, Canadians, Mexicans, and southern blacks to threaten older workers. To many immigrant laborers, life in a steel mill was better than life in the old country, and there were always more immigrants searching for jobs. The companies tried to cooperate with the skilled workers, offering them subsidized housing, incentive bonuses, pensions, and stock purchase plans. Also, the unions lacked the backing of public opinion, often appearing as antiworker and anti-American. The American people at this time were to a large extent for business and against unions.

The result was that in good times wages went up, and in bad times there was widespread unemployment. Companies gradually brought down the salaries of the highest paid, highest skilled positions. Safety and health problems continued to plague the industry, although U.S. Steel had introduced a safety-first program in 1912 and gradually began paying more attention to worker health and safety. Finally, in 1936, the Congress of Industrial Organizations (CIO) invested in a $500,000 fund to support the Steel Workers Organizing Committee (later the United Steelworkers of America). In the next year there was a long and often bitter steelworkers strike against U.S. Steel. At last, in

March 1937, U.S. Steel signed with the union, deciding it did not want to face a costly strike at a time when it detected a recovery from the depression. During the following two years, other companies followed and recognized the union, sometimes after brutal strikebreaking attempts by the companies. One of the reasons for union recognition was the understanding that the union leaders had the ability to shut down the industry. And the public had moved away from its pro-business orientation, recognizing that the failure of business leaders had in part brought about the depression.

When the United States entered World War II, its steel industry was operating significantly below capacity and had aging and obsolete equipment after a decade of limited investment in new technology and plants. Yet the country was in great need of iron and steel in order to win the war. The industry performed very well. From an output of 38 million tons of raw steel in 1935, the country produced 79 million tons in 1945 and continued this expansion after the war to produce 117 million tons of steel during the postwar year of 1955. The steel industry's ability to produce the material for the ships, planes, tanks, guns, trucks, and other items needed by the country to win the war demonstrated, despite how things might have seemed, its health as well as the workers' and management's capabilities. Bethlehem Steel, in its shipyards, produced more than 1,100 naval and merchant vessels during the war and repaired, serviced, or rebuilt more than 38,000 ships of all types. The production of all other steel companies was equally impressive, and the steel industry contributed significantly to the U.S. victory over Japan and Italy. All told, the United States manufactured 297,000 airplanes, 86,000 tanks, 6,500 naval vessels, 64,500 landing craft, 5,400 cargo ships, 315,000 artillery pieces, 4.2 million tons of artillery shells, and 17 million rifles during the war.[12]

With the end of the war, the steel industry converted to peacetime applications and expanded production as the country boomed. Automobiles, home building, construction, and other applications required steel. By 1955, steel output was 30 percent over the peak output of 1944. Irving Olds, in 1951, said:

> U.S. Steel is expanding capacity and increasing steel production to enable it to do its part towards meeting the Nation's pressing need for more steel. ... The steel industry of the United States has put no limits on its eventual size. ... That the Nation should never go off the Steel Standard, if it lies in our power to prevent it, is the pledge of all of us at U.S. Steel on this, our Golden Anniversary.[13]

The first half of the twentieth century had been the glory days of steel. It had also given the industry a false sense of prosperity. The next fifty years would be a time of reality.

The Decline of the Steel Industry (1950–2000)

Steel had grown in this country because American steelmakers had led the world in technology; new national markets for steel had opened; new sources of raw materials and energy were discovered and developed within the country; entrepreneurs and inventors were attracted to the industry; major investments had been made in this growth industry so that American manufacturers had the most modern plants in the world; American manufacturers had learned to compete and sell their products worldwide; immigration provided workers for the jobs that were created and American wages were competitive; government developed pro-business policies, working with management to expand the position of American industry; and finally, strong management led the industry. The industry declined because, after 1950, most of these factors were no longer part of the picture. Although it is fashionable to blame external factors for the decline of "king steel," including the Japanese, Korean, German, and other foreign steel industries that were operated to further their own national interests, the illness was, to a very large extent, internal. The U.S. steel industry declined in health because it coasted for too long. It assumed that things would never change, that management, labor, investors, the public, and the government could all get a bigger share of the pie. Meanwhile, no one worried about making more pie. The textile industry and the railroads had declined for the same reasons, but the lesson had not been learned by the steel industry.

In the early 1950s, the U.S. steel industry was the largest and most efficient in the world. Since then, its fortunes have declined sharply. New technologies, including the basic oxygen furnace, the electric furnace, and continuous castings were applied by many world competitors before the leading U.S. producers made commitments to them. There was now a diffusion of steelmaking capability throughout the world. Overseas producers and American mini-mills became more formidable competitors. Market conditions changed as customers learned to use less steel or switched to lighter and stronger materials such as aluminum and plastics. A new generation of entrepreneurs developed young industries around silicon—not around steel, as had been the case during the first half of the century. There were changes in sources, costs of raw materials, and costs of energy and shipping. The industry maintained obsolete mills for long periods in the belief that the capacity would be required in periods of booming demand. Earnings were insufficient to simultaneously support the modernization of the industry and new government requirements in areas of pollution and workplace rules. Labor peace was purchased at a price that neither the industry nor labor could afford, and jobs were eliminated in great quantity. The government changed from being a strong supporter of the industry to a neutral observer and then an adversary. And finally, management failed in a number of areas to provide a strong sense of direction. Conglomerates bought steel companies without understanding the industry. Major producers diversified in new directions. Without strong leadership, the industry lost its way.

For a century, from 1860 to 1960, steel had been produced using the Bessemer and the open-hearth methods, which together accounted for 90 percent of the steel made during most of this period. As was shown in Table 3.1, the Bessemer process was the leading method of producing steel through 1895 and then declined in importance over the next fifty years. The open-hearth process grew in importance and was the major method of producing steel through the 1960s. After World War II, there were significant changes in technology as the electric furnace and basic oxygen furnace became the principal methods of making steel. These two technologies accounted for 12 percent of the steel produced in 1960 and almost 90 percent two decades later. Technologies change, and when they do, industry leadership often changes. The iron makers of 1850 had been succeeded by steelmakers in 1890. One hundred years later, a similar phenomenon was occurring. The United States had led the world in the change from iron to steel and the application of the new technology. The major American producers did not, however, lead the world in the development of the new steel technology. A study on capital expenditures in the steel industry indicates that technological innovation has not been of primary importance in affecting capital expenditures. Most technological innovations were known for years before they were widely adopted by the American steel industry, which meant that ultimately, it was not ready for competition.

The electric furnace has a long history. In 1909, the first large-scale electric furnaces were constructed in America. The electric furnace largely replaced the crucible process for making high-quality specialty steels such as stainless and tool steel. The electric furnace is now capable of producing a whole range of carbon steel, and not just high-price, high-quality steel. With an electric arc furnace, scrap steel, including shredded automobile bodies as well as pig iron, are loaded into a furnace and electrical currents are passed from one electrode through the scrap steel to another electrode. The primary cost saving in this technology comes through the use of recycled scrap steel as the major material. In normal times, the price of scrap steel is lower than the cost of making iron in a blast furnace. In times of business expansion, however, the cost of scrap steel can rise significantly and become unavailable in sufficient quantities. Another reason for the increasing importance of electric furnaces has been the development of pollution control laws for open hearths, coke ovens, and blast furnaces. Electric furnaces do not require hot metal and therefore can meet environmental control laws at a lower investment cost. Today, almost 40 percent of steel is manufactured using electric furnaces.

The Linz-Donawitz (LD) converter , or basic oxygen furnace, was named after the plant in Austria where it was first used. Pure oxygen, which is blown through a water-cooled lance at high speed and high pressure directly into the center of molten pig iron in a brick-lined converter, refines pig iron and scrap. The advantage in this process is that it combines the benefits of a converter process—high productivity, low operating cost, and low construction cost—with the advantages of an open-hearth process—more precise control of the quality of steel. The basic oxygen process, which only became feasible with the bulk production of oxygen in the years between 1929 and 1960, offers much shorter heat times and therefore requires much less labor and investment per ton of output. The time required to make steel decreased from an average of five to ten hours in the normal open-hearth process to less than one hour.

The first American basic oxygen furnace was built at the McLouth Steel Corporation near Detroit in 1954. Over the next thirty years, the industry increased the number of plants using this process, a transition accomplished by a decline in the production of the open-hearth process. Basic oxygen furnaces must use less scrap than open hearths or electric furnaces, unless the scrap is preheated, which means a substantial increase in cost. Thus, the electric furnace is important in its use of available excess scrap iron, and both the basic oxygen furnace and electric furnace processes grew together.

A third major innovation in the last thirty years was the introduction of continuous casting. This process casts molten iron continuously into a ribbon of steel that is gradually cooled and rolled into semifinished shapes—a process that bypasses the costly and time-consuming ingot stage. This process improves the yield of finished product per ton of raw steel, gives higher product quality, and provides energy and labor-cost savings. The amount of energy required to produce a ton of steel could be reduced up to 50 percent. By 1990, more than 90 percent of American steel was cast continuously.

Japan, because it had lost many factories and had to replace its steelmaking capacity after World War II, took advantage of this new technology. After the war, most Japanese production employed the basic oxygen furnace and the continuous caster. Germany and other European steelmakers also had to replace the steel mills that had been destroyed in the war, and they, too, chose the most modern technology.

In the United States, a new type of steel mill, the mini-mill, was developed—in large part by entrepreneurs. The mini-mill companies, including Nucor, Gallatin Steel, Ipsco, Worthington Industries, Kentucky Electric Steel, Steel Dynamics, and Carpenter Technology, grew to become significant competitors in the steel industry. A mini-mill plant using an electric arc furnace combined with a continuous casting machine could be established for a limited capital investment. These integrated plants use scrap metal as the major raw material and can be established in areas where both scrap metal is available and where a local market for the finished steel exists. Mini-mills produce a limited range of products but have captured a growing share of the American steel market. They are among the most efficient steel manufacturers in the world. The mini-mill has two other advantages: they need only a relatively small crew, usually very flexible in their work assignments and often on incentive pay, and they employ local management able to make quick decisions about product quality, mix, pricing, and delivery. Not only have mini-mills garnered a larger share of the steel market, some suppliers have even been able to maintain profitability during recessions when the large integrated mills suffer huge losses. As this is written, there are about 100 mini-mills in 33 states.

In order to understand some of the problems of the steel industry, it is worth looking at some market changes during the past half century. Steel is a commodity, and there is very little product differentiation within the industry. Almost all steel products are manufactured to standard specifications; that is, there are few differences in steel produced by different firms or, for that matter, by different countries. United States, German, Japanese, Indian, Russian, Chinese, and Korean steel are similar. The competition among steel manufacturers is therefore related to price, including all delivery and extra charges; customer service, including technical advice, delivery, and storage procedures; and financing arrangements.

After World War II, pent-up demand for products, including automobiles, appliances, and buildings, caused a surge in steel utilization. The industry was also affected by major construction projects such as the building of the interstate highway system. Eventually, however, the demand slackened, and the steel industry found itself with excess capacity.

When the Japanese auto industry increased its share of the U.S. auto market as desribed in chapter 5, it affected not only Ford and General Motors, but also the U.S. steel industry. Japanese automakers use Japanese steel, just as Korean shipbuilders use Korean steel, and German machinery makers use German steel. Thus, the U.S. steel industry is affected by the health and growth of a number of other United States industries—railroad and highway construction, agricultural and electrical equipment, machinery, appliances, automobiles, aircraft, and construction. As the manufacturers in these industries lost market share worldwide or manufactured products overseas, it directly affected the health of the U.S. steel industry.

Another factor affecting the U.S. steel industry is product downsizing. When the price of petroleum began to increase in the early 1970s, automobiles were redesigned to save gasoline. This was partially a market consideration—a desire to give the customer a more fuel-efficient automobile. But it was also a result of fuel consumption standards written by the federal government, which, for the first time, told the automobile companies what kind of cars they could build. Starting with a desire to save gasoline, the change ended up saving a lot more: steel, rubber, glass, and other materials. In six years, Ford reduced the weight of its automobiles more than 1,100 pounds and decreased the amount of iron and steel used in its average car by 1,000 pounds as the automaker switched from steel to plastics and aluminum. Other industries were also building lighter products and using materials other than steel.

With any industry, as with any company, there is always competition. There are other ways of doing things and a customer can use less of a product. The amount used is to some extent related to the way things have previously been done, which is why a new company or industry has to overcome customer inertia in order to succeed. But in time, newer products or processes replace older ones. Steel had replaced iron just as iron had replaced wood, and eventually steel was affected by product substitution. Reinforced concrete replaced steel in some applications in the construction industry. Aluminum, glass, and paper replaced steel in containers, and plastics and aluminum replaced steel in a variety of other applications.

Finally, there is the issue of imports and the competitiveness of the American steel industry. The United States is no longer the dominant steel producer in the world. In 1890, the United States passed Great Britain as the world's leading steel producer. After World War II, the United States was passed first by the Soviet Union and then, in 1973, by Japan as steel producers. In 2000, China was the leading steel-producing country, followed by Japan and the United States. Because of the breakup of the Soviet Union, Russia is now the fourth largest producer.[14] The United States, according to the American Iron and Steel Institute *Annual Statistics Report,* produced 57 percent of the world's raw steel in the unusual postwar year of 1947, 26 percent in 1960 and 1965, 16.4 percent in 1975, 14.2 percent in 1980, and in 1982, the United States produced only 10.5 percent of the world's steel. In 2000, the United States produced 12.0 percent of the world's steel, and in 2001, 10.6 percent. From 1965 to 1982, U.S. steel output delivered to the following industries declined more than 50 percent: automobile, machinery, rail transportation, industrial fasteners, ship-building, and aerospace. When entrepreneurs built the automotive and appliance industries, for example, the steel industry benefited. As these and other industries have declined, the steel industry has also suffered.

After World War II, it became necessary for the United States to develop additional sources of iron ore. Annual consumption of ore had increased signif-icantly and it was believed that the ore in the Mesabi Range would be insufficient to supply the needs of the country through the remainder of the century. Hence, new sources of iron ore were found in Australia, Brazil, Chile, India, Labrador, Liberia, Peru, South Africa, and Venezuela. Methods were also pursued to use the lower-grade ores found in abundance throughout the United States. Concentration plants were built in Minnesota where billions of tons of taconite, a low-grade iron-bearing rock, were found. Companies learned how to crush rock and then pelletize the ore so that it would hold up under the high pressures of blast furnaces. Large bulk-cargo carriers capable of handling 100,000 tons or more of iron ore were built, reducing the cost of shipping ore to steel plants around the world. The U.S. steel industry had grown in the early twentieth century not only because of a large home market, but also because of the availability of rich sources of minerals, an excellent bulk transportation system of railroads and barges, and the building of plants with a large scale of operation. In the late twentieth century, the newer steel producers of the world opened up richer ore fields than the Great Lakes district, learned how to move minerals worldwide on a low-cost basis, and could operate large steelmaking plants that are as good as their American counterparts.

Exports and Imports

For the entire twentieth century until 1959, the United States was a net exporter of steel; that is, it exported more steel than it imported. In that year, partially due to a long strike in the industry, the United States imported more steel than it exported, and every year thereafter, the United States was a net importer of steel. Imports grew rapidly, and the country imported 5.6 percent of its supply in 1962, 12.2 percent in 1967, 16.6 percent in 1972, 17.8 percent in 1977, and 23.0 percent in 1984. In 1965, the United States imported 10 million tons of foreign steel; by 1978, it imported 21 million tons. And by 1984, foreign manufacturers produced a quarter of all steel sold in the United States.[15]

During the 1980s, more than 400 American steel mills were closed. Within a quarter century, the United States went from being the world's largest exporter of steel to the world's largest importer. Imports came from three areas: Japan, the European Economic Community (EEC), and the Advanced Developing Countries (ADC), including Mexico, Brazil, India, Turkey, and Korea. The story of worldwide steel production at the end of the century is told in a few paragraphs.

Japan's steel industry began in 1858, and its first integrated steel plant was built by the government in Yawata in 1901. By 1929, Japan's output was less than 2 percent of the world's production. Throughout the 1930s, Japan built its steelmaking capability on importing scrap iron from the United States and pig iron from Manchuria and India. As a result of World War II, Japan lost much of its steelmaking capacity, its ships capable of delivering raw materials to Japan, and sources of raw materials throughout Asia. Changing American government policy after the war had much to do with the rebuilding of the Japanese steel industry.

In 1950, the occupational government dissolved the Japan Iron and Steel Company, the country's dominant steel company, by applying American antitrust policy to postwar Japan based on its excess concentration of economic power. The assets of Japan Iron and Steel Company were then divided between

Yawata and Fuji. This reorganization led to intense competition in the Japanese steel industry among the six leading integrated steelmakers: Yawata Iron and Steel, Fuji Iron and Steel, Kawasaki Steel, Nippon Kokan, Sumitomo Metals, and Kobe Steel. Twenty years later, Yawata and Fuji were recombined into Nippon Steel Company, and in time, the firm became the second leading steelmaker in the world—larger than U.S. Steel Corporation—with fiscal 2000 revenues of $25.4 billion and profits of $106 million.

The early rivalry in Japan forced each company to compete aggressively for the local market by using the best iron and steelmaking technology. The Japanese developed a philosophy of searching out the best practices in the world and then improving on them. This philosophy had first been introduced into the steel industry by Andrew Carnegie more than a century prior but had been forgotten by the American steelmakers. The leading Japanese company, Yawata Iron and Steel, adopted a new steelmaking process, the basic oxygen converter, which was being developed in Austria. Nippon Kokan independently did the same. For competitive reasons, other steelmakers soon followed. Later, the Japanese steelmakers constructed advanced rolling mills and built bulk-cargo carriers.

The Korean War stimulated the modernization of the Japanese steel industry. In 1950, President Harry Truman pressured the American and Japanese steelmakers to expand production by using scrap-consuming open-hearth furnaces. Between 1951 and 1961, the six Japanese integrated steelmakers bought American scrap in increasing amounts, and the price of scrap iron soared. In February 1957, the U.S. Commerce Department announced a suspension of export licensing of all kinds of iron and steel scrap. The Commerce Department urged the Japanese steel industry to construct large blast furnaces and basic oxygen converters and arranged the financing of this modernization of the Japanese steel industry through the International Bank for Reconstruction and Development and the Export-Import Bank of the United States.

As the Japanese steel industry successfully used this new technology, it began to aggressively sell its steel to a world market. Japan bought coal from Australia and the United States and iron ore from all over the world, especially Australia, Brazil, Canada, and India. At the end of World War II, Japan was producing less than 1 million tons of iron and steel. By 1973, its production had increased to 119 million tons, second only to the Soviet Union. By 1985, one-quarter of all steel in international trade came from Japan. Japan became the lowest cost steel producer. In 1983, Nippon Kokan, Japan's number-two steelmaker, bought 53 percent of National Steel, America's seventh largest steelmaker, and began to apply Japanese technology and capital to a major American company.

Western Europe also rapidly expanded and modernized its steelmaking capacities after World War II, especially in West Germany, France, and Belgium. For a time, the EEC lacked sufficient steelmaking capacity to satisfy its internal requirements, but gradually, excess capacity developed. Operating a steel mill below capacity results in high unit costs. With Japan's policy of lifetime employment for its workers and the European government's policy of making it difficult to lay off workers, there was a tendency to ship excess production overseas at below cost in order to keep plants operating at full capacity. European and Japanese firms cut prices when they had excess capacity. American steelmakers preferred to follow full-cost pricing strategies. It was the issue of Carnegie and Schwab versus Judge Gary's philosophy on pricing carried out on an international level.

Government-owned steel firms may be operated indefinitely from public funds in order to maintain employment. A number of European steelmakers were unprofitable but were subsidized by governments through direct subsidies, low-interest loans, low-cost shipping and storage, import duties, and quotas.

After the war, some developing countries began to develop a national steel industry. Countries such as South Korea, Ukraine, Brazil, Mexico, India, Taiwan, Turkey, and Argentina initially created steel industries to use local iron ore or other raw materials. Eventually, excess capacity was achieved, and steel was then exported to the United States and other world markets.

As steel imports to the United States increased, the American steel industry asked the government to take action to protect the domestic industry. Hence, in the late 1960s, the United States pressured Japan to agree to voluntary restraint agreements—essentially, a quota system. Moreover, dumping and other unfair labor practices had already been restricted under the General Agreement on Tariffs and Trade (GATT). An antidumping duty was used to raise prices in the United States. Furthermore, Trigger Price Mechanism (TPM) has supplemented existing antidumping laws and has been used to cut off steel imports from Japan and other countries above a certain level. The quota system and TPM were used to buy time for the domestic steel industry to modernize, but some in the industry failed to act and were still noncompetitive. The result of these actions was an increase in steel costs for the consumer without any long-term benefits to the industry.

The issue finally is the relative costs of manufacturing and how competitive each company and country is in the world market. Whereas tariffs and legal barriers to imports can buy time, ultimately American suppliers must be able to match their competitors worldwide. For decades, the U.S. steel industry had the technical, financial, and marketing strengths to modernize and could have competed anywhere. From 1940 to 1970, there were significant increases in productivity in the U.S. steel industry. The United States had good technology and operating practices, but eventually Japan and other countries caught up and ultimately required less labor to produce steel. The continuation of grossly inefficient technologies such as open-hearth furnaces and slow adoption of more modern processes hurt the American steel industry. Capital investment was used for maintenance of mandated pollution equipment for older plants. Poor investment choices were made. Wire rod production is more advantageous in mini-mills, and yet for many years few large producers invested in this technology. In fact, large producers are now closing mills devoted to bar capacity, the main product of mini-mills. Japan invested in continuous casting, for example, and in 1990 cast 75 percent of its raw steel. In addition, at the turn of the twenty-first century, the EEC cast 45 percent of its raw steel, whereas the United States only cast 25 percent. This, of course, has an impact on relative costs.

It is difficult to justify protecting a domestic industry with tariffs or legal barriers so that the industry can maximize its profits by attempting to defy the laws of supply and demand. As a result of such practices, the U.S. steel industry now lacks funds for modernization and the latest steelmaking technology to revive its competitive edge.

During this fifty-year period, the unions faced a time of transition. Labor, ultimately, is dependent on the health of the business. Although any company can grant wage increases, it doesn't matter how much workers are making if the plant closes and they lose their jobs. The cost of production eventually influences the ability of a company to grow, maintain the status quo, or survive. For more than two decades, escalating wage and benefit costs have been a major factor in placing the steel industry in a noncompetitive situation against the Japanese and nonunion domestic mini-mills, and a significant number of jobs have been lost.

Total employment costs (salaries and benefits) in the steel industry started to escalate during the 1970s. In 1982, steel labor costs were more than $23 per hour, more than double the average for all employees engaged in manufacturing in this country at that time. Steelmakers' labor rates were 60 percent above those in Japan, twice those in Europe, and more than six times those of other Asian competitors. Although labor costs can be higher if labor productivity is higher, because of a lack of investment in modern technology and obsolete work rules, this was not the case in the American steel industry, hence it could not continue its lead in productivity. In the 1980s, less labor was required to make a ton of steel in Japan than was required in the United States. The high labor costs in the United States were partially a result of a cost-of-living adjustment (COLA) given to the union in the 1970s and 1980s in return for a pledge not to strike. COLA was responsible for 60 percent of the increase in wages in the 1970s and early 1980s. Labor peace had been purchased at a price that neither the industry nor the union could long afford.[16]

While the industry agreed to wage increases that rose faster than in other manufacturing industries, the penetration of the American market by foreign producers had been rising. Employment in the steel industry declined by more than 100,000 employees in a ten-year period starting in 1969, and, in 1982, the fifteen largest integrated producers laid off an additional 40 percent of their workforce. Employment in Pittsburgh, Youngstown, Buffalo, Cleveland, Gary, Toledo, and other cities in the Northeast rapidly declined, leading to economic problems in the so-called "rust belt." United States Steel Corporation now has fewer workers than it did in 1902.

The industry in the 1980s began to realize that its survival was at stake, and management and labor worked together to improve the competitive position of the industry. The industry attempted to obtain wage and benefit concessions in order to reduce labor costs. In return for these concessions, the companies agreed to reinvest labor savings in the business. Management and labor finally had to recognize their interdependence, as plant after plant was closed and the industry had its worst performance since the depression.

Changing Role of Government, New Competition

In many other countries, the steel industry has either been owned, subsidized, or indirectly controlled by the national government. The U.S. steel industry has always had an independent industry, which, for most of its history, benefited from a friendly government. But since the 1950s, the federal government has gone from supporter to a frequent adversary—usually to no one's gain. For much of this period, depending on who held political power, the government oscillated from a position of supporting a free market economy to one favoring more government control of the steel industry.

For example, in 1952, during the Korean War, President Harry Truman seized the steel mills. He believed that steel companies, engaged in a labor dispute with the United Steelworkers of America, would be shut down by a strike and the war effort would suffer. There already had been a major steel strike of fifty-four days' duration in 1952, and Truman sought to avoid a strike by taking over the mills in the name of national interest. The Truman administration vigorously defended itself against criticism for the move leveled by both Congress and the press. The action was overturned by the Supreme Court, which in a six to three decision, agreed with an injunction issued by Judge Pine of the District Court that Truman had exceeded his authority as president.

During World War II, the government established price controls for steel and other major products. After the war, the government continued a strong interference in pricing decisions, allowing neither market conditions nor the steel industry to freely set prices. At times, the government took the role of "jawboning," or trying to talk the industry out of raising prices, whereas at other times, the government actually established mandatory controls or used its purchasing power to force price increases to be rescinded. In 1951, the Federal Trade Commission sued the American Iron and Steel Institute and certain of its members regarding pricing practices within the industry. Presidents Harry

Truman, John Kennedy, and Richard Nixon all confronted the steel industry regarding increases in steel prices, and for a time, President Nixon instituted price controls. It was partly as a result of all of these actions that the industry did not invest sufficient capital to introduce more efficient technology and modernize the industry. The government in the nineteenth century had used tariffs as a way of supporting the growth of the U.S. steel industry. It had become an advocate of free trade, even if some nations competed unfairly. In the mid- to late twentieth century, government policy was in favor of encouraging the lowest prices and was no longer in favor of industrial and economic growth, more manufacturing jobs, or the development of a strong domestic steel industry.

Iron making and steelmaking inherently are polluters of air and water. When federal policy began to reflect environmental concerns with the passage of the Clean Air Act of 1963 and the Clean Water Act of 1965, for example, the burden fell heavily on these industries. The Occupational Safety and Health Act (OSHA) also had a major effect on the steel industry. And although many in the industry felt that there were excess governmental controls and regulations, there was no question that major capital investment was required to meet new environmental and workplace standards. Unless market and government considerations allowed the manufacturers to pass on these costs to their customers, funds had to be diverted from the modernization of the industry.

One method of increasing industry efficiency was through company mergers. However, the Justice Department blocked most mergers on antitrust grounds. For example, in the 1950s, the attempted merger of Bethlehem and Youngstown Sheet and Tube was denied. In the 1980s, when the industry was in major trouble, the Justice Department turned down the merger of U.S. Steel and National Steel, and caused a delay in the merger of Republic Steel and Jones and Laughlin. The government did, however, allow the acquisition of integrated steel companies by large conglomerates, as well as permit Japanese steelmakers to purchase large amounts of stock in National Steel and Wheeling Pittsburgh. Although there may be some logic in denying the right of strong American steelmakers to take over weak ones while at the same time allowing American companies to be controlled by foreign companies, there is no doubt that the logic could not easily be explained to the early industrialists and labor and government leaders. There are many people who found the government's reasoning unusual, if not blatantly damaging to the industry.

In 1997, American iron and steel imports were $11,285 million, whereas exports were $5,637 million, a net trade imbalance of $5,648 million. In 2000, American iron and steel imports were $34,800 million and exports were $6,200 million, a net trade imbalance of $28,600 million. In 2001, President George W. Bush imposed a tariff of up to 30 percent on steel imports in order to provide temporary relief to the U.S. steel industry, claiming that foreign producers were dumping steel in the U.S. market at below their costs. This was judged illegal under the General Agreement on Tariffs and Trade (GATT) and before penalties were assessed on American exports, the president rescinded the tariffs. Beginning in 1998, more than twenty-five steel producers, including National Steel, Wheeling Pittsburgh, Bethlehem, Republic Technologies, and LTV/Jones and Laughlin—representing about 25 percent of U.S. capacity—filed for Chapter 11 bankruptcy as the industry lost money in record amounts, owing, in part, to substantial increases in imports, often dumped at prices below cost.

Ultimately, the government has to decide whether a strong domestic steel industry is important, whether it supports market pricing or wants government interference in pricing decisions. It must decide who should pay for desired environmental and workplace rules, whether to provide guarantees of employment or improved international competitiveness, and what to do with workers whose jobs have been eliminated.

Last, but by no means least, the role of the leading steel companies' management must be examined. The Japanese, the Germans, and other nations of Western Europe rapidly expanded and modernized their steel capacities after World War II, and they did so admirably. The American entrepreneurs who decided to enter the steel business at that time built mini-mills and captured a significant part of the U.S. market. Advanced developing nations such as Korea, India, and Mexico built strong national steel industries that then started to enter the export market. The leading American steel companies, with strong financial, technical, marketing, and labor strength, had a lot of options for proceeding. However, despite plentiful resources, they accomplished very little, preferring to continue business as is, spending earnings on dividends and on expanding existing capacity, not on new technology. They withdrew from the international marketplace and then tried to shelter the U.S. market through government action. Like the iron manufacturers of the nineteenth century or the vacuum-tube manufacturers of the mid-twentieth century, strong resources did not compensate for weak management decisions.

Management did not make the required commitments when it had the resources and the market. It is now paying the price for its complacency. After the war, United States Steel Corporation was opposed to borrowing for new plants and equipment. As a result, it was able to reduce its long-term debt to $62 million, less than one-third of what it had been before the war. But this early preservation cost the company a great deal. By 1974, long-term debt had risen to $1,361 billion and in 1983, it was more than $7,100 billion—partially to finance the acquisition of Marathon Oil, a company outside of the steel business. A failure to invest early in the new technologies and make difficult decisions about plant modernization and closings resulted in the company losing market share and having to invest later when the cost of modernization had risen significantly and when much revenue and market share had been lost to other companies.

As the steel industry began to get into trouble, two very different approaches were taken to improve profitability. Some companies, such as Allegheny Ludlum Steel Corporation, diversified away from the steel industry. U.S. Steel Corporation attempted the same thing with its acquisitions of Marathon Oil and Texas Oil and Gas. Some steel companies were acquired by large conglomerates. Examples include the acquisition of Jones and Laughlin by LTV and the acquisition of Crucible Steel by Colt Industries. All of these actions reflect the concerns expressed by Charles Schwab at the beginning of the century regarding the rise of the "financial man" at the expense of the "operating man" in the steel industry. Conglomerates all too often are run by managers who know how to buy and sell companies, but not, in many cases, how to run them. Mere mergers or acquisitions do not, in themselves, accomplish anything. The key is what is done with the resources available to management.

For, ultimately, the role of top management is to know how to run the business, develop a coordinated and integrated marketing and product strategy for the business, and then implement that plan. Management must decide how much of the earnings to reinvest in the growth of the business and what to return to stockholders in the form of dividends. Too much milking of the business through excess dividends, and a company will eventually decline. Sufficient resources must be devoted to the modernization and competitiveness of plants. A "financial man" may be predisposed to focus on the numbers at the expense of the business. A leader, whether a founding entrepreneur or a professional manager, must understand the steel business because he or she is competing against others who do.

The U.S. steel industry grew not only because of technological, market, and financial reasons but also because of leadership. However, good management was succeeded by complacency and then sometimes by mismanagement. Expensive modernization programs lacked integrated planning with respect to plant structure and organization. American steel companies did not objectively evaluate the capabilities of the plants they already had and those they acquired. Recommendations on steelmaking from some of the industry's technical people from the 1920s through the 1970s were ignored. Large amounts were spent on a piecemeal expansion of poorly located and laid-out plants. Steelmaking capacity was increased at a time when it was not advisable since consumption was on its way down. Industry capacity, which had been as high as 150 million tons, had to be decreased significantly. The industry needed retrenchment as a policy.

The industry would do well to learn from Andrew Carnegie. Rather than fixing prices, Carnegie cut costs and improved efficiency. Although many in the steel industry may not be comfortable with this approach, there is no question that the Japanese and other steelmakers are following many of both Carnegie's and Schwab's philosophies. For example, ways of reducing costs include closing obsolete and inefficient plants, undertaking joint ventures, and raising cash through the sale of assets and new financing to allow the industry to modernize, using the best steelmaking technology. A smaller, cost-competitive steel industry has much to recommend it.

The Future: Downsizing and Modernization

The steel industry has come full cycle. From a time of many small and local plants, the industry moved to several giants created out of these small plants by the financiers, and now the industry has partially returned to small, local plants—the mini-mills, which now control a significant share of steel production. For a long time, major suppliers were adding capacity; they are now reducing their steel output. From a time when the industry wanted protection from foreign competition through tariffs because it was too small to compete, the American steel industry grew to dominate the market worldwide through a policy of free trade. And it now wants protection from foreign competition because the industry has overcapacity and continues to lose many jobs. From a time when workers were exploited and without unions, unions have become too strong or management too weak, salaries have become too high or productivity increases too small—partially through work rules—and companies have been forced to reduce employment significantly. From a time when the industry was dominated by entrepreneurs who took risks, raised money, developed markets and plants, and built an industry, a point has been reached now where management is so comfortable and so hesitant to take risks or develop a well-conceived and coordinated strategy, that their companies lose to those who do—the entrepreneurs who started the mini-mills, the Japanese, and other foreign steel manufacturers, as well as the management of conglomerates who acquire the weaker steel companies for paper stock. Yet, the world market for steel products has continued to grow. In 1975, world production of steel was 506.9 million metric tons, and worldwide exports represented 25.6 percent of production. In 1985, production worldwide had grown to 599 million metric tons, and exports were 28.5 percent of production. By 2000, production had reached 747.9 million metric tons, and exports equaled 40.5 percent of production.[17] The world's largest producer and user of iron and steel is now China, and Asia will be a very large growth market in decades to come.

However, employment in the steel industry has declined significantly during this period. The European Union lost 81 percent of its steel industry employment in the years between 1975 and 2000, the United States 67 percent, and Japan 57 percent. Clearly, efficiency has been forced on the industry. By closing older plants and investing in newer technology, the industry is now running at more than 80 percent of capacity.[18]

The failure of the steel industry is not fundamentally a failure of technology or a failure of market. It is a failure of planning, a failure of will, and a failure of leadership. A reading of the annual reports of U.S. Steel for the last eighty years, or of many publications of the American Steel Industry, indicate both a company and an industry that have been complacent, oblivious at times to what was happening in the world, have played it safe, and have been ready to blame the government, the unions, the investment community, foreign steelmakers, and even environmentalists for what has happened.

The leadership of an Andrew Carnegie or a Charles Schwab at the right company could have made a substantial difference. Yet, it is still not too late for the industry to face its future. But without plans to modernize the industry, decrease industry capacity by closing or replacing inefficient facilities, increase productivity, reduce costs, and become more efficient, without leadership to implement these plans and without risk taking, the industry will have only continued decline and problems ahead.

The lessons of the steel industry can be applied to other industries examined in this book: the automobile industry, the electronics and the computer industry—or, for that matter, any industry. A business may be looked at on a worldwide basis, with competing companies and competing technologies carefully scrutinized. A business must make enough profit to be able—after paying taxes, interest, and dividends—to invest in its future. Increased wages are important to everyone, but they only have long-term value if the company or industry is able to provide jobs. Rather than being adversaries, government and business must work together. Although there are obvious differences in roles between the two, they both benefit from a healthy industry and a healthy economy.

Ultimately, success or failure in any enterprise is the long shadow of management. Any business that can be managed can be mismanaged. The steel industry has seen both. And in business as in life, there is no such thing as a free lunch—for management, for labor, or for the government. They all share in success. Or in failure.

CHAPTER 4

Andrew Carnegie (1835–1919)
Partner and Benefactor

There is properly no history; only biography.
—Ralph Waldo Emerson

Let us dare to read, think, speak and write. ... Let every sluice of
knowledge be opened and set aflowing.
—John Adams

Andrew Carnegie was born to a working-class family that had to borrow to immigrate to the United States, and yet he earned and gave away more money than anyone of his day. Forced to leave Scotland because of the effects of one industrial revolution, he led another. He achieved a senior position with the world's leading company and then left to start his own—a company that later became the foundation of America's largest company. His workers loved him, yet his Homestead factory was the scene of one of the major labor battles of the nineteenth century. Although he attended school for only five years, he educated himself and wrote more than ten books, several hundred magazine articles, letters to newspapers, and speeches. Because of the more than 2,000 public libraries he helped finance, he had a greater effect on the education of the American people than any person before or since. An industrialist, an investor, a motivator of people, a philanthropist, a writer and speaker whose varied ideas influenced political leaders and scholars throughout the United States and Europe, his works, legacy, and influence continue today, more than 165 years after his birth.

Biography

Andrew Carnegie was born in Dunfermline, county of Fife, Scotland, in the attic of a small, one-story house, on the corner of Moodie Street and Priory

Lane, on November 25, 1835. He was the first of two sons of William and Margaret Morrison Carnegie. A sister died in infancy and his brother, Thomas, was eight years younger than Andrew.

Carnegie's mother took on most of her eldest son's training, and she taught him the value of hard work. Andrew did not start school until he was more than eight years old, when he attended a one-teacher school near his home. His teacher, Robert Martin, was also a taskmaster who often said, "Ye hae na been put into this world to enjoy yoursel', but to do yair duty."[1] Andrew, however, was no dour Scot and strongly believed that "a sunny disposition is worth more than fortune."[2] His open and friendly manner served him well throughout his life.

Dumfermline was essentially a one-industry town, with more than half of the population dependent on linen weaving. With the introduction of damask-cloth weaving in 1718, Dumfermline became the center for the damask trade. Dunfermline was long renowned as the most liberal town in the kingdom and prided itself on being the first capital of a united Scotland. The town was active in the charter reform movement of the 1830s and 1840s, with its demands for political equality and universal suffrage.

The population in large part was composed of men who were small manufacturers, each owning his own loom or looms. They were not tied down to regular hours, their payments being piecework. They got spindles of thread from the larger manufacturers and did their weaving at home. The linen weavers regarded themselves as craftspeople and looked down on those who were slaves to a machine, as were the cotton weavers of Manchester. The Scottish weavers had feared union with England, believing that the English woolen interests would dictate to the Scottish linen industry. But after union, the linen industry continued to grow. William Carnegie, a damask weaver, prospered and used his savings to purchase three additional looms, staffed by apprentices.

The flax growers of Scotland could not completely meet the increasing demand for more thread, and the weavers sought direct government action to protect their sources of raw material. During the 1800s, however, wool and linen producers found themselves in increasing competition with a new textile—cotton; for, in the eighteenth century, a series of inventions affected the spinning and weaving of cotton—the beginnings of the industrial revolution. Lower-cost cotton began to roll off Britain's power looms.

The only way linen could compete with the low prices of cotton was through industrialization, but this would mean the end of the hand weavers' craft. In 1835, the Dumfermline weavers still had pride in their craft and a strong sense of continuity with the past. Nevertheless, linen thread, once produced by hand spinning in the district, was now imported from the large powered spinning factories in Belfast and Leeds. The next step was the power loom.

In his autobiography Carnegie later recalled: "The change from hand-loom to steam-power loom weaving was disastrous to our family. My father did not recognize the impending revolution, and was struggling under the old system."[3] By 1840, economic conditions had worsened, and even the master weavers faced hardship. William was forced to dismiss his apprentices, sell three of his four looms, and move into a small cottage. Carnegie wrote: "Mother opened a small shop in Moodie Street and contributed to the revenues. She helped to keep us comfortable and respectable."[4] In 1847, a large steam-powered factory began operation in Dunfermline. The day of the hand-loom weaver was over.

On May 17, 1848, William Carnegie auctioned off his remaining loom and furniture, and, at age forty-three, the tired and beaten man—with his wife, Margaret, thirty-three, and sons Andrew, thirteen, and Tom, five—left Dunfermline to join Margaret's two sisters in Pittsburgh. A loan of £20 from a friend made the journey possible. The family took a train to Charlestown, a steamer to Glasgow, and sailed across the Atlantic on the *Wiscasset* to New York City. Since there were no railroad connections to Pittsburgh, they took the night steamer up the Hudson to Albany, canal boats from Albany to Buffalo (a journey covering 364 miles and taking ten days), a lake steamer west to Cleveland, another canal boat down the Ohio River and a canal to Akron, then east to Beaver, Pennsylvania, on the Ohio, and finally, a river steamer to Pittsburgh. The 3,700-mile journey took ten weeks.

The family settled in the town of Allegheny, now a part of Pittsburgh, in two small rooms of the house owned by Margaret's sister Annie. Will Carnegie, unable to endure work in a cotton mill, earned some money weaving and selling linens. Margaret Carnegie earned a living by binding shoes, a trade she had learned in Scotland. Starting as a bobbin boy in a cotton textile mill at $1.20 per week, Andrew Carnegie got a job working in the bobbin factory of another immigrant from Dunfermline. He fired and ran the boiler and cleaned the factory. One day, Carnegie's boss, John Hay, needed a clerk and asked Andrew to show him his handwriting. As a result, Carnegie was appointed clerk and given the job of making out the weekly statements and answering correspondence, in addition to oil-treating the finished bobbins. At this time, he took night classes in Pittsburgh and studied double-entry bookkeeping.

In the spring of 1850, the family heard about an opening for a messenger boy in the Pittsburgh telegraph office run by David Brooks, a family friend. Andrew was hired at $2.50 a week to deliver messages around the city. He began to learn the locations of all the businesses in town and came to know many of the businesspeople. He also delivered messages to reporters at various newspapers and developed a strong desire to work for a newspaper. Carnegie, a voracious reader, continued to educate himself. He was able to use the free, 400-book library that Colonel James Anderson had established for the city's working boys. When the library was turned over to the city, a new librarian interpreted the bequest as applying only to bound boys and demanded that Carnegie and other working boys pay $2 per year to use the facility. Carnegie wrote a letter of protest to the editor of the *Pittsburgh Dispatch,* presenting his case to the public. The rule was changed, and Carnegie had his first experience seeing his name in print.

During this time, Carnegie was assigned some routine administrative responsibilities at the telegraph office. He studied the telegraph instruments and soon was allowed to receive messages. The telegraph was the major link to the outside world and the source of much news and business communication. Carnegie was soon promoted to telegraph operator. His performance improved in both speed and accuracy until he was the best telegrapher in the office, and businessmen began to ask for him by name to send out their most important messages. His salary was raised to $25 per month. He then began to make an additional $1 per week by making duplicate copies for the newspapers of all the foreign news received over the telegraph. This new income enabled the Carnegies to buy the house his mother wanted.

Young Carnegie continued to prosper. His father, however, did not advance, and tried to sell his weaving on profitless selling trips. On October 2, 1855, Will Carnegie died at age fifty-five. In his autobiography, Andrew Carnegie wrote: "My father was one of the most lovable of men ... not much of a man of the world, but a man all over for heaven."[5] Andrew Carnegie was twenty years old when his father died.

In 1852, the management of the Pennsylvania Railroad announced that they had officially opened to trade and travel a single-track railroad between Philadelphia and Pittsburgh that connected the headwaters of the Ohio River with the Atlantic seaboard. Pittsburgh was no longer isolated and was now known as the "Gateway to the West."

Thomas A. Scott, the superintendent of the line's Western Division, was dependent on the telegraph for communication and was a frequent visitor to the Pittsburgh telegraph office. Within a few weeks, Scott realized the necessity of having his own telegraph and an open line to Altoona and points east. He offered Carnegie the position of telegraph operator and personal secretary. Tom Scott became mentor and friend to "my boy, Andy," who was now in the railroad business.

Railroads formed the base for his steel career. Carnegie later recalled:

When I became a railroad man, the Pennsylvania Railroad was not yet finished to Pittsburgh. By means of some miles of staging between two points, and a climb over the mountains by means of ten inclined planes, the passenger was enabled to reach Philadelphia by rail. The rails on the mountains were iron, fourteen-feet lengths, imported from England, lying on huge hewn blocks of stone, although the line passed through woods and wooden ties would have cost little.

We had small locomotives and the roadbed was something to frighten one. It was laid with light rails and cast-iron joints were used. I have known 47 broken joints found one morning in winter on my division, and it was over such a line that we ran our trains. It is no wonder that break-downs were frequent. We had no cabooses on freight trains. Trainmen had to be out in all weathers. It was single track, and not having a telegraph line, in case of delays trains ran curves; that is, a flagman went and the train followed and met when they could, and sometimes met with consid-erable force, on the sharp curves. There is nothing apparently that takes so long to learn by the average railroad man as this proposition that two trains cannot pass each other successfully on a single track. We never did quite learn that lesson, even on the Pittsburgh Division.[6]

Carnegie quickly learned the basics of railroading. As telegraph operator, he had the opportunity to review every message and learn a great deal about the business activities of the railroad and its customers. He handled payrolls and took charge of the railroad telegraph wire when it was constructed. He wrote the rulebook for telegraphers, hired and trained telegraph operators, and hired the first woman telegraph student to work for a railroad.

Once, there was an accident on the line, and all traffic came to a halt, await-ing orders. When Scott could not be located, Carnegie took matters into his own hands and, signing Scott's name, sent orders for each train to move to its proper station. When Scott arrived and discovered the situation, he reviewed the dispatches and then, shaking his head, he left. That night he was heard bragging to a friend about "what that little white-haired Scotch devil of mine did."[7]

In the fall of 1856, Scott was promoted to general superintendent of the Pennsylvania Railroad and took Carnegie with him to Altoona. Early in 1859, Scott was promoted to vice president of the company, and the twenty-three-year-old Carnegie was made superintendent of the Pittsburgh Division. Carnegie was a tough taskmaster, going out in all kinds of weather, delegating no authority in emergencies, working very long hours, and expecting those under him to do likewise. For Carnegie, the important thing was to keep the traffic flowing no matter what the cost to people or material. He showed no favorites and drove his workers very hard.

Years later, in a more philosophical mood, he wrote:

In those days the superintendent had to do everything; there was no divi-sion of responsibility. We went out to every wreck, worked all night; often I was not at home for a week at a time, scarcely ever sleeping, except for a few snatches, lying down in a freight car. I now look back and see what poor superintendents we were. It took me some time to learn, but I did learn, that the supremely great managers, such as you have these days, never do any work themselves worth speaking about; their point is to make others work while they think. I applied this lesson in after life, so that business with me has never been a care. My young partners did the work and I did the laughing, and I commend to all the thought that there is very little success where there is little laughter. … When you see a president or superintendent or treasurer loaded down with his duties, oppressed with care, with a countenance as serious as a judge uttering a death sentence, be sure that he has more responsibility than he is fit for and should get relief.[8]

During his years with the Pennsylvania Railroad, Carnegie became an investor. He took his first step in 1856, when Tom Scott offered him the opportunity to buy shares in Adams Express and then lent him the money to make the investment. In 1858, Carnegie joined John Edgar Thomson and Tom Scott, the president and vice president of the Pennsylvania Railroad, in investing in the Woodruff Sleeping Car Company. In 1861, he joined William Coleman in forming Columbia Oil Company. In addition, Carnegie invested in other oil companies, the Piper and Shiffer Bridge Company, the Freedom Iron Company, the Central Transportation Company, the Lochiel Iron Company, and the Pittsburgh Manufacturing Company. The Central Transportation Company was subsequently merged into the Pullman Palace Car Company, and the Piper and Shiffer Company was later recapitalized as the Keystone Bridge Company.

In 1856, Carnegie had $817 of borrowed capital. By 1868, he owned securities worth $400,000 that paid dividends of $56,000 per year. He had learned to minimize risks by using borrowed money and investing in companies whose dividends exceeded the cost of the loan. In addition, his friendship with businesspeople throughout Pennsylvania enabled him to choose his partners carefully and invest early in promising ventures.

Carnegie wrote: "Thenceforth I never worked for a salary. A man must necessarily occupy a narrow field who is at the beck and call of others. Even if he becomes president of a great corporation he is hardly his own master unless he holds control of the stock." In the spring of 1865, he left for a one-year tour of Europe to acquire culture and learn about the world. Carnegie believed in vacations for both education and pleasure. He shared his observations through books originally written for private publication and meant for those friends who stayed at home and worked.

In 1868, in the Saint Nichols Hotel in New York, Andrew Carnegie took stock of his life and wrote one of the more remarkable documents by any American businessperson, a complete analysis of himself and a plan for his life:

> *Thirty three and an income of $50,000 per annum. ... Beyond this never earn—make no effort to increase fortune, but spend the surplus every year for benevolent purposes. Cast aside business forever, except for others. Settle in Oxford and get a thorough education, making the acquaintance of literary men ... pay special attention to speaking in public. Settle then in London and purchase a controlling interest in some newspaper or live review and give the general management of it attention, taking a part in public matters, especially those concerned with education and improvement of the poorer classes. Man must have an idol—The amassing of wealth is one of the worst species of idolatry. ... I will resign business at 35.[9]*

But he continued to work. When the Civil War broke out, Tom Scott was called to Washington as assistant secretary of war. He was assigned to keep the railroads open from the North to Washington and to move men and supplies. Carnegie for a time became special assistant to Scott, in charge of military railroads and telegraphic service. He then returned to Pittsburgh to his old job and expanded the business, following the philosophy that was the basis of his professional life: reduce prices by reducing costs.

"During the Civil War the price of iron went up to something like $130 a ton. Even at that price it was not so much a question of money as of delivery."[10] The railroad lines were fast becoming dangerous for lack of new rails. And Andrew Carnegie took advantage of this opportunity.

In 1865, independently wealthy because of his investments, Carnegie resigned as superintendent of the Pittsburgh Division of the Pennsylvania Railroad. It had been a time for learning. During the last half of the nineteenth century, the railroads' need for capital led to modern investment banking and the growth of the stock market. The railroads were also responsible for many modern management techniques, including new operating methods, cost controls, scheduling and maintenance techniques, and accurate cost accounting. By the time Carnegie left, the Pennsylvania Railroad had become the largest business firm in the world in terms of revenues, employees, and physical assets. And, under President Abraham Lincoln, the federal government had passed the Homestead Act, the Railroad Act, the Merrill Protective Tariff, and the National Bank Act. These laid the foundation for rapid industrial expansion after the Civil War.

In 1870, when he was thirty-five, Carnegie was even more active in business. He had interests in telegraphy through his holdings in the Pacific and Atlantic Company; was an investor in the Pullman Car Company; was acting as agent for American companies, selling their railroad and bridge bonds to banks in London and Germany; and through Keystone, he was building bridges. He showed no sign of slowing down. And he became more involved in the steel industry. "I determined that the proper policy was 'to put all good eggs in one basket and then watch that basket.' The men who have succeeded are men who have chosen one line and stuck to it. Invest in your own business."[11]

Andrew Carnegie and Steel

Andrew Carnegie entered the steel business based on two of his interests: railroads and bridge building. And, as described in chapter 3, Andrew Carnegie not only entered the steel industry, he dominated it. Initially, Carnegie's main interest was in finished products. Keystone Bridge needed a low cost and guaranteed source of supply. In railroads, iron was starting to give way to steel. On certain curves of the Pennsylvania Railroad, iron rails had to be replaced every two weeks. Hence, the Pennsylvania began to convert to steel rails, and U.S. suppliers had to compete with the British.

The Keystone Bridge Company continued to expand. Additions had also been made to the Union Iron Mills, successor of two earlier firms he had invested in. In 1866, Carnegie helped establish the Pittsburgh Locomotive Works. That same year, the Freedom Iron Company, formed in 1861, was renamed Freedom Iron and Steel Company, and later started the conversion to the Bessemer process. By 1866, Carnegie had to devote a great deal of his attention to iron manufacture.

The years after the Civil War were challenging for the U.S. iron industry. The British, with better technology and larger and lower-cost furnaces, were dominating the market with their Bessemer steel. Americans sought tariff protection, and Congress cooperated, but with limited effect. The dominant figures in the iron industry had been merchants who controlled the flow of materials from one manufacturing plant to another. Large amounts of money were tied up in inventory, with many brokers each taking a cut. Few people knew their costs. More important, there was no science of metallurgy. The making of iron and steel was still an art, with the blast-furnace manager forced to diagnose the condition of a furnace based on experience and instinct. Varieties of ores, limestone, and coke were supplied with little or no regard for their component parts or knowledge of their effects.

It was also a time of great opportunity. The demand for iron and steel was soaring. The opening of high-quality iron ore fields in upper Michigan, the increase in coal supplies, and the availability of railroads to haul the raw materials and finished products meant a good future to those who succeeded. It was a time ripe for the leadership of Andrew Carnegie.

In 1872, Carnegie visited Bessemer plants in England and realized that he would have to build a large Bessemer production facility to make steel. With the backing of several railroad executives, Carnegie and his old associate William

Coleman—now his brother Tom's father-in-law—formed Carnegie, McCandless & Company. Carnegie aimed for the best plant in the world and the most dedicated management. He hired Captain William Jones from the Cambra Iron Works in Johnston, Pennsylvania, to run his new company. Carnegie gathered his financial resources and sold some of his stock in Pullman and Western Union. In August 1875, he opened the Edgar Thomson Works, named after the former president of the Pennsylvania Railroad. In 1876, this firm was merged with other holdings into the Edgar Thomson Steel Company, and in 1881, it became Carnegie Brothers and Company.

Essentially a marketer, Carnegie delegated supervision of manufacturing to men like Captain Jones, Henry C. Frick, and Charles Schwab, while he traveled around the world selling steel products to railroads and governments. Carnegie's aggressive sales efforts and relentless demand for more production led to his success. He worked unceasingly to produce a better product at a lower cost and to become the lowest cost producer. To lower costs and increase volume, he hired the best skilled steelworkers and made them plant managers. He spent money on new equipment and then ran it until it failed. He based promotions on success in getting costs down:

> As I became acquainted with the manufacture of iron I was greatly surprised to find that the cost of each of the various processes were unknown. I insisted upon such a system of weighing and accounting being introduced throughout our works as would enable us to know what each man was doing, who saved material, who wasted it, and who produced the best results.[12]

Andrew Carnegie applied some of the management techniques he had learned with the Pennsylvania Railroad to the manufacture of steel. He defined his philosophy as follows: "One of the chief sources of success is the introduction and strict maintenance of a perfect system of accounting so that responsibility for money or materials can be brought home to every man."[13] Constant efforts were made to reduce labor costs. Steel manufacturing was revolutionized by the Bessemer and open-hearth furnaces and by basic inventions. New machinery could make 60 percent more steel than the old. Costs continued to decline.

From 1876 to 1880, the production of steel rails exceeded those of iron rails, with most made in the United States. Iron tracks were replaced, and, by 1890, 80 percent of the country's railroad tracks were made of steel. Steel also revolutionized the size and character of the locomotive and freight cars. Better track and locomotives increased a train's carrying capacity from 200 tons in 1865 to 2,500 tons in 1900, and speed from twenty-five miles per hour to sixty-five miles per hour. In 1865, the weight of a freight car was 65 percent of its laden weight, and by 1900, it had dropped to 26 percent. Freight-car capacity went from 10,000 pounds to 110,000 pounds, and transportation costs were reduced by 60 percent, from 1 cent per ton-mile to 0.4 cent.

The business continued to grow. In 1883, Carnegie bought the Bessemer Steel Company at Homestead, the most modern Bessemer steel plant in the country. In 1889, Captain Jones was killed in an industrial accident, and a young associate, Charles Schwab, was appointed superintendent. Carnegie Brothers made almost everything in steel, from a wire nail up to a twenty-inch girder. According to Carnegie, "A manufacturing concern in a growing country like ours begins to decay when it stops expanding. One great advantage which America will have in competing in the markets of the world is that her manufacturers will have the best home markets."[14] Carnegie developed the Law of the Surplus: extra products where standardized can be exported. By 1898, one-third of Carnegie's production was being sent out of this country.

Steelmaking deals with the problem of moving large amounts of material from one place to another. In one speech, Carnegie described the problem:

> *To make a ton of steel—$1^1/2$ tons of iron ore has to be mined, transported by rail a hundred miles to the Lakes, carried by boat hundreds of miles, transferred by rail 150 miles to Pittsburgh; $1^1/2$ tons of coal must be mined and manufactured into coke and carried 50 miles by rail; and one ton of limestone mined and carried 150 miles to Pittsburgh. The Steel must be manufactured and sold, without loss at three pounds for two cents.[15]*

To be successful, you must make steel by the thousands of tons.

Carnegie was proud of America's progress in steelmaking. He wrote:

> *The republic's progress and commanding position as a steel producer can be told in a few words: In 1873, the United States produced only 198,796 tons of steel, and Great Britain, her chief competitor, 653,000 tons, more than three times as much. Twenty-six years later, in 1899, the republic made more than twice as much as the monarchy, the figures being 10,639,857 and 5,000,000 tons respectively, an eight-fold increase for Great Britain and fifty-three fold for the republic, and it made almost 40 per cent of all the world steel.[16]*

Throughout the last half of the nineteenth century, Carnegie Steel grew. Even though the price of rails went steadily downward, costs decreased even faster, and profits continued to increase. Carnegie had never paid dividends, believing that the best use of profits was in expanding the business. He began to integrate backward by purchasing or leasing coke and coal fields; buying an interest in Henry Frick's Coke Company, iron ranges, and shipping lines; and making special contracts with railroads. Carnegie wanted to control his sources of supply. When Tom Carnegie, Andrew's brother, died in 1886 at age forty-three, Frick took his position in management

In 1898, the Carnegie Steel Company was making more than 200,000 tons of steel per month, and in 1900, it produced more than the entire British steel industry. Meanwhile, J. P. Morgan had created Federal Steel and the National Tube Company. He wanted to establish a trust to control the steel industry but discovered that Carnegie was prepared to undercut the competition. Morgan approached Schwab to see if Carnegie would be prepared to sell the business. By this time, Carnegie was sixty-five and ready to start with his plan to give away his fortune. He wrote a figure on a piece of paper. It was shown to Morgan. "I accept his price," came the reply. Andrew Carnegie was now out of the steel business.

In April 1901, the House of Morgan and a syndicate merged the Carnegie properties with others into the U.S. Steel Corporation. It was the largest corporation in the world and well capitalized. The Carnegie Company received $492 million for its properties, with Andrew Carnegie's personal share in excess of $300 million. Carnegie insisted on payment in 5 percent gold bonds, acquiring a mortgage that insured his right to reclaim his property should the company fail.

On Management

Few, if any, businesspeople have written so extensively, had as major an influence with their writings, or reflected their times more completely than Andrew Carnegie. In many respects, Carnegie the writer is more interesting than Carnegie the industrialist. He wrote to influence his contemporaries, and influence them he did. He wrote on a variety of subjects, sent letters to newspapers, private friends, and public figures, and wrote numerous books and articles. His collected works cover eleven volumes. Much of his writing belongs to his time and is best left to historians of the period. But much applies equally to today's business leaders.

On the subject of quality, he wrote in reference to two of his operations:

Make nothing but the very best. We organized Keystone Bridge Company in 1863 to make iron bridges. We were our own severest inspectors. Build safe structures or none at all. A high standard of excellence is easily maintained and men are educated in the efforts to reach excellence. The effect of attention to quality, upon every man in the service, from the president of the concern down to the humblest laborer, cannot be overestimated. I have never known a concern to make a decided success that did not do good, honest work, and even in these days of the fiercest competition, when everything seems to be a matter of price, there lies still at the root of great business success the very important factor of quality. The surest foundation of a manufacturing concern is quality. After that, and a long way after, comes cost. [17]

On the subject of management: "For my epitaph 'Here lies a man who was able to surround himself with men far clever than himself.'"

He also said: "Mr. (J. P.) Morgan buys his partners, I raise my own." And many people became partners and made significant amounts of money when Carnegie Steel was sold to form U.S. Steel.

On the subject of a career, he wrote:

I believe that the true road to preeminent success in any line is to make yourself master in that line. My advice to young men would be not only to concentrate their whole time and attention on the one business in life in which they engage, but to put every dollar of their capital into it. [18]

Carnegie wrote on both public matters and personal philosophy. His book *Triumphant Democracy* was a statement of his beliefs—a sort of social Darwinism, a belief that poverty was useful in developing manhood, that opportunity was within the reach of everyone, and that wealth could be achieved by all who had the energy and intelligence to pursue it. It was written to inform Americans and others, mainly the British, of the great work America had done and was doing in the world. It sang the praises of America and the country's spectacular growth. It was a highly successful book and was revised and reissued ten years later, after the 1890 census, to include a look at the last decade and the future. Relatively few businesspeople have written so extensively on politics, government, economics, or personal philosophy, and perhaps none has had so much influence on contemporaries.

Carnegie's relations with labor, however, were mixed. Carnegie had written, in two famous articles, that capital, labor, and employer were a three-legged stool, none before or after the others, all equally indispensable. He had established a new incentive system of pay in which workers shared in the output of the mill. "Of all the services rendered to labor, the introduction of the sliding scale is chief. It is the solution of the capital and labor problem, because it really makes them partners—alike in prosperity and adversity."[19] In addition, in 1881, Captain Jones had persuaded Carnegie to abolish the twelve-hour day and instead staff the mills with three eight-hour shifts. Carnegie also offered promotions to a large number of workers based on their ability, and some had done quite well. Nevertheless, many were burned out from working in the steel mills. Furthermore, wages, which had gone up in good times, started to decline.

In 1892, there were major labor problems at the Homestead Works. The company, after negotiating unsuccessfully with the union on a new contract, dissolved the union and locked out the workers. Pinkerton Detective Agency guards were brought in by barge, and in a bloody battle, several people were killed. Seven hundred strikebreakers were hired, the union was broken, and many of the union leaders were unable to ever work again in the industry. The reputation of the company and that of Carnegie suffered greatly, but management had succeeded in their objectives. Until the 1930s, there were no more unions in the steel industry. Carnegie was in Scotland at the time of the trouble. He wrote: "The policy I had pursued in cases of differences with our men was that of patiently waiting, reasoning with them, and showing them that their demands were unfair; but never attempting to employ new men in their places—never."[20] However, he had supported the action of his management. Salaries were reduced, and Homestead Works was put back on a twelve-hour shift.

The Legacy of Andrew Carnegie

Andrew Carnegie retired in 1901, some thirty years later than he had planned. But instead of an income of $50,000 per year, he retired with a net worth of hundreds of millions of dollars in gold bonds. He now wanted to give it away.

In 1900, Andrew Carnegie published *The Gospel of Wealth,* a collection of articles that he had written between 1886 and 1896. In this book, he described his philosophy of the obligations of wealth. Few people have written and acted on such an approach to life:

> *This then is held to be the duty of the man of wealth: To set an example of modest, unostentatious living, shunning display or extravagance; to provide moderately for the legitimate wants of those dependent upon him; and, after doing so, to consolidate all surplus revenue which comes to him simply as trust funds, which he is called upon to administer in the manner which, in his judgment, is best calculated to provide the most beneficial results for the community.[21]*

> *In bestowing charity, the most consideration should be to help those who will help themselves; to provide part of the means by which those who desire to improve may do so; to give those who desire to rise the aids by which they may rise; to assist but rarely or never to do all. The man who dies thus rich dies disgraced.[22]*

Philanthropy, however, was hard work, and Carnegie worked as hard in giving money away as he had in earning it. He wrote that "$950 of every $1000 given to charity is better thrown into the sea—many don't take time to think. Don't give unless the object is deserving."[23]

Carnegie started by giving $4 million to his workers for pensions and accident relief, and he made extensive donations to build halls for workmen. He supplied private pension funds that eventually supported more than 500 beneficiaries who were deserving of assistance in their old age.

Andrew Carnegie donated money to assist many communities in establishing free public libraries.

Father had been one of the founders of a circulating library in Dunfermline. Colonel James Anderson, founder of Free Libraries in Western Pennsylvania had allowed me to use it. The fundamental advantage of a library is that it gives nothing for nothing. Youths must acquire knowledge themselves. No use to which money could be applied is so productive of good to boys and girls who have good within them and ability and ambition to develop it, as the founding of a public library in a community which is willing to support it as a municipal institution.[24]

Carnegie donated more than $5 million for sixty-eight libraries in New York City and twenty libraries in Brooklyn. Eventually, he contributed to 2,811 free public libraries, 1,946 in the United States and the remainder in Britain, Canada, South Africa, New Zealand, Australia, and the British West Indies.

He established the Carnegie Institute in Pittsburgh with a gift of $28 million, and he founded chairs or libraries in the names of friends and associates at Lehigh University, Kenyon College, Case Western Reserve University, Brown University, Dickinson University, and a number of other schools. He made donations to the Hampton and Tuskegee Institutes, the University of Pittsburgh, and the Cooper Union.

Carnegie also established a Railroad Pension Fund, the Mount Wilson Observatory, Carnegie Hall in New York City, a Hero Fund in both Britain and the United States, the Carnegie Trust for the Universities of Scotland, a private pension fund for aged university professors, and the Carnegie Foundation for the Advancement of Teaching. In addition, he made scores of bequests to research hospitals as well as bequests for more than 7,600 church organs and for parks. Because the U.S. government was unwilling to act, he organized a private pension program to assist former president William Howard Taft and the widows of former presidents Theodore Roosevelt and Grover Cleveland.

Carnegie became interested in the cause of peace. He endowed the Carnegie Institution in Washington, D.C., with $25 million and organized the Carnegie

Endowment for International Peace, the Pan American Union Building, in Washington, D.C., the Central American Court of Justice in Costa Rica, and the Temple of Peace in the Hague. During World War I, he made gifts to the Red Cross and other organizations.

He established the Carnegie Corporation for the Advancement of Knowledge with an endowment of $125 million, leaving the trustees free to spend it as they saw fit. When Andrew Carnegie died in Lenox, Massachusetts, on August 11, 1919, at the age of eighty-three, he had given away more than $350 million. Of the $30 million left at his death, two-thirds was willed to the Carnegie Corporation and the remaining $10 million went to various other charities.

He had believed that it was more blessed to give than to receive and that a rich man dies thus disgraced. He had given away an extraordinary amount during his lifetime. Andrew Carnegie had truly lived by his gospel.

A businessperson, like everyone else, is dependent on the economic, cultural, social, governmental, and philosophical environment in which he lives. Carnegie had lived at a time of rapid change in materials, technology, energy, transportation, capital, population, and markets. The United States had a strong feeling of national and economic superiority and a need for economic growth. In this, perhaps, Andrew Carnegie had been lucky.

But businesspeople, like political and other leaders, are measured by how they use available resources to create something of value. Entrepreneurs control the use of economic, technological, and other factors in the various stages of business. The growth or decline of a business is therefore largely dependent on management and leadership. Carnegie had been an outstanding business leader.

In death as in life, Andrew Carnegie casts a long shadow. After he died, the steel industry continued to grow. By 1910, American steel output was 28 million tons, and in 1918, it was 45 million tons. At that time, German output was 14 million tons and British production, about 9 million tons. It can be claimed that the United States industrial capability had much to do with successes in the First and Second World Wars.

Yet somehow, the lessons of Andrew Carnegie were forgotten. His belief in the need to invest in the best machinery and a desire to become the lowest-cost producer were ignored by the steel industry, and dividends were increased at the expense of investments in the business. By 1959, the United States had once again become a net importer of steel. By 1962, imports were 5.6 percent of supply, and by 1984, the United States imported 23 percent of its steel. The industry's production declined to 50 percent of capacity. U.S. Steel and other producers began to cut production, closing less efficient mills and laying off workers.

Carnegie's message of the sliding wage scale was forgotten as steel management bought union peace at the expense of ever-higher wages. Average hourly wages, which were $7.08 per hour in 1972, reached $13.04 per hour in 1977 and $23.00 per hour in 1982, significantly higher than in other industries. Beginning in the 1970s, the industry has been desperate to buy labor peace at any price. Without the leadership of an Andrew Carnegie, the U.S. steel industry has fallen further behind Japan and other competitors.

Andrew Carnegie may be missed even more in his role as a writer. For the last century, there has not been a businessperson of equivalent stature with the talent, the time, and the thought to present the views of business to the general public. Discussions about jobs, business, and finance have been left to the academicians, politicians, and journalists. Perhaps that has something to do with the anti-business climate that exists in major segments of this country— and this apparent paradox: a desire for more jobs and less business.

The results of Andrew Carnegie's philanthropy continue today. For example, the Carnegie Corporation, with an initial endowment of $125 million, has made substantial contributions over the last eighty years, and today its assets total more than $325 million, about the same as Carnegie's original fortune. His other gifts have also been substantial and continue to grow.

But it may be in Andrew Carnegie's first love that the greatest benefits have been accomplished. Because of Carnegie, 2,811 free public libraries have been in existence, some for almost a century. And during that time, tens of millions of people of all ages and conditions have been exposed to books, to new ideas and experiences, and have received a continuing education. This may be the greatest gift of all. Andrew Carnegie may be as influential in death as in life. The shadow of the man is long indeed.

CHAPTER 5
————•◆•————

Automobiles
Everybody Wants at Least One
(1860–2000)

*We should all be concerned about the future because we will
have to spend the rest of our lives there.*
—*Charles Franklin Kettering*

The chief business of the American people is business.
—*Calvin Coolidge*

There is probably no product in history that had as much influence on the
average American as did the invention and production of the automobile.
The development of the automobile affected where people could live and work,
where they shopped and went to school, where they vacationed, the people they
knew, and even how they viewed the world. It changed how products were delivered to market and gave farmers more independence, freeing them from rural
isolation. The automobile enabled people to look at a much larger universe for
jobs, for opportunities, and for their future in a growing and changing country.

Using railroads or trolleys to bring large numbers of people into a city is a
very efficient method of handling commuting. But providing each person with
an automobile also can be efficient and, in most cases, is preferred by the individual because of the additional flexibility automobiles provide. However,
widespread use of the automobile had results that went far beyond a decrease in
the use of mass transportation. Much of modern America—the suburbs, shopping centers, vacation travel, occupations, education, and even family
income—has been affected by the automobile.

Background and Early Days of the Automobile

The steam engine was invented to solve the problem of pumping water from mines. Then it was used as a source of power that was applied to the textile industry and later to transportation, first on steamships and then railroads.

Both of these applications decreased the time required for travel and the costs of moving large amounts of materials. They allowed more of the country to be settled and increased communication through the United States. But they both had major disadvantages. Steamships could only go on major lakes and rivers; rapids and mountains rendered them useless. Furthermore, water levels and winter weather conditions could make their use difficult even in suitable areas. The train could climb hills and go into new parts of the country, but it could only run where tracks had been laid. This was also true of the electric trams or trolley cars that were used in cities during the nineteenth and early twentieth centuries.

For other areas, the horse and wagon was a major method of hauling people and freight from the railroad to the countryside across the very bad roads of America. Could a steam engine be applied to a wagon? Was it possible to develop a horseless carriage? And was the country prepared to improve roads so that the vehicle could get from the farm to the village or between towns?

There were many difficulties to overcome. The weight of the early steam engine could be as much as the wagon and would not allow room for freight or passengers. In addition, steam engines required a long time for the coal fire to boil water and generate steam. Many technical advances had to be made before the time was ripe for the automobile.

In 1769, the Frenchman Nicolas Cugnot developed a steam-driven three-wheel vehicle as a gun-towing tractor for the army and drove it through Paris. In 1786, John Fitch made a model of a steam carriage but then turned his attention to steamboats. In 1802, Richard Trevithick developed a steam-propelled road carriage. On August 26, 1791, Nathan Reede of Warren, Massachusetts, received a patent for a land carriage for "a simple method of moving land carriages by means of steam." Oliver Evans also worked on the problem and in 1789 received a patent on a steam-powered land vehicle. One of his steamboat prototypes in 1805 was an amphibious steam-powered dredge, which he drove through Philadelphia before going into the Schuylkill River. It weighed some twenty tons and was self-propelled. In 1822, Julius Griffiths built the world's first steam-driven bus for commercial service. In England between 1828 and 1838, Walter Hancock built six passenger steam carriages. In the 1820s and 1830s, there were steam-driven carriages in Gloucester, London, and Glasgow, with British engineers designing boilers, furnaces, and gears for them. The development of steam carriages continued through the 1850s and 1860s. In 1868, Richard Dudgeon built a steam vehicle in New York that could carry ten passengers.

Jean Joseph Lenoir in 1860 developed an internal combustion engine using illuminating gas and put it on a small wagon to power it. In 1865, Siegfried Marcus developed a car driven by a two-cycle benzene vapor engine. Nikolaus Otto from Germany developed a four-stroke gasoline engine, and six of these engines were demonstrated at the Philadelphia Centennial Exposition in 1876. In 1879, George B. Selden filed a patent for a gasoline-powered automobile that had a clutch, a foot brake, and a muffler, even though he had not yet built one. The patent was granted in November 1895. Karl Benz in 1885 developed a motorcar and the following year drove it through the streets of Munich. In 1886, he received the first patent for a gas-fueled car, and by 1900, his company, Benz & Cie, was the world's largest automobile manufacturer. Gottlieb Wilhelm Daimler developed a gasoline-powered high-efficiency engine, and in 1885, he connected his engine to a bicycle, making the first motorcycle. Two years later, he attached the engine to a four-wheel vehicle, creating one of the early automobiles. At the Paris World's Fair in 1889, about sixty gas engines were exhibited. In 1891, Emile Levassor designed and tested a gasoline-powered vehicle. In 1896, Britain passed a law that eliminated the requirement for a motorcar to be preceded by a person waving a red flag to warn people that the car was coming. The law allowed motor carriages to travel at higher speeds than the previous British speed limit of seven miles per hour. The annual London to Brighton race celebrates this forward-looking legislation.

Thomas Blanchard of Springfield, Massachusetts, and Richard Dudgeon of New York City built early steam carriages. Sylvester Hayward Roper of Roxbury, Massachusetts, announced his development of a steam car in *Scientific American* in 1863 and built about ten vehicles. His steam carriage had room for two passengers and enough coal under the seat for an entire day. In 1868, Roper was operating a steam-driven bicycle in Massachusetts. Other early steamers were developed in Wisconsin, New Jersey, Pennsylvania, Vermont, Arizona, and Ohio. Ransom Eli Olds built two steamers, one in 1887 and the second in 1890. Perhaps the most famous steam-car manufacturers were twins Francis E. and Freelan O. Stanley. On August 31, 1899, F. O. Stanley and his wife, Flora, drove their motor carriage to the top of Mount Washington (4,600 feet) and came down using the vehicle's primitive brakes. By the turn of the century, one of the Stanley steam-driven cars had been driven to the top of Pikes Peak in Colorado. Early electric automobiles were made by William Morrison of Des Moines, Iowa, in 1890 and the Electrobats made in Philadelphia in 1895 by Henry Moris and Pedro Salom.

Bicycles, which came on the scene in the late nineteenth century, convinced people that they wanted to go long distances by themselves and needed a self-propelled vehicle. How, then, to satisfy this demand for independent transportation? A large number of inventors and businesspeople began working on the problem of how to build a horseless carriage. In the auto industry, the challenges at the turn of the twentieth century included how to power an automobile, what kind of fuel to use, how to steer an automobile (with a tiller or steering wheel?), how to stop a car, how many passengers could be carried, and how the chassis would support the passengers. None of those questions had a given answer. There were no auto supply companies, and all parts had to be built from scratch. As a result, there were a variety of designs, manufacturers around the country, and types of cars.

On September 21, 1893, Charles and Frank Duryea built a car at Russel's Machine Shop and ran their first successful gasoline-powered American automobile on the streets of Springfield, Massachusetts. The U.S. automobile industry was born in 1896 when Charles and Frank Duryea formed an automobile company and made thirteen cars from the same design. Altogether the brothers made fewer than twenty vehicles. By 1899, there were about sixty American companies making automobiles.

In the 1890s, people throughout the United States were trying to make electric-, steam-, or gasoline-powered engines and automobiles. People such as David Buick, Charles and Frank Duryea, Elwood P. Haynes, Hiram Percy Maxim, Ransom Eli Olds, the Stanley brothers, Alexander Winton, and countless others were entering the field, some from bicycle manufacturing, some from designing marine engines, some from manufacturing carriages, and others as trained machinists. It was a very challenging time. There were no available products such as spark plugs, carburetors, valves, pistons, automobile wheels, axles, brakes, crankshafts, bearings, gears, belts, distributors, starters, automobile chassis, or automobile engines. Everything had to be adapted or made from the ground up by the automobile designer. There were no standard parts and this affected not only the designer but also the owner of an automobile.

Choosing how to power an automobile was not easy. Steam (Stanley), electricity (Studebaker), and gas (Pierce Arrow) were all contenders at the beginning of the twentieth century. Automobile registration in 1900 shows that 40 percent of the cars were steam, 38 percent were electric, and 22 percent gasoline. Meanwhile, technology developments were occurring in the design of all three automobile types.

Steam vehicles took time to start up, as the boiler and burner had to be heated. Once started, however, they had significant power, which was of special value in mountainous regions. They were also freer from noise, smell, and vibration than the early gasoline engines. Steam engines used the exhaust of one cylinder in another before exhausting it into the air. A condenser was used to condense the exhausting steam, and most of this was turned back as hot water into the boiler. The invention of the flash boiler in 1899 enabled a steamer to reach full power in seconds rather than minutes. But the water in steamers could freeze up in winter, and on long trips automobiles had to be stopped often for refills. At first, steamers had to have water added every fifty miles, but by 1915, they could go up to 300 miles or so—not much different from some gasoline-powered cars today.

The trolley car took its power from an electric wire overhead, with a storage battery for special conditions. An electric automobile had to have a rechargeable storage battery for power. The electric car had to be frequently recharged and hence was used in cities and townships. Range of the vehicle between charges was around sixty miles. The electric car could go at a fast speed for short distances or at lower speeds for somewhat longer distances. The cars had limited range, but few people needed to go far. Moreover, country roads would not allow them to go great distances. The electric car's top speed of twenty miles per hour was acceptable. Its engine design was much simpler than the gasoline engine, and an electric was easy to drive.

The first car to go a mile a minute was an electric. In 1899, outside Paris, an electric car reached a speed of 65.8 miles per hour. The first car to go two miles a minute was a steam car, the Stanley Steamer, which held the world speed record in 1906 of 127.66 miles per hour. In 1907, the Stanleys' driver, Fred Marriot, tried again at Ormond Beach in Daytona, Florida, and reached a speed of 197 miles per hour before the car bounced, broke up, and the boiler went one mile down the beach. Marriot lived, but he was badly injured, and the Stanley brothers never again tried for a speed record.

Two types of gasoline engines were developed in the early twentieth century. In one, the gasoline was burned under a steam boiler to generate steam. In the other, the gasoline was burned directly in the cylinder that drove the vehicle.[1] Gasoline engines also had to be cranked to start, a disadvantage not shared by electric and steam automobiles.

In 1898, the first motor exhibition was held in Boston with ten vehicles on display. Two years later, the first auto show was held in New York City. The 1900 census reported the production of 4,192 cars—1,681 steam powered, 1,575 electric, and 936 powered by gasoline. There was a choice of models, many produced by very small companies. Worldwide, fewer than 10,000 automobiles were made that year.

In January 1904, *Frank Leslie's Popular Monthly* listed the major new cars of that year. A review of the list gives a feeling for the breadth of manufacturing. The list is divided into three groups: gasoline carriages, steam carriages, and electric carriages. Neither a propulsion system nor an industry manufacturing center had yet been settled on. Based on the information in 1904, it would have been difficult to predict the proper technology or where future autos would be built. The cars listed in Table 5.1 were made by sixty-four manufacturers, used three different methods of power, were guided by both steering wheels and tillers, carried between two and seven people, weighed between 500 and 3,600 pounds, and ranged in price between $425 and $9,700, at a time when the average annual salary was $500.[2] Which technologies and which manufacturers would dominate the future?

Table 5.1. The new 1904 cars and their city of manufacture

Car	City	Type	Cost
Apperson	Kokomo, IN	gasoline	$3,500
Auburn	Auburn, IN	gasoline	1,000
Autocar	Ardmore, PA	gasoline	1,700
Baker Runabout	Cleveland, OH	electric	850
Baker Stanhope	Cleveland, OH	electric	1,600
Berg	New York, NY	gasoline	3,500
Buffalo Golf Brake	Buffalo, NY	electric	2,200
Buffalo Stanhope	Buffalo, NY	electric	1,650
Buffalo Tonneau	Buffalo, NY	electric	5,000
Cadillac	Detroit, MI	gasoline	850
Clement	New York, NY (Imported)	gasoline	5,000
Columbia Brougham	Hartford, CT	electric	3,500
Columbia Coupe	Hartford, CT	electric	3,500
Columbia Hansom	Hartford, CT	electric	3,500
Columbia Surrey	Hartford, CT	electric	1,500
Columbia Touring	Hartford, CT	gasoline	4,500
Columbia Victoria	Hartford, CT	electric	1,600
Columbia Victoria PH	Hartford, CT	electric	3,000
Compound	Middletown, CT	gasoline	8,000
Courier	Sandusky, OH	gasoline	700
Covert	Lockport, NY	gasoline	750
Crestmobile	Cambridge, MA	gasoline	850
Cudell	New York, NY (Imp)	gasoline	4,500
Daimler	Long Island City, NY	gasoline	7,500
Darracq 4 Cylinder	New York, NY (Imp)	gasoline	7,000
Darracq 2 Cylinder	New York, NY (Imp)	gasoline	3,500
Decauville	New York, NY (Imp)	gasoline	6,000
De Dietrich	New York, NY (Imp)	gasoline	9,700
Dion Bouton	Boston, MA (Imp)	gasoline	3,000
Duryea Phaeton	Reading, PA	gasoline	1,350
Duryea Tonneau	Reading, PA	gasoline	1,750
Eldridge Runabout	Belvidere, IL	gasoline	750
Eldridge Tonneau	Belvidere, IL	gasoline	2,000
Elmore Runabout	Clyde, OH	gasoline	650
Elmore Runabout	Clyde, OH	steam	800
Elmore Tonneau	Clyde, OH	gasoline	1,400
Ford	Detroit, MI	gasoline	750
Franklin	Syracuse, NY	gasoline	1,300
Freedonia	Youngstown, OH	gasoline	1,250
Freedonia Runabout	Youngstown, OH	gasoline	1,000
Grout	Orange, MA	steam	2,000
Haynes Apperson LC	Kokomo, IN	gasoline	1,550
Haynes-Apperson T	Kokomo, IN	gasoline	2,400
Holley	Bradford, PA	steam	650
Knox	Springfield, MA	gasoline	2,000

continued next page

Table 5.1. The new 1904 cars and
their city of manufacture (continued)

Car	City	Type	Cost
Locomobile	Bridgeport, CT	gasoline	2,000
Locomobile Runabout	Bridgeport, CT	steam	850
Matheson	Grand Rapids, MI	gasoline	5,000
Mors	New York, NY (Imp)	gasoline	8,000
National Tonneau	Indianapolis, IN	electric	1,500
Niagara	Wilson, NY	gasoline	850
Northern	Detroit, MI	gasoline	750
Oldsmobile	Detroit, MI	gasoline	650
Orient Buckboard	Waltham, MA	gasoline	425
Packard, Model L	Detroit, MI	gasoline	3,000
Panhard	New York, NY (Imp)	gasoline	8,500
Peerless 35 hp	Cleveland, OH	gasoline	6,000
Peerless 24 hp	Cleveland, OH	gasoline	4,000
Phelps	Stoneham, MA	gasoline	2,000
Pierce Arrow	Buffalo, NY	gasoline	2,500
Pierce Stanhope	Buffalo, NY	gasoline	1,200
Pope-Toledo	Toledo, OH	gasoline	3,500
Pope-Waverly	Indianapolis, IN	electric	1,100
Premier	Indianapolis, IN	gasoline	2,500
Rambler Model K	Kenosha, WI	gasoline	1,000
Rambler, Model L	Kenosha, WI	gasoline	1,350
Renault	New York, NY (Imp)	gasoline	6,000
Robinson	Hyde Park, MA	gasoline	5,000
Rochet-Schneider	New York, NY (Imp)	gasoline	7,500
Royal Tourist	Cleveland, OH	gasoline	2,300
Sandusky	Sandusky, OH	steam	650
Santos Dumont	Columbus, OH	gasoline	1,500
Smith and Marbley	New York, NY	gasoline	5,500
Stanley Runabout	Newton, MA	steam	670
Stearns	Cleveland, OH	gasoline	3,000
Stephens-Duryea	Chicopee Falls, MA	gasoline	1,300
Saint Louis	Saint Louis, MO	gasoline	1,200
Studebaker Runabout	New York, NY	electric	975
Studebaker Stanhope	New York, NY	electric	1,175
Thomas	Buffalo, NY	gasoline	1,250
White	Cleveland, OH	steam	2,500
Winton	Cleveland, OH	gasoline	2,500
Woods Stanhope	Chicago, IL	electric	950
Woods Victoria	Chicago, IL	electric	3,500
Yale	Toledo, OH	gasoline	1,500

Source: "The Automobiles of 1904," *Frank Leslie's Popular Monthly,* January 1904.

In these early days, there were a variety of automobile choices for the customer: the Apperson, Babcock, Buick, Cadillac, Duryea, Fischer, Franklin, General Electric, Glide, Great Arrow, Haynes, Howard, International (Harvester), Knox, Northern, Packard, Peerless, Pierce Arrow, Pontiac, Pope-Robinson, Rambler, Red, Selden, Stanley Steamer, Stearns, Studebaker, Triumph, Waverly, White, Winton, and many others. A buyer could also choose between the Alamobile, Clarkmobile, Gasmobile, Lancamobile, Buzmobile, Locomobile, Oldsmobile, Rushmobile, Steamobile, and the Mobile. If the customer wished to support a local company, he or she could buy an Akron, Bethlehem, Buffalo, Chelsea, Cincinnati, Cleveland, Holyoke, Knickerbocker, Marlboro, Milwaukee, Niagara, Pawtucket, Pennsylvania, Phoenix, Reading, Rochester, Rockaway, Sandusky, Shelby, Saint Louis, Syracuse, Tauton, Toledo, or an Illinois, Louisiana, Maine, Maryland, Bay State, or New England motorcar.

There have been more than 1,500 automobile manufacturers in the United States located in more than forty states.[3] Buffalo, New York, was one early center of car manufacture, with the Buffalo Electric, Stanhope, Thomas, and Pierce Arrow. Cleveland was another center of the early automobile industry with at least eighteen automobiles, including the Winton, Stearns-Knight, Peerless, Hupmobile, White, Baker, Chandler, Royal, and Star. There were more than 100 automobile manufacturers in Massachusetts alone in the years between 1895 and 1925, producing cars such as the Beverly, Stevens-Duryea, Knox, Waltham-Orient, Crestmobile, Rolls-Royce in Springfield, and the Stanley Steamer, made in Newton. From 1908 to 1912, even Sears, Roebuck made several models of automobiles. These cars were priced below $500 and came with a ten-day return policy. Cars decreased in price and performance improved, trends that were repeated in the computer industry almost a century later.

Some Entrepreneurs

When the first cars came out, the United States was already the richest market in the world and growing fast. Unlike steel, which is a commodity, automobiles are unique and reflect both on their designer and their owner. It is worth reviewing the story of some of the early pioneers in the industry as well as their contributions to automobile development.

John (1864–1920) and Horace (1868–1920) Dodge started off as bicycle manufacturers, even designing and patenting their own ball bearings. They then made transmissions for many companies and in exchange for stock, became a sole supplier to Ford. They quit the supply business and opened up their own firm, Dodge Brothers. Their 1914 Touring Car was very popular, and more than 45,000 were sold that year.

Elwood P. Haynes (1857–1925) was a college-educated engineer who had to do a lot of traveling in his job as superintendent of Indiana Gas and Oil Company. He made his first car in 1894 in Kokomo, Indiana, using a marine engine. He then formed the Haynes-Apperson Company, which made cars from 1895 until 1924.

Henry Martin Leland (1843–1932) started in the firearms manufacturing business where he learned about interchangeable parts. A gifted machinist, he owned a machine tool factory that made internal combustion engines for boats. Leland took over when Henry Ford was fired from the Ford Engineering Company and the company was renamed Cadillac. In 1906, Cadillac was the first company to offer closed bodies as standard equipment. Partly because he used interchangeable parts, Leland and his Cadillac cars became symbols of quality. In 1908, three Cadillacs were sent to England, where they were dismantled. The parts were mixed and then the cars reassembled. The cars ran perfectly, demonstrating to the English the value of interchangeable parts in automobile manufacturing. In 1907, Leland established the first school to train machinists, technicians, and toolmakers. He left Cadillac in 1917 and organized the Lincoln Motor Company, which was purchased by Henry Ford in 1922.

Jonathan Dixon Maxwell (1864–1928) started as a bicycle manufacturer and then helped found the Maxwell-Briscoe Company in 1903. His first cars, the Maxwell Tourabouts, were made in Tarrytown, New York. Maxwell designed the Oldsmobile and Northern automobiles and worked in the field until 1913. The Maxwell was made from 1903 to 1923, and then the name disappeared for a while as it was absorbed into Chrysler, returning as the Chrysler 50.

Charles W. Nash (1864–1948) started in the carriage business. He then joined with Billy Durant in 1905 to help run Buick and became its president. In 1912, Nash became president of General Motors but left in 1916 to purchase the Thomas Jeffrey Company where he began to manufacture Nash cars. He was president until 1930, when the company merged with Kelvinator. He became chairman of the resulting company.

Ransom Eli Olds (1864–1950) began as a partner with his father and brother in a firm that manufactured steam engines in Lansing, Michigan. He built steam vehicles in 1886 and gas-powered vehicles in 1894. He started Olds Motor Vehicle Company in 1897 and built eleven models in a two-year period, some electric and some gas. In 1901, he introduced the first Oldsmobile, the "curved dash," priced at $650 and nicknamed because of the elegant contours of its front. The cars he built from 1901 through 1904 were the first commercially successful American autos. He sold his company to General Motors in 1907 and started the Reo Motor Company, named for his initials.

James Ward Packard (1863–1928), an electrical engineer, bought an early Winton, but it broke down. Disappointed, he decided to build his own car, and in 1893, he and his brother Warren introduced the first automobile, the excellent 1899 Packard Model A. By 1902, the Packards were entering and winning races, including the New York to Buffalo and the New York to Boston races. In the 1920s, the Packard emerged as a leader in the luxury car market.

Albert Augustus Pope (1843–1909), a major bicycle manufacturer, began to manufacture electric runabouts in 1896 and controlled three companies in the auto business. His autos bracketed the market from the low-cost Pope-Toledo, the Pope-Tribune, and the Pope-Hartford, all gasoline powered, to the Pope-Waverly, a luxury electric automobile. In 1895, Pope hired Hiram Percy Maxim, an MIT graduate and the son of the Maxim gun inventor. Two years later, they began large-scale production, making 500 electrics and 40 gasoline cars in the next two years.

Francis E. (1849–1918) and Freelan O. (1849–1940) Stanley, twin brothers, were born in Kingfield, Maine. They were inventors who developed a home gas generator, X-ray equipment, and a photography dry-plate coating machine, which they patented on July 13, 1886, and sold for a substantial sum to George Eastman. They moved to Newton, Massachusetts, where they designed the Stanley Steamer in 1897. The brothers showed the car in an auto show in Boston on November 9, 1898, and drove around a bicycle track at a world record–breaking time of two minutes, eleven seconds, or twenty-seven miles per hour. A car that was easy to handle, safe, and reliable, the Steamer had little vibration and lots of power. The boiler provided the pressure to drive a two-cylinder engine. The car did not have a transmission or gearshift; one gear engaged the crankshaft to directly power the rear wheels. In 1903, the Stanleys sold several cars to the Boston Police Department. At Daytona, they set records of one mile per minute and then two miles per minute. In 1908, they introduced the Stanley Roadster, a steam car similar to the one that had set the world's speed record in Florida. They redesigned the steam engine to recycle water, since watering troughs were being eliminated as fast as the horse. In 1918, F. E. was killed in an accident, and his brother retired. Others tried to carry on the business, but the last Stanley Steamer was made in 1925. Early in 1903, F. O., struck by a severe recurrence of tuberculosis, went to Colorado, where he summered there every year. He bought 6,000 acres in Estes Park and began construction of a grand hotel, the Stanley, near Rocky Mountain National Park. He also built a power plant to supply electricity to the hotel, with enough left over to electrify the town. F. O. Stanley died in October 1940.

John Mohler Studebaker (1833–1917) began with an 1852 wagon manufacturing company that made chuck wagons, artillery wagons, and Conestoga wagons for more than half a century. He returned home from California, where he had made wheelbarrows for gold miners while his brothers were building wagons for the U.S. Army and expanding the wagon business through the Civil War. By the 1890s, Studebaker was the largest vehicle manufacturer in the world. Studebaker started in the auto business in 1899 by building car bodies. In 1902, the company made its first electric car, and in 1904, it produced the Studebaker Touring Car, which had a gasoline engine. The brothers started to make cars in large quantities in 1912 using the Studebaker name, producing 28,000 cars that year.

Windsor, Rollin, and Walter White's father owned the successful White Sewing Machine Company. The brothers introduced in 1900 the White Steamer, which was built under a Stanley license. It used gasoline as fuel for the boiler, and the car could go 200 miles on one filling of the boilers. By 1911, they were producing a line of luxury town cars and limousines, both gasoline and steam powered. A White automobile was the first White House car, with a model delivered to President William Howard Taft in 1909.

John North Willys (1873–1933) sold bicycles and later automobiles— including Pierce, Overland, and Rambler—in Elmira, New York. In 1906, Willys organized the American Motor Company as the marketing outlet for Overland Company. He then acquired the Pope-Toledo Company. By 1910, he was the third largest automobile manufacturer, and in 1915, Willys-Overland was second only to the Ford Motor Company. Willys bought a company that made engines, renamed it Willys-Knight, and by the 1920s was making more sleeve-valve engines than all other car manufacturers combined.

Alexander Winton (1860–1932) was born in Scotland and settled in Cleveland in 1886. Another bicycle manufacturer, he entered the auto business in 1897 when he built his first motor carriage. He delivered 22 cars the next year and 100 in 1899. Winton developed the eight-cylinder motorcar, a storage battery, and other technological advances and pioneered the ideas of spare parts and service stations for repairs. He entered the first American car in a French race in 1899. (Few American road races were held due to the poor roads.) In 1900, Winton won the first Cleveland to New York race in thirty-eight hours, thirty minutes, at an average speed on 20.8 miles per hour.

These and other pioneers developed a number of automobile features. Early horns were brass bugles that honked when squeezed. Car bodies came in myriad styles. Brakes were a particularly difficult problem. Some of the early cars had no brakes, and the driver had to steer the car into the side of the road to stop it. Others used shoes that rubbed against the wheel rims—the same braking system used on horse-drawn carriages. These usually acted on the front wheels and were made of leather. Eventually, other braking systems were tried, including slowing down the transmission drive, braking all four wheels rather than just two, moving air into an expanding drum, and finally, using cast-iron shoes to press against the wheels and slow them down. Passengers in the early automobiles were exposed to rain and weather, but this was not worse than riding in horse-drawn buggies.

Gasoline engines required a crank or starting handle. Hand cranking a gasoline automobile was too difficult and dangerous for women, for young people, and for many men. Steam and electric cars started instantly. Manufacturers tried all sorts of schemes to eliminate this problem with gasoline engines—springs, compressed air, and gas with valves—but none worked reliably. The 1912 Cadillac offered an electric self-starter as well as electric lights to replace gaslights.

By 1905, American cars had been sold in Great Britain, Japan, China, South Africa, and Mexico. Europeans had great automobile designs, but Americans had low cost. Cheap raw materials and a shortage of skilled labor in America led to automation that required standardization, enabling the United States to pull in front of the pack. By 1913, the United States was producing 80 percent of the world's automobiles.

Once there were a number of automobiles and automobile manufacturers, racing became important. The first challenge was whether it was possible to drive a car from point A to point B, reflecting not only the performance of the car but also the roads. A second issue was how much time was required to go from point A to point B. Early races went from New York City to Buffalo, New York City to Boston, Chicago to Waukegan, Illinois, and San Francisco to New York City. Finally, there was the issue of speed on a closed and prepared track. Not surprisingly, many of the early auto designers also participated in races either as drivers or as support crew in order to demonstrate the performance of their automobiles.

Frank Duryea won an auto race in 1895. On November 28, 1895, the first scheduled race was run from Chicago to nearby Waukegan, Illinois. The winner completed the ninety-two miles in nine hours and twenty-two minutes. In 1902, young Roy Chapin, a future secretary of commerce for Herbert Hoover, and John Maxwell, the future automobile designer, drove an Olds from Detroit to New York City to arrive in time for the Auto Show. Because the roads were poor or nonexistent, the trip took seven days, and the car frequently got stuck in mud. The adventurous driver often had to carry his own gasoline, extra tires, spare parts, and block and tackle because there was little help or supplies outside of the larger towns.

On July 26, 1903, sixty-four days after leaving San Francisco, a Winton automobile driven by Dr. H. Nelson Jackson and Sewell K. Crocker arrived in New York City. That year, two other cars completed the trip, including a Packard driven by Tom Fetch and Marius Krarup in fifty-three days. In 1904, a trip was planned between New York City and Saint Louis to celebrate the Louisiana Purchase Exposition. Of the seventy-one cars that started, fifty-nine completed the 1,200-mile trip. In 1909, driver Alice Huler Ramsey and three female companions, none of whom could drive, took a Maxwell from New York City to San Francisco in fifty-three days.

Races were held in conjunction with many of the early automobile shows, including the 1900 Chicago show and many of the New York and Boston shows. In 1901, there was a challenge between Henry Ford and Alexander Winton over a twenty-five-mile course in Grosse Point, Michigan, and Ford won. Henry Ford continued to race until his wife put her foot down, and Ford hired Barney Oldfield, a racing cyclist, as race-car driver for his Model 999.

On October 27, 1901, Ransom Olds and Alexander Winton met on the sands of Ormond Beach in Daytona, Florida, for a race that began a racing tradition. In 1896, the first automobile racetrack in America was built in Narragansett, Rhode Island. In 1909, a track was built in Indianapolis, and the Indianapolis 500 was first raced in 1911 and won with a locally built car, the six-cylinder Marmon. The following year, another Indianapolis-built car, the National, was first across the finish line.

In the early part of the twentieth century, steam-, electric-, and gasoline-powered vehicles were all vying for supremacy. At the time, more than 50 percent of the cars registered in New York in 1902 were steam powered. Electric cars also were widely supported, especially in the cities. But gasoline was to win out.

The first gasoline wells had been drilled in Pennsylvania in the 1860s. In 1900, the entire output of petroleum in the United States was 64 million barrels a year, with most used for lamps. In 1901, an oil discovery at the Spindletop oilfield in Texas came in, and the price of crude petroleum dropped significantly to just 5 cents a barrel. In the first year, Texas oil fields produced 17 million barrels. Low-cost gasoline and the development of large energy companies supported the gasoline engine as the power source for the growing automobile industry.

The Engineering and Production Phase: The Ford Motor Company

If the automobile was the most important product of the twentieth century, there is most assuredly no individual who had more influence on the history of the automobile industry than Henry Ford. Henry Ford read about the gas engine that had been developed by Nikolaus Otto and wanted to learn how the engine worked. Otto had obtained a patent for this revolutionary motor in August 1877, and the Otto Engine had been shown at the Paris Exhibition in 1878. Henry Ford and many others throughout the United States began to think about the gasoline engine.

Henry Ford started the Ford Motor Company in 1902 at the age of thirty-nine. He had already had one bankruptcy and been fired from a second company. There were hundreds of other automobile manufacturers and no reason to believe he would succeed. In 1903, Ford employed a dozen workers in an assembly area that measured 250 feet by 50 feet. He depended on suppliers for components and then assembled the autos.

Ford entered the automobile business at a time of rapid development. In the United States, there have been more than 1,500 different automobile manufacturers. In 1902, there was one automobile for every 1,500,000 people in the country, but soon thereafter, the industry began to grow rapidly. In 1908, the auto industry built 65,000 cars; in 1915, the number jumped to 1 million.

Henry Ford, with his strengths and weaknesses, his accomplishments and his failures, provides a good example of the influences one individual can have on the economy, on technology, on jobs, and on the character and direction of a country. Ford built a major company and an industry from an idea. Attention has been paid to Henry Ford in the later years of his life, and his life will be discussed in the next chapter. Certainly, his company faced a number of major crises in the 1930s and 1940s, but Henry Ford, his son, Edsel, and his grandson, Henry II, solved these problems, and the company continued to advance. For a very long time the Ford Motor Company has been one of the five largest American companies and one of the largest manufacturing organizations and employers in the world.

Ford's first car, the Model A of 1903, was fairly standard. In the 1904–1905 year, the Ford Motor Company expanded, and the Model A was replaced with the Model C, which sold for $800. In addition, a new touring car, the Model F, was introduced and sold for $1,000. In order to appeal to a wealthier customer, the company introduced a new heavier and faster car, the Model B, which sold for $2,000. It was the first of the company's four-cylinder cars and was replaced in time by the Model K. In 1906, the Ford Motor Company took its first major step toward industry leadership with the introduction of the Model N. Henry Ford wanted to make a very low-priced car by building cars in high volume using standardized parts and one chassis. The Model N had an engine in front under the hood, two lamps on the radiator, mudguards covering the wheels, and could achieve a speed of forty-five miles per hour. This good-looking four-cylinder car, weighing 1,050 pounds, had a list price of $600 and was one of the best cars of its time. The Model R and the Model S also used the same chassis but had slightly different appearances. The Model K and the Model B were soon discontinued.

The Model N reached dealers in the fall of 1906 and was a great success. In the ten months after October 1906, 11,500 cars were built. Some industry observers called the Model N the car of the year. The company did a significant amount of advertising under James Couzens's direction, and this helped build the image of Ford as a national company. Low cost, simplicity, durability, and quality were the Model N's advantages. Henry Ford believed that other manufacturers, who had several chassis and introduced new designs every year, would soon go broke. He followed this philosophy for the rest of his life, sometimes successfully and sometimes not.

Ford's company grew by leaps and bounds. He built 8,300 cars in 1906, 32,000 in 1910, and 170,000 in 1912. His production in 1910 was four times that of all English manufacturers combined. By 1921, Henry Ford was supplying more than one-half of the automobiles sold in the United States. In his lifetime, the Ford Motor Company sold almost 35 million cars, or one automobile for every man, woman, and child living in the United States in the year of Henry Ford's birth.

Ford had never been enthusiastic about the Model B, which had been supported by his partner, Alexander Malcomson. Moreover, the Model K, the Model B's successor, had very disappointing sales. This six-cylinder car had major trouble with its transmission, and at a price of $2,500, it was moving the company away from Henry Ford's idea of the low-cost automobile for the mass market. Disagreements developed between Ford and Malcomson, and in 1907, Henry Ford bought out Malcomson and was elected president of the company. Ford now owned a majority of the stock and was clearly in charge. James Couzens also increased his ownership share in the company with 11 percent of the stock.

At the 1904 New York Auto Show, Detroit was well represented by Cadillac, Ford, Northern, Olds, Packard, and Wolverine. The presence of Henry Ford, Ransom Eli Olds, and Henry M. Leland; the existence of wagon manufacturers and machine shops; the availability of low-cost labor; and the city's strategic location all helped Detroit to boom. During 1909, twenty-two new automobile companies were organized in Detroit as other companies joined the new industry. The city was becoming the center of the automobile industry.

Competition continued to change as new companies were formed and some of the older ones got out of the business. Every year, some of the prior year's entries in the New York Auto Show were not there, and new companies made their debut. (This two-decade turnover of competition was not unlike that seen in the computer industry at the National Computer Show more than seventy years later.) In 1908, leadership in the industry passed to four corporations— Buick, Ford, Reo, and Maxwell-Briscoe—and together they sold as many cars as all the other manufacturers combined. There was the start of a shakeout as competitors continued to disappear. Overland Company failed but was bought by John North Willys. William Durant started to form General Motors and talked to Henry Ford about merging.

Meanwhile, the Ford Motor Company continued to advance. For two years, a dozen people in the Ford organization had been working to build a new, simpler, more useful, cheaper, and more efficient car. On March 19, 1908, the Model T was announced and was first shown at the London and Paris Auto Shows that November. This now legendary car, the most popular in history, had a twenty-horsepower four-cylinder engine, could achieve speeds of forty-five miles per hour, had a fuel consumption of better than twenty-five miles per gallon, and was about half the price of its competitors. When the Model T was announced, it was manufactured in black, red, gray, green, and blue, but by

1914, black became the only available color. Black was used because color finishes could not be mass-produced on the metal chassis parts and on the wooden bodies of the Model T.

The initial price of the Model T was $825, but by 1914, it had been reduced to $440. By 1926, the Model T could be purchased for $260. The car was built around the concept of interchangeable parts and was easy to build, operate, maintain, and repair. With the Model T, a mechanic was often not needed. Anyone could take the car apart with a wrench, buy new parts, and then reassemble the car.

The Model T moved the Ford Motor Company into leadership in the auto industry. The company sold off all older models and concentrated on the Model T, planning 25,000 cars for its first year of production. The car had a good engine; was rugged, durable, and low cost; could be serviced by the buyer; and sold well in both urban and rural areas. In 1914, the company increased production to 200,000 cars while decreasing its number of employees by 10 percent. It made 750,000 vehicles in 1919, and in 1923, 2 million.

Henry Ford was himself a skilled mechanic with an extraordinary instinct for mechanical design. He studied all competitors' cars and borrowed ideas from them. He used new materials, including vanadium steel alloy and other heat-treated steels, to reduce the car's weight. He combined many ideas and was able to produce a basic, high-quality, no-frills automobile at the lowest price. The American public bought his direct, commonsense approach, and Henry Ford became a symbol of the company. At age forty-five, after working on the design of cars for more than eighteen years, Henry Ford became an "overnight success." And with the growth of the Model T, Henry Ford became a national and an international figure.

In 1908, the labor required for the final assembly of a Model T totaled twelve hours, twenty-eight minutes. By 1914, it had been reduced to one hour, thirty-three minutes. The mass-production techniques that Ford had used at the Picquette Avenue Plant—his first major plant—with the Model N were put into use at the Highland Park Plant with the Model T. The Highland Park factory was made for mass production. Soon, Henry Ford started assembling cars at branch assembly plants around the country and shipping subassemblies from Michigan.

In January 1914, because of productivity gains, Ford announced the $5 per day, eight-hour shift, which doubled the wages of his workers and cut their workday by 20 percent. Ford workers had twice the purchasing power of their average American counterparts, and six times that of British workers. Henry Ford wanted his workers to be able to purchase his cars.

In addition, as the son and grandson of farmers, Henry Ford wanted to make farming life easier. Ford started work in 1907 to build a light and cheap tractor that most farmers could afford. The Model T became the basis for this tractor, which Ford introduced in 1916. The tractor, also called the Model T, could seed, plow, harrow, and pump water. It could also act as a snowplow and haul products to market. The life of the farmer was changed forever. On July 27, 1917, a company was incorporated under the name Henry Ford & Son for the large-scale manufacture of tractors, agricultural implements, and appliances. The company was wholly owned by the Ford family. In 1917, Ford accepted an order for low-cost, reliable tractors from the British government to assist in feeding people during the war. By April 1918, Ford had delivered the entire order of 7,000 tractors to the British to help solve their food crisis. By June 1918, he had American orders for 13,463 tractors, with 5,000 already delivered. By 1922, the company had delivered almost 200,000 tractors.

After World War I, the company grew overseas. Ford established sales and service branches first and then, when volume dictated, local assembly plants. The first assembly plant outside of the United States was built in Manchester, England, in 1911. By 1928, Ford had assembly plants in Canada, England, Ireland, Germany, France, Italy, Belgium, Denmark, Finland, the Netherlands, Sweden, Spain, Argentina, Brazil, Mexico, Colombia, Australia, New Zealand, South Africa, and Japan.

At its Highland Park facility, the Ford Motor Company led the world in the development of mass production. New manufacturing methods and new machines resulted in higher production at lower cost. Significant capital investment was made in order to increase the output of each worker. The manufacturing process was divided into a large number of reproducible steps. The design of an assembly line, however, was a very complicated procedure requiring standardization and precise planning of the work. The assembly line had to move at the right speed, on just the right level, through just the right sequence of activities. Subsidiary lines had to produce the right parts, which had to arrive at the worker's station at just the right moment. Nothing should be wasted, and everything had to arrive on time. The lack of one part could cause the entire production line to shut down, causing large financial repercussions.

Henry Ford also wanted to vertically integrate, not only controlling all of his sources of raw materials, including iron and steel, lumber, coal, limestone, and silica sand, but also owning mines, forests, foundries, steel mills, glass factories, power sources, railroads, and shipping fleets. He wanted to acquire raw materials and bring them to Ford plants on Ford ships. In this way, he had the greatest chance of guaranteeing that the production lines would keep running. In 1915, Ford purchased 2,000 acres of land in the Rouge River area outside of Detroit, and planning started for the largest factory in the world. The design of the facility was based on the concept of continuous flow, bringing all raw materials and parts to the manufacturing point where they were needed at the time they were needed.

Work was soon started at the Rouge River Plant making Eagle Boats for the U.S. government during World War I. By 1918, there were 8,000 employees at the facility. After the war, the plant was retooled for automobile and tractor pro-duction, and for the next dozen years, the plant expanded. The Rouge Plant took in raw materials, produced much of its own iron and steel in its blast furnaces, processed all the coke it needed, provided lumber for the Model T bodies, gen-erated power in its power plant, and made most of the parts with its foundries fashioning the iron, brass, steel, and bronze castings. This material was then used to manufacture automobiles, trucks, and tractors. The Rouge Plant cost Henry Ford more than $115 million, which he paid out of company earnings.

In order to allow ships and barges to reach the plant, Henry Ford built a canal and dredged the Rouge River, doubling its width to 200 feet and its depth to 21 feet. By 1925, ocean ships were able to steam into the plant from any port in the world. In the 1930s, the plant's capacity was further increased. Ford bought a railroad, the Detroit, Toledo & Ironton, and, after improving its operations, sold it to the Pennsylvania Railroad at a price seven times what he had paid for it. He invested in glass plants in Pennsylvania and Minnesota, coal mines in Kentucky and West Virginia, and, with Harvey Firestone, new sources of rubber in Brazil. Without any obligations to partners or shareholders, Henry Ford was able to move the company in any direction he chose.

By the 1920s, the Model T had a number of disadvantages relative to its com-petition. It needed constant care and adjustment. The car vibrated and gave a rough ride. The Model T had no shock absorbers. Moreover, it had no water pump, so its radiator boiled under moderate engine strain. It had no gas or oil gauge, and four-wheel brakes were never available. The Model T had a hand accelerator instead of a foot accelerator, and, with its planetary transmission, the driver had to keep a foot on a pedal in order to keep the car in low gear, a significant disadvantage in city driving. The car had a flywheel magneto that caused the brightness of its headlights to vary depending on engine speed—at times almost going out when a motorist came up to an intersection at night and took a foot off the accelerator. Although electric starters had been first used by Cadillac in 1912, the Model T still had to be hand cranked, and if the car was accidentally left in gear, it could run over the driver when the car was cranked. (After 1919, electric starters did become available on the Model Ts as optional equipment.) It could take up to twenty minutes to put up the side curtains in a Model T, and, if the weather changed suddenly, both the driver and the passengers were likely to get wet.

For a variety of reasons, then, the day of the Model T began to pass. Ford did not value marketing since he believed the Model T sold itself. In 1923, there were five times as many Fords sold as Chevrolets. By 1926, however, Ford's mar-ket share had dropped, and there were only twice as many Fords sold as Chevrolets. Model T owners traded up to more comfortable cars. American tastes changed. People began to be interested in style, comfort, and looks in an auto-mobile as well as in engineering and reliability. They wanted roomier interiors, upholstery, fashion, and beauty. Women began to have a greater influence in the purchase of an automobile, and many women were more interested in how a car looked and drove than in how it operated. Speed and power became important, and the six-cylinder car began to replace the four-cylinder car because of its quicker acceleration, greater power, and reduced engine vibration. People wanted a smoother ride, better cushioned by springs and balloon tires. The closed-model car began to replace the open model, and, by 1924, closed models represented one-half of all new car sales, and sales were increasing.

The price differential closed between the Model T and other cars—including the Overland 4, the Chevrolet, and the Dodge—as other manufacturers adopted Ford's ideas of cost-cutting mass production of a single chassis. These cars had different design and comfort features than the Model T and offered better performance at only a slightly higher price. Chevrolet began to advertise its competitive strengths over Ford and gain market share.

Henry Ford believed in the Model T, the most successful automobile in history, and his son Edsel had to fight him to make changes. Edsel was sensitive to a car's design, whereas Henry only cared about what made a car run and how its costs could be reduced. The restyled Model T, introduced in 1925, helped for a time, but the need for a major change became apparent. Ford kept cutting costs to stimulate demand but, after a while, it no longer increased sales. When Edsel pressed Henry to build an entirely new car, recognizing that times had changed, Henry responded by withdrawing from his son, and for a time, only communicated to him through others. At one point, he even ordered his production manager to tell Edsel to go to California and stay there until he was called back.

In 1926, the Ford Motor Company's sales had decreased to 34 percent of the industry's total production. Henry Ford became more inflexible and began to blame the company's problems on the mental attitude and lack of faith of his managers and dealers. Ford added new dealers and cut those that disagreed with his programs. He established competing dealers in the same territory. But the days of the Model T were passing and other than Henry Ford, all members of management wanted a new car.

On June 4, 1924, the 10 millionth Model T had been made. On Tuesday, March 26, 1927, the 15 millionth Model T was built. But in the last week of May 1927, all dealers were notified that the final Model T had left the assembly line. The final number of cars made was 15,007,003. In March 1927, nineteen years after the first Model T was built, there were more than 11 million of the cars registered in the United States—proof of their durability. As late as 1949, there were more than 230,000 registered, a number greater than the total number of cars in the United States the year the Model T was introduced.

The days of the Model T were over, but Henry Ford had entered the last months of production without the design of a successor car ready. Ford had no research facilities or centralized engineering to design new cars, as Alfred P. Sloan Jr. had given General Motors. The American public wondered if the Ford Motor Company could come back. Henry Ford, at age sixty-four, had to start over again.

After the Model T was discontinued, the Highland Park Plant was shut down and more than 60,000 Ford workers were laid off. Around the country, several hundred thousand workers were affected by plant closings and production cutbacks. The Ford Motor Company had been using approximately 10 percent of the country's iron and steel, aluminum, tin, nickel, and copper, and more than 35 five percent of the country's plate glass and rubber. Numerous subcontractors suffered badly, and the Ford dealers had nothing to sell until a new car was in production.

Henry Ford, however, was happy as he had a very challenging design project ahead of him. He gathered a few trusted employees and started the design of a new car in mid-1926. Henry and Edsel agreed quickly on the wheelbase, external size, and other dimensions of the car and then began the difficult job of engineering. Edsel was in charge of the overall design and styling of the car, and his father worked on every part of the car's operation. Edsel knew exactly what he wanted. Since 1913, Edsel had been keeping a scrapbook of information about cars he admired, and he wanted the replacement Ford automobile to measure up to these vehicles. The first rough sketches and blueprints of the new car were quickly done, and the prototype was built and tested over the next few months. On August 10, 1927, Edsel Ford announced that the first Model A car had been tested and was ready to enter production.

The Model A was an advanced car for its day. It had four cylinders and used a sliding transmission instead of the planetary transmission used in the Model T. Features of the car included a standard gearshift and foot throttle, battery ignition instead of a crank to start the car, four-wheel brakes, automatic windshield wipers, brake lights, speedometer, gas and oil gauges, a water pump to cool the engine, hydraulic shock absorbers, and safety glass, the first automobile with this feature. All of the disadvantages of the Model T had been eliminated in the new design. The Model A was well styled, and its inside was comfortable and roomy. Edsel's experience with the design of the Lincoln car and his accurate evaluation of other manufacturers' cars resulted in a beautiful automobile. The Model A was available in four colors and seventeen body styles. Station wagon versions were produced after 1929, and in 1932, a V6 was introduced.

The Model A, although a much more advanced car than the Model T, was announced at Model T prices and at decidedly lower prices than the Chevrolet. Some industry historians consider the Model A the best car, dollar for dollar, ever made in the United States.

The results of the Model A's announcement were unbelievable. It was introduced on December 2, 1927, and more than 10 million people saw the Model A during the first thirty-six hours the car was shown. Ford display rooms and automobile shows nationwide were jammed, and the company received orders for 400,000 cars with cash deposits in the first two weeks. The company soon announced Ford's first finance company, Universal Credit, to help customers buy the new cars. Henry Ford had disliked installment selling but had been convinced by Edsel and others that it was necessary.

The new car required different tools, complete adjustment of assembly methods, and retraining of all workers. Thirty-four assembly plants in the United States and Canada, twelve overseas factories, and the shops of major independent suppliers all had to be retooled. Almost all the 5,580 Model A parts were new. Beginning in the summer of 1927, thousands of toolmakers and other skilled employees were recalled to prepare for production. For the next two years, production volume was built. By December 1927, daily production reached 100 automobiles. Week by week, production climbed, and by midyear 1928, production of the Model A reached 4,000 cars per day. Orders for 800,000 automobiles had been received by the spring of 1928.

The Ford Motor Company had had a close call. In the first half of 1927, Chevrolet had sold 700,000 cars, more than its entire production for 1926. In 1928, Chevrolet sold 1 million cars to Ford's 800,000. That year, Ford lost $70 million, whereas General Motors made a very substantial profit. But by 1929, the Ford automobile was back in first place, shipping 1.85 million cars, 34 percent of the industry's production, while Chevrolet sold about 1.4 million cars. In 1930, Ford outsold Chevrolet two to one. Despite the depression, 4.5 million Model A cars were sold in its first four years. A V8 Model A was developed in 1932, and in 1935, more than 1 million of these were sold. Furthermore, in 1933, Henry Ford started annual model changes.

The Ford Motor Company had recaptured its position of producing the number-one car in the industry. After spending more than $250 million on the new model for design and tooling, the company had turned the profit corner.

The Marketing, Styling, and Financial Phase: General Motors

The other major figure of the early automobile industry, William (Billy) Crapo Durant, was born in Boston on December 8, 1861. His father was an investment banker who abandoned the family soon after Billy's birth. When Billy Durant was nine, his family moved to Flint, Michigan, where his grandfather, a former Michigan governor, lived and was a leading citizen.

A natural salesman and promoter, Billy Durant started the Durant-Dort Carriage Company to make carriages in 1885. By the end of the century, the company had fourteen branch plants, hundreds of sales agencies, annual sales of more than 150,000 vehicles, and was the largest manufacturer of carriages in the country.

In November 1904, Durant bought the bankrupt Buick Motor Company and within four years was selling more cars than anyone, including Ford. He expanded production from 28 Buicks built in 1904 to 2,300 in 1906, and in 1908, the company built 8,487 cars. On September 16, 1908, the same year that Henry Ford developed the Model T, Billy Durant founded General Motors. Durant planned on building a company by acquiring the biggest automobile manufacturers and suppliers. He quickly bought Dow, a wheel company, Weston Mott, which made axles, and then Elmore, Ewing, Oldsmobile, Cadillac, Weston, Garland, Marquette, Rainier, Oakland (which became Pontiac), Carter, Randolph, Sheridan, and Welch, as well as majority stake in Fisher Body. Between 1908 and 1910, Durant brought about twenty-five companies into General Motors. Eleven were automobile companies, two were electric lamp companies, and the remainder were auto parts and accessory manufacturers. Durant's goals were to provide a variety of cars at different prices, diversification, and to increase integration by manufacturing parts and accessories used in cars. He acquired most companies for stock. The exception was Cadillac, which cost $4.5 million in cash. Durant offered to buy Ford Motor Company for $8 million, but Henry Ford would not sell.

Durant believed that expanding sales and profits would provide the capital required for acquisitions and rapid growth. However, he was forced out in 1910 when he had to go to bankers to meet a temporary cash shortage. The bankers took over the business, appointing Charles Nash as president. Walter Chrysler, manager of the American Locomotive Works, was then brought in to replace Nash as president of Buick. From 1910 to 1915, the bankers ran General Motors.

Meanwhile, Durant funded Mason Motors and Little Motors in 1911. He then backed Louis Chevrolet, a race-car driver, in experiments with the design of a light car and named a new company after him. The first Chevrolet was a 1912 six-cylinder with lots of power. The car and company were both successes. In 1915, Chevrolet introduced the 490, complete with electric lighting and an electric starter. Chevrolet built 13,292 cars in 1915, and 62,898 in 1916, putting the company in sixth place in the auto industry. In 1919, the company went into second place with 123,272 cars.

Durant began to buy up General Motors stock to regain control, as did Pierre DuPont, who had much cash to invest from his family's World War I munitions business. When Chevrolet was well established, Durant formed a holding company and offered to trade five shares of Chevrolet for one share of General Motors. There were so many takers that the offer was soon closed. The Chevrolet Motor Company, Durant, and DuPont now owned a majority of General Motors shares. Nash resigned as president on June 1, 1916, and Durant again became the president of General Motors, backed by the DuPonts, who assumed a significant equity position. By the end of 1918, the DuPont

Company owned 26.8 percent of General Motors. By 1921, the company owned 36 percent of the common stock of General Motors.

Durant soon developed General Motors Acceptance Corporation to assist customers with financing. Up until then, car purchases were on a cash-only basis. Durant bought new parts suppliers, including Fisher Body, Delco, and Hyatt Roller Bearing. Hyatt's president, Alfred P. Sloan, soon became a corporate vice president of General Motors. By 1920, General Motors had a line of seven automobiles as well as supporting companies, including Champion (AC) Spark Plug, Delco, Hyatt Roller Bearing, Harrison Radiator, and Dayton-Wright Airplanes. Nevertheless, Ford controlled 61 percent of the American auto market and General Motors had 12 percent. Moreover, Ford held 70 percent of the low-cost market.

Durant was an entrepreneur, a builder of a company and an industry. A born salesman, he relied on intuition and imagination rather than facts and analysis. With one-man rule, he lost relationships with his key associates. Charles Nash left to start his own company. The Lelands left Cadillac to form Lincoln Motors. Walter Chrysler left because he believed Durant was too disorganized and mercurial, a man who ignored facts and relied on his own judgment.

By 1920, motor vehicles were the nation's largest industry. They influenced the growth of the glass, rubber, and steel industries and had a strong relationship with road building and oil production. Durant assumed that the auto industry would always grow. But in the fall of 1920, there was a recession that affected the auto industry, and Durant was unprepared. General Motors came close to bankruptcy. The company's stock price dropped, and DuPont and the bankers asked for Durant's resignation, which he gave on November 20, 1920. Meanwhile, Pierre DuPont was sent in to protect the family's investment, and he appointed Alfred P. Sloan as vice president of operations. In 1921, all General Motors product lines, except Buick and Cadillac, were losing money. In 1923, Sloan became president of General Motors as DuPont became chairman.

After leaving General Motors, Billy Durant started Durant Motors in January 1921 with financing of $7 million. He brought out several models of automobiles and also bought the Willys Corporation. But the market had changed, and he couldn't attract top talent because he was difficult to work for. The company failed, and Durant filed for personal bankruptcy in 1936. Later, he went into the supermarket business in New Jersey and opened a chain of bowling alleys in the Midwest. William Durant died in New York City on March 18, 1947. He once said: "Money? What is Money? It is only loaned to a man; he comes into the world with nothing and leaves with nothing."[4] It is a suitable epitaph for him—and for many other entrepreneurs.

If Henry Ford was the dominant figure in the automotive industry in the first quarter of the twentieth century, Alfred P. Sloan Jr. was the dominant figure in the next. Whereas Henry Ford was the ultimate engineer and tinkerer, and Billy Durant the ultimate salesman and one-man show, Sloan was the man of organization, business planning, and financial measurement and control.

Born on May 23, 1875, in New Haven, Connecticut, Alfred P. Sloan Jr. was the son of a well-to-do businessman. In 1885, his father moved his business to New York City. After attending public school and the Polytechnic Institute in Brooklyn, Sloan received a bachelor's degree in electrical engineering from MIT in 1895, graduating in three years.

That year, Sloan joined Hyatt Roller Bearing, a company with twenty-five employees and $25,000 in annual sales. When the firm got into trouble, Sloan's father and a partner helped the business survive and then expand. Sloan became general manager and revived the company by manufacturing steel roller bearings for a variety of customers. He then began to get orders from new companies in the automobile industry, particularly the Ford Motor Company, Buick, Cadillac, Reo, and Willys. Hyatt became an industry leader in the manufacture of bearings and a profitable company. By 1916, Hyatt was a growing company with 4,000 employees. That same year, the company was sold to Billy Durant for $13.5 million, half in General Motors stock and half in cash. Durant made Sloan president of United Motors, a group of parts and accessory manufacturers owned by General Motors. Two years later, the company merged with General Motors and Sloan became a General Motors vice president and a member of the Executive Committee. In 1920, Sloan was appointed chief operating officer of General Motors and president and chief executive officer in 1923. He held this position and that of chairman for thirty-three years and built General Motors into the world's largest corporation.

Sloan proved to be an outstanding administrator and began a program of innovations not only in automobiles but also in business management. Whereas Ford had one boss, Henry Ford, General Motors was organized with dozens of product divisions. To manage the company's various divisions, Sloan organized the modern management system using centralized control for decentralized operations. Each operating division was headed by its own chief executive officer and was complete in every necessary function, including sales, production, and engineering. A central or general corporate office established overall policy, coordinated the divisions' works, allocated capital, and evaluated financial results. Sloan originated the idea of systematic management, defined responsibilities, and organized communications and decision making.

Sloan developed a new marketing strategy: "A car for every purse and purpose." In 1921, there was no established policy for the car lines as a whole, but Sloan quickly changed that. There would be a General Motors car in each price range, and there would be no competition between divisions in the market steps. There were now nine divisions, each with their own dealers and price range:

Cadillac, LaSalle, Buick, Marquette, Oldsmobile, Viking, Oakland, Pontiac, and Chevrolet. General Motors introduced the annual model change in 1927, with an emphasis on styling, multiple car colors, and planned obsolescence, encouraging the customer to trade up. Automobiles were no longer purchased based only on price. Customers now considered power and performance, styling, comfort, reliability, dealer organization, and financing.

Sloan expanded the General Motors Acceptance Corporation to finance customer installment purchases and to help dealers fund corporate expansion. Since the automobile industry did not grow significantly after 1924 (and would not until the years after World War II), one company's growth was at the expense of another. The key now was to get owners to upgrade their automobiles—not to get someone to buy a first car, but to get someone who already had a car to buy a new one. Sloan established the annual model changes with different designs in the automobile industry, increasing sales tremendously. He knew that, to survive, it was essential for General Motors to become the most efficient competitor and the lowest cost producer.

The 1929 *General Motors Annual Report* gives an indication of Sloan's progress in building a financially successful business. Net sales, which had been $96.2 million in 1917, reached $1,054.4 million in 1929, and net income, which had been $14.2 million in 1917, reached $248.2 million. The company had sixty-three subsidiaries in the automobile business and had 137 styles and body types in its ten models, ranging in price from $495 to $9,700 at the factory.

The automobile industry, according to this report, had produced 5,622,000 motorcars and trucks in 1929. General Motors dealers had sold 1,860,643, or one-third of them. There was no mention of an engineering or technical advance in the forty-page annual report.

General Motors developed its business worldwide as an exporter and as a manufacturer. By 1929, the company had opened operations in Argentina, Australia, Belgium, Brazil, Denmark, Egypt, France, Germany, India, Indonesia, Japan, London, New Zealand, Poland, South Africa, Spain, and Sweden, and it had just opened its first operation in Shanghai, China. In 1938, sales outside the United States exceeded 350,000 vehicles.

Alfred Sloan's memoir, *My Years with General Motors*, was published in 1963 when Sloan was eighty-seven years old. It is one of the better books on management ever written. Its chapters deal with organization, product policy, styling, the annual model change, finance, and marketing. There is little about technology or engineering, subjects that were Henry Ford's main concerns. And there is no mention of Japanese carmakers or government regulations, subjects that would concern Sloan's successors in the last third of the twentieth century. According to Sloan,

During the early years of the automobile industry, the immediate goal of the engineers and inventors was simply reliability—to get a car to go somewhere and come back under its own power. ... Great as have been the engineering advances since 1920, we have today basically the same kind of machine that was created in the first twenty years of the industry.[5]

So in the auto industry, as in many others, innovation is highest at the beginning. In the auto industry, market saturation coincided with a slowdown in technological innovation, with technical changes becoming small and incremental.

Alfred Sloan was detached from personalities and focused on facts. But he was not just a man of numbers, he was also people oriented and developed intense loyalty and respect among his subordinates. When he retired from General Motors, Sloan devoted his life to philanthropy and endowed the Alfred P. Sloan Foundation, which especially supported the Sloan-Kettering Institute for Cancer Research in New York and the School of Management at MIT, his alma mater. He died in 1966 at the age of ninety.

Through his innovations and management, Sloan made General Motors into the world's largest corporation. When he took control of the company it had a 12 percent share of the market. When he retired in 1956, General Motors had a 52 percent share of the U.S. market. And overseas, the company owned Vauxhall in England, Opel in Germany, and Holden in Australia. In 1962, General Motors manufacturing plants produced about 10 percent of the passenger cars and trucks made outside the United States and Canada in the free world.

In his book, Sloan credits his major decisions as follows: "New elements: installment selling, used car trade in, the closed body and the annual model. I would add improved roads if I were to take in the environment of the auto."[6] But perhaps Sloan's most important contribution was in organization and developing the science of management. He established the organizational structure under which General Motors still operates today, with independent operating divisions and a central operation that establishes overall policy, coordinates the divisions' strategies, and measures results.

Lest it be thought that there was no technical innovation at General Motors, one only has to mention the career of Charles F. Kettering. Born in 1876, Kettering began his career as an engineer for National Cash Register. He left to start Detroit Engineering Laboratories Company (Delco) and in 1911 developed an electric automobile self-starter. Henry Leland bought the starter for his 1911 Cadillac, making the car attractive to a larger group of customers. In 1916, Delco was sold to the United Motors Company, which was managed by Sloan. The General Motors Research Corporation was established in 1920, and "Boss Ket" became head engineer. In 1923, ethyl gasoline, developed by General Motors, went on sale. A new company, Ethyl Gasoline Corporation, was formed by General Motors and Standard Oil of New Jersey, with DuPont in charge of manufacturing the gasoline additives. Moreover, the 1928 Cadillac had a synchronized gearshift, making it easy to change gears. Other innovations from the Research Laboratories included quick-drying paint, the first engine-driven generator, balloon tires and front-end suspension, and more efficient and powerful engines. After World War II, Kettering designed new and better V8 engines with higher compression. When Alfred Sloan retired, General Motors had more than 19,000 engineers and scientists working on technical issues. But the annual model change had modified the role of engineering from the early days. The importance of design and styling changed the technical staff's function, and styling, engineering, and production went to a three-year cycle.

Automobile engineering in the industry's first fifty years went through three phases: getting a car to work, getting an efficient car to go and come back, and paying attention to what a car looked like. In the third phase, the engineer focused on getting the parts into the selected auto body. In that sense, the change is similar to the changes between the first textile machines described in chapter 2 and the fashion industry today.

The 1920s to the 1950s:
The Industry, Chrysler, and Other Manufacturers

By the 1920s, the automobile industry had made most of its engineering decisions. The last steam car was built in 1929, the last electric car, the Berwick Electric, in 1927. The Dobie, the last of the steam cars, could go from zero to seventy-five miles per hour in ten seconds and travel 1,500 miles on one twenty-four-gallon tank of water. But the gasoline engine had won. Most cars had closed bodies, and steering by wheel, brakes, rubber tires, and automatic starters all had become standard features. The next decades involved design, market position, and finance.

During the 1910s and 1920s, some manufacturers began to leave the industry as the market became more competitive and Ford began to dominate with its low-price car. Still, there were many choices of car, with other major manufacturers including Austin, Briscoe, Buick, Cadillac, Chalmers, DeSoto, Essex, Franklin, Hudson, Hupmobile, Kissel, Harmon, Maxwell, Oldsmobile, Oakland, Packard, Paige, Peerless, Pierce Arrow, Reo, Studebaker, White, Willys-Overland, and Wolverine. As some car companies left the field, new ones were established. Among the newcomers were Billy Durant's Chevrolet, the Lincoln, the Oakland, the Star, the Nash, the Winton, the Chrysler, and the Dodge. In 1915, Ford was the largest manufacture, John N. Willys was second, and General Motors third, manufacturing the Buick, Chevrolet, Oldsmobile, Oakland, and Cadillac. Relative industry positions changed frequently during the next two decades.

Henry M. Leland had built Cadillac into a significant competitor. When General Motors purchased Cadillac in 1909, Henry Leland and his son, Wilfred, had stayed on to run the division for General Motors. In 1917, after a disagreement with Billy Durant, the Lelands left and founded the Lincoln Motor Company. Lincoln built the Liberty engine for the war effort and, in 1920, introduced the Lincoln automobile. The car did not sell well, partially because of its poor styling and partially because of a poor automobile market after the war. When the company got in trouble, it could not arrange refinancing and went into receivership. Henry Leland asked Henry Ford to purchase the company, and Ford bought it for $8 million in February 1921. Henry Ford later assumed an additional $4 million of the company's debt, although he had no legal responsibility to do so. He asked the Lelands to run the company for him but, within a few months, disagreements arose between the Ford and Lincoln people. By June 1922, the Lelands had left the company and Lincoln was integrated into the Ford organization. Edsel Ford took over Lincoln's management and had designers redesign the automobile until it was done to his satisfaction. Edsel said to a friend: "Father makes the most popular car in the world, I would like to make the best car in the world." The company soon began manufacturing the Lincoln car in larger quantities.

The third major automobile manufacturer, and the last to be formed, was Chrysler. Walter Percy Chrysler was born in 1875 and worked for American Locomotive, where he rose to manage one of its plants. He purchased his first car, a Locomobile, took it apart, figured out how it worked, then put it back together and learned how to drive. Chrysler entered the auto industry with Buick in 1911 when Charles Nash offered him a job as plant manager at a reduced salary. When Nash left to start his own firm in 1917, Chrysler became president of Buick. He left General Motors because of disagreements with Durant but was called back by the bankers and returned to work heading Willys and later Maxwell Chalmers in 1925, both of which he saved from bankruptcy.

Walter Chrysler bought Maxwell with a loan and renamed it Chrysler in 1924. The Maxwell was made from 1904 to 1925; Chrysler built them until his new car was ready. In January 1925, he introduced the new car, the first Chrysler automobile. Chrysler then acquired Dodge Brothers in 1928, eight years after the brothers had died, and also added DeSoto in 1928 and Plymouth the same year. The company became one of the big three with its low-price Chrysler and Plymouth and the midlevel DeSoto and Dodge. Starting in the 1930s, Chrysler developed a reputation for solid engineering.

By 1928, the auto industry had been reduced to three major competitors: General Motors, with assets of $1,098 million; Ford, with assets of $742 million; and Chrysler Dodge, with assets of $236 million. No one else even came close. In 1916, automobile production passed 1 million units. By 1929, 5.3 million units were produced, with General Motors, Ford, and Chrysler accounting for 80 percent of new car sales. Nevertheless, it is worth noting the status of several other independent car manufacturers.

The Hudson was made from 1909 until 1957. The company introduced the four-cylinder Essex with closed-coach bodywork in 1925, and in 1932, the Teraplane, a lower cost version. Hudsons were excellent hill climbers, set records at Pikes Peak, and set speed and endurance records at Daytona Beach. The Nash Brothers made cars from 1917 until 1957. In 1918, the Nash 681 was an excellent car. In 1929, Nash offered an eight-cylinder engine. The Packard was made from 1899 until 1958. An American luxury car, in 1915 Packard introduced a large 12-cylinder car with great acceleration. In 1919, the car set a speed record of 150 miles per hour on Ormond Beach in Daytona, and also raced at Indianapolis. Packard built six- and eight-cylinder cars during the depression, both sport sedans and convertibles. By 1947, Packard had built its millionth car. The Pierce Arrow, another American luxury car, was manufactured from 1901 until 1938, when it ceased production, another casualty of the depression. Studebaker started making cars in 1912 and through the 1960s was a significant producer. The company had good market position at the beginning of the depression with the Studebaker Rockne. In 1933, the company went into receivership but emerged the following year. During World War II, Studebaker built B-17 Flying Fortresses. Stutz manufactured cars from 1912 until 1934. Barney Oldfield, who also raced for Henry Ford, raced a Stutz at Indianapolis in 1914 and came in sixth. In 1922, Charles Schwab of Bethlehem Steel fame gained control of Stutz. Willys-Overland started making cars in 1908 and made them until 1951. The company had major strike and lockout in 1919 but recovered and built excellent cars for years. During World War II, Willys designed and built the famous Jeep.

Four million cars and trucks were sold in 1923, and the number remained fairly level throughout the 1920s. But then came the depression, and it hit the automobile industry hard. During the 1930s, sales declined, with most cars sold at the low end. General Motors had sales of $1.5 billion in 1929, but they fell to $983 million in 1930. In 1929, 5,337,087 passenger cars were made; by 1932, production had declined to 1,103,557, the worst figures since the war year of 1918.

The depression was a very difficult time for the Ford Motor Company, its automobile dealers, and its suppliers. In the years between 1929 and 1933, Ford's revenue, number of cars produced, and number of employees declined by approximately 70 percent. By 1935, Ford had dropped to third place behind General Motors, which had 43.1 percent of the American market and Chrysler, which had 25 percent. Ford only had 22.4 percent of the market. Not until 1941 were the auto manufacturers able to sell as many cars as they had in 1929, and Ford remained in third place through 1941. In the ten years between 1921 and 1930, the Ford Motor Company had built 15.5 million cars. In the ten years between 1931 and 1940, the company built 9.4 million cars, a 40 percent decline in production.

In order to increase sales during the depression, car prices were reduced and manufacturers put pressure on the automobile dealers. Manufacturers cut dealer commissions and drove a lot of them out of business. The Ford Motor Company always had the lowest commissions in the industry since Henry Ford believed the Model T and the Model A sold themselves. The company put even more pressure on the dealers to either improve their performance or quit. Many left the industry.

Overland and Studebaker went into receivership. During the first years of the depression, many of the remaining independent automobile competitors disappeared, including Chandler, De Vaux, Elcar, Gardner, Jordan, Kissel, L&E, Locomobile, Harmon, Martin, Moon, Stearns-Knight, Viking, and Windsor. Still, as many were leaving the industry, others manufacturers were entering.

August and Fred Duesenberg made their name with racing cars, first under the Mason name in 1912 and then under their own name starting in 1920. Five hundred Duesenbergs were built that first year. In 1921, their cars finished second, fifth, and ninth at Indianapolis. Then Errett Cord bought the company in 1926 but let the brothers continue to design cars. They designed cars until Fred died in 1932, and the name was retired in 1937. The "Dusey" was the height of luxury cars and was very popular in Hollywood. Errett Lobban Cord was a Los Angeles businessman who took over the almost bankrupt Auburn Automobile Company and built high-quality cars in Indianapolis. He was responsible for some of the best automobiles and most stylish cars ever made— the 1932 Auburn Bobtail Speedster, the 1930 Duesenberg Model J, and the Cord L-29, 810, and 812 Phaeton. All of these cars became classics. The Cord was made from 1929 until 1932 and then again from 1935 until 1937.

In 1939, Powell Crosley, a radio and refrigerator maker, introduced the Crosley, a small car. It held four passengers and cost $350. It was sold through department and appliance stores that sold his refrigerators.

Throughout the 1930s there were advances made in technology. The 1931 Buick had drum brakes and independent front-end suspension, and the 1935 model introduced hydraulic brakes. The 1934 Reo had an automatic transmission. Four years later, Oldsmobile and Buick introduced automatic transmissions, and before World War II, the use of automatic transmissions became common. Electric starters, disc wheels, enclosed bodies, and stronger engines made automobiles of interest to a broader portion of the population. The first car radios was introduced in 1927 under the Philco name. During the 1930s, car radios became widespread even though radio stations could not be heard in much of the country. In 1924, there was one car for every seven people, and by 1936, the Department of Commerce reported that 54 percent of all U.S. families owned a car.

The depression was also a very difficult time for workers in the industry. Almost half of the automobile workers in Detroit were laid off in 1930 and 1931. More lost their jobs in 1932 and 1933, and others went to part-time work. The Ford Motor Company had almost 174,000 workers in 1929; in 1933, there were fewer than 49,000 workers on the payroll. Not surprisingly, the 1930s were a time of increased union activity in the industry.

In May 1935, the United Auto Workers (UAW) had their founding convention in Detroit. In 1936, the UAW prepared for the total unionization of the auto industry. Before 1933, General Motors had no experience with labor unions. A sit-down strike at a General Motors plant in Flint, Michigan, ended in February 1937, when General Motors recognized the United Auto Workers as the union representing the workers. A month later, in March 1937, Chrysler workers won a sit-down strike for union recognition. The conflict now moved on to Ford.

Labor conditions had deteriorated at Ford, as wages had fallen behind General Motors and Chrysler. Hiring and firing practices were arbitrary and often unfair. There was a lack of seniority and uncertainty of tenure. Workers could be discharged at any time for any reason. Edsel Ford wanted to solve the problems with the workers, but Henry Ford told him to stay out of the matter. Ford promoted Harry Bennett, a tough administrator, to deal strongly with the unions. Edsel Ford wanted to work with the union, but Henry and Bennett wanted to obstruct the Wagner Act, which guaranteed workers the right to unionize, and fight the union. Bennett's men tore union buttons off workers, and union organizers suffered physical abuse. Henry Ford took any criticism of Bennett's policies as criticism of his own management. Edsel Ford, a firm and quiet leader, could not get along with Bennett, and became sick at heart. He felt his father's judgment was deteriorating with age.

On May 26, 1937, Ford thugs beat UAW organizing officials, including Walter Reuther and Richard Frankensteen who became leaders of the union, and Ford worker volunteers as they distributed leaflets outside the Ford River Rouge plant. The National Labor Relations Board filed complaints against Ford, supported by news reporters' graphic testimony. Ford was accused of unfair labor practices in nine plants, including the beatings of workers and union organizers by strong-arm squads. Both the National Labor Relations Board and the U.S. Circuit Court judged the Ford Motor Company guilty. Sporadic violence continued. After a two-year battle for recognition by the union, in a supervised election in 1941 more than 97 percent of the Ford workers asked for union representation. Henry Ford stated that this was the worst disappointment in his life. After much soul-searching and pressure from his wife, Henry Ford finally signed with the union on June 19, 1941.

Because of World War II, all automobile companies stopped production of civilian cars on February 9, 1942. The auto producers then turned their attention to the production of war materials: 2 million army trucks; 86,000 tanks; 300,000 planes; 456,000 aircraft engines, mines, and torpedoes; and 17 million weapons, including machine guns and carbines, bombs; and steel helmets. The manufacturing capability of the U.S. auto industry helped win the war.

After World War II, Detroit returned to auto production and found a tremendous pent-up demand for cars and enjoyed a large increase in production. The automobile industry needs a good economy for the market to expand, and it found that economy in the years between 1946 to the 1950s. In 1949, U.S. auto production was at 6,253,651, breaking the record set in 1929. In 1951, the 100 millionth passenger car was built in the United States. In 1955, the American auto industry produced 9,204,049 cars and trucks. By 1965, automobile production reached 9,335,277 units, and truck/bus production reached 1,802,603 units, both records.

For a time, new manufacturers entered the business. Crosley sold 65,000 cars between 1946 and 1950. Henry Kaiser entered the auto business, bringing the same manufacturing know-how that had worked for him in building ships during the war. Sears, Roebuck, which had left the automobile business in 1910, made another attempt in 1951. And Preston Tucker raised a significant amount of money but produced fewer than sixty automobiles.

After World War II, automatic transmissions, radios, and softer and quieter rides were introduced as standard features. These new automobiles were reliable, well-produced cars, with comfort and convenience. In 1960, some new compact cars were introduced but did not find a market. The postwar period was defined by larger automobiles, turbines, and tail fins, and the muscle cars of the 1965 to 1973 era. Cars became heavier, more powerful, and more expensive. These cars were also more luxurious—air conditioning, rearview mirrors, longer, wider, lower bodies, better suspension, and headlights that dimmed automatically.

The independent manufacturers had controlled 20 percent of the market in 1929, 13 percent in 1952, and barely 4 percent in 1954. That year, there were three mergers. Nash-Kelvinator and Hudson Motors merged to become American Motors, Studebaker Corporation and Packard Car Company become Studebaker-Packard Corporation, and Willys merged with Kaiser. The 1961 Studebaker Lark was a good car, with disc brakes, sunroof, reclining seats, and tachometer. It was not enough. In 1963, Studebaker announced plans to cease all production of motor vehicles in the United States and moved across the border because of Canadian government financial incentives. The company quit auto production in March 1966 after 64 years as a producer and 114 years of vehicle production.

The German, French, and Japanese automobile plants had been destroyed in World War II, and for the years following the war, America dominated worldwide. In 1970, the U.S. auto industry had an annual production of 6.5 million cars—more than double that of its closest rival, Japan.

But trouble was brewing for the American auto industry. There were too many cars—two for every five people in the United States. In addition, Japan had become a significant competitor. From fewer than fifty cars a year in the mid-1950s, Japan's exports soon reached half a million cars per year. Furthermore, Americans were producing gas-guzzlers with lots of defects.

It is worth mentioning America's love affair with the automobile. For the first third of the twentieth century, an American had wide variety of choices in automobiles, manufacturers, and features. For many, car was their most precious possession and helped define them as individuals. And that love affair with the early cars continues today. There are more than 150 automobile museums in the United States. There are countless automobile clubs, by make, model, manufacturer, steam, electric, or hot rod. And automobile racing continues to be one of the most popular sporting events.

Improved Roads and Their Impact on America

The United States was a vast land with scattered communities and a need for better transportation. A steamship could run on the smooth surface of lakes and rivers. The railroads ran on smooth tracks. The auto also had to run on a smooth surface, or at least one smoother than open land. This section could be called the "road and tire review," for without good roads and good tires, the automobile would have made little impact on America.

America had bad roads. It took three months for a wagon to get across the country during the California gold rush of 1848. Roads were wagon or horse tracks, and some went across private land where one had to open and close gates as one traveled.

The development of roads was necessary for the development of the auto industry. At the beginning of the twentieth century, streets existed in the cities and towns, but there were only dirt roads and trails in the country leading from cities to the surrounding farms, with nothing beyond. Moreover, these country roads were impassible in the winter and spring months, when snow and rain turned them into pools of mud. Attempting to drive on these bad roads resulted in broken transmissions, flat tires, and boiled-over engines. Most roads were dirt. Where there was pavement, it might be asphalt, brick, concrete, granite, macadam, tar, or wood blocks.

The first concrete road outside a city was built in 1908 when Woodward Avenue in Detroit was extended a mile past the city limits. But for most of the country, roads consisted of wagon ruts across the prairie. Until better roads could be built, automobiles were only for the city. And who would pay for these new roads—the town, the county, or the state?

Table 5.2 shows figures from the *Engineering News* of 1912, indicating just how bad the road situation was. Almost all finished roads were in the cities.

Table 5.2. February 1, 1912, U.S. public road mileage [7]

	1904	1912
Total mileage	2,151,379	2,199,645
Mileage of improved roads		
Stone	36,818	59,237
Gravel	109,925	102,870
Other materials	6,807	28,372
Total	153,530	190,479
% all roads improved	7.14%	8.66%

Source: Engineering News (New York: Hill Publishing Company, 1912)

In 1912, Carl Fisher of Indianapolis proposed a coast-to-coast highway system, complete with route markers and directional signs. The fledging automobile manufacturers and their customers immediately backed the idea. Since there were no national highway funds and few local sources of finance, Fisher proposed an organization, later known as the Lincoln Highway Association, to fund the national road. The choice of a route was announced in Colorado Springs on August 1913, and work began shortly thereafter. The Lincoln Highway started in New York City and then went across New Jersey, Pennsylvania, Ohio, Indiana, Illinois, Iowa, Nebraska, Wyoming, Colorado, Utah, and then on to San Francisco. Over the next few years, the 3,300-mile Lincoln Highway was completed and then improved so that by the depression it was paved most of its length. The army sent heavy vehicles over the road in 1919 to show its potential for military use, and the federal government took over responsibility for finishing and maintaining the road in 1923.

The Federal Highway Act of 1921 authorized the Bureau of Public Roads to provide funding and help state highway departments to construct paved two-lane interstate highways. But, in general, roads did not keep up with automobile developments. Whereas city streets and surrounding suburbs had adequate roadways, travel over longer distances was another story. From the 1920s through the 1950s, a coast-to-coast automobile trip involved numerous two- and three-lane highways, frequent stops, and top speeds of forty miles per hour, often through the centers of cities and towns. Most goods were shipped by railroad, and most long-distance travel was by train. Clearly, improved roadways would allow improved auto performance.

General John J. Pershing had originally proposed the concept of an interstate highway system in 1918 on military and national defense grounds. The German autobahn, built by Hitler in the 1930s as a military highway, set the standard for roads and was the first major national highway.

Until the end of World War II, there were only minor improvements in American roads, although there were some good individual roads built, including the Pennsylvania Turnpike, the parkways north of New York City, and U.S. Routes 1, 40, 50, and 66. The national routes often went through small towns, benefiting local businesses but slowing the traveler down considerably. The Pennsylvania Turnpike sped the driver across Pennsylvania but then dumped the car onto narrow highways on both the turnpike's western and eastern sides.

President Dwight Eisenhower signed into law the Federal Highway Act of 1956, which sponsored an Interstate Highway System and authorized the construction of a 42,000-mile national highway system. Justified partially on national security grounds and partially as a public works project, this highway system unified the country, changed the face of America, and was one of the most important events of the twentieth century. Road building would lead to growth in many areas, from construction and leisure activities to the cement and steel industries. The federal government agreed to pay 90 percent of the cost using revenue from gas taxes, with state and towns paying the remaining 10 percent. The system committed federal and state highway spending of $33.5 billion, financed by a penny-a-gallon tax on gasoline over the next dozen years. These taxes were increased over time, and the Federal Highway Trust Fund had annual receipts of $3 to $5 billion in the 1960s and now runs at about $35 billion per year. This amount is raised by taxes on gasoline, gasohol, diesel, and special taxes on trucks and trailers and the sale of tires.

Good roads and good automobiles were of no value without better and safer tires. Early tires might last only a few hundred miles. John Dunlap, a Scottish veterinarian, invented and patented in 1888 the pneumatic tire, which combined a rubber tube with air pressure. The Hartford Rubber Works of Connecticut began to make pneumatic tires for cars in 1895. Harvey Firestone started making tires for the carriage and bicycle trade in the 1890s, then switched to automobile tires. An order from Henry Ford to Firestone in 1906 led to the widespread use of the pneumatic tire. Charles Goodyear provided tire innovation and vulcanizing that gave rubber durability and elasticity. The Michelin brothers developed France's first pneumatic tire and introduced tire tread patterns, low-pressure balloon tires, and steel-cord tires. In 1915, the average tire's life span was nine months. By 1930, it had risen to two years. In 1922, balloon tires were introduced. In 1949, Goodrich offered puncture-sealing tubeless tires, and in 1961, most tire manufacturers introduced two-ply tires for compact cars. That year, Goodyear announced a new synthetic rubber that promised to double the life of tires. Tire improvements continued throughout the remainder of the century.

Without improved roads and tires, the automobile would have remained a toy for the rich city dweller. Speeds in the city would have been in the twenty-mile-per-hour range and travel in the country would have been for the adventurous. Instead, it is possible to travel almost anywhere in the United States at very reasonable speeds. There are currently more than 200 million cars, trucks, and motorcycles registered in the United States, and trucks now carry more than 900 million ton-miles of freight annually.

But the story is more than numbers. Better automobiles, tires, and roads have changed the way Americans live. At the beginning of the twentieth century, cities and towns were the center of commerce, those on railroad hubs were the trading centers, and much of the country's population lived in rural isolation, going to a town infrequently and then only to buy or sell goods.

Building a national road system made the suburbs possible, allowing more people to own homes. It changed how products were delivered to market, giving farmers and rural dwellers more independence. Shopping malls, service stations, restaurants, motels, and many other aspects of modern life would not be possible without the automobile and the roads to service them. Employment and types of jobs, vacations, outdoor recreation, education for Americans who do not live in the cities, family economics, and even an understanding of the country have been strongly influenced by the national road system and the development of the automobile.

The Government and a Changing Relationship to the Industry

In the days of Andrew Carnegie, the government was the steel industry's best friend, protecting it with import duties and quotas. Then, for a variety of reasons—some the fault of steel industry leaders—the government, starting with President Harry Truman's administration, passed a series of laws to control the industry (see chapter 3).

In the 1960s and 1970s, the same thing happened to the auto industry. New laws and regulations affected auto safety, gasoline efficiency, and auto emissions. There were many reasons for the federal government to get more involved in automobile design—some of these factors were real, and some reflected the classic Washington view that any problem could be solved with a new law that wouldn't cost anybody anything.

Ralph Nader, a young Washington lawyer, wrote a magazine article in 1959 about auto safety. In 1965, he published *Unsafe at Any Speed*, accusing General Motors of hiding safety defects in its cars. General Motors handled the accusations badly and lost support in Congress. Nader's chief target was the General Motors Corvair and later the Pinto. It was the beginning of the modern consumer movement.

In 1966, Washington passed the National Traffic and Motor Vehicle Safety Act and established the National Traffic Safety Administration and the Department of Transportation. The regulations required safer vehicles and set national safety standards. In the 1970s, the federal government passed a further series of safety laws that greatly affected the auto industry. These included a requirement for seat belts, head restraints, energy-absorbing steering columns and dashboards, and then later airbags and child restraint seats. Many of these were mandatory changes in car design and some were voluntary. The changes reduced injuries, and the fatality rates per 100 million miles of travel has been cut in half since the 1970s.

There are major costs for increasing automobile safety, with a high penalty for manufacturers that economize in this area. Large jury awards, lawsuits including punitive damages for victims and their families, and more lawsuits with lawyers working for a portion of the settlement began in the 1960s and have increased yearly. The Ford Explorer/Firestone tire problem of the 1990s is but one of the latest examples.

The second area for legislation involved auto mileage. Up through the 1950s, the United States produced most of the oil it needed. However, from 1960 to 1980, increased petroleum consumption was not met with increased domestic production. The large automobiles made in Detroit in the 1950s were energy inefficient. As long as gasoline was plentiful and cheap, most Americans paid no attention. But the increasing dependence on foreign oil and then the oil embargo that resulted from the Israeli–Arab conflict and gasoline price increases by OPEC countries in the 1970s brought about new legislation.

In 1976, the Energy Conservation and Oil Policy Act was passed, mandating average fuel economy for all automobile manufacturers. Penalties were set for manufacturers that didn't meet specified averages, and these gas-guzzler taxes could range as high as $7,700 per vehicle. Gasoline mileage figures were specified by legislation, resulting for a time in smaller and lower-weight cars, with less steel and more plastic. In 1974, the federal government passed a law mandating a fifty-five-mile-per-hour speed limit to save fuel and reduce injuries. This law made sense inside the Washington Beltway and in eastern cities where it was difficult, if not impossible because of traffic, to ever get above fifty-five miles per hour, but was deeply resented in the West, with its vast distances and lower traffic patterns. The law was eventually repealed in 1995.

The auto industry set goals for improving fuel efficiency. In 1970, the average American car was getting fourteen miles per gallon, and the goal was 27.5 by 1985, a figure that was finally reached in 1995. For a time, cars were downsized and their performance reduced. However, fuel-efficient cars may be smaller cars, and small cars are not as safe as large ones in an accident. This may partially explain consumers' increased purchases of recreational vehicles and small trucks. Everyone wants to be the survivor if there is an accident. Yet larger vehicles use more fuel.

The third area of legislation dealt with the emission of pollutants. The Clean Air Acts, passed in 1965 and 1970, forced manufacturers to reduce the air pollutants from auto exhaust. In Los Angeles, Houston, and many other American cities, there was terrible smog that resulted from a combination of sunshine and auto emissions. For health reasons, it became necessary to reduce the amounts of hydrocarbons, carbon monoxide, and oxides of nitrogen from car exhaust. Catalytic converters changed exhaust into water, nitrogen, and carbon dioxide, but carbon dioxide increased the greenhouse effect and may increase global warming.

In 1974, California passed its own emission laws mandating catalytic converters and setting higher emission standards than the national laws. The manufacturers had to meet these standards if they wanted to sell automobiles in California. Again, car prices increased.

Much of American auto design responsibility went from Detroit to Washington, which set the standards for fuel consumption, exhaust emissions, and safety. The Department of Transportation, established on October 15, 1966, in 2001 had 63,400 employees and an annual budget of $43 billion, a six-fold increase since 1970. For comparison, Ford Motor Company had worldwide revenues of $162 billion and 350,000 employees to design, manufacture, sell, and support all automobile production. So as auto employment decreases, the number of people regulating the industry increases, a situation similar to the Department of Agriculture and the number of farmers.

All of these laws and regulations were perhaps necessary, but they were hardly free. The cost of an entry-level Ford car has increased from less than $1,800 in the early 1960s to more than $15,000 today, with many cars priced above $30,000. Over the last half century, the consumer has seen the auto world change from an individual's freedom to choose among many manufacturers and automobiles to government domination and fewer manufacturers.

California's most recent law required that, in order to help clean the air, 2 percent of all new vehicles sold there could not emit any harmful particles. The only feasible way to meet this goal was with electric vehicles, and the industry feared that the first vehicles could cost $6,000 to $10,000 more than gasoline cars. Furthermore, research and design for alternative ways of powering automobiles stopped in the 1920s, when the gasoline engine won out over steam and electricity.

The industry needs lighter cars that are environmentally friendly and have improved fuel economy and lower pollutants. This change could have both positive and negative effects on the industry and automobile costs. But will the consumers buy such vehicles, no matter what the bureaucrats decide?

The Challenge from Japan and Germany

As mentioned previously, the German, French, and Japanese automobile factories were destroyed during World War II. In the 1950s, the American auto industry took advantage of this fact and built worldwide manufacturing dominance in automobiles just as it had done in steel.

The British gave the Germans back their remaining automobile factories in 1949, and the Germans then staked everything on one car, the Volkswagen Beetle, which soon dominated the mass markets of the world. The Volkswagen entered the U.S. market in 1955 and, although laughed at by the powers in Detroit, it developed a loyal customer base. At that time, many American cars were getting about twelve miles per gallon, but the Beetle got more than thirty miles per gallon. By 1972, worldwide Beetle sales passed the 15 million units of Ford's Model T. The Germans then introduced the first mass-produced front-wheel-drive car, the Volkswagen Rabbit.

Other early imports were European luxury and sports cars: Mercedes, Rolls Royce, Bentley, Bugatti, Fiat, Renault, MG, Porsche, Triumph, BMW, and Jaguar. Detroit seemed willing to give away that small part of the automobile market.

Whereas the Germans had a century-long tradition of innovative automobile design and manufacturing capability, the Japanese did not. But it was the Japanese that changed the rules and became the world's automotive leader. The Japanese traditionally made very small cars specifically for their narrow roads. However, a combination of excellent leadership and marketing conditions ultimately moved the Japanese auto manufacturers into first place worldwide.

One of the first Japanese automobiles was the Mitsubishi Model A, made in 1917, based on the Italian Fiat. The Toyoda (now Toyota) Model AA was developed in 1936 based on Chevrolet engineering. Many other early Japanese automobiles were developed as a result of foreign business relationships. World War II not only severely damaged the Japanese automobile industry, it also restricted the availability of steel, rubber, and other materials the industry needed, cutting production to one-half of its prewar level. There were cutbacks in production and employment at the end of the 1940s, resulting in strikes at all the major producers. Only orders from the U.S. government at the beginning of the Korean War in 1950 kept some companies in business. In the 1960s, older Japanese companies expanded their automobile business and new companies were established. These included Daihatsu, Honda, Isuzu, Mazda, Mitsubishi, Nissan/Datsun, Suzuki, and Toyota. Several individuals were instrumental in promoting this growth.

Born in 1906, Soichiro Honda was a mechanic who started a piston-ring production factory in 1934. He produced motorcycles in 1948, and over the next half century, his firm would become one of the world's leading manufacturers of motorcycles and automobiles. Motorcycles require far less steel than automobiles and were suitable for the roads of Japan. By 1960, Japanese motorcycle production was almost 1.5 million units annually, making Japan the world's leading manufacturer and exporter. Honda opened a Los Angeles office in 1959 to introduce his motorcycles and imported his first car, the N600 two-door sedan, to America in 1969. Cars improved in quality and performance and by 1980, Honda started making cars in the United States. By 1995, Honda had sold more than 10 million cars in America and was exporting cars from its factories there to other countries, including Japan. By 1997, cumulative Honda automobile production reached 30 million units.

Sekichi Toyoda invented a power loom in 1902 and built a textile company. His son, Kiichiro, set up a car manufacturing business in 1936 and traveled to Detroit to spend a year studying Ford's manufacturing operations. He established new equipment and processes that could deal with smaller quantities, creating what became known as "just in time" manufacturing. His cousin, Eiji Toyoda, helped develop innovative manufacturing procedures that dealt with the material shortages after the war and set standards for quality and design. Toyoda developed the Crown in 1955, the first Japanese-made passenger car for family use, and the Corolla in 1966. The name of the company was changed to Toyota. Others who influenced the company included Taiichi Ohno, who developed innovative production systems after reading Henry Ford's autobiography, and the American W. Edwards Deming, who helped establish quality control systems in Japan, including total quality management and continuing improvements with worker participation.

In September 1955, Japan became a member of the General Agreement on Tariffs and Trade (GATT). Looking forward to trade liberalization, Japanese capital became available to build automobile exports, and large-scale investments were made in plants and equipment. The June 1967 GATT reduced world import tariffs by half. Japan's auto industry was ready to start growing.

In 1964, Japanese exports to the United States totaled about 12,600 cars. That year, Japanese worldwide auto exports passed 100,000 cars, putting the country in sixth place as a manufacturer. By 1975, Japan became the world's largest exporter of passenger cars, with 1,800,000 automobiles. Early successes were the Subaru 360 in 1958, the Datsun Bluebird in 1960, the Mitsubishi Colt in 1971, and the Honda Civic in 1973. Most Japanese companies had ties with overseas companies—Nissan with Austin, Isuzu with Hillman, Nissan with Renault, and Mitsubishi with Willys. In 1971, Isuzu had new agreements with General Motors, Mitsubishi with Chrysler, and later Ford with Mazda.

Japan's domestic market also grew. After the war, most cars in Japan were cabs or used by business or government. In 1962, one in seven cars in Japan was for personal use; by 1970, the figure was one in two. By 1970, Japan had become the world's second-largest economy after the United States.

As Japan's automobile use increased, air pollution became a major problem. The Ministry of Transportation in July 1966 passed the first government automobile controls. In December 1972, new pollution regulations were introduced in Japan to control exhaust emissions. Further rules were passed in 1978, forcing Japanese automobile manufacturers to invest heavily in exhaust research and in decreasing the carbon monoxide, hydrocarbons, and nitrogen oxide emissions by more than 90 percent.

The Japanese studied the American market very carefully. They found ways to improve on American designs. Shorter development time allowed the industry to change with the market, and changeable machine tools allowed manufacturers to modify their production lines quickly. New Japanese cars featured styling, durability, higher quality, and more standard features. The Toyota Corolla was introduced in 1966 and the Datsun 510 in 1968. The Datsun 240Z, a value-oriented sports car, was introduced the following year. The Japanese introduced affordable, economical small cars with lots of basic features; affordable sports cars; and performance sedans. Compact pickup trucks were soon to follow.

The 1973 oil crisis had a major impact on Japan, as the country depended on the Middle East for 80 percent of its oil. The price of gasoline tripled in Japan, and the Japanese gross national product decreased. Japanese engineers began looking at energy efficiency and conservation as well as ways to increase miles per gallon. They redesigned their cars, changed materials, and developed better fuel-injection systems.

When the oil shock of the 1970s occurred in the United States, it was the Japanese who had the right cars because they had faced the issue earlier. The Americans were producing large cars with poor gas mileage. The Japanese had much more energy efficient automobiles, and when oil prices doubled in the 1979 to 1982 period, the Japanese cars looked even better. Their cars were higher quality than the lowest cost Fords and Chevrolets. American manufacturers had to respond with higher quality cars or risk losing their markets.

In 1904, the United States had surpassed France as the worldwide leader in the production of automobiles. In 1911, U.S. automobile imports totaled $2,446,248, mainly from France, and exports totaled $21,636,661, mainly to British territories, including Canada. The Americans had a positive balance of trade in automobiles for more than the next half-century.

However, in 1980, Japan took first place in automobile manufacturing, a position it has held ever since. Japanese production rose from 4 million cars in 1972 to 7 million in 1980. In 1990, the American automobile manufacturers had 60 percent of the U.S. domestic market, the Japanese 27.5 percent, and the Europeans 12.5 percent.[8] Japan developed a substantial balance of trade surplus, which exceeded $55 billion in 1997. The trade imbalance was so high that for a while, the Japanese established voluntary export quotas to limit exports. Then they began to build plants in the United States—Honda in Ohio, Nissan in Tennessee, and Toyota, Mitsubishi, Mazda, and Suzuki in both the United States and Canada.

For years, Detroit had focused on luxury vehicles, and Americans had been complacent until the Arab oil embargo. And for decades, because of their position, U.S. automakers had not invested enough in machine tools and research and development, which were less important to them than short-term profits. The Japanese design, automation, and manufacturing techniques put them way ahead of the United States.

U.S. domestic production, which was 9.3 million in 1965, dropped to a little more than 7.4 million in 1980, the year that Japan took over first place in the auto industry. By 1987, 31.1 percent of all cars sold in the United States were imports. The American automakers temporarily or permanently were closing plants and laying off workers. There was a lack of confidence by Americans in American-built cars. Japanese autos, it was felt, offered much higher quality and a better value.

It was the late 1980s before Detroit responded fully with higher quality, better fuel performance, and more muscular power trains. General Motors started the Saturn division to directly compete with the Japanese. In fact, the Japanese emphasis on quality had forced all of the American competition to make more reliable automobiles. But by 2001, Honda alone had produced cumulatively 7 million units in the United States.

The American Automobile in a World Market

American-made cars peaked at 11.1 million in 1965 and then dropped to 8 million cars in 1980, with imports rising from 17.7 percent to 27.9 percent. American auto companies invested in Japanese auto companies at the same time they were investing in plants in North America. In 1998, Daimler-Benz acquired Chrysler for $56 billion. Ford invested in Mazda, General Motors in Isuzu, and DaimlerChrysler owned 37 percent of Mitsubishi. Currently, the growth in the market is not predominantly in the United States and Europe; it is in China, India, the Pacific Rim, and South America.

There is now a worldwide automobile market. Parts are built in factories around the world and can be shipped somewhere else to be assembled. The auto industry is very large. Of the world's top 200 companies, General Motors comes in at number 3, Ford at 6, DaimlerChrysler at 7, Toyota at 8, Volkswagen at 19, Hitachi at 28, Honda at 29, Nissan at 39, Fiat at 47, Peugeot at 49, Renault at 98, Mitsubishi at 106, Toyota at 190, Hyundai at 193, Volvo at 217, Mazda at 218, Suzuki at 253, Kia Motors at 348, and Isuzu at 400. Together these nineteen companies had 2001 revenues in excess of $1 trillion.[9]

If one were to add in revenues from the companies dependent on automobiles for the majority of their sales—petroleum companies such as Exxon Mobil, Royal Dutch, and British Petroleum; tire manufacturers such as Bridgeton,

Goodyear, and Michelin; and steel manufacturers such as U.S. Steel, Nippon, and Kobe Steel—the total would exceed $2 trillion. The auto industry is the biggest customer for the oil industry, steel industry, and a significant customer for electronics, glass, aluminum, plastics, and many other parts.

In the last half century, worldwide auto production has grown significantly.[10] In 1950, there were about 8 million new automobiles manufactured and a worldwide fleet (number of cars on the road) of 53 million vehicles. In 1960, 12.8 million were made, and the fleet had grown to 98 million. In 1970, 22.5 million new autos were made, and the fleet had reached 193 million cars. By 1980, 36.5 million cars were made, and the fleet had grown to 320 million cars. By 1990, 36.3 million new cars joined a fleet of 445 million. And at the turn of the twenty-first century, 40 million new cars were made, and the fleet had reached 532 million vehicles. Eighty-one percent of these automobiles were in developed countries. Worldwide, however, there were three times as many bicycles being produced as automobiles.

According to one industry estimate, the market is saturated, with the automobile industry having a capacity of 80 million vehicles and demand worldwide of 55 to 60 million.[11] Industry growth currently is estimated at 1 to 2 percent per year.

In 2001, American automakers sold 17.2 million vehicles in the United States, with an estimated market size of $378.4 billion, a decline of 1.3 percent from 2000. Although the auto companies are profitable, profits are because of sales of SUVs, small trucks, and luxury models with the higher markups—not from the simple low-cost cars of Henry Ford. And now, the Japanese are beginning to compete at the higher end.

The cost of new cars has been going up. As a result, people are keeping their automobiles longer. The average age of automobiles in use was less than six years in 1970 and ten years at the turn of the century. Because of cost, the idea of annual model change has disappeared. Purchasers throughout the country have a choice of Japanese quality cars or European luxury automobiles in addition to the traditional U.S. suppliers.

Purchase through the Internet and national chains of dealers are changing the way customers buy cars. Consumers can now thoroughly research and purchase automobiles electronically. And there is less need for large amounts of inventory on the dealers' lots to attract customers. Because there are fewer differences in features and performance between manufacturers and fewer service issues with the better designed automobiles, the consumer may purchase based on price alone. Or perhaps, just as in the early days, there will once again be more choices for the consumer.

At the beginning of the twentieth century, there were questions about how to power an automobile. Gasoline won because of its ready availability and very low cost. And for most of the twentieth century, little research was done on alternative fuels. But as the twenty-first century begins, the matter is being reevaluated. The higher cost of petroleum and the country's dependence on Middle East oil has caused many scientists and engineers to review the earlier engineering and build on that. America's transportation system is currently 95 percent reliant on petroleum as fuel (the exception being electric-driven trains and trolleys). Sixty-seven percent of the petroleum consumed in the United States is used for transportation. However, there are now in use 100,000 electric and hybrid vehicles made by Toyota and Honda.

Today, engineers are looking at electric cars, hydrogen fuel cells, solar power, and energy-efficient and environment-friendly cars. But the issue is one of both technology and of supply. For example, drivers would need to find a source of hydrogen—a problem faced a century earlier with gasoline. Methanol is a fuel produced from coal or natural gas that produces little in the way of hydrocarbons and so does not result in hydrocarbons (smog), but it is high in carbon dioxide output.

Although design and finance are important issues, engineering is also important. Perhaps somewhere there is a Ransom Eli Olds, a pair of Stanley Brothers, an Alexander Winton, a Henry Ford, or a Soichiro Honda who will provide the leadership and innovation for the next generation of automobiles. Perhaps in the automobile industry as in other industries, bigger is not necessarily better, nor are traditional ways better than making continued investments in research and development.

CHAPTER 6

Henry Ford (1863–1947)
Getting the Costs Down

Old men are always advising young men to save money. That is bad advice. Don't save every nickel. Invest in yourself. I never saved a dollar until I was forty years old.
>—Henry Ford

The older I grow the more I distrust the familiar doctrine that age brings wisdom.
>—H. L. Mencken

Henry Ford was the best-known businessman of the early twentieth century. His automobile changed the way America lived and his company, for a long time, dominated the industry. The man, the automobile, and the company were identical in the minds of many people. His career shows the influence that one man can have on a company, an industry, and a nation.

Biography

Henry Ford's grandfather, John Ford, his wife, Thomasina, their seven children, his mother, Rebecca Jennings Ford, and his brother, Robert Ford, and family, left their home near the town of Clonakilty, County Cork, Ireland, in 1847 to escape the famine and follow their brother to Michigan. Thomasina died in Canada on the trip, and the remainder of the family proceeded across Lake Ontario to Buffalo and then by lake steamer to Detroit. William Ford, the oldest son, was twenty-one years old when he arrived in Michigan, and he assumed major responsibilities in helping his father support the family. He cleared land for the family farm, working at times on the farm and at times for the railroad. As the farm prospered, William's father sold him some land and he acquired other land elsewhere.

On April 25, 1861, William Ford married Mary Litogot, the daughter of William Litogot, who had been killed in an accident. After her father died, Mary was adopted at age three by Patrick O'Hern and his wife, who were childless, and they raised her. At the time of her marriage, Mary was twenty-two years old and the groom was thirty-five. The young couple moved in with the O'Herns, who shared their home with their growing family.

Henry Ford was born July 30, 1863, on a farm near Dearborn, Michigan, the second child of William and Mary Ford. Their first child had died in infancy. Later, the couple would have five more children: John, Margaret, Jane, William, and Robert.

Henry Ford grew up on the farm close to nature. At the age of seven, he started school, walking the three miles each day, where he learned to spell, do arithmetic, and write, studying *McGuffey's Readers*. The books of William Holmes McGuffey, with their old-fashioned moral values, had a significant influence on Henry as they did on generations of children. From his earliest days, however, Henry was more interested in mechanical things than in farming, more interested in working with his hands than in reading. At the age of twelve he received a watch. Years later he said: "By the time I was fifteen I could do almost anything in watch repair, although my tools were of the crudest."[1]

Very early on, Henry Ford's father recognized his son's mechanical ability and allowed him to use and repair items on the farm. Henry loved to examine machinery and learn how it worked. Once, he expressed his views on this subject:

> *It is not possible to learn from books how everything is made—and a real mechanic ought to know how nearly everything is made. Machines are to a mechanic what books are to a writer. He gets ideas from them and if he has any brains he will apply those ideas.*[2]

In March 1876, Mary Litogot Ford gave birth to her eighth child. The baby died, and, twelve days later, so did thirty-seven-year-old Mary, leaving her husband with six children, ages three to thirteen. The family was devastated but tried to pull together. Henry Ford years later said that the house without his mother was like a watch without a mainspring.

Henry Ford by his teenage years had grown tired of farm work and wanted to go to town. On December 1, 1879, at the age of sixteen, he left the family farm and went to Detroit, less than a half day's walk from the farm. He stayed at first with his aunt, Rebecca Ford Flaherty, and worked at the Michigan Car Company. He left this job after six days and joined James Flower and Brothers Machine Shop. He soon got an additional part-time job repairing watches. After nine months, Henry Ford changed jobs again and went to work at the Detroit Drydock Company, the largest shipbuilding firm in Detroit, where he was trained as a machinist.

Henry left Detroit in 1882 when his father wanted him to return to the farm and help take care of the family. During the next nine years, he worked on the farm, found part-time work repairing machines, and set up Westinghouse Engine Company traction engines, which were used for threshing and sawing wood. He also had a variety of other jobs since his younger brothers were now able to assist their father on the farm.

Early in 1885, at a dance in Greenfield Township, Henry Ford met Clara Jane Bryant, a friend of his sister Margaret. Clara was the oldest of ten children. Her mother, Martha Bench, had come to Michigan in the 1860s from Warwickshire, England, with her parents. Her father, Melvin Bryant, had been born in Greenfield, Michigan, in 1836, and was the son of John Bryant, who had been born in Canada but had come to Michigan in the 1830s. Henry Ford was married to Clara on April 11, 1888, her birthday. They were to be married for four days short of fifty-nine years.

William Ford had given Henry forty acres of timberland. On this site, Henry cleared the timber and built a small house. Here, he operated a sawmill and was busy in his shop, repairing machinery and doing mechanical work for the farmers in the area. He continued to read about steam- and gasoline-driven vehicles. In September 1891, Henry and Clara moved back to Detroit. Ford wanted to learn about electrical power and became an engineer for the Edison Illuminating Company. He started at a substation where he shoveled coal, watched gauges, and repaired steam engines when they failed. By 1895, he had become chief engineer responsible for maintaining electric-light service twenty-four hours per day to residences in the city and providing lighting power for street lamps. In Detroit, the Fords' only child, Edsel, was born on November 9, 1893. He was named after Ford's boyhood friend, Edsel Ruddiman.

As soon as he got to Detroit, Henry Ford started to design a gasoline engine. He did all the work in his spare time after his job at Edison. Almost every spare dollar went to buy tools and materials. By the end of 1893, he had an experimental engine working, although it lacked an ignition system and a method of mixing the fuel. For the next three years, Ford worked on the remainder of his automobile in a shed at his home. He eventually had to knock out a wall to get the vehicle out. Ford tested his first car, which he called a "quadricycle," on June 4, 1896, driving it on the streets of Detroit. The car had a twin-cylinder engine with a belt drive and achieved speeds of twenty miles per hour. The body was wooden, and it was a light car, weighing only 500 pounds. Henry started replacing wood with metal in order to strengthen the vehicle and then began work on a second car.

In August 1896, Henry Ford was sent to New York for a convention of the Edison Companies. Although the companies were promoting the use of electric power for automobiles, Ford discussed his work with Thomas Edison, who encouraged him to continue work on the gasoline engine. In 1899, Ford's second car was finished, weighing in at 875 pounds. With this second car, Henry Ford had his first press interview, and a story with pictures appeared in the *Detroit Journal.*

Henry Ford resigned from the Edison Company to devote his full time to designing automobiles. One week later, on August 5, 1899, Ford's first company, the Detroit Automobile Company, was incorporated with $15,000 capital. Ford was a small stockholder and superintendent of the new company. In early January 1900, the first vehicle was ready, a gasoline-powered delivery wagon that weighed 1,200 pounds and sold for $1,000. The company had planned to make two automobiles per day but was only able to build about twenty cars total, due to part shortages and Henry Ford's continual redesign of the vehicle. The company folded in November 1900, when the original stockholders declined to make additional investments in the company.

Four people bought the old company, and it was reorganized on November 30, 1901, as the Henry Ford Company. The company now had $30,500 in capital. Clarence A. Black was named president, and Henry Ford was named chief engineer and had a one-sixth interest in the firm. The investors wanted to build a company that produced a high-quality, high-price automobile. At this time, Henry Ford was preoccupied with automobile racing and started working on a race car. Henry M. Leland, a very successful engineer and machine shop director, was brought in to help finish the design of a commercial car and start production. Leland had been trained at the Colt factory, at Brown and Sharpe, and now had his own business, Leland and Faulconer, a leading company in precision engineering and manufacturing.

Ford, a "cut and try" engineer, had little in common with the precise Leland, and they clashed frequently. Ford was also dissatisfied with his stock ownership and wanted more control. Henry Ford resigned from his company on March 10, 1902, less than four months after it had been formed, and was given the drawings for the race car, $900 in cash, and a promise that the company wouldn't use his name anymore. The company was renamed Cadillac and, under Leland's direction, achieved more than a little success.

At this point, Henry Ford wanted to spend all of his time automobile racing. His goal was to develop a race car and drive a mile in thirty seconds. He designed a racing car and in October 1901, entered his first race at Grosse Pointe, Michigan, and won. He then improved the design of his car. On October 25, 1902, Barney Oldfield, a bicycle racer who had just learned to drive, drove a Ford car to victory at Grosse Point in a five-mile race in five minutes, twenty-eight seconds—an American record. This was the start of Oldfield's auto racing career and enhanced Ford's reputation as a designer. Henry Ford continued racing and in January 1904 drove the 999, a modified Model B without clutch or gears, on the ice on Lake Saint Clair near Detroit, and set a record of thirty-six seconds for one mile. Three days later, he repeated the race with official timers on hand and covered a mile in 39.4 seconds, then an official American record. The publicity helped the company attract more customers.

In 1903, Henry Ford was forty years old. His first two attempts at starting companies had ended in personal failure. There were several hundred companies already making automobiles, with several hundred more about to enter the marketplace. The previous year, more than 4,000 cars had been manufactured, with three-fourths of them steam and electric. New England, the Mid-Atlantic states, and the Midwest all were locations of automobile manufacturing.

Obviously, there was already an automobile for every taste. There was little reason to believe that Henry Ford or, for that matter, Detroit, would play much of a role in the future of the automobile industry.

On August 20, 1902, Henry Ford formed a partnership with Alexander Malcomson, a Detroit coal merchant, to develop a low-cost automobile. Based on his success in racing, Henry Ford began to attract attention, and on June 16, 1903, the Ford Motor Company was incorporated with Ford and Malcomson the largest stockholders, each owning 25.5 percent of the stock. The company was capitalized with $100,000 of stock, but only $28,000 of new cash was invested in the business. There were twelve stockholders in the company, including the Dodge Brothers and Malcomson's clerk, James Couzens, who received stock and became a key employee for the new firm. Couzens was responsible for the business side and Henry Ford for engineering and production. John S. Gray, president of the German American Bank, was made president of the Ford Motor Company.

Henry Ford designed the Model A, a two-cylinder car with an under-floor-mounted engine and a control-chain drive. The car could achieve speeds up to thirty miles per hour. The Model A was priced at $850, $100 more than the Cadillac, but cheap enough to put Ford on the low end in the contest between the big expensive cars and the small inexpensive models. The Ford Motor Company stressed low cost, reliability, and safety. Cash was very tight for the first weeks, but then the company began to receive deposits and orders from customers. In its first four months, the company was profitable; in November, it paid a 10 percent dividend; and in its first nine and a half months, it had earnings of nearly $100,000. In its first year, the company shipped more than 1,700 automobiles.

The new Ford Company was one of more than 300 automobile companies nationwide, and, within the state of Michigan, it was one of twenty-four. Yet Ford's company pushed immediately and rapidly to the front, and, within ten years, it dominated the industry. From 1914 to 1925, Ford manufactured more than 40 percent of the cars in the United States (for several years it produced more than half the industry's output) and, at times, earned more than the rest of the automobile industry combined.

The company prospered, paying dividends and returning to the stockholders within the first year almost the entire $100,000 of capitalization. Additional earnings were used to expand the business, so the company did not need to borrow money or sell more stock. Couzens started to make arrangements with a number of dealers in order to build sales. Henry Ford, the chief mechanic and designer, worked in the factory, provided leadership in engineering and production, and knew most of the employees by name.

In October 1903, George B. Selden, a Rochester, New York, attorney and the Electric Vehicle Company filed a suit against the Ford Motor Company for infringement of Selden's 1895 patent application for a road carriage. Henry Ford, alone among automobile manufacturers, fought the concept of a master patent in the industry. After an eight-year court battle, Ford won the case in 1911, and with it, a considerable amount of publicity as the champion of the small company against the monopoly.

If the company was going to grow by mass production of a low-cost car, then the Ford Motor Company had to make more of its own parts. Ford and Couzens decided they no longer wanted to be dependent on the Dodge Brothers for engines and gears. Hence, on November 22, 1905, they incorporated the Ford Manufacturing Company to make engines, gears, and other automobile parts. Cash investment in this new company was $10,000, with Henry Ford owning 58 percent of the stock. Henry Ford was in complete control.

Ford furnished price lists of spare parts to consumers, a major innovation at the time. The spare parts business produced significant profits for the company over the next decade. By 1924, there were more than 40,000 outlets for the sale of Ford parts. Meanwhile, James Couzens worked on expanding the branch offices and the dealer network. The Ford Motor Company had the largest dealer network in the industry, and by 1913, there were more than 7,000 Ford dealers across the country, with representation in almost every town in America. Ford cars and Ford service were available only from authorized Ford dealers, another industry innovation. To support the dealers, Ford introduced a major advertising program. In order to communicate with the customers, the *Ford Times* was introduced semimonthly in 1908 and then monthly in 1911, running until the publication was suspended in 1917 during the war.

In 1913, worker reforms began. Continued improvements in worker safety measures were made, and a 13 percent wage increase boosted daily wages up to $2.34 per day. At this time, there was no unionization since there was an abundant supply of workers, many of them foreign born, and a strong opposition to unions by Detroit industrialists. The Ford Company enjoyed a rapid growth in profits and had a profit-sharing program as early as December 1905. In December 1913, Henry Ford called a management meeting to talk about increasing wages in order to share the company's prosperity with the workers. Various salary increases were discussed.

In January 1914, the Ford Motor Company shocked the world by announcing that it was reducing the workday to eight hours, converting the factory to three shifts instead of two, and instituting a $5 per day minimum basic wage rate. James Couzens convinced Henry Ford to apply the same rules to office workers and staff. Doubling salaries for fewer working hours brought the company major publicity. Labor turnover at the company decreased significantly. Ford Motor Company suddenly had one of the most advanced labor policies in the world and was looked up to by workers worldwide. In 1919, Ford announced a $6 minimum daily rate and, in 1929, a $7 rate—another well-publicized move.

Henry Ford looked at his employees as possible customers for his cars. By 1926, he wrote: "I have no doubt that the workers in the Ford Industries in the United States own more automobiles than are owned in the whole world outside of this country."[3]

Ford began operations with $28,000 in cash. All other financing had been from retained earnings. By 1917, $54.5 million had been paid in dividends. As the Ford Motor Company grew, Henry Ford wanted to run the organization his way, with no outside interference. He believed that the boss was the boss and shouldn't have to explain anything to anyone. He did not believe in sharing power or responsibility. In the late 1910s, he took complete charge.

James Couzens built the company with Henry Ford. For a long time, he had acted as a counterbalance to Ford. In 1915, he disagreed with Ford about using the *Ford Times* to publish Henry's views on pacifism and America's relationship with the Allies, and on October 12, 1915, Couzens resigned as vice president and treasurer and left the business. (Later, Couzens became a U.S. senator.) Henry Ford now had a free hand to run the company as he saw fit, with no internal restrictions.

The Dodge Brothers manufactured engines for Ford, and he was their only customer. They were worried about their dependence on one customer and decided to build their own car using their Ford stock dividends to finance the business. However, they became worried when Ford kept cutting prices on his cars and spending earnings on expansion instead of dividends. The Dodges wanted Ford to keep dividends high instead of reinvesting in the business. They believed that if he would not continue the high dividends, he should buy their stock for a good price. Ford balked, and the Dodge Brothers sued Ford to force the profits to be distributed. Ford lost the suit, and $19 million of profits were distributed to the stockholders, of which Henry Ford received $12 million.

In 1918, Ford appointed his son, Edsel, as president and announced that he was planning to start a new company. Other shareholders panicked, but Ford revealed that he might be willing to buy them out. Ultimately, he bought out all seven stockholders, including the Dodge Brothers and Couzens, for $105,820,895 and borrowed $60 million from a syndicate of banks. By April 1921, Henry Ford had paid off the debt out of retained earnings. The Ford family was now the sole owner of the business, making the Ford Motor Company the largest family-owned business in the world. Henry owned 55 percent, Clara 3 percent, and Edsel 42 percent of the company.

During this period, Edsel Ford's role increased. Edsel had wanted to go to college, but Henry thought that this was nonsense, since he himself had not gone. At the age of twenty-one, Edsel was appointed secretary of the Ford Motor Company, and at age twenty-five, he became president. Later, on November 1, 1918, Edsel Ford and Eleanor Lowthian Clay were married. Their three sons, Henry II, Benson, and William Clay, would eventually take on major roles in the company's management.

Edsel had great talent as an executive. Where Henry Ford was autocratic and did not like to hear objections to any of his ideas, Edsel listened to the ideas of all around him. He was energetic, a good leader, intelligent, analytical, fair, and had a complete grasp of the company's business. He led the company day to day, focusing on administration, sales, marketing, the international business, and running the Lincoln division. Whereas Henry was concerned with the design and production costs of an automobile, Edsel was concerned with styling and marketing. Whereas Henry was concerned with doing things his way, Edsel was concerned with building an organization. Many managers stayed with the company, waiting for Edsel to take over. The father and the son were a good team, even if Henry did not realize it.

In 1926, Ford reduced the price of his cars to $260, the lowest price in automotive history, to stimulate demand. Competitors were forced to follow suit, although they complained bitterly. Their reaction helped Ford's image, as the price cuts were seen as a noble gesture to fight postwar inflation. As the 1920 recession hit the industry, the Ford Company had major layoffs. Cash was conserved by reducing inventory, selling raw materials and subproducts, and cashing Liberty Bonds. Ford dealers were forced to accept cars and pay immediately based on the terms of their contract. There were offers of aid, including one suggestion—which gained some popularity—that all Ford Model T owners lend the company $100. When a banker came to arrange loans to the company, he was listened to for a while and then shown the door. Henry Ford was upset that the banker wanted to name the treasurer of the company and not the chief engineer, which he believed a much more important position. He immediately made Edsel the treasurer of the company in addition to Edsel's job as president.

> *You will note that financiers propose to cure by lending money and not bettering methods. ... This is the danger of having bankers in a business. They think of a factory as making money, not goods. They want to watch the money, not the efficiency of production. They cannot understand that a business never stands still, it must go forward or back.*[4]

In December, business got better, and by April 1921, the Ford Company was in good shape and had paid off all debts. The millionth car was turned out on December 10, 1915; on May 21, 1921, the company manufactured its 5 millionth car; and on June 24, 1924, Ford produced its 10 millionth vehicle. Henry Ford had started his company with 125 workers in 1903. By 1925, the company had grown to an average employment in excess of 155,000 workers. In addition, a significant number of other people—working for suppliers, dealers, in automobile repair, auto insurance, at service stations, and a variety of other service-related industries—owed their employment to the success of Henry Ford.

Henry Ford applied his engineering and production genius to fields other than automobiles. In 1910, a Ford employee had built an experimental airplane that interested Henry Ford, and in the 1920s, the company became active in aviation. Henry and Edsel Ford had, together with some friends, invested in the Stout Metal Airplane Company, which was organized by William B. Stout. The Fords eventually bought out Stout and his investors, and expanded into the aviation field.

On August 11, 1925, Charles Lindbergh gave Henry Ford his first airplane ride in the *Spirit of St. Louis.* Henry immediately became interested in the design of airplanes and wanted to see what could be done. He was less interested in the financial results than in the technical challenge of this new field. In 1925, the Ford Motor Company established a commercial airline between Detroit and Cleveland. It also won two airmail routes, one between Detroit and Cleveland and one between Detroit and Chicago.

In 1925, a Ford plane entered a 1,900-mile, thirteen-city race and won at an average speed of 100 miles per hour against fifteen other entries. Next, the company built an experimental trimotor, all-metal airplane and in 1926, based on its reputation, sold thirty-six of its trimotors to Pan American, Northwest, and Transcontinental Air Transport, the airline that eventually became TWA. In 1929, the company sold eighty-six planes, making it one of the country's leading aircraft manufacturers. Sales then began to fall during the depression and the company cut back its investment.

The Ford Company could have become one of the major airline manufacturers, but Henry Ford eventually tired of the project. He also interfered too much in the design process and, one by one, the best airplane designers left the company. Yet Ford Motor Company had a number of significant credits in the field, including the introduction of scheduled mail service, Ford's passenger and airfreight lines, the development of the first trimotor built in the United States for commercial purposes, and some of the first engineering studies of large-volume airplane production.

Henry Ford, the Public and Private Man

As the Ford Motor Company grew, Henry Ford began to play more of a role on the national scene. When he was outside his field of expertise, he relied on his intuition, did very little reading and little listening, and frequently delivered poor judgments with absolute conviction. He had strong prejudices and was suspicious of things he did not understand, and these traits often led him into trouble.

In 1915, Henry Ford became active in the peace movement. He wanted President Woodrow Wilson to call a peace conference of neutral nations to work for a peace acceptable to all belligerents. When Ford discussed the appointment of a neutral commission with the president, Wilson was not interested, and Ford immediately decided to take the lead himself. He told the nation that he hoped to negotiate the end of the war by Christmas and immediately chartered a peace ship to head for Europe. Henry Ford approached a number of leading Americans, including Thomas Edison, John Burroughs, Helen Keller, William Jennings Bryan, Jane Addams, William Howard Taft, and more than a hundred other Americans to join him on this crusade for peace. Almost all declined to go, although many expressed support for the project.

On December 2, 1915, Ford's peace ship, the *Oscar II*, departed Hoboken, New Jersey, for Norway. The ship carried a few public figures, some ministers, teachers, socialists, lecturers, and college students. About half the passengers were writers. There was an immediate division between those who wanted to be complete pacifists and those who wanted the United States to be prepared if war came. Ford welcomed all to the peace crusade. When the ship landed in Norway, Henry Ford was sick, and he returned to America after a week. The remainder of the group visited Sweden, Denmark, and Holland and established relations with other pacifists in these countries. By May 1916, a conference had issued an initial report, and for more than a year, negotiations continued between representatives of a number of neutral countries and the belligerents to find a way out of the war. Although his trip was unsuccessful, many people gave Ford credit for trying to achieve peace.

Despite his strong pacifist views, by January 1917 Henry Ford had been convinced of the need to prepare for war. When Congress declared war on April 6, 1917, Henry Ford threw his energy and the resources of his company into the war effort. The Ford Motor Company built ambulances, tanks, armor plate, Eagle Boats, a submarine detector, and did other work for the government.

Henry Ford spent a few years in the political world. In 1914, the Bull Moose progressives in Calhoun County, Michigan, endorsed Henry Ford as a candidate for governor, and several Michigan politicians also supported him as a vice presidential candidate. In 1918, Ford ran as a candidate for U.S. senator from Michigan, entering both the Republican and the Democratic primaries. Although he lost the Republican primary, he won the Democratic. In the runoff election, he lost to the Republican candidate, Truman H. Newberry, by 1 percent of the vote.

Ford had not waged any campaign, yet a switch of 2,200 votes out of almost 430,000 cast would have resulted in Ford's election. His opponent, backed by financial interests opposed to Ford, exceeded the election spending limit. There were also some election irregularities and charges of fraud and conspiracy. Senator Newberry was tried and convicted of conspiracy to violate the Federal Corrupt Practice Act and sentenced to two years in prison. The conviction was later thrown out by the Supreme Court on constitutional grounds. On November 18, 1922, Newberry submitted his resignation to the governor of Michigan. Although Henry Ford had not won the election, neither had his opponent.

Ford's devotion to peace and his agrarian ideals led to a "draft Ford for president" movement, starting in 1922. Henry Ford liked the idea for a while but then backed out and supported Calvin Coolidge. His decision may have been influenced by the fact that his wife, Clara, stated in public that "if Mr. Ford wants to go to Washington he can go but [I will] be on the next boat to England."

In 1917, Henry Ford filed a $1 million suit against the *Chicago Tribune* for an article it had written about him. In May 1919, Henry Ford appeared as a witness at the trial and showed his complete lack of knowledge about American history, literature, and world affairs. Henry Ford became a target of humor, and his reputation suffered badly during the trial. However, the jury found the *Tribune* guilty of libel and awarded Henry Ford six cents. Both sides claimed victory in the case.

Based on his experiences in politics, Henry Ford decided to enter newspaper publishing. In 1918, he purchased the *Dearborn Independent,* a country weekly. He wanted to make certain the country could read his opinions without having them interpreted by the press. The weekly publicized Henry Ford's views on a number of subjects, including pacifism, prohibition, social justice, education, rural life, antimonopoly, the opportunities available for all Americans, and his feelings regarding national and world affairs, and the current presidential administration.

Writing, however, also brought out Ford's darker side, including his anti-Semitism. In May 1920, the *Independent* ran an unsigned article about the Jewish threat. Similar articles were published in subsequent issues. Ford's diatribes against Jews caused Hitler to call Henry Ford a great man and, on his seventy-fifth birthday, Ford received the Grand Cross of the German Eagle. Reactionaries from France to Russia used his remarks against Jews. Ford was sued for libel, and he then apologized to the Jewish community. The *Independent* finally ceased publication at the end of 1927.

Henry Ford loved to travel around the country with a few friends. Ford, John Burroughs, Thomas Edison, Harvey Firestone, and others traveled and camped out together. Comments Ford made about two of his colleagues tell a lot about the man and his views on life: "John Burroughs was never too old to change. He kept growing to the last. The man who is too set to change is dead already. The funeral is a mere detail."[5] And:

Thomas A. Edison is interested in every conceivable subject and he recog-
nizes no limitations. He believes that all things are possible. At the same
time he keeps his feet on the ground. He goes forward step by step. He
regards impossible as a description for that which we have not at the
moment the knowledge to achieve.[6]

Like Andrew Carnegie, Henry Ford did not believe in charity, asking: "Why should there be any necessity for alms giving in a civilized community?"[7]

Despite this philosophy, Ford gave a great deal to charitable institutions, including the Henry Ford Trade School in Dearborn, the George Washington School in Georgia, and the Ford Hospital in Detroit. In September 1923, Ford bought the Wayside Inn and 2,667 acres in Sudbury, Massachusetts. The inn had been made famous by Henry Longfellow in his *Tales of a Wayside Inn.* Ford restored the inn; had a farm, blacksmith shop, gristmill, and sawmill established on the site; and moved an old church, the Martha Mary Chapel, to the area. He even had the main road, Route 20, relocated at his own expense to protect the inn from the automobile he had done so much to popularize. He paid $1.6 million and spent $2.8 million more on the inn over the next twenty years.

Henry Ford wanted to preserve the rural values he had loved in his boyhood, and to help accomplish this, he built Greenfield Village in Dearborn, Michigan, as a living museum. He gathered items from all over the country to show how average Americans had lived since the country was founded and provided a new kind of American history. He established four schools, including the Henry Ford Trade School for young people. He moved Thomas Edison's laboratory from Menlo Park, New Jersey, to Dearborn. On October 21, 1929, the fiftieth anniversary of Edison's invention of the electric light, Ford invited the aged inventor, now eighty-two, and a number of celebrities, including Madame Curie, Albert Einstein, Orville Wright, Jane Addams, Charles Schwab, William Green, Will Rogers, and President Herbert Hoover to the official opening of Greenfield Village. Ford continued to expand the village throughout his lifetime.

From 1917 to 1947, Henry and Clara Ford gave more than $40 million to charitable causes. After Henry Ford's death, far more was donated. The Ford Foundation, originally created in January 1936 to escape high estate taxes, was the great legacy of Clara, Edsel, and Eleanor Ford to America. The Ford Foundation in its first two decades gave more than $2 billion to a variety of organizations and programs and has since given many times that amount.

During the 1930s, the Ford Motor Company lost its leadership position, and the causes of the company's decline were becoming apparent. Henry Ford could not bear to surrender power. As he got older, he became more autocratic, his temper got worse, and he fought change of all sorts. He disliked the rise of marketing in the industry, the New Deal, government regulations, and organized labor.

Edsel Ford continued to provide leadership as president, making decisions on administration, manufacturing, and sales. Modest, capable, and energetic, he remedied all problems he saw in the organization, unless blocked by his father. The father, however, frequently undercut the son. Henry Ford was still the ultimate authority. Henry Ford would not build an organization or establish clearly defined responsibilities and authority. Ambitious people sought power, and Henry Ford played them one against the other. As a result, many talented people left the company.

Henry Ford suffered a stroke in 1938 and a second stroke in 1941. He never recovered from the second stroke. In 1941, when the war started, he still had not turned the company over to his son. As he got older, Henry Ford's worse characteristics sometimes overshadowed his best. He frequently persecuted and humiliated his own son. Henry Ford was seventy-eight years old, but he refused to let go.

On May 26, 1943, at the age of forty-nine, Edsel Ford died after a one-year battle with stomach cancer, undulant fever, and stress. All who knew Edsel loved him and were holding on until he succeeded his father. In many ways, he had contributed as much to the development of the company as had Henry.

After Edsel's death, Henry Ford, at eighty years old and in declining health, was chosen president of the company until a permanent solution could be found. The company was in trouble, and the U.S. government was worried about Ford's productivity in support of the war effort. Henry Ford II was released from the navy and joined the company in 1943, assuming responsibility for sales and advertising. Meanwhile, Henry Ford's health continued to deteriorate.

Eleanor Clay Ford had watched her husband, Edsel, suffer from the problems with his father. She now fought for the rights of her sons. At this point, she and Clara Ford were very influential directors of the company, and on September 21, 1945, the board of directors held a meeting, and Henry Ford II was appointed president, succeeding his grandfather.

With Henry Ford's resignation as president, an era had ended. He had built the company from an idea, and the company had been very successful. The final years had not treated him well. Once he had said: "I don't believe in quitting work. Happiness is on the road, not in reaching the peak. I am on the road and I am happy."

Ford was a very complex man, and his difficult later years would have to be judged alongside the creative decades. He was representative of some of the best and the worst of America in the twentieth century.

On April 7, 1947, at 11:40 P.M., Henry Ford died at age eighty-three in his home in Dearborn of a cerebral hemorrhage. A flood had covered the local power plant, depriving the home of electricity, heat, and telephone. When he died, only his wife and a maid were with him in the darkened home. The only light was from a burning candle.

More than 100,000 people passed through Greenfield Village where Ford's body lay in state. The nation paid homage to him as a great man and as a man of the people. Three years later, on September 27, 1950, Clara Ford at eighty-four years of age followed him in death. On their fiftieth wedding anniversary, when a reporter had asked Ford if he had any good advice to offer, Henry had replied: "Pick a good model and stick with it. I've been sold on one model for half a century." They were a very good team.

On Management

Henry Ford was motivated by traditional American values and the Puritan work ethic. He said:

> *For the day's work is a great thing! It is at the very foundation of the world; it is the foundation of our self respect. And the employer ought constantly to put in a harder day's work than of his men. The employer who is seriously trying to do his duty in the world must be a hard worker.*[8]

Ford shared with Thomas Edison, his idol, the view of persistence and innovation: "If you keep on recording all your failures, you will shortly have a list showing that there is nothing left for you to try—whereas it by no means follows that because one man has failed in a certain method that another man will not succeed."[9]

Ford reflected that, "I determined absolutely that never would I join a company in which finance came before the work or in which bankers or financiers had a part."[10] And:

> *Industry is not money—it is made up of ideas, labor and management and the natural expression of these is not dividends, but utility, quality and availability. Money is not the source of any of these qualities, though these qualities are the frequent source of money.*[11]

Henry Ford valued the hard worker and avoided the expert:

> *None of our men are "experts." We have most unfortunately found it necessary to get rid of a man as soon as he thinks himself an expert—because no man ever considers himself an expert if he really knows his job. A man who knows a job sees so much more to be done than he has done, that he is always pressing forward and never gives up an instant of thought to how good and efficient he is.*[12]

It is not easy to get away from tradition. That is why all our new operations are always directed by men who have no previous knowledge of the subject and therefore have not had a chance to get on really familiar terms with the impossible. We call on technical experts to aid whenever their aid seems necessary, but no operation is ever directed by a technician, for always he knows far too many things that can't be done. Our invariable reply to "It can't be done" is "Go do it."[13]

Perhaps the above quote partially answers the question raised earlier of why established companies do not cope very well with technological innovation. They may rely on too many experts.

Henry Ford shared with many Americans a distrust of lawyers and financial people. His comments on the stock market should be read by all entrepreneurs. "People are led to conclude that business is good if there is a lively gambling upwards in stocks and bad if the gamblers happen to be forcing stock prices down." And:

The stock market as such has nothing to do with business. It has nothing to do with the quality of the article which is manufactured, nothing to do with the output, nothing to do with the marketing, it does not even increase or decrease the amount of capital used in the business. It is just a little show on the side.

Stock speculation is not without value—some really good men lose at it and in consequence are compelled to go to work. The stock market takes too many men's minds off their legitimate business.[14]

He opposed borrowing. Ford said: "I regard a bank principally as a place in which it is safe and convenient to keep money."[15]

We are not against borrowing money and we are not against bankers. We are against trying to make borrowed money take the place of work. We are against the kind of banker who regards a business as a melon to be cut. ... Money is only a tool in a business. It is just a part of the machinery. You might as well borrow 100,000 lathes as $100,000 if the trouble is inside your business. Only heavier doses of brains and thought and wise courage can cure. A business that misuses what it has will continue to misuse what it can get. The point is—cure the misuse.[16]

Lawyers, like bankers, know absolutely nothing about business. They imagine that a business is properly conducted if it keeps within the law or if the law can be altered or interpreted to suit the purpose in hand. They live on rules. ... Business cannot be conducted by law.[17]

It is not good management to take profits out of the workers or the buyers; make management produce the profits. Don't cheapen the product; don't cheapen the wage; don't overcharge the public. Put brains into the method, and more brains, and still more brains—do better than ever before; and by this means all parties to business are served and benefited. And all of this can always be done.[18]

The Legacy of Henry Ford

Who was the real Henry Ford? The young man who taught himself how to design and build an automobile? The forty-year-old man who started Ford Motor Company after two failures and made it into one of the world's great corporations? The sixty-four-year-old man who started again in 1927 after the Model T had to be replaced and designed an even better car, the Model A? Or the old man who, as his physical and mental health deteriorated, turned inward and became even more autocratic? The mechanic, the production genius, the entrepreneur, the businessman, the politician, or the public figure who often showed his lack of education and the depths of his prejudices?

The fact is that Henry Ford, like all leaders—in fact, like all human beings—must be examined through an entire life in a variety of roles. As one of the most influential people of the twentieth century, his positive exploits should be considered as much, if not more so, than his personal failures, for he had such a great influence on the American people.

Henry Ford had a highly original mind and personality. He may have been the supreme individualist of his time. He was full of ideas, both good and bad, but always his own. He read little. He was that rare person, a man who took time to think and experiment. "A man who cannot think is not an educated man, no matter how many college degrees he has. Thinking is the hardest work anyone can do."[19] Yet Ford's mind leaped directly to a conclusion, based on hunches and intuition rather than logical process. He was a man at home in direct action rather than in the world of ideas.

Henry Ford had a vision of where he wanted to go. He knew that the American people needed cars in the millions, and a single reliable model, built in quantity and sold at ever-lower prices, could meet that demand. Ford was determined to continuously expand the plant, production, and sales in defiance of those who wished to stop. He wanted to make as many cars as possible at the lowest prices, whereas others wanted to restrict production and raise prices. He believed that mass production could furnish millions of cheap vehicles, that price reductions meant market expansion, and that high wages meant high buying power. At the time, none of these ideas was widely believed in by the experts. Henry Ford accomplished things because he listened to himself and not to other people. He had a remarkably intuitive mind. He wanted complete and personal control and would not share power or responsibility. He had great faith in common humanity and would take ordinary humans and from them train skilled workers and plant executives. These characteristics were both his strength and his weakness.

"I do not think a man can ever leave his business. He ought to think about it by day and dream about it by night." Ford's intense concentration on engineering, on design, and on the manufacturing process does much to explain why he so far outstripped the competition. His almost infallible grasp of detail and mechanical vision made him very effective and swift of action. While others talked about and studied a problem, Henry Ford moved ahead.

Henry Ford became a symbol of many things to the world. For many rural families, he was the symbol of the end to isolation. For many Americans, he was one of them: an agrarian rebel, a likable person, the man who had no use for bankers and financial people, the common man who offered them better products at lower prices. He also became the symbol of tedium in work, the mass-production era, satirized by Aldous Huxley in *Brave New World* and Charlie Chaplain in his films.

In the Ford legend, the man became confused with the product. Henry Ford believed that he must constantly keep his name before the public for his company to expand. The image was of an ingenious, determined, self-willed mechanic with a rural education, a set of firm agrarian prejudices, a belief in old-fashioned simplicities joined with technological changes, a faith in hard work combined with broad leisure, and a devotion to honesty and moral integrity.

Henry Ford had an uncanny knack for sensing the mood of the times and of the public, and a great dramatic flair for playing the media along with his interests. He had a strong desire for headlines, publicity, and popularity.

When Ford turned to fields in which he lacked skill and experience, his intuition led him astray. He commented on a range of subjects about which he had no understanding. Outside his field, he delivered hasty judgments with absolute finality. Impulsive, intuitive, and arbitrary, he tended in his later life to neglect the field he knew best for those outside his horizon. There was a conflict between Ford the countryman and Ford the industrialist. Ford the artist, the dreamer, the visionary wanted to create the world in his image. He therefore had the conflicts many dreamers and artists have.

Henry Ford never could let go of his company and turn it over to others to run. As his vigor and capabilities waned, as times changed, he refused to let go. Like other autocrats, he could not bear to surrender power. He allowed others to turn his plants into places of injustice and violence against his workers. The worst tragedy, however, was in his relationship with his son, whom he loved but did not understand. Edsel was a man of the finest qualities. He was honest, capable, people oriented, and highly intelligent. But Henry Ford thought he lacked toughness, and that led him to be hard on his own son. He set others against Edsel and broke Edsel's heart.

Despite his personal weaknesses, Henry Ford accomplished a great deal in his life. Many of his ideas remain pertinent, and he has much to say to today's entrepreneurs, managers, leaders, and historians. He wrote three books with Samuel Crowthers, penned many articles, and spoke often during his life. Let the words of Henry Ford indicate some of how the man thought and how he approached life.

In the first chapter of this book, questions were raised about the nature of an entrepreneur and the creation of job opportunities. Henry Ford spoke about the role of the pioneer:

There are always two kinds of people in the world—those who pioneer and those who plod. The plodders always attack the pioneers. They say that the pioneers have gobbled up all the opportunity, when as a plain matter of fact, the plodders would have nowhere to plod had not the pioneers first cleared the way.

Think about your work in the world. Did you make your place or did someone make it for you? Did you start the work you are in or did someone else? Have you ever found or made an opportunity for yourself or are you the beneficiary of opportunity, which others have found or made? [20]

Henry Ford wrote of his distrust of organization, a tendency that helped him for much of his career but hurt him badly as he got older:

That which one has to fight hardest against in bringing together a large number of people to do work is excess organization and consequent red tape. ... To my mind there is no bent of mind more dangerous than that which is sometimes described as "the genius for organization." This usually results in the birth of a great big chart showing, after the fashion of a family tree, how authority ramifies. The tree is heavy with nice round berries, each of which bears the name of a man or an office. Every man has a title and certain duties which are strictly limited by the circumference of his berry. [21]

Titles in business have been greatly overdone and business has suffered. One of the bad features is the division of responsibility according to titles, which goes so far as to amount to a removal of responsibility. And so the Ford factories and enterprises have no organization, no specific duties attached to any position, no line of succession, very few titles and no conferences. We have only the clerical help that is absolutely required; we have no elaborate records of any kind, and consequently no red tape.

Henry Ford and his management philosophy were complete opposites of the style and performance of Alfred P. Sloan and General Motors. Both management styles have succeeded at times with some leaders, and both have failed at other times with other leaders.

Perhaps Henry Ford's most famous quote is about history. "History is bunk." It is therefore interesting to write about Henry Ford in a book of business history. Yet a complete reading of what Ford said provides a lot to think about. And most businesspeople and historians can agree with his ideas about using the past to guide the present.

> *I don't know anything about history, Henry Ford once said to an interviewer, Charles Wheeler, and I wouldn't give a nickel for all the history in the world. The only history that is worth while is the history we make day by day. Those fellows over there in Europe know all about history; they know all about how wars are started; and yet they went and plunged Europe into the biggest war that ever was. And by the same old mistakes too. Besides history is being rewritten every year from a new point of view, so how can anybody claim to know the truth of history.[22]*

> *"History is more or less bunk. It is tradition. We want to live in the present, and the only history that is worth a tinker's dam is the history we make today."*

> *The principle of service are these: an absence of fear of the future and of veneration of the past. One who fears the future, who fears failure, limits his activities. Failure is only the opportunity to begin again. There is no disgrace in honest failure; there is disgrace in fearing to fail. What is past is useful only as it suggest ways and means of progress.*

Henry Ford never feared failure. For more than half a century he tried, and in his trying, he made history. Henry Ford grew up in a world of national isolation and united the country with the automobile. People could now live, work, shop, travel, visit, and ship their goods and products where they wanted. America's views of itself and its values changed. Henry Ford built a world of mass production, which provided the foundation for much of America's economic and military progress in the twentieth century. He raised the salaries of workers to a new level so that the working class became a consuming class, owning automobiles, homes, appliances, and other items.

No matter that Henry Ford got old, and in his aging, lost his vitality, his vision, and his flexibility. No matter that he maintained a singleness of direction and could not abandon the sole purpose of his life. The changes he made in America went on without his leadership. And the country was never the same again.

Henry Ford, more than almost any person of the twentieth century, made history.

CHAPTER 7

Electronics

The Basic Material (1880–2000)

Things are always at their best in their beginning.
        —Blaise Pascal

A high degree of enthusiasm should be encouraged at all levels;
in particular the people in high management positions must not
only be enthusiastic themselves, they must be able to engender
enthusiasm among their associates.
        —David Packard

Wood was the basic building material from the fifteenth through the eighteenth centuries. Iron and steel became the industrial building blocks in the nineteenth and early twentieth centuries. But the building blocks of the twentieth and twenty-first centuries were and continue to be the electron and electronics—first with vacuum tubes, then germanium transistors, and finally silicon, both as transistors and later integrated circuits. During the earlier centuries, mechanical devices were used as gears, valves, switches, and controls for operating machinery. In the late twentieth century, these would largely be replaced by electronic devices.

Electronics made possible many of the advances of the last century: in communications with telephones, radio, and television; in manufacturing and process control; in transportation; in the exploration of space and below the sea; in finance and medicine; and in education and computers.

Of course, as with the other technologies described in this book, electricity and electronics have a history that significantly predates the twentieth century.

Electricity

Early humans looked to the skies and saw lightning. The Greek philosopher Thales discovered around 600 B.C. that amber (elektron) when rubbed could attract other materials, such as feathers. In the eighteenth century, static electricity that could draw sparks was of interest to many observers. It was discovered that when glass was rubbed, it attracted paper and feathers, which then were repelled from the glass after touching it. Static electricity is familiar to all who rub their shoes on a rug on a dry day and then draw sparks when they touch something or someone.

In 1600, William Gilbert published the first scientific study of electricity and magnetism. In 1745, Ewald Jurgens von Kleist and Petrus van Musschenbroeck in Leyden, Netherlands, stored electricity in a glass full of water and discovered the Leyden jar, a storage mechanism to build up a substantial charge of static electricity. The Leyden jar could generate a shock significant enough to cause those who received it to jump. In 1752, Ben Franklin's famous experiment with a kite demonstrated the shared identity between electricity and lightning. Franklin advanced the single-fluid theory of electricity, worked on improving the Leyden jar, originated the plus and minus symbols for electricity, invented the lighting rod, and became famous in both Britain and France as a major scientist. In 1785, Charles Augustin de Coulomb demonstrated that electrical attraction and repulsion followed an inverse square of the distance law. In 1799, Alessandro Volta developed the first electric battery. Volta's battery, or voltaic pile, was a series of copper and zinc discs interleaved with cardboard or cloth soaked in brine. Steady current electricity could now be obtained from a chemical source. In 1800, Volta's work was communicated to the Royal Society in London, and the following year, Volta gave a demonstration of his battery to Napoleon. By the 1880s, batteries were being used to light railway carriages.

Andre Ampere established a mathematical theory of electricity. In 1808, Humphrey Davy demonstrated the earliest electric arc and incandescent lights. In 1820, Hans Christian Oersted discovered that the needle of a magnetic compass could be diverted by electricity and that a current could influence magnetic properties. In 1827, Georg Simon Ohm discovered that there was a resistance to the flow of electricity and wrote his famous law that voltage is equal to current times resistance, or $E = IR$.

In the 1820s, Michael Faraday discovered electromagnetic induction and invented the electric motor, a device for transforming rotary motion into an electric current. Between 1829 and 1844, Joseph Henry, who later became the first director of the Smithsonian Institution, ran a number of experiments on magnetic induction. When electric current was run through coils of wire wrapped around an iron core, the wires influenced magnetic properties. Henry built some of the first transformers, in which signals in one wire would cause current to flow in another wire.

In 1873, James Clerk Maxwell published *Electricity and Magnetism,* in which he stated the mathematical principles of modern electromagnet theory and deduced the nature of light as waves of electromagnetic radiation. In 1886, Elihu Thomson invented arc welding and brought electric welding into general use. In 1887, Heinrich Rudolph Hertz demonstrated the existence of radio waves by using a spark transmitter to send and receive them. And in 1894, Oliver Lodge demonstrated the use of radio waves for communication.

The first widespread application of electricity was in telegraphy. The next major applications were in lighting and powering machinery. In the nineteenth century, homes were lit using candles, whale oil, kerosene, and coal-gas or natural-gas lamps. In 1879, after trying almost 6,000 materials, Thomas Alva Edison demonstrated his practical electric light, which soon replaced gaslights.

Thomas Alva Edison, America's—and the world's—outstanding inventor, was born on February 11, 1847, in Milan, Ohio, and moved to Gratiot, Michigan, when he was seven. He was partially deaf and was taught at home by his mother, who was a schoolteacher. He remembered everything he read, and he was a very fast reader. Edison worked on the family farm and then as a newsboy on a train in Michigan, where he not only sold newspapers, he printed them—on the train. In 1863, Edison went to work as a telegraph operator, traveling around the country. He was extremely fast and accurate as a telegrapher and ended up in Boston, where he got his first patent in 1869. Edison worked for Western Union for one year and then left to devote the rest of his life to inventing.

From the late 1860s until his death in 1931, Edison was the owner or co-owner of 1,093 patents. Most of modern industry is dependent, in some way, on the creativity of Edison, who has been called the world's greatest experimenter. Edison also established the first modern research laboratory.

From 1870 to 1876, Thomas Edison had his own engineering business in Newark, New Jersey. Early inventions included wax paper, the mimeograph machine, and improvements in telegraphy. Edison also worked on inventions for the telegraph and the stock ticker developed for the Gold and Stock Telegraph Company. A contract with Western Union on multiple telegraphy on the same wire gave Edison the money to build a laboratory for research and development in Menlo Park, New Jersey. Here, Edison worked on additional telegraphic inventions, acoustic telegraphy, competing with Alexander Graham Bell to improve the telephone, the incandescent lamp, light, and power systems, storage batteries, the phonograph, early phases of radio, the microphone, electrical railways, kilns for making cement, the typewriter, vacuum tubes, the kinetoscope—a forerunner to talking motion pictures—and numerous other inventions. In 2,500 notebooks, Edison kept complete records on his observations, and according to David Sarnoff, "No inventor ever did more to enrich the world."[1] In fact, three of the entrepreneurs described in this book were influenced by Edison's work: Andrew Carnegie and David Sarnoff started as telegraph operators, and Henry Ford worked for Thomas Edison's Detroit operation.

For electrical lighting to develop widely, an efficient and inexpensive source of power was needed. Thomas Edison designed an entire system for providing electricity and obtained a series of patents for ways to generate and distribute electrical current for light, heat, and power. These included generators, cables, transformers, dynamos, motors, hydroelectricity, lightbulbs, lamps, fuses, switches, regulators, conductors, and meters, as well as the organization of services to supply electricity to customers.

The Edison Electrical Light Company was incorporated in 1878 and opened a business office in New York in 1881. In 1882, Edison begins operating his Pearl Street Station, whose steam-driven generator provided enough power for 7,000 lamps. In its first decade, the company sold or established 1,500 lighting plants or central stations, powering about 750,000 lamps. Many other companies also supplied electricity for illumination for both municipal and private use around the country. But by 1889, the largest was the Edison General Electric Company, which in time became General Electric (GE).

Edison believed that the best solution for power distribution was direct current, or DC, which flows in only one direction. However, due to transmission losses, direct current required power stations every few blocks. A power system using high voltage DC would require fewer generating stations, but there was no way of adjusting a direct current's voltage. The alternative technology was alternating current, or AC.

In terms of electric power, high voltage producing a low current is no different from a low voltage producing a high current. But low currents require smaller wires. By using transformers, it was possible to transform alternating current from high to low voltage and vice versa. Transformers take a strong low voltage alternating current and turn it into a weaker high voltage current. For long-distance transmission, the transformer could step up an alternating current to high voltage, and at the receiving end, a transformer could lower the current's voltage for use in electrical lighting. This process was not possible with direct current, which required larger wires and could only supply power for short distances.

Nikola Tesla was born in Croatia and immigrated to the United States in 1884. He worked for a year for Edison but quit to work on his own. In 1888, Tesla was issued a patent for an induction motor, which caused a magnetic field to rotate by supplying it with alternating currents. An inventive genius with 700 patents to his credit, Tesla advanced the AC system and developed a rotating motor, a polyphase alternating current power system, generators, dynamos, and transformers. He also worked on radio, telegraph, and telephone applications.

George Westinghouse was the business leader credited with the development of alternating current as a major power source. Through Westinghouse's innovations, generators would turn magnetic discs through the poles of a permanent magnet. Power was supplied by falling water (hydroelectricity), by steam produced in boilers using coal or oil as a fuel (steam turbines), or by internal combustion engines (diesel generators). Westinghouse, another brilliant inventor, had 400 patents in his name, such as the railroad air brake, railroad signals, more efficient steam engines, and a variety of other inventions for the railroad industry. Westinghouse bought the patent rights for alternating current from Tesla, and in 1886, George Westinghouse put the first commercial AC power system in general service in Great Barrington, Massachusetts. Tesla and Westinghouse converted hydropower to electricity at Niagara Falls, and in 1895, the first of the Niagara Falls generators was sending power to Buffalo, New York, twenty-two miles away. Power from the generator was stepped up to 220,000 volts, sent to the city on elevated power lines, and then step-down transformers reduced the voltage to 110 volts before entering customer homes.

Edison and Westinghouse had disagreements over patents and the efficiency and safety of alternating current. In time, Westinghouse and alternating current won the day. In 1892, Westinghouse underbid GE to provide power for the 180,000 incandescent lamps at the 1893 Columbia Exposition in Chicago. Twelve 1,000-horsepower two-phase generators supplied the raw power. Transformers stepped up the voltage, transmission lines connected all parts of the exposition, and local transformers reduced the voltage to drive motors and lighting. This system clearly demonstrated the advantage of alternating current and polyphase systems. Today most electricity is generated and distributed by three-phase, 60-cycles AC power.

Another early scientific leader was Charles Steinmetz. Steinmetz was born in Breslau, Prussia, on April 9, 1865. He studied in Zurich and Berlin, where he received his Ph.D. in 1888. He immigrated to the United States, settled in Schenectady, New York, and worked for General Electric for thirty-one years. He pioneered studies of alternating current theory, found a method for reducing magnetic loss in transformers, and applied mathematics to put the design of electrical systems on a scientific basis.

By the mid-1880s, applications for electricity were increasing, and the technology was becoming more available. In 1882, the first electric elevator was developed for a textile mill and then for other buildings. Electrical machinery and support accessories were designed. Within two years, a central lighting system was installed in San Francisco. In 1888, Frank J. Sprague completed America's first electric streetcar in Richmond, Virginia, revolutionizing urban transportation.

By the late nineteenth century, many cities had lighting and power machinery. Westinghouse generators powered streetcars with Westinghouse air brakes on the cars. By the turn of the century, the electric power industry was well developed. To understand the magnitude of these developments, one only has to consider what modern cities would be like without lighting, electrical power, or electric elevators.

The National Electric Light Association meeting on June 10, 1912, in Seattle dealt with issues such as the growth of the industry, power distribution, street illumination, waterworks, electrical vehicles, commercial heating and cooling, electricity on the farm, standardization, safety, and public commission and electricity rates—subjects that would be discussed at engineering meetings today.[2]

Most of the early issues of power generation and distribution had been solved. The next decades dealt with the issues of reliable power networks, system efficiency, broader power distribution, and lower costs in order to support the increasing power needs for lamps, radios, televisions, appliances, machinery, and equipment around the United States.

Communications: Telegraph and Telephone

For a message to be sent from one person to another, a number of factors have to be considered. Reception is dependent on the loudness of the sound, the amount of noise (consider talking in a noisy restaurant), the distance to the receiver, the listener's hearing, and any mechanical or electronic amplification. For centuries, people used drums, megaphones, smoke, and beacon fires to communicate over distances longer than voices can carry. Flag signals were used between ships at sea. In Britain, people also used semaphore, in which an observer on a hill would see a distant signal and then send it on to another viewer, effectively amplifying the signal by generating it again.

Using electricity to communicate information was a major development. In the late eighteenth century, there were a number of proposals for using electricity to transmit messages. The electromagnetic telegraph, which drew sparks from a magnet, was a major mid-nineteenth-century invention. In England, Charles Wheatstone and William F. Cooke patented the first electric telegraph in 1837, and the first telegraph was installed in the Great Western Railway between London and West Drayton in 1838. In 1851, the stock exchanges in Paris and London were connected by telegraph so that stock prices could be compared.

The major American figure in the development of the electromagnetic telegraph was Samuel Finley Breese Morse. Morse overcame electrical design flaws and improved information flow to enable the telegraph to become a viable system of communication. Morse used an electromagnet, a device that becomes magnetic when activated by a current and hit against a metal contact. A series of short electrical pulses repeatedly made and broke the magnet and tapped out the message. Morse also introduced relays, devices to reproduce or amplify the signal. Telegraphy transmitted defined pulses of electricity, with the dash having a longer pulse than the dot. Morse developed a code wherein the most popular letters were easiest to send—or example, *E* equals dot and *T* equals dash, whereas the infrequently used letter *Q* equals dash, dash, dot, dash. His new code sped up both transmission and signal decoding.

Morse tried to raise money privately for his invention but was unsuccessful. After a six-year struggle, he received $30,000 from Congress for developing the telegraph, and on May 24, 1844, he demonstrated his telegraph by sending a message between Washington and Baltimore on two wires, one to send the signal and the other for a return. Eventually, he found he could use only one wire if the other transmitter and receiver wires were grounded, i.e. physically connected to a plate buried in the earth.

By 1846, a telegraph line had opened from Philadelphia to Jersey City, where messages were ferried across the Hudson River to New York City. By 1850, New York City had telegraph lines to Albany, Buffalo, Boston, Cleveland, and Chicago. The major customers were investors, businessmen, and newspapers.

By 1861, the telegraph spanned the continent and thousands of miles of wires had been strung. Railroads were using telegraphs for signaling, controlling traffic, and scheduling. Businesspeople were sending out information on shipments, orders, and prices. Small communities were obtaining the latest national news by telegraph. In order to unify the various independent telegraph companies, Hiram Sibley organized Western Union in 1851.

The telegraph not only spread across the country, it joined the United States with Europe. In 1856, Cyrus M. Field established the Atlantic Telegraph Company and two years later, the first Atlantic telegraph cable was laid, but it failed after twenty-six days. A new stronger cable was laid in 1866, and messages could now be sent between the Old and the New Worlds.

During the Civil War, the telegram was very important. The North, with better technology and transportation, was able to string and maintain wires, communicate with armies, and send messages back to Washington. Telegraph could only handle one message at a time on a wire. Eventually Alexander Graham Bell and Thomas Edison each helped develop a harmonic telegraph system that could transmit many telegraph messages over a single pair of telegraph wires. In 1898, the Weather Bureau began to transmit forecasts and weather information around the country by telegraph. But communication was only possible where wires had been strung. Furthermore, it was dependent on an operator at each end, translating messages into Morse code and sending the code across the lines. Periodically, an additional operator had to listen to the message and then repeat it by transmitting it down another pair of wires to yet another operator who had to decode the message. An experienced operator might be able to send or receive text at fifty words per minute. The most important factor in communications is not speed but reliability of transmission, and mistakes were often made.

The next major innovation was the telephone, which sent audio messages down a pair of wires. Its purpose was to provide direct verbal communication between people separated by physical distance. Alexander Graham Bell was born and educated in Edinburgh, Scotland, the son and grandson of speech teachers.

While studying in London, he became a teacher of the deaf. He moved to Canada and then the United States, where he became a young college professor teaching vocal physiology at Boston University and where he also founded his own school for the deaf. His study of speech guided him, and he wanted to create an electrical signal, a continuous current whose intensity would vary in exactly the same ways as the sound waves of speech patterns.

Bell worked from his boardinghouse at 5 Exeter Place, Boston, where he demonstrated that people could talk to each other over a distance. He obtained a patent for the telephone on March 3, 1876—patent number 174,465, one of the most important American inventions. At the Philadelphia Centennial Exposition of 1876, Bell demonstrated the telephone. It was a major event at the show and impressed many visitors, including Emperor Don Pedro II of Brazil and Lord Kelvin of England.

In 1876, Western Union had turned down an opportunity to buy all of Bell's patents for $100,000, and the Bell Telephone Association was incorporated the next year. Within two years, Western Union was challenging the Bell patents as the market developed.

Early telephones were noisy, due in part to the electrical static from power distribution, electric lights, and street railways in the city. There was no central switching office, so all users had private lines. The first switchboard was installed in 1877 in the office of the Holmes Burglar Alarm Company of Boston, with all phones connected to it for security purposes. The first telephone exchange was opened on January 28, 1878, in New Haven, Connecticut. Potential customers wondered why they should have a phone if there was no one to talk to, so growth was dependent on signing many customers (a situation repeated a century later with the Internet). The telephone system required that many customers have a telephone in their home, in their name, with a local exchange, and pay a monthly fee for the privilege. Telephone calls went to a local or main exchange, and the call was then routed on, similar to the way letters are sorted and sent on to another post office, which sorts and delivers the letter. By 1887, there were almost 1,200 phone exchanges staffed by operators who connected customers' calls through a switchboard.

The fledgling industry was entangled in both technical and political issues since various government organizations were deciding who could have permission to establish telephone companies in their areas. Consequently, by 1902 there were almost 300 independent phone companies with incompatible systems—sometimes two or three companies in the same city. Some users had several phones, depending on whom they wished to call.

Theodore Newton Vail was born in Ohio in July 1845 and became a postal clerk in Omaha. He moved up to assistant superintendent of the post office's railway mail system in 1873. In 1878, he was hired as business manager of the Bell

Company, and three years later of American Bell Telephone Company. Vail, an expert telegrapher, had faith in the telephone. He went to work for Bell and received a very small salary for a long time as the Bell system grew. Vail wanted anyone, anywhere to be able to talk to anyone, anywhere—a national system that supports everyone. In 1885, American Telephone and Telegraph company was formed as a subsidiary of American Bell to build and operate the long-distance network. The Bell system soon developed both locally and nationally, and in 1884, phone service was started between San Francisco and Sacramento, California—a distance of eighty miles. By 1887, the company had 170,000 subscribers.

Having built a strong organization, Vail retired from business in September 1887 to his farm in Vermont. He traveled, and on a trip to Buenos Aires installed electric lighting and telephones in that city.

By 1900, Bell had 800,000 telephones in service. The Bell system got into financial trouble, and J. P. Morgan and associates took control of the company from New England investors. Vail's wife died in 1905 and his only child the following year. In 1907 he was called back to run the company. His leadership was also needed due to increased competition as Alexander Graham Bell's telephone patents expired. Although J. P. Morgan was the chairman, Vail had effective control of the company. Vail continued as president until 1919 and built the modern American Telephone and Telegraph Company (AT&T) out of Bell.

The long-distance company was AT&T, and Vail once again became its president. In his new capacity, he focused not on telephones but on the telephone system. Vail quickly raised $21 million, and a total of $250 million in the next few years, to expand the business. He had a vision of where the company should go. Vail's plan was universal transcontinental telephone service. His philosophy was one policy, one system; universal service; and build the telephone system ahead of demand. He believed that the telephone industry should be a regulated monopoly. Vail consolidated research and development in the Western Electric subsidiary and, in order to have the best information to lead the company, he listened to Bell officials from around the country on their problems and requirements.

In 1910, AT&T bought working control of Western Union, and Vail became its president as well. To compete with the post office, Vail wanted to provide "teleletters," messages sent by the phone and telegraph system at night to the nearest telephone or telegraph office for manual delivery. However, Vail and AT&T were blocked by the attorney general on antitrust grounds.

In its first years, the Bell system increased significantly. There was a growth in the number of phones, from 237,000 in 1880 to more than 6 million in 1907, when the Bell company had 3,130,000 phones, compared to 2,987,000 for independent phone companies. That year, almost 1.5 million rural users had phones and were no longer isolated. Furthermore, because of better design, telephones and telephone lines now had less noise associated with them. Operators could connect senders' call to the recipient, and manual switchboards were slowly being converted to mechanical switchboards. On January 25, 1915, the first transcontinental telephone call took place between New York and San Francisco, with the signals amplified by vacuum-tube amplification. The telephone had interconnected the United States.

In 1962, Telstar, the first communication satellite, was operational and an indication of the future. In the mid-1970s, AT&T started to install the first electronic telephone switches to replace electromechanical switches. By 1975, there were 358 million phones in the world, with 156 million of them in North America. The development of fiber-optic technology from Corning to increase the bandwidth of telephone lines was well underway. AT&T was the world's largest corporation when the federal government broke it up in January 1982 on antitrust grounds. The company had 182 million phones and almost 1 million employees. AT&T was separated into twenty-two local operating companies. The next two decades saw new competitors enter the industry and then start to recombine into larger and larger communications companies.

Vacuum Tubes

A vacuum tube is a glass envelope with the air removed, with a filament or heater similar to a lightbulb, and one or more additional plates. The tungsten filament, when heated, produces a cloud of electrons around it, and if a positively charged metal plate is near the filament, it will attract electrons. The first tubes were made in the nineteenth century. In 1875, G. R. Carey invented the phototube, and in 1895, William Roentgen invented an early version of the X-ray tube.

In 1882, Thomas Edison was developing the electric light and noticed that the filament life of a bulb was short because bulbs quickly were blackened. He then entered a second electrode in the light and discovered that current could flow through space from a filament to an electrode in an incandescent bulb when there was a positive charge on the second electrode. This "Edison effect" became the foundation of the vacuum tube.

John Ambrose Fleming was a student of James Clerk Maxwell. He became a professor of electrical engineering at University College, London and worked as a consultant to Edison and then to Guglielmo Marconi. He built on Edison's discovery of the Edison effect, and in 1904 invented the first electronic rectifier, the diode, or "Fleming valve," to control high frequency alternating current. Fleming connected alternating current into the filament and noticed that only one-half of the cycle was passed. It was rectified and produced a direct current, since current would only flow one way in the diode.

Lee De Forest got his Ph.D. at Yale while studying Heinrich Rudolph Hertz's electromagnetic waves. In 1906, De Forest invented the three-electrode vacuum tube. The triode, or audion, tube had a control electrode placed between the filament and collecting plate. The first tubes, however, provided poor performance. H. D. Arnold then enhanced the design by improving the vacuum and changing to an oxide-coated filament, which greatly improved performance. Radio was limited by the sensitivity of the detector. But the triode could amplify weak radio signals and increase the distance over which they could be received by at least a factor of a hundred. The triode made modern radio possible. Small change in grid voltage could vary the electron flow far more than a large change in plate voltage. Amplification took a feeble electric signal and made it a larger one, thus improving long-distance telephone transmission. By 1913, AT&T was installing audions to boost voice signals as they went longer distances around the country. Voice signals were routinely amplified along the way by repeaters.

De Forest, who had more than 300 patents, also discovered regenerative feedback, which added an interconnection between the input and output circuits, thus refreshing the signal. He later started American De Forest Wireless Telegraph Company, which initially could send Morse code by radio at least six miles and for a time was the largest radio company in the United States. Using De Forest's equipment, United Fruit built a radio chain between Costa Rica and Panama. In 1921, De Forest discovered a way of recording sound on movies. However, motion picture studios were not interested, and sound was not put in movies until 1927, and then using a different technology.

Initially, there were two types of vacuum tubes—the diode and the triode. In time, however, other types of vacuum tubes were developed with their own electronic characteristics that a circuit designer could use. Chief among these were the tetrode, in which a second grid was inserted between the control grid and anode, and the pentode, in which a third grid was used. The tetrode and pentode were widely used in radio and radar. During the 1930s and 1940s, tubes were miniaturized and their performance greatly improved.

By 1901, the following eight companies had been established and provided much of the growth in the electricity and electronics industries for the next several decades: American Telephone and Telegraph (1885), Western Union (1856), Westinghouse Electric (1886), General Electric, Philco, Sprague, Sylvania, and Western Electric.

The Edison Electric Light Company was organized on October 15, 1878. The Edison General Electric Company was organized in 1889, and it acquired many of the local Edison Companies. In 1892, General Electric was formed from the merger of the Edison General Electric Company and the Thomson-Houston Company. General Electric started as an electrical company but quickly expanded into other fields. In its first annual report in 1891, General Electric reported that its number of control power stations around the country was 1,277, supplying electricity to more than 2.5 million lamps. Charles Coffin was the chief executive officer of GE from 1892 until 1912 and built the company into a leading American corporation.

Philco, started in 1892 as Helios Electric Company, became Philadelphia Storage Battery Company, and then Philco in 1919. It manufactured batteries and then entered the radio business. Frank J. Sprague had worked for Edison, and in 1888, after completing his electric streetcar, he established Sprague Electric to make electrical components. Frank Poor became a partner in 1901 in the Merrit Manufacturing Company, which renewed or refilled lightbulbs and grew to become Bay State Lighting Company, later renamed Sylvania. Sylvania shipped radio tubes and radio batteries and then made radios in the 1920s.

Western Electric was founded in 1869 as a partnership, reorganized in 1872 as the Western Electric Manufacturing Company, and became the manufacturing and supply unit of the Bell system. It developed telephones, amplification units from vacuum tubes to transistors, sound broadcasting, radio telephones and switching networks, and conducted research that led to the semiconductor industry and most forms of the modern communication industry.

Communications: Radio, Phonograph, and Home Entertainment

The telegraph and telephone improved communication immensely, but they both required wires to connect the sender and the receiver. The next challenge was to develop a wireless communication so that two people could use signals to communicate with each other over a distance.

In 1895, an Italian, Guglielmo Marconi, developed a radio transmitter and receiver using spark transmitters and gave the first demonstration of sending radio waves. In 1899, he transmitted a Morse code signal thirty miles across the English Channel. In 1901, Marconi transmitted the first transoceanic radio signal from Cornwall, England, to St. John's, Newfoundland. In 1903, a message from President Theodore Roosevelt was sent from Cape Cod to England. In 1910, Marconi opened regular telegraph service between the United States and Europe, and in 1912, the first trans-Pacific service was started between San Francisco and Hawaii. These systems were point-to-point communication. In 1905, Germany adopted the distinctive Morse-code string, SOS (three dots, three dashes, three dots) for signaling distress at sea, and it soon became the standard used by other nations.

In November 1906, Reginald Fessenden, a professor at the University of Pittsburgh, conducted the first radio broadcast of speech and music using a high frequency continuous wave alternator designed by Ernst Alexanderson and built by General Electric. He used continuous transmission and amplitude modulation with a signal sent from Brant Rock, Massachusetts. It was received at many surrounding locations, including ships at sea hundreds of miles away. Fessenden holds numerous radio patents and can be considered one of the founders of the radio industry.

Most early radio work used spark transmissions (short bursts of energy) that could only send dots and dashes. Speech transmission using a spark transmitter was noisy. Radio needed a continuous transmission for the complicated patterns of voice, not the short bursts of telegraphy signal. There are many excellent histories of radio.[3]

The U.S. Navy started evaluating radio as early as 1892 for navigation and communication purposes. The navy had traditionally used semaphore to communicate between ships, but at the turn of the century it began to equip its entire fleet with radio and trained sailors to work as radio operators. In 1907, President Theodore Roosevelt sent a fleet of twenty-four navy ships around the world to demonstrate American military power. Lee De Forest's Radio and Telephone Company built the wireless telephones (radios) for the fleet. By 1908, ships were communicating both by Morse code and voice signal. Radio equipment was also being made for the new airplanes of the U.S. Army Signal Corps, commercial ships, and private yachts. Commercial wireless was concerned with intercontinental and marine services, that is, ship-to-shore communications.

Meanwhile, experimental and amateur radio moved forward. The Wireless Association of America had 3,000 members, or "hams," by 1909. At first, amateurs were restricted to transmitting at 1,599 kilohertz, which had a limited range. In 1912, the government made available to amateurs selected wavelengths of radio frequencies, but there was no licensing or regulation of radio transmissions, so amateurs were free to set up stations wherever they wanted to. Radio waves can be transmitted at different frequencies long waves (lower frequency), medium waves, and short waves (higher frequency). Amateurs used Morse code first and then voice on the short waves, or higher frequencies, which were supposed to have no commercial value, while professionals used the longer waves, or lower frequencies. Transmission frequency relates to transmission distance, with low frequencies requiring long antennas for transmission.

Anyone could now build and operate equipment, and radio amateurs could talk to people anywhere. A number of amateur stations made contact over very long distances, including between the United States and France, and between England and New Zealand. Radio messages were not private since anyone could listen in. The name of the technology was changed from "wireless" to "radio" to signify electromagnetic waves radiating from a transmitter. Simple radiophone transmitters were produced by Western Electric during World War I. During the war, amateur broadcasts were forbidden by the governments of both Great Britain and the United States, both of which feared the transmission of classified information.

The reception of radio signals is dependent on several factors: the output power of the transmitter, the frequency on which the signal is sent, the type and directional property of the antenna, and the capability of the transmitter and receivers. An oscillator and transmitter produce a radio signal, which is combined with a sound signal as it is transmitted.

Early crystal detectors used a semiconductor of galena (lead sulfide), carborundum (silicon carbide), or silicon to gather a signal, and a small connector called a "cat's whisker" to tune the receiver for a particular frequency of a station. The receiver has to adjust the frequency for the station to be picked up and eliminate unwanted frequencies. This was done by adjusting the tuning capacitance or inductance to the frequency desired. These radios could only receive a few stations and were initially limited to receiving stations five to fifty miles away. The early crystal radio sets suffered from a lack of sensitivity and crystal instability. Systems were noisy due to the squeaks, crackles, and hums of both nature and the transmitter, as well as interference from other stations. Vacuum tubes, quartz crystals, and regeneration made it possible to compensate for inefficient detection of a weak signal, control the frequency, and lower the noise.

In 1915, more than half of the American population lived in towns with fewer than 5,000 inhabitants. Information came from newspapers, mail, and word of mouth. Radio changed that. The first vacuum tube radios began to appear that year. Vacuum tubes had become cheaper and more reliable, and they could amplify signals and more easily adjust stations in the receiver. Circuit design with vacuum tubes became better. In 1920, RCA began manufacturing the first commercial vacuum tubes, and factory-produced receivers replaced home-built models. In June 1921, Westinghouse introduced a crystal set radio receiver that came with headphones, cost $25, and had a range of up to fifteen miles. Westinghouse's next radio set had vacuum tubes and sold for $60.

In the fall of 1916, Lee De Forest transmitted Enrico Caruso's voice from the stage of the Metropolitan Opera Company and started what he called "radio phone concerts." During this period, there were many experimental stations. The first woman announcer may have been Eunice Randall in 1920 broadcasting from Tufts College in Massachusetts on 1XE, an experimental station owned by American Radio and Research Company.

The first commercial radio station, KDKA in Pittsburgh, went on the air on November 20, 1920, and announced the results of the Warren Harding and James Cox presidential race. It then started a daily program of music and news. In May 1922, the British Broadcasting Company (BBC) was formed and took over a British Marconi station in London. By the end of 1921, there were twenty-eight stations in the United States, many broadcasting on the same frequency. By the end of 1922, there were 570 licensed stations in the United States, but fewer than 2 million homes had radios. Improvements were made in radios as they shifted away from requiring headsets to using speakers so that the entire family could listen to a program. They also moved from wet/dry batteries to AC power, and to being enclosed (possibly with a phonograph) in a mahogany or walnut cabinet, making them major pieces of furniture.

The use of radio sets grew rapidly. From 5,000 home radios sold in 1920, the number grew to 100,000 in 1922, 500,000 in 1923, and 2.5 million radios in 1924. Originally most of these were crystal sets. Crystal detectors were tube-less radio sets, selling for about $2.25, aimed at amateurs who built their own low-quality systems. But by 1925, an all-electric radio set, operated off of home current and with vacuum tube and loudspeakers, could detect many broadcasts and amplify stations' signals. In 1923, Sears, Roebuck and Montgomery Ward offered the first radios.

Radio moved into the home, and by the mid-1920s, many types of companies had gone into broadcasting—department stores, music stores, other retailers, radio manufacturers, colleges, newspapers, large companies, and entrepreneurs. Stations were financed by a parent company or had to sell advertising to exist. In 1927, the first trans-Atlantic radiophone call was made at a cost of about $200 per minute. That same year, there was a radio broadcast from New York City of Lindbergh's triumphant return from Paris.

Radio broadcasting was beginning to develop as an industry. Westinghouse, a manufacturer of broadcast equipment, developed preassembled radios. The company then realized that a radio station would increase the number of radios sold and, in 1920, opened KDKA in Pittsburgh with an output of 50,000 watts. Programs were soon broadcast on a scheduled basis. Westinghouse also opened WJZ in Newark, New Jersey, and WBZ in Springfield, Massachusetts, where it had factories. By the end of 1922, the Commerce Department had granted licenses to 600 radio stations. For radios to sell, there had to be programming—music, drama, news, and sports.

There were now hundreds of manufacturers. Early radio manufacturers included Atwater Kent, which made ignition systems and radios, Columbia, Decca, Edison, GE, Kennedy, Majestic, Philco, Philips, Pope, RCA, Spartan, Western Electric, Westinghouse, and Zenith. In 1928, Paul Galvin purchased a battery eliminator company that allowed radios to work on household current. The company started making car radios in 1930 and adopted the name Motorola.

The depression increased the number of radio listeners because tabletop models became more affordable and radio provided free entertainment. By 1939, there were 1,465 stations in the United States and four networks. In 1926, NBC was founded by RCA and had two networks: the Red, taken over from AT&T, and the Blue. In 1927, William Paley founded CBS, and in 1934, Mutual Broadcasting was formed. Stations were linked by telephone lines leased from AT&T. In 1943, NBC sold the Blue network, and it became the American Broadcasting Company. In 1946, the Dumont network was established. Networks were profitable as advertisers wanted to develop a national market. NBC sold $10 million of radio advertising in 1928 and $15 million the next year. Advertising revenues continued to grow through the depression as retail companies looked for ways to increase business.

Technical advances continued. The superregenerative receiver could whistle and oscillate if the regeneration control was turned on too loud. Louis Hazeltine invented a radio receiver that eliminated the squeaks and howls of the early radio receivers, and by 1927, 10 million of these sets were in operation.

In 1918, Edwin Howard Armstrong, while at Columbia University, invented regenerative feedback, in which an incoming signal was fed back on itself and the signal strengthened. Later, he invented the superheterodyne and super-regenerative circuits for radio receivers—the basis for modern radio and radar communications. In 1933, Armstrong received patents for wideband frequency modulation (FM). A high frequency radio signal is combined with a sound signal as it is transmitted, that is, modulated by amplitude (AM) or by frequency (FM). A detector in the receiver extracts the signal from the carrier and reproduces the sound. Frequency modulation (FM) solved the problems of noise (static), which was inherent in the AM broadcasts and caused by a variety of factors, from lightning storms to motors. David Sarnoff of RCA became aware of FM in 1933, but did not encourage it. Armstrong built the first FM station himself and in 1940, gave the first demonstration of FM to the Federal Communications Commission (FCC). Sarnoff wanted to continue to produce AM radios and use the profits for investing in television, and he fought Armstrong's patents in court. RCA had been supreme in the radio field because it held exclusive rights to so many inventions. When there was too much trouble with the authorities, RCA licensed the technology but continually purchased the rights to inventions of others or fought them in the courts.

In the very early days of radio, amateur radio operators as well as experimental stations could transmit signals on any frequency. But interference between stations was a problem, especially as some stations increased their power. In 1922, Secretary of Commerce Herbert Hoover, who was responsible for radio, convened the first radio conference in Washington. In 1924, the Department of Commerce allocated the band from 550 Kilocycles (KC) to 1,500 KC and power output up to 5,000 watts for commercial radio stations. In 1927, the Federal Radio Commission (which became the FCC in 1934) was made responsible for frequency allocation, station transmission times, and power output. Some stations then in service had to change frequencies or surrender their licenses.

As the number of radio stations increased and their power levels grew, the performance of radio receivers had to improve, especially in signal selectivity and noise suppression. By 1930, there were 14 million radio sets in American homes, about twenty-five years after radio's advent. By 1933, there were 605 broadcasting stations in the United States, 36 in Canada, and 39 in Mexico. By 1934, radio was reaching 60 percent of American homes and there were numerous radio manufacturers.

Radio stations, by regulation, had to broadcast programs free of charge to the public. Stations broadcast music, religious services, sports, news, farm crop and market reports, children's programs, and talk shows. And radio programs created an entirely new form of entertainment. For example, in vaudeville, a performer could use the same songs or jokes throughout a career. Radio required new material constantly. Soap operas were developed to entertain housewives during the week. Programs such as *Ma Perkins, The Romance of Helen Trent, One Man's Family,* and *Lorenzo Jones* soon attracted their own national audience. Listener loyalty and fan letters became part of the American scene.

Popular music also was broadcast nationally and helped make "hit" songs. In the early 1930s, classical music was broadcast nationally—the Philadelphia Orchestra led by Leopold Stokowski, Serge Koussevitzky and the Boston Symphony, and Arturo Toscanini and the New York Philharmonic. By 1938, the radio opera audience was estimated at 12 million listeners. For those who listened to radio in the 1930s and 1940, it was the center of entertainment. In music, people from Paul Whiteman and Rudy Vallee to Glen Miller, from Toscanini to the Grand Ole Opry, and radio personalities, including Edgar Bergen, Fanny Brice as Baby Snooks, Kate Smith, Fibber McGee and Molly, Lum and Abner, Henry Aldrich, The Shadow, Sam Spade, Jack Armstrong, Kate Smith, Bob Hope, Bing Crosby, Eddie Cantor, Jack Benny, Fred Allen, and numerous other people, became well known.

Radios were not only entering the home in great quantity; they were also going into automobiles. In 1929, General Motors had developed a way of installing radios in its autos and introduced radios as a standard feature, even though, in much of the country, there were no radio stations that could be heard by drivers. A joint venture for car radio manufacture was owned by GM (51 percent) and RCA (49 percent). There were about 100,000 car radios in 1932, and more than 700,000 were sold in 1934. In 1940, 2.3 million car radios were made.

Radio manufacturers now included Avco, Belmont, Crosley, Emerson, GE, Hoffman Radio, Magnavox, Meissner, Motorola, Noblitt Sparks, Packard Bell, Philco, Raytheon, RCA, Sears, Roebuck, Sentinel, Stromberg Carlson, Sylvania, Temple, Westinghouse, Zenith, and many others. Most had settled with the estate of Edwin Armstrong regarding his frequency modulation patents, and FM was becoming more widespread.

Throughout the 1930s and 1940s, radio was the principal method of communication. In the 1928 presidential election, Herbert Hoover and Al Smith gave election eve speeches to about 40 million listeners. Campaigning began to change, and the networks began to charge for time on political talks. During the depression, President Franklin Delano Roosevelt communicated to the country on the radio with his "fireside chats."

Advertising became the principal way of supporting radio expansion. The first commercial was broadcast on August 22, 1922, when New York City WEAF sold ten minutes for $50 to an apartment-house development in Queens. Eventually, most local radio stations started making money through advertising.

National news was of interest during the 1930s, and H. V. Kaltenborn and Walter Winchell had loyal audiences. But with Pearl Harbor, radio assumed much more importance. During World War II, CBS's broadcast reports by Edward R. Murrow in London, Eric Sevaried from China-Burma, Howard K. Smith and William Shirer from Germany and Switzerland, and Winston Burdett from North Africa became a way in which Americans learned of progress in the war.

Radio allowed people in the cities and suburbs to be entertained, educated, and to receive news and information in the privacy of their homes. By 1940, 80 percent of U.S. homes had radio. But it was not until after the World War II that radio broadcasts reached some rural areas.

On June 27, 1945, the FCC decided that frequency programs would have to move from their established frequencies to a different bandwidth to make way for television stations. Consequently, fifty transmitting stations and half a million FM sets licensed by Edwin Armstrong were now obsolete. Americans had to purchase new sets. By the end of WWII, 95 percent of all homes had a radio. Radio continues in importance today, with 13,000 AM and FM radio stations as well as nearly 20,000 Internet radio stations.

The West Coast, especially the San Francisco Bay Area, has had a long history of electronics development. The U.S. Navy established wireless stations along the West Coast in the early twentieth century. Lee De Forest established a San Francisco office in 1910. Magnavox was established in Oakland in 1917 as a radio receiving company. In 1925, Stanford University started teaching courses in electronics. During the 1920s and 1930s, a number of important electronics companies were established in the Bay Area. Charles Litton started producing glass tubes and formed his own business, Litton Engineering Company, in 1931. Philo Farnsworth demonstrated his early work in television in San Francisco. In 1938, William Hewlett and David Packard started their own company in Palo Alto, California, and designed an audio oscillator, an electronic instrument, to test sound equipment. In his book *The HP Way*, David Packard talked about the company philosophy of an open-door management style, trust in people, paying as you go without incurring substantial debt, and a commitment to innovation. Hewlett-Packard (HP) grew to be one of the great electronics companies of the twentieth century, with sales passing $30 million in 1958 and $365 million by 1970. Sigurd and Russell Varian developed airborne radar for Britain's Royal Air Force using klystron microwave technology. After the war in 1948, they founded Varian Associates. Russian-born Alexander M. Poniatoff started Ampex in 1944 to manufacture motors and generators for radar-scanning antennas. And dozens of new companies and many established companies began operations on the West Coast due in large part to significant government funding for defense programs.

Electronics in World War II and Beyond

In 1940, the United States had many companies and inventors working in the field of electronics. But the country's needs during World War II significantly advanced the field as new technologies and products were developed and many people were trained in electronics.

Radio was improved significantly with better radio systems and antennas, stronger signals, and coded messages. Two-way radio was needed to communicate with ships, submarines, and aircraft over longer distances. Army commanders and troops needed more timely information. In 1940, Motorola developed the first handheld two-way radio, the SCR-536 "handy-talkie." Then, in 1943, Motorola developed an FM two-way radio, the "walkie-talkie." It weighed thirty-five pounds and had a range of ten to twenty miles. Army commanders could now communicate directly with troops in the field, and local units could more easily request support when needed.

Radio was important for navigation. Early in World War II, German aircraft followed radio beacons to their targets. Like lighthouses, each with its own call signals, directional wireless onboard a plane could fix its position from the angles where two of these signals intersected. The British soon jammed these radio beacons with false stations. The Germans then developed beacons on the Continent that pointed to the target, leading the German bombers to their destination. The British then jammed the beams and diverted the bombers to dump their loads in empty fields.

A major electronics development was in radar (radio detecting and ranging). Robert Alexander Watson-Watt had patented his first electronic device in 1919, and in 1935, he patented radar for meteorological purposes. A key man in the Battle of Britain, Watson-Watt was appointed director of radio research at the British National Physical Laboratory in 1935. John Randall invented the magnetron tube in 1940 to produce microwaves that were used for radar signals.

The British focused its radar technology on aircraft detection and early warning systems for approaching aircraft, and the Germans focused on aircraft navigation systems. But the use of radar quickly spread to other applications. For example, anti-aircraft batteries were soon fitted with radar to assist in defense. Search radar were used on ships for tracking enemy aircraft, including low-flying planes. Antisubmarine radar systems were also introduced. Planes were fitted with airborne radar systems as blind-bombing devices so planes could bomb from higher altitudes in bad weather and find targets on the ground. Planes were also equipped with ground-approaching-systems radar to make flying and landing safer. Radar countermeasures were developed by both sides, ranging from complex radar-jamming stations to dropping films of tinfoil from planes to confuse ground radar.

Early in the war, Britain shared the invention of the magnetron with American scientists. In 1940, the Radiation Lab at MIT was established for wartime radar development. During the war, the Radiation Lab developed more than 100 models of radar and did research on radar, navigation, microwave theory, and systems engineering. During World War II, almost 1 million radar systems were produced in the United States.

Another major invention was precision long-range navigation (loran), developed between 1940 and 1943. Loran's creation was supported in part by Alfred Lee Loomis, a great amateur in science who financed a private American laboratory. In 1942, the first loran system was installed along the East Coast and was used to direct surface ships and aircraft-attacking submarines. With loran, pulsed radio transmissions from two ground stations were displayed on a ship's cathode-ray tube, and the distance between the two waves corresponded to the time distance of arrival of signals from the two stations. Another set of transmitters repeated the process and the position of a ship could be determined within a few kilometers.

An additional important technology was sonar (sound navigation ranging). Transmitted and reflected sound waves could locate submerged objects, such as a submarine or mines, as well as measure distance underwater. It could also find U-boats, and acoustical depth charges could then destroy them.

By the end of the war, the U.S. Army, Navy, and Air Corps had developed and used far more electronics than they had used in the 1930s. Hundreds of thousands of young men and women had been exposed to electronics in the military. In the United States, many engineers and scientists had now been trained in electronics, and many organizations had received research-and-development contracts from the military that improved the company's capabilities significantly. These developments led to the rapid expansion of electronic products after the war with many new companies.

Bill Hewlett joined the army in 1941 as an army signal corps officer. He then became head of an electronics section of the Development Division. When he returned to Hewlett-Packard in 1947, the company's revenue was $851,287, and it had just over a hundred employees. Hewlett was now prepared to introduce electronics into many of the future HP products. Thomas Watson Jr. was also exposed to electronics in his military career. When he rejoined his father at IBM, he pushed for electronic solutions to problems rather than the mechanical solutions favored by Thomas Watson Sr. The son soon took over IBM and led it to its dominance of the computer industry. Another young serviceman was Ken Olsen. After the war, his father wanted him to become a machinist, but Olsen went on to MIT and then founded Digital Equipment Corporation (for his story, see chapter 10).

In the late 1940s, much of the wartime technology was converted to peacetime uses. Improvements in radio systems, antennas, vacuum tubes, electronics, navigation, and other areas soon resulted in commercial applications. For example, the magnetron, a new source of microwave energy for early warning radar, led to the development of the microwave oven at Raytheon. Motorola's work on military communication led to improvements in police radios.

After the war, there was a pent-up demand for housing, cars, and other consumer items, which led to a major economic boom in the late 1940s and the 1950s. One of the major production developments during World War II had been the widespread use of the assembly line with interchangeable parts. After the war, many companies used this technique to satisfy consumer demand for goods, appliances, and even houses in suburbs such as Levittown, New York.

There are three new industries that should be specially noted. The first is the computer industry, which is described in chapter 9. The second is the airline industry. After World War II, the number of trained pilots, navigators, and ground crew, as well as performance improvements in airplanes, made possible the rapid expansion of the airline industry, uniting the country. Airline expansion would not have been possible, however, without the air traffic control system that required hundreds of radar systems, airborne radios, display screens, communication networks, and trained personnel, all of which were improved during the War. The third business is television, which is described next.

Television

In the nineteenth century, people were informed by the print media—newspapers, magazines, and books—or if they lived in larger cities, by attending museums and public lectures. In the twentieth century, people all over the country could receive information by telephone, radio, and television. The technology that had the greatest impact was undoubtedly television.

Like all technologies, television had a long history with many inventors and companies contributing to its development. In 1872, Joseph May discovered that selenium's conductivity was enhanced by light. Paul Nipkow of Germany made one of the early proposals for a mechanical television system in 1883. His scanning disc had a spiral of holes, and the information on each hole could be coded. As the disc spun, the eye blurred all the points together to re-create the picture. In 1897, Karl Ferdinand Braun invented the first cathode-ray tube, and within ten years, it was being used to produce pictures.

To transmit a television picture, an image had to be scanned and the information transmitted by electronic signals. The receiver had to obtain the signal and then decode it to re-create the original picture. Television transmits a series of pictures, perhaps thirty per second, and the eye merges these into a moving picture. The quality of the picture can be described based on the number of lines that are scanned as well as the number of scans per second required to communicate. A moving image requires more scans than a static one.

Early television sets were not all electronic, however. Charles Jenkins, who held more than 400 patents, demonstrated a mechanical wireless television system in June 1925, which he called radiovision. The display had a small motor with a spinning disc and a neon lamp. He began to broadcast movies from Washington, D.C., in July 1928, sending an image of forty-eight lines per inch with synchronized sound.

In 1926, John Logie Baird, a graduate of the University of Glasgow, demonstrated television using the Nipkow mechanical scanning disc, initially with thirty lines per picture. Baird was a very creative individual who demonstrated many new television ideas and sent the image of a face across the Atlantic in 1928. From 1929 to 1935, the BBC used the Baird mechanical television system with a picture of 200 lines per frame and started regular television service in 1932. In 1936, the BBC switched to an electronic system using 405 lines per minute. Later in life, Baird, an independent inventor, improved his system and developed a 600-line color television system.

In 1923, Ernst Alexanderson started work on television at General Electric, and GE gave a demonstration of a mechanical television set in April 1927. Pictures of Herbert Hoover, the secretary of commerce, were sent from Washington, D.C., to New York City. The fifty-line picture was transmitted at eighteen frames per second and shown on a tiny screen. General Electric began experimental television broadcasting in 1928, but mechanical systems for scanning limited picture quality and the size of the reproducible image.

In 1927, Philo Farnsworth, a Utah-born inventor, developed the first all-electronic television system at the age of twenty-one and held the first public demonstration of such a system the following year. Farnsworth then founded the Farnsworth Television and Radio Corporation and was transmitting experimental television programs to about fifty homes in Philadelphia. Farnsworth, who held 165 patents, fought with RCA and David Sarnoff over patents throughout the 1930s and prevented RCA from dominating the television patent arena. In fact, RCA was eventually forced to pay a patent license fee to Farnsworth. This story of the battles between Farnsworth and Sarnoff is well documented.[4]

The first experimentation with television broadcasting began in the 1920s, with both black-and-white and color transmissions in Great Britain and the United States. In 1928, the first regularly scheduled U.S. television programs were transmitted six hours per week in Schenectady, New York. In 1929, David Sarnoff, president of RCA, made a long-range commitment to television. Under Sarnoff's leadership, RCA invested many millions of dollars in technology development.

Vladimir Zworykin was born in Muron, Russia, came to the United States, and worked for Westinghouse. In 1923, Zworykin developed the first electronic television tube, the kinescope. In 1925, he described a working system to his bosses at Westinghouse, and when they were unresponsive, he left and joined

RCA in 1927. There, he developed the iconoscope, an early television camera tube introduced by RCA in the late 1920s. By 1938, an improved television camera was developed that was much more sensitive to light and was used for aircraft applications during the war.

In the 1930s, early television broadcasts were made in Germany and England. The 1936 Berlin Olympics were televised using American equipment supplied by RCA and by Farnsworth. This was the first broadcast of a sporting event and was sent from the stadium to viewing locations in Berlin and Potsdam. In 1937, the coronation of King George VI and the Wimbledon tennis tournament were broadcast in England.

NBC started experimental television broadcasting in 1934. In 1936, RCA demonstrated an electronic system, 343 lines and 30 frames per second. David Sarnoff appeared on the first public demonstration of television, shown at the 1939 World's Fair in New York. At the fair, Franklin Roosevelt became the first president to be televised. In June 1940, both RCA and Philco televised the Republican Convention. But there were only a few hundred television sets in operation at that time, so the audience was limited. Sarnoff worked hard to push the FCC to institute technical standards and approve the commercialization of television. In 1941, the FCC announced television standards of 525 lines, 30 frames per second. The United States and Japan decided on a 525-line standard, whereas in most of the rest of the world the standard was 625 lines. NBC began commercial broadcasting in 1941, but technical and financial difficulties and World War II delayed television's introduction to the public until 1946.

Allen B. Dumont had been chief engineer for the De Forest Radio Company but left to start his own company. He developed cathode-ray tubes in the early 1930s and offered a fourteen-inch television set in 1938. He started a television network to compete with NBC and the Dumont network continued in business until 1955.

By 1940, there were twenty-three experimental television broadcasting stations operating in the United States. On March 22, 1941, the FCC suspended RCA's limited commercial authorization, accusing it of developing a monopoly. In April 1942, the federal government banned further commercial development and production of television equipment as scientists and engineers were needed for war work. Almost all television transmission ceased. By end of the war, there were about 7,500 receiving television sets in New York City, Schenectady, and Philadelphia.

After the war, television expanded significantly. In the spring of 1945, Sarnoff told his senior managers that RCA had one priority: television. Whatever resources were needed would be provided. In 1947, there were 47,000 sets in metropolitan New York City and 13,000 sets in the rest of the country. The same year, the first World Series game was telecast and *Meet the Press* premiered. But there were very few television sets in the market, and most sets were in stores or bars. By 1948,

RCA had operating stations in Chicago, Los Angeles, New York City, and Washington. Other television manufacturers or networks, including ABC, CBS, Crosley, Dumont, General Electric, Philco, Raytheon, Stromberg Carlson, and Westinghouse, were opening television stations. Also starting television stations were newspapers, including the *Atlanta Constitution, Kansas City Star, Louisville Courier-Journal, Los Angeles Times, Milwaukee Journal, Oregonian, New Orleans Times-Picayune,* and *San Francisco Chronicle* as well as Hearst and Scripps-Howard. No one wanted to be left behind in this communication revolution.

The first RCA television sets were manufactured in Camden, New Jersey, in 1946. In that first year, RCA sold 10,000 sets at an average price of $385. By 1947, 250,000 sets had been sold by the entire industry. By August 1949, there were 2 million television sets in the country, with more than 700,000 of them in New York City. Industrywide manufacturing increased rapidly, from about 5,000 sets per month in 1947 to 400,000 sets per month in 1950 to 600,000 per month in 1953. By 1950, there were almost 8 million sets, and by 1960, 46.7 million.

In 1950, there were about 100 television stations serving 9 percent of the American households. Less than thirty years later, there were 680 stations serving 95 percent of American households. In 2002, there are more than 1,600 television stations in the United States.

Television communication links initially were established between New York, Philadelphia, Washington, and Boston. In 1950, AT&T opened a microwave system between New York and Chicago, and a year later the system reached California. Television broadcasting spread across the country as new stations were set up. In 1952, *The Today Show* and *I Love Lucy* debuted, and the Rose Bowl was first broadcast in 1954.

Early television sets were made by Dumont, Farnsworth, General Electric, Jenkins, Philco, RCA, and Westinghouse. Later, Admiral, Capehart, Crosley, Emerson, Heath, Magnavox, Motorola, Packard Bell, Silvertone, Sylvania, Warwick, Zenith, and many other manufacturers joined them. Ultrahigh frequency stations (UHF) started in 1952. By 1962 television sets had to receive both VHF (Channels 2–6) and UHF (Channels 7–13) programs.

All early television had to be broadcast live, and sometimes twice—once for the East Coast and once for the West Coast. The industry needed a machine that could record video signals using low-cost tape. To allow for tape delay of a television program, Alexander M. Poniatoff and Ampex developed a machine that recorded broadcasts on a two-inch magnetic tape. Ampex grew, but its engineers were vacuum tube people and did not understand transistors. They licensed the technology to a small Japanese company called Sony. In 1969, Sony announced a videocassette recorder, and soon Ampex was out of the television recording business.

Lower costs and more programs put a television set in every home. Americans watched *I Love Lucy, Leave It to Beaver, Father Knows Best, Your Show of Shows,* and Ronald Reagan's *General Electric Theater.* By 1978, more than 95 percent of American households had television sets.

Television, like radio, enabled the public to be entertained and educated in their homes. Sharing events at a distance changed the way people perceived the world and themselves in it. Much of television is banal, superficial, and repetitive. But when television achieves its potential, it can have major influence. In 1960, the Kennedy-Nixon debates were broadcast nationally and helped elect John Kennedy president. In the 1960s, the Vietnam War was broadcast nightly and affected political opposition to the war. On July 20, 1969, 600 million people worldwide viewed the first television broadcast from the moon. Both of the Iraqi wars were covered live and twenty-four hours per day, giving the American people a firsthand look at the power and violence of war.

People had thought about color television for a long time. In theory, it was simple. All one had to do was scan each frame three times, one for each primary color. The three scans then would be sent as independent signals to a television set that decoded the information and rebuilt the colors. But it took a lot of work to make the theory practical. Most early color systems used a spinning disc that scanned the image with alternating lines of red, blue, and green.

Sarnoff channeled vast amounts of RCA capital into research and development of color television. To focus on color television took self-confidence, a vision, and a lot of time and money. Again, Sarnoff's vision paid off with sales and profits.

CBS, founded in 1927 and led by William Paley, had been, for a time, a junior competitor to RCA and NBC. But it took the lead in the development of color television. CBS fought RCA's transmission and reception standards. In 1940, Peter Goldmark of CBS announced a color system consisting of a part electronic, part mechanical spinning system, using a disc of three filters—red, green, and blue. Signals were sent to a black-and-white set and viewed through a second rotating color wheel. The two wheels were kept synchronized so that the receiver saw the same color image as the camera. CBS then requested that the FCC adopt its color system standards. However, CBS's system was incompatible with existing black-and-white sets that had 525 and not the 405 lines of the CBS system. RCA fought the standards, but the FCC accepted them in September 1950. CBS broadcast the first commercial color program, a one-hour *Ed Sullivan Show* in June 1951, but it was not widely watched since it couldn't be seen on the existing monochrome sets.

After World War II, NBC and CBS had developed competing color systems, and the FCC had to decide on the new standards. Should a color television system be compatible with the existing black-and-white sets? In 1947, the FCC ruled that the CBS color system was premature, but in 1951, the FCC approved the CBS system because it had superior color. CBS was now free to start commercial broadcasting. However, the Korean War caused shortages of some materials required for color sets, and all color production of television was suspended during the war.

Meanwhile, the number of black-and-white sets continued to increase. By 1953, there were 25 million sets in the field that could not receive the CBS color. RCA appealed to the FCC for acceptance of compatible transmission standards. In order to receive CBS color, existing black-and-white sets would require an adapter that used a mechanical spinning color wheel. There was much political pressure and infighting, and in 1951, RCA broadcast color programs with the first color system compatible with black-and-white systems. On December 17, 1953, RCA won its victory in the color wars when its standards were adopted for an all-electronic color system. The FCC accepted the standards proposed by RCA and the electronic RCA compatible color system, reversing its prior decision to accept the CBS mechanical system.

Color sets were expensive, costing more than three times what a black-and-white set cost. Westinghouse introduced the first color set in April 1954, and it cost $1,295. Shortly thereafter, RCA introduced its first color set, the CTC-100 with a twelve-inch screen, for $1,000. RCA had a forecast that 75,000 sets would be sold, but because of its high price, fewer than 5,000 were distributed, many to company employees.

Today, with satellite and cable transmission of signals, the number of American homes with television is in excess of 98 percent, with the majority having two or more color sets. So for the last half century, television has boomed. But whereas many companies have shared in its success, the early pioneers, in general, have not. First, conglomerates bought some of the leaders and did not provide the proper kind of leadership. Philco was purchased by Ford Motor Company, Sylvania by General Telephone and, as will be seen in the next chapter, RCA by General Electric.

Meanwhile, foreign companies have come to dominate consumer electronics in the United States. From Japan, Sony, Hitachi, Matsushita, Sanyo, Sharp, JVC, Toshiba, and Mitsubishi produced excellent consumer products at very reasonable prices. From Europe, Thompson of France and Philips of the Netherlands moved strongly into the television business. By 1987, fewer than 20 percent of Americans' television sets were being produced in the United States. (There is a very good account of this story in a chapter titled "Consumer Electronics: Japan's Paths to Global Conquest," in *Inventing the Electronic Century*.)[5] A company especially worth studying is Sony. Founded in 1946 by Masaru Ibuka and Akio Morita as the Tokyo Telecommunications Engineering Corporation, Sony made audio and video equipment, televisions, and other products and grew rapidly. Meanwhile, most of the United States electronics companies had shrunk or left the television business.

But it was not only through selling television equipment that the world changed, change also occurred because of content distribution resulting from cable television and growth in direct broadcast satellite television.

Cable television started in the 1940s as a way to reach customers in areas that had trouble receiving broadcast signals. Antennas on mountaintops were used to pick up stations in remote locations and relay the signal locally. The first cable location was in Pennsylvania in the spring of 1948. In 1953, Bill Daniels built his first cable system in Casper, Wyoming. By 1962, almost 800 cable systems serving 850,000 subscribers were in business. Some of the first cable companies were in the western United States, since long distances from cities and the presence of mountains made early television signals from the big cities inaccessible to much of the region. Consequently, Denver became an early center for the cable industry with many cable companies including Tele-Communications, Inc. (TCI) led by Bob Magness and John Malone.

For a long time, the government couldn't decide what to make of cable companies. Were they television companies required to supply their broadcasts free of charge to all who could receive their signals as radio and television stations were? Or were they utilities like the telephone and electrical companies, providing a monopoly in their territory but with rates and services subject to government approval? For forty years, the FCC wrote and rewrote regulations.

Cable was the first home of pay-TV sporting events. By 1973, the industry was using satellites to relay signals to local cable companies. By 1973, 1,200 cable systems served 1 million homes. Fiber optic cables, developed by Corning, increased the number of both signals and stations during the 1970s and 1980s. In 1976 Ted Turner's WTCG in Atlanta became the first satellite-delivered national broadcast station. In 1982, Ted Turner's Broadcasting Company announced the premiere of Cable News Network (CNN), the first twenty-four-hour news channel, which was initially connected to 1.7 million American homes. In the 1980s, direct broadcasting satellites were available, sending the signals directly into the home. New channels and new companies became available to the consumer. Disney, Financial News Network, Discovery Channel, Weather Channel, A&E, HBO, American Movie Channel, Home Shopping Network, and many others were started.

As the decades passed, cable and satellite bandpass (frequency of transmission) became broader and signal strength increased. Signals were scrambled for security. Channel capacity expanded to eighty channels and then up to several hundred channels, resulting in greater choice of programs for the consumer and increased revenue for the providers. By 1989, industry revenue reached $15 billion with new entrepreneurs and new jobs.

The three remaining television networks, NBC, CBS, and ABC, saw their market share decrease. Meanwhile, cable companies witnessed growth domestically and internationally, and began to supply digital video, entering the telephone business and computer high-speed data communications. In February 1983, a fiber optics phone system was started between New York City and Washington, D.C. By 1984, all phone companies were investing in long-distance fiber optic lines but were forbidden by regulators from entering some of the new communication markets.

Changes in technology not only has direct effects, it can also have very indirect effects. Worldwide television has changed what people perceive and know, how they get their information, and what they may wish for themselves and their children. If knowledge is power, then the rapid and simultaneous dissemination of information on a worldwide basis gives power in new ways and takes away power from established sources. This has certainly been true with television, as new competitors have entered the marketplace and established ones have faded away. Today there are more than 600 million television sets throughout the world. Many of them share the same programs, getting entertainment, information, and often an unrealistic view of American life and culture.

Semiconductors

For the first half of the twentieth century, the functions of amplification, switching, and control were performed mechanically by relays or electronically by vacuum tubes. Advances in radio, television, radar, and other electronic applications were possible because of improvements in vacuum tube design and use. But tubes had significant disadvantages that restricted the growth of electronics. Vacuum tubes used a lot of power and created heat. Equipment temperatures could increase, and to cool a system to manageable temperatures, high ventilation or air-conditioning might be required. Tubes were large, and miniaturization was achieved only with difficulty and at great expense. Tubes were expensive, so the prices of electronic equipment could not be reduced below certain limits. Most important, tubes had a short life. A short life span was not a big problem with a radio that might have five to eight tubes. When the radio failed, the owner could bring the tubes down to the drugstore or electronics shop, test the tubes one by one on a tube tester, and purchase a replacement. But with more complicated systems, such as television sets, telephone networks, military aircraft, and computers, the lifetime of the individual vacuum tubes could limit total system or equipment reliability to unacceptable levels. A smaller and more reliable device was needed.

Since the 1930s, Bell Telephone Laboratory was the largest industrial research organization in the world. In 1939 and 1940, Russell Ohl of Bell Labs investigated crystal detectors, especially silicon, for radar and radio systems. He asked Bell chemists to prepare pure silicon as well as silicon crystals with controlled amounts of impurities. Ohl developed a silicon photodetector by building a barrier in a silicon crystal that would generate a current when light was shined on it. This discovery was the forerunner of solar cells and a step along the way to today's semiconductors.

In the summer of 1945, Bell Lab's Murray Hill Facilities started a research project on semiconductors as possible amplifiers. William Bradford Shockley headed up the solid state physics group. John Bardeen, a theoretical physicist, and Walter Houser Brattain, who physically built and conducted the experiments, were the key researchers.

Bardeen and Brattain demonstrated the first transistor on December 23, 1947. Theirs was a point contact transistor—a germanium crystal touched by two gold-point contacts, or "cat's whiskers," just a fraction of a millimeter apart. The design was improved and announced to the world on June 26, 1948, and it was reported in the *New York Times* several days later. It was called a transistor because it acted as a resistor that could amplify electrical signals as they were transferred through it (transresistance). Applications were limited since each point contact transistor had slightly different electrical characteristics, and they were difficult to manufacture. In June 1950, Bardeen and Brattain received a patent for the point contact transistor.

In early 1948, a few weeks after Bardeen and Brattain's announcement, William Shockley developed the concept of the junction transistor, an electrical sandwich of sorts in which a thin layer of electrically positive germanium is sandwiched between two electrically negative ends or vice versa, i.e. junction transistors could be positive-negative-positive (pnp) or negative-positive-negative (npn) germanium. The electronic properties of semiconductors were tailored by the inclusion of small, controlled amounts of impurities. Positive material was doped with group 3 atoms with fewer electrons than pure germanium; negative material was doped with group 5 atoms and had more electrons than pure germanium. Shockley filed for a patent on the junction transistor two weeks after Bardeen and Brattain applied for their patent, and he received it in September 1951.

With the invention of the transistor in 1948 at Bell Telephone Labs under the leadership of John Bardeen, Walter Brattain, and William Shockley, the world changed. For this invention they won the Nobel Prize in physics in 1956, joining two other electronics pioneers, Guglielmo Marconi and Karl Ferdinand Braun, who had won the Nobel Prize in physics in 1909 for their work in early radio. John Bardeen left Bell Labs in 1951 to join the University of Illinois. He also shared the 1972 Nobel Prize in physics for work on superconductivity, becoming the first person to win two Nobel physics prizes.

Experimental point contact transistors were soon being made in laboratories around the country. The transistor was a three-terminal, solid-state electronic device, in which current or voltage between two of the terminals could be controlled by sending a signal to the third terminal. In 1948, Raytheon introduced a point contact transistor, the CK 703, and in 1953, the first transistor sold to the public, the CK722, a germanium junction transistor. The early transistors sold for $6 to $25, when a vacuum tube sold for about $1. By 1955, however, prices for transistors had dropped significantly. Early transistors were made of crystalline semiconductor material, initially germanium, but in 1954, the first transistors were made from silicon. Throughout the early 1960s, most transistors in use were germanium, and more vacuum tubes were sold than transistors.

Initial point contact transistors were noisy and could not operate at frequencies higher than a few megacycles per second. But gradually, component performance improved. The earliest transistors had an average life of 70,000 hours, many times that of vacuum tubes, and reliability quickly improved even further. Unlike vacuum tubes, transistors were resistant to mechanical shock and vibration. Moreover, transistors operated more efficiently and used less power in circuit design, producing much less wasted heat, and consequently, equipment had no heating problems. Transistors did not have the warm-up time of a vacuum tube, which often had to have power continuously applied so the system was always ready to operate. Transistors were more efficient electronic devices and made more complex electronic systems possible.

Perhaps no scientific area had a greater influence on life in the second half of the twentieth century than the semiconductor industry. Its impact was widely felt in transportation, communications, medicine, manufacturing, and the information industries. Transistors were first used commercially in hearing aids and radios, applications for which their small size and lower weight were important. The first transistorized hearing aid was made available in 1952 by Sonotone and sold for $230. In October 1952, Bell put the first transistors in service as components in a direct-dial phone system in Englewood, New Jersey. Vacuum tube radios were big, often the largest piece of furniture in a living room. Regency made the first commercial transistorized radios in 1954 at a price of $49.95, using transistors made by a small Dallas company, Texas Instruments. Transistorized radios from RCA and Philco soon followed. In the ensuing years, many transistorized portable radios were made. There were 15 million car radios in 1950, all made with vacuum tubes, and 40 million by 1960, many transistorized. Early transistors were also used in calculators. The first electronic handheld calculators were developed in the 1960s—first relay-based calculators by Casio, then transistorized ones by Sharp, Wang Laboratories, Texas Instruments, and Hewlett-Packard. Size and price came down and performance improved.

In 1954, a small Japanese company, Tokyo Tsushin Kyogo, the Tokyo Telecommunications Engineering Corporation, licensed the Bell Labs and Western Electric patents for making transistors. In August 1955, the company, now renamed Sony, took the design of the Regency Radio, improved it, and made the TR-55, its first pocket radio. The following year, Sony made the TR-72, TR-6, and TR-63. In 1957, the latter was introduced around the world and became a major success. The radio had six transistors, leather case, battery, and earphone. Under the leadership of Akio Morita, Sony soon became the leader in small radios with the TR-620 and other models. By 1985, Sony had 44,000 employees, revenues of $6.7 billion, and profits of $669 million. It became a leader in producing audio equipment, televisions, video equipment, and semiconductors.

In 1955, William Shockley left Bell Labs for California and started Shockley Semiconductor Laboratory, funded by Arnold Beckman of Beckman Instruments. Shockley hired many of the most talented scientists in the country. He wanted to be near Stanford University, where he had graduated, encouraged in part by Professor Frederick Terman, who had supported Hewlett-Packard and Varian as well as other startups in what later came to be called Silicon Valley. Shockley Semiconductor had a short life as an organization and was sold to Clevite Transistor in April 1960.

Shockley made the key decision to use silicon rather than germanium as the base material and to use diffusion rather than alloying as the key fabrication technology. He ruled with an erratic hand, was a difficult person to work for, and his personality drove eight of the brightest people out of Shockley Semiconductor, including Gordon Moore, Bob Noyce, Eugene Kleiner, and Jay Last. Together, they founded Fairchild Semiconductor, financed by Fairchild Camera and Instrument, which was working in missile and satellite systems and owned by Sherman Fairchild. Fairchild started as a manufacturer of silicon diffused transistors and over the next several decades became one of the leading semiconductor companies.

Texas Instruments was founded in 1941 as Geophysical Services. In 1950, its revenue reached $7.6 million. In 1952, the company entered the semiconductor business and was soon renamed Texas Instruments. It bought a license from Bell Labs and in 1954 began to mass-produce germanium transistors. The company introduced the first silicon transistors, which could perform at higher temperatures and were ideal for military and space use.

Motorola also entered the semiconductor business in the early 1950s, producing audio power transistors for its automobile radios and military communication systems. Within a few years, Motorola introduced transistorized walkie-talkies and later portable cellular radio-telephones, leading to today's pagers and cell phones. Another early company was National Semiconductor founded in Danbury, Connecticut, in 1959 by six former Sperry Rand engineers. In 1965, it opened a facility in Santa Clara, California, and became a major player. Other early semiconductor manufacturers included CBS, Clevite, General Electric Labs, General Transistor, Germanium Products, National Union, Philco, Radio Receptor, Raytheon, RCA, Sylvania, Transitron, and Western Electric. Early Japanese firms included Hitachi, NEC, and Sony. By the early 1960s, transistors were available in both germanium and silicon. They were manufactured and sold as amplifiers and switches to companies that assembled them in circuits and equipment.

There were major developments in manufacturing technology during the transistor's early years. Early point contact transistors were expensive to make and were replaced by junction transistors. Semiconductor firms tried various designs including alloy junction, alloy diffused, surface barrier and mesa transistors. By laying patterns over the crystal, parts of the crystal could be etched away and impurities added where needed. A raised surface, or mesa, stuck up as depressions were etched into the germanium or silicon. In 1959, Fairchild developed the planar process in which the silicon surface was entirely flat, allowing for the silicon to grow an insulating silicon dioxide film on its surface. Transistors were no longer made individually but in batches through an optical lithography technique. In 1962, RCA introduced metal oxide semiconductor field effect transistors, which were easier to make, and in time, became the preferred manufacturing method. In 1963, Fairchild introduced the 907 diode transistor logic and later National Semiconductor and Sylvania introduced transistor-transistor logic, in which the transistor performed logic functions. Meanwhile, yields were increasing, costs were coming down, and individual transistor performance was improving. Computer-aided design made the development of Fairchild chips faster and more reliable and became essential for the development of future sophisticated semiconductors.

The semiconductor industry reached $100 million in sales in 1957 and $1 billion in sales in 1964. The years between 1948 and 1968 were challenging for those who designed circuits, systems, and equipment. Originally, designs that had worked with vacuum tubes were modified for transistors, and new circuit configurations were developed. To use early semiconductors, electronics engineers designed circuits with transistors, diodes, resistors, capacitors, inductors, delay lines, and other devices to perform the functions they wanted and then soldered them together on circuit boards. From the early 1950s until the end of the 1960s, circuit designers learned how to use transistors for the gates, flip-flops, amplifiers, oscillators, and other electronic functions that previously had been performed by vacuum tubes. Because of the transistor's capabilities, designers were able to create better circuits at lower prices. First the germanium transistor replaced the vacuum tube, next, silicon transistor replaced the germanium transistor, thin film and other technology was used for miniaturization, and then integrated circuit replaced individual transistors and components.[6] By 1970, circuit technology had stabilized and the major advances since then have been in the size, cost, and component density on a silicon chip, from individual transistors to a few hundred transistors in the mid-1960s to many millions today. This improvement in cost and performance in the semiconductor industry led to the rapid expansion of the computer and communication industries over the last decades of the twentieth century.

For many of us who were circuit designers during the third quarter of the twentieth century, an annual pilgrimage was necessary to visit Phoenix (Motorola), Dallas (Texas Instruments), and the San Francisco Bay Area (Fairchild, National, Intel, and others) in order to learn the latest technology. As computers, television, special systems, and other products became more complicated, engineers were puzzling over the "tyranny of numbers"—the large number of electronic components needed for sophisticated products. They needed better, smaller, and more reliable building blocks.

In July 1958, Jack St. Claire Kilby, an electronics engineer at Texas Instruments, conceived what has been called the "monolithic idea," or integrated circuit, where multiple components could be integrated on a single semiconductor chip. His first design on a germanium wafer was an oscillator that converted direct current into alternating current with wires connecting various parts of the silicon. An integrated circuit (chip) is a wafer of material to which impurities have been added in the right patterns so that the entire chip is a circuit made up of many transistors, diodes, and resistors all etched into it at once and interconnected. Kilby, who owns more than sixty patents, won the Nobel Prize in physics in 2000 for his invention of the integrated circuit.

In 1959, Robert Noyce, working independently, had the same idea, and his microchip design was the first to use silicon with evaporated interconnections. Kilby's patent was first by five months over Noyce's, but they both deserve equal credit for this major innovation. The importance of this watershed development was not recognized at the time, in part because transistor yields were so low that is seemed impossible to contemplate building an array of any size. Nevertheless, over the next decade, Fairchild and Texas Instruments led the way and developed the commercial production and application of the integrated circuit, or microchip—the incredible miniaturized electronic circuit produced on a single crystal of silicon. Costs came down and applications increased as microelectronics revolutionized the computer and electronics industries.

Perhaps no man was more central to the changing world of semiconductor technology than Bob Noyce. Born in Burlington, Iowa, Noyce received his bachelor's degree from Grinnell College in 1949 and his Ph.D. in physical electronics from MIT in 1953. He was a research engineer for Philco in Philadelphia where he helped to develop germanium transistors when he flew out to California to ask Shockley for a job. He and others built the semiconductor industry. In 1957, Noyce helped to found Fairchild Semiconductor and was its general manager for six years. Gordon Moore was head of research and development and led the company forward. Fairchild, along with Texas Instruments, National Semiconductor, Signetics, and Motorola changed the world, as transistors, integrated circuits, and microprocessors became the building blocks of the information age.

Frustrated with Fairchild's communication breakdowns and poor decisions by its parent company, Noyce, Gordon Moore, and Andy Grove left Fairchild and founded Integrated Electronics (Intel) in July 1968. Bob Noyce became its chairman and Moore became head of research and development. Intel went on to become the world's leading semiconductor firms, thanks to its continued technological innovation and manufacturing capability. Intel was a high capacity producer of computer chips, including the first dynamic random-access memory. These semiconductor memory chips had their first widespread application in computers in the early 1970s and ultimately replaced other types of computer main memories.

In his later life, Noyce worked to improve the competitiveness of the U.S. semiconductor industry. In the 1980s, the Japanese manufacturers, with major government and company support, passed the U.S. manufacturers in semiconductor sales volume. If American companies had cooperated, however, they might have been in violation of U.S. antitrust laws. Then, in 1984, Congress passed the Cooperative Research Act, which enabled a new entity, SEMATECH, to fund university research for industry members. SEMATECH, formed in 1987, was a consortium of more than fourteen companies, formed to help U.S. chipmakers overtake Japan in semiconductor manufacturing. Bob Noyce became SEMATECH's president in 1988. The United States retook the lead from the Japanese in semiconductor volume in 1993 and has maintained it since. Among numerous awards, Noyce received the Charles Stark Draper Prize from the National Academy of Engineering for his work on the integrated circuit. Bob Noyce died of heart failure in 1990 at the age of sixty-two.

Memories and Microprocessors

To illustrate more completely the development and expansion of the semiconductor industry, it is helpful to describe three activities. The first is semiconductor memory, the second is the microprocessor, and the third is the building of many semiconductor firms, especially in northern California, which in many cases were offshoots of Fairchild and therefore of Shockley Semiconductor.

In these days of personal computers with 250 million bytes or more of main memory, it is difficult to remember that early computers had 4,000 to 8,000 bytes of storage. (For that story, see chapter 9.) What follows is a description of the semiconductor industry and its influence on storage in computers and communications.

Early computers used magnetic core memories for storage. Cores were made individually, as were the first transistors, and were then strung together in arrays. Cores were fast, inexpensive, and performed the job well. But it was impossible to get the cost of computers below a certain point because the costs of core memories and of circuitry could not be decreased. From the 1970s to the 1980s, semiconductor memories were to replace core memories.

Information could be stored in individual flip-flop circuits that stored one bit of memory, in core memories that stored thousands of bits, or on magnetic tape or discs that could store millions of bits of information but which were relatively slow. The first commercial semiconductor memory was the Fairchild 4100, a 256-bit static random-access memory introduced in 1970 that provided comparable performance to core memories but at a significantly higher cost. When Intel was founded, its initial product focus was on semiconductor memories. In its first two years, it produced a 64-bit static memory, the 3101, and a 256-bit memory, the 1101. It was hoped that the advantages of semiconductor memories—smaller size, lower power consumption, and greater performance— would compensate for their higher costs.

Semiconductor memories really started to develop when the Intel 1103 was introduced in 1970. The 1103 was the first 1,024-bit dynamic random-access memory. A dynamic memory requires regular refreshing of the chip to boost the charge in the memory cells, but system designers learned to design computer memories around this limitation. Over the following decades, memory capacity of a chip increased while the cost declined. In 1976, Mostek introduced the 4116, a 16,000-bit dynamic random-access memory; in 1977, IBM developed the first 65,536-bit dynamic memory, which was used in IBM's computers; and in 1981, IBM introduced a 294,912 dynamic random-access memory. Today, a memory chip might store 32 million bits and cost about $2, and computers that cost less than $1,000 are available with 250 million bytes (each of 8 bits) of main memory.

Over time, more and more transistors could be placed on a piece of silicon. This development was possible due to an increase in the silicon wafer's size from less than one inch in diameter to eight or more inches, and also to the decrease in line width of the smallest dimensions that could be fabricated in silicon. Sizes also decreased as a result of better design and manufacturing technology, which effect diffusion, the oxide masking process, lithography and etching, and therefore the separation of semiconductor regions. On April 19, 1965, Gordon Moore, a founder of both Fairchild and Intel, presented a paper in *Electronics* magazine about the future of the semiconductor industry. In what came to be known as Moore's Law, he pointed out that the number of transistors on a piece of silicon had doubled every year while the price remained the same. He predicted that 65,000 components would someday be created on a silicon chip. Although progress later slowed to doubling every eighteen months, this law has remained true for forty years and explains both the tremendous improvement in semiconductor performance and decrease in cost. Starting at a few dollars per transistor in the early 1950s, today the same amount will buy several million transistors. From an average of fifty elements on a chip in 1965, the number has increased significantly. In no area is this more apparent than that of microprocessors.

In 1969, Busicom, a Japanese calculator company, asked Intel to design a variety of chips for their new calculators. Marcian (Ted) Hoff, a young engineer at Intel, was assigned to work on the project and developed the first microcomputer, or microprocessor. Instead of developing many semiconductor chips, each to perform a specific function such as input, instructions, calculation, and storage with all chips interconnected externally, Huff designed a small computer and programmed it to act like a calculator. Intel reduced the chips to four, a read-only semiconductor memory, a small random-access memory, a shift register, and a microprocessor. The result was the Intel 4004, a 4-bit microprocessor, with 2,300 transistors on a chip introduced in 1971. This development made it possible to include data-processing capability in thousands of applications for the first time. The microprocessor was a complete computer central processor on a single integrated circuit or chip. Today, microprocessors are in computers, cars, phones, watches, games, and even appliances as costs continue to decline and performance improves.

The ENIAC, one of the first early computers, described in chapter 9, had about 18,000 vacuum tubes. That number of active switches was soon exceeded by the new microprocessors. In 1972, Intel introduced the 8008, an 8-bit microprocessor with 3,300 MOS transistors. This was followed in 1974 by the Intel 8080, an 8-bit general-purpose microprocessor. Texas Instruments offered the TMS 1000, a system that did not need memory or input/output chips, and was used in calculators, games, toys, and appliances. Within a few years, more than 100 million of these chips had been sold. National Semiconductor introduced the PACE, a 16-bit microprocessor, and Signetics introduced the 2650, an 8-bit processor used extensively in video games. Zilog offered the Z-80, an 8-bit microprocessor, and Motorola the 68000 16-bit microprocessor used widely in industrial control applications. Hewlett-Packard offered a 32-bit microprocessor, as did Motorola with its 68000 and National Semiconductor with the 16000.

To give an indication of how fast the industry developed, it is useful to examine the products of one company. In 1978, Intel introduced the 8086, a 16-bit processor with 29,000 transistors, more electronic power than was in the ENIAC computer and significantly faster than the ENIAC at a tiny fraction of the cost. In 1982, the Intel 286 had 134,000 transistors and ran at twelve megacycles. In 1985, the Intel 386 had 275,000 transistors and ran at thirty-three megacycles, followed in 1989 by the Intel 486, which had 1.2 million transistors and ran at fifty megacycles. In 1993, Intel introduced the Pentium processor with 3.1 million transistors. Two years later, the Intel Pentium Pro had 5.5 million transistors and ran at 200 megacycles, followed in 1999 by the Intel Pentium 3, which had 28 million transistors and ran at 733 megacycles.

For forty years, one innovation has led to another in the semiconductor industry, and costs have decreased while performance has increased. New companies changed the world as transistors, integrated circuits, and microprocessors became the building blocks of the information age, reducing size and power and increasing reliability.

This continued improvement in performance had major advantages for customers. Every few years, they could purchase significantly more computer power at the same or a lower price. But semiconductor companies, with their revenue per function declining, had to run very fast to stay in the race. All the winners have had increased revenues despite the fact that the cost of keeping up with the technology kept increasing.

When Fairchild was started in 1957, the eight founders invested $3,500 of their own money, and Fairchild Camera invested $1.5 million to enter the semiconductor business. By 1980, a vice president of Texas Instruments stated that it cost $40 million to set up a new manufacturing line.[7] Today, a semiconductor plant can cost more than $1 billion to establish. Clearly, the cost of entry has gone up.

This increase, however, has not stopped companies from entering the semiconductor business. There are many companies that were founded by Fairchild alumni (sometimes called Fairchildren) or by alumni of these companies. Estimates of the number of these range from 50 to more than 125 enterprises, and they include Advance Micro Devices (AMD), Cirrus Logic, Computer Microtechnology, Four Phase, Intel, Linear Technology, LSI Logic, National Semiconductor, Sierra Semiconductor, Signetics, VLSI Technology, and Zilog. Each of these companies, founded by entrepreneurs, created jobs.

Furthermore, a number of established semiconductor companies expanded: General Instruments, Harris, Motorola, RCA, Sylvania, and Texas Instruments. In addition, a number of new firms entered the business: American Microsystems, Analog Devices, Intersil, Linear Technology, Mitel, Micron Technology, Monolithic Memories, Mostek, Nvidia, Siliconix, Solectron, Solid State Scientific, and Vishay Intertechnology. At the same time, the Japanese and Europeans invested heavily in building their semiconductor industries. Major companies include Fujitsu, Hitachi, NEC, Philips, Siemens, and Toshiba. The Japanese success in consumer electronics was based in large part on their ability to mass-produce transistors. Meanwhile, some major American companies, including AT&T, Digital Equipment, General Electric, Hewlett-Packard, Raytheon, and especially IBM built all or many of their semiconductor devices. Digital Equipment invested heavily in semiconductors, and their 64-bit Alpha product line processed 10 million transistors on a thin wafer chip. IBM also provided major capability in their microprocessors and semiconductor memories.

While some companies grew greatly in this environment—Intel's revenue reached $4.8 billion in 1991, $11.5 billion in 1994, and $25 billion in 1997—

some companies did not grow and folded or were sold to international companies. Worldwide semiconductor revenues reached $200 billion in 1990. New companies entered the business and old ones left. This has been an exciting and challenging business, and management's understanding, leadership, and a little luck has been required for success.

In all businesses, product development, marketing and sales capability, and production issues are at the heart of the corporate strategy. But these issues are more important in the semiconductor industry than in almost any other. Success in the semiconductor industry is a by-product of taking chances. Calculated risks have been essential, and many older semiconductor companies failed because they could not make decisions fast enough to keep up.

Product and market identification is difficult in a fast-growing and changing world. Simply because the scientists and engineers can do something does not mean that it should be done or, if it is, that customers will purchase the product. Change is difficult for many, especially in large organizations, and large organizations have been the market for many products.

The semiconductor industry has influenced and benefited from the entrepreneurs who have established other industries. It is no coincidence that the growth of the semiconductor industry has coincided with the establishment of new organizations in communications, computers, entertainment, networks, multimedia, wireless, and many other areas.

There have been many advances in semiconductors during the last several decades. More transistors have been placed on a silicon chip, and the transistors use less power, are faster, and cost less. Yields of good units have grown from perhaps less than 10 percent of the chips manufactured in the early years to more than 80 percent today. Machines rather than people now handle the wafers, and automation isolates workers from physical and chemical hazards. Through the use of computer-aided design, productivity has improved but it is just keeping up with increased complexity and microprocessor performance.

But none of this matters if the chip design does not meet a need, is priced too high, or if the intended market doesn't develop. The choice of which products to develop or acquire is very important, but so are production considerations. Long-term planning is required for manufacturing capability. Factories have to be planned several years in advance. Capacity has to be built with a long lead time, and by then demand for a product may be greater or less than the supply. Moreover, there are semiconductor capacity cycles. Strong demands can lead to capacity overexpansion. There are marketing and economic cycles in which customer issues lead to a drop in demand for chips. For example, downturns in demand in 1985 and in 2001 resulted in industry excess capacity, with many companies losing significant amounts of money. Or, a company might be developing chips for the game or cellular phone market and those particular games or phones then go out of fashion. Timing is everything.

The semiconductor industry is a voracious consumer of money. Money is required for increasing factory capacity and for product development. Consequently, these companies have high fixed costs. There is initial pricing to stimulate new markets, with pricing of initial units below costs, hoping that volume increases and experience can result in very substantial reductions in manufacturing costs. A manufacturer will cut prices at the right time to stimulate demand and try to have their chips designed into their customer's high-volume products. Sale of a few thousand devices doesn't help with semiconductor manufacturing costs. The goal is to sell chips in the millions. The industry focuses on technical literature and advertising to convince the design engineers that this new chip is the major chip for the next decade. In short, the industry sometimes has to innovate to continue to exist. Some firms have had good growth with poor or no profits. They can't survive a semiconductor capacity or customer marketing downturn. An industry downsizing leads to consolidation or companies closing their doors. In 1985, Intel had fourteen strong competitors in the microprocessor industry. Today, there are only a few.

Nevertheless, new companies have entered the semiconductor industry and have provided excellent and needed products—in semiconductor storage devices; for cell phones; in communication and networking products; in digital cameras, watches, and games; in entertainment; in 3-D graphic capability; in analog circuits; in radio frequency and wireless integrated circuits; in power circuitry; in sensors and discrete devices; and in specialized circuitry for a variety of customers. Semiconductors have also moved into auto controls and displays and are moving into biomedical sensing. Most of these applications were not possible a few decades ago. Other companies have been organized to serve the semiconductor companies and have achieved large sales volume through manufacturing systems for processing silicon wafers, process control and yield management, outsourcing packaging, and test equipment. Other organizations have been established as manufacturing companies that interconnect semiconductor products into configurations required by their customers. In that role, they are performing the function of a module supplier as did Digital Equipment Company and Computer Control Company (described in chapters 9 and 10)—except with bigger building blocks.

Electronics and Twenty-First Century America

Semiconductors have had impact in transportation, communications, medicine, manufacturing and the computer/information industry.

There are millions of transistors for every person in the world, but that is like saying that in 1900, there were so many hundred pounds of steel for every American. The real issues are how silicon affects our lives and what the future holds.

Certainly, this is a semiconductor world. Radio, television, and entertainment have gone digital, and the entertainment technology of the mid-twentieth century is no more. Now, it is a world of Web radios, DVDs, music downloads, movies on demand from satellites billed to our accounts, and television news from around the world, available anywhere, anytime. None of this would have been possible without the advances in semiconductors, including microprocessors.

One hundred years ago, a phone call required an operator to manually plug in connections. First, there were mechanic switchboards and routing systems, then telephone networks went digital, and finally, cellular phones and the Internet became possible with semiconductor advances. Today, it is an integrated world where digital, audio, and video data can be communicated to anyone, anywhere. E-mail is automatically routed to the addressee without knowing where the person resides.

Advances in computers, typewriters, word processors, and personal computers and the impact of semiconductors in these areas are described in chapter 9. But it is sufficient to say here that the sheer volume of computers and power would not be possible without advances in the semiconductor industry.

Process control in petroleum, paper, plastics, metals, textiles, glass, beverages, food, and other substances and the manufacturing of parts made from all sorts of material would be different if not for advances in electronics. Controllers, signal sensing devices, analog integrated circuits, operational amplifiers, and other electronic advances have changed the way manufacturing processes are monitored and things are made. The machine tool industry, which Ken Olsen's father encouraged him to enter, bears little resemblance to that of the 1940s, due in part to the work of Ken Olsen at Digital Equipment Corporation and others.

Americans also face the impact of electronics in daily interactions with the retail industry. Fast-food restaurants now use electronic cash registers. Digital scales and electronic scanning in supermarkets establish not only customer bills but provide point of sale and inventory control information to headquarters as well as providing information on consumer buying habits. Most people use ATMs for banking. Data is gathered, communicated, and analyzed. Magnetic ink characters were put on checks in 1958, magnetic strip credit cards were introduced in 1968, and bar code readers in supermarkets in 1990. This world is wildly different from that of fifty years ago.

This section will close with two industries everyone interacts with—transportation and health care—and look at how electronics has affected both. The design and operation of automobiles are quite different from the world of Henry Ford. Today's automobiles are designed using computer-aided design (CAD) and computer-aided manufacturing (CAM). Use of CAD and CAM means that alternative designs can be evaluated and cars can be manufactured more efficiently and to greater tolerance.

Whereas once the future of the automobile and the steel industry were interdependent, today the automobile and electronics are interdependent. Perhaps 20 percent of car cost is now in electronics, for communication, controllers, sensors, and subsystems. Trends in automobile electronics are now the subject of international engineering conferences, and auto manufacturers, including BMW, Ford, DaimlerChrysler, General Motors, and Toyota, have electronic Web sites. Whereas once almost every part of a car's performance was manual or mechanical, today many are electronic, as those who try to tune their cars themselves quickly find out.

Electronic sensors measure those items that impact an auto's performance and efficiency. Semiconductors keep continual records of auto performance and problems, and a trained technician can use them to look at the car's history and performance. Microprocessors measure and control electrical distribution, battery management, electrical power systems, energy storage, enhanced power steering and control, heating and cooling controls, valve lift, clutch motion, turbocharger speed, power trains, and emission post treatment. System performance is adjusted as required.

The driver has digital processing of radio, mobile telephone, navigation, and even control information on mileage efficiency, miles to an empty tank, the status of all liquids, pressures and tires, distance covered, and perhaps distance to the destination and what restaurants are on the way. Automobiles today may have better navigation help than was available to ships and planes during World War II.

The trip home may now be smoother. Control of traffic lights has gone digital, detecting the number of waiting cars and adjusting signals accordingly. None of this would be possible without advances in semiconductors.

In the early twentieth century, steam, electricity, and gasoline competed as power sources for automobiles. Now, 100 years later, electric automobiles and hybrids are once again being considered and built.

Significant advances have also occurred in medicine. The most obvious area is in patient recordkeeping. Medical information and patient information, including medical history, drugs prescribed, and possible complications, are now available to doctors, nurses, and other health professionals through computer terminals.

But it is in the less obvious areas that the most medical advances have occurred. Doctors once listened to a patient's heart and made a diagnosis. They might have listened to the heart before and after exercise and stress tests. Now the cardiologist can watch videotape of a patient's heart. Magnetic resonance imaging, remote pressure monitoring, and enhanced EKG devices monitor present and past heart measurements. Electronic pacemakers can adjust the heart's performance.

Many other electronic systems assist the physician in diagnosis. They include ultrasound to detect abnormal blood flows, diagnostic imaging for evaluating breast cancer and other diseases, patient monitoring systems such as those in maternity and geriatric wards, microelectronic sensors, and image archives. Treatment can range from programmable insulin delivery systems to electronic pacemakers. Patients can be monitored in the doctor's office, the hospital, or the home. Electronic hearing aids and optical reading programs for the blind help thousands.

Many medical schools and universities now offer courses in medical electronics, a field that was unknown a few decades ago. There are significant numbers of companies doing research and developing products in this new field.

Semiconductor advances have affected most professions, from education to insurance to agriculture to journalism to the design of appliances and equipment. Advances in the electronic field have changed how people live.

The last forty years have been exceptional in terms of semiconductor performance, cost, and application. This has been due not only to the imagination and capabilities of those in the semiconductor industry, but also to their customers, many of whom were not in business a half century ago.

Whether the next few decades will see continued improvements and growth or whether the semiconductor industry, like the steel industry, will have peaked as the demand for their products stops growing, is something for a future historian to discuss.

CHAPTER 8

David Sarnoff (1891–1971)
The Practical Dreamer

New opinions are always suspected, and usually opposed, without any reason but because they are not already common.
—John Locke

Never tell people how to do things. Tell them what to do and they will surprise you with their ingenuity.
—General George Patton

D avid Sarnoff was involved in the founding of two industries— radio and television—which had major influence on all Americans. Both required not only technical vision but also the ability to imagine a system approach to a new way of living.

Biography

David Sarnoff was born on February 27, 1891, in Uzlian, Russia, a small Jewish village, or *shtetl*, southeast of Minsk, and now a part of Belarus. David was the oldest of five children, four boys and a girl, the first three born in Russia. Their father, Abraham, was a housepainter and paperhanger. Their mother, Leah Privkin Sarnoff, was a descendant of a long line of rabbis. Russian villages were cold, impoverished, and isolated. Peasants were the majority of the population, and the Jews were at the bottom of the economy, opposed by the government, the Cossacks, and the other peasants. There was little hope for advancement. When David was five, Abraham Sarnoff left for the United States with hope for a better life, planning to send for the family when he was settled.

After his father left, David's mother sent him to the remote village of Korme to live with a granduncle, Rabbi Schlomme Elkind, and study to be a Jewish scholar. The young Sarnoff spent four years studying the Talmud in Aramaic and

209

the prophets in Hebrew. He memorized several thousand words every day. Life was a serious affair, never to be wasted. David learned intellectual discipline and developed an outstanding memory.

It took four years for Abraham to save the $144 to bring his wife and three sons, David, Morris, and Lew, to the United States. In 1900, the family followed Abraham to America. To minimize costs, the four members of the Sarnoff family took a train trip from Minsk to the port of Libau on the Baltic Sea, got on a boat to Liverpool, England, were in steerage on the 3,000-mile trip to Montreal, then took a train to Albany, New York, and went down the Hudson by steamboat to New York City. They settled in a tenement on New York City's Lower East Side.

In the decade between 1900 and 1910, 8,795,000 immigrants came to the United States, the most in any decade in American history. They joined the 76 million Americans listed in the 1900 census, and by 1910, 14.7 percent, or one in seven, of the total U.S. population was foreign born. Many were Jewish, as almost 2 million people immigrated from eastern Europe to the United States in the forty years between 1890 and 1930. Many immigrants headed west to new jobs in steel, railroads, or factories or to become farmers on the available land.

When he was nine years old, David Sarnoff faced the challenge most immigrants faced—how to help provide some financial support for the family and to learn English. His father was ill and much of the family's money was earned by Leah Sarnoff and her oldest son.

Each morning, David Sarnoff sold Yiddish-language newspapers, and within four years, he had his own newsstand in the Hell's Kitchen section of New York. He also earned money singing in his synagogue choir. Young David enrolled in night classes for immigrants at the Educational Alliance, where he studied English and public speaking. In June 1906, he graduated from the eighth grade.

His father continued to be in bad health and soon died of consumption. At sixteen, David became the family provider and needed a job with a regular paycheck. His first employment was with the Commercial Cable Company, the American arm of a British company that had undersea cables to London, Paris, and Rome. David was a messenger boy, delivering cablegrams around Manhattan. He also practiced with a telegraph key. However, Sarnoff was fired when he took time off on a Jewish holiday to sing in the synagogue choir.

Sarnoff's career in the next few years was strangely similar to that of Andrew Carnegie. Both men learned to send and receive telegraph signals, learned aspects of business as they worked, and became protégés of business leaders—in Carnegie's case, Thomas Scott and in Sarnoff's, Guglielmo Marconi.

In September 1899, Guglielmo Marconi had arrived in New York with his invention, a wireless telegraph capable of sending messages from ship to ship and from ship to shore. Although Marconi was born and raised in Italy, he started his Wireless Telegraph Company in England since he couldn't get financing in his home country. Telephone and telegraph were dependent on where wires could be laid. They obviously couldn't be laid at sea, and so the new technology of radio was essential if contact was to be made with a ship. In 1900, two ships, the *Republic* and the *Florida*, collided in a fog off New York. One thousand six hundred and fifty passengers were saved when another ship, the *Baltic*, received an SOS distress signal. By 1903, Marconi was able to transmit radio signals across the Atlantic Ocean. By 1914, naval transmitters were sending signals around the world.

On September 30, 1906, David Sarnoff joined the Marconi Wireless Telegraph Company of America as an office boy. He had many jobs, including cleaning the office, administrative duties, organizing the payroll, and scheduling the staff. He learned everything he could about the business, and also about Guglielmo Marconi.

In December 1906, Marconi came into the New York office, and Sarnoff met him. Thereafter, Sarnoff was Marconi's errand boy whenever he was in town. Sarnoff soon became a junior telegraph operator at a salary of $7.50 per week and took advantage of every opportunity to improve his telegraphic skills. In 1908, he became a telegraph operator at the Marconi station in Nantucket. In 1909, he was sent to Coney Island, where he received messages for the Marconi ship-to-shore installation. In 1911, Sarnoff served as wireless operator and ship's officer on the SS *Beothic* out of Newfoundland for a seal hunting expedition to the Arctic ice fields. He also served for a time on the SS *Harvard*. Later, he helped establish radio communications with railroad trains on the Erie Lackawanna line.

In 1910, the John Wanamaker Company wanted to install Marconi wireless stations atop their Philadelphia and New York department stores. Sarnoff worked days as a telegraph operator at Wanamaker and as Marconi's personal errand boy when Marconi was in town. In addition to his workload, Sarnoff took evening courses in electrical engineering at Pratt Institute.

On April 12, 1912, the British ship *Titanic* hit an iceberg and sank, killing 1,517 people. David Sarnoff was the manager of the Wanamaker station when they picked up news of the *Titanic* from rescue ships. Over the next days, the station received the names of survivors and relayed them to anxious relatives waiting for word of their loved ones. As a result of their help in the disaster's aftermath, David Sarnoff and Marconi received a great deal of positive attention. The U.S. government now realized the importance of radio telegraphs on all ships and soon required wireless communication on all large passenger ships. Because of the publicity he received for his help with the *Titanic* disaster, Sarnoff was promoted to radio inspector and an instructor at the Marconi Institute. He also became the commercial manager of Marconi. In 1916, Sarnoff proposed to Marconi's president a "radio music box," suggesting that radios be used to broadcast music and information to many receivers at different locations instead of using them only as point-to-point communicators. But he was ahead of his time, and the idea was ignored.

Sarnoff next became chief engineer for Marconi and was responsible for procuring technology for the company. He read voraciously from all the technical journals he could find. He continued to take correspondence courses, and from 1915 to 1918, he was the secretary of the Institute of Radio Engineers.

On July 4, 1917, David Sarnoff married Lizette Hermant, a vivacious blonde who had been born in Paris and had recently emigrated from France. The couple had three sons, Robert in 1918, Edward in 1921, and Thomas in 1927.

Marconi's business boomed during the World War I. American Marconi got orders from the U.S. Navy to send messages to its fleet and sold radios for naval communications. The navy believed it should control the radio world.

Prior to World War I, most radio consisted of Morse code messages to and from ships and of trans-Atlantic signals. When war started in 1914, the British cut all undersea cables between Germany and the United States and radio became the only way to communicate. During World War I, the U.S. government took over all radio telemetry. The navy also nationalized all amateur and commercial radio stations not belonging to the army signal corps and shut many of them down. The war convinced Assistant Secretary of the Navy Franklin Delano Roosevelt that American radio patents should be under U.S. control, and during the war, there was a moratorium on new patents for radio.

The navy saw the virtue of monopoly and, after the war, wanted to maintain control of the radio industry. The navy wanted the government to control American overseas communications. Congress wanted it returned to private industry.

In 1919, General Electric received several orders from British Marconi to purchase electronic equipment. Owen D. Young, vice president and general counsel of General Electric, notified the navy of his intention to sell alternators and vacuum tubes to Britain. The U.S. government didn't want radio under the control of a foreign government and forbade General Electric to sell the equipment to Marconi. General Electric was then asked to take over the lead in developing an American radio company.

On October 17, 1919, Radio Corporation of America (RCA) was incorporated in the state of Delaware as a wholly owned General Electric subsidiary to hold and license radio and communication patents. The navy was willing to put its patents and those of General Electric into a new company since it wished to counter the United Kingdom's domination of worldwide communications. To the navy, the virtue of a monopoly in international radio communications was obvious.

General Electric then bought Marconi Wireless Company of America from Marconi's Wireless Telegraph Company and transferred the ownership to Radio Corporation of America. The staff of American Marconi was also transferred to RCA. Owen D. Young became chairman of the board while continuing as a General Electric vice president, Edward Nally was named president, and David Sarnoff became commercial manager. The new company acquired some radio stations and hundreds of installations on ships. RCA also inherited the ship-to-shore business and started transoceanic radio service.

Young believed that battles over patents would slow the development of radio. He decided to move RCA into domestic telegraphy. At the request of the government, AT&T received stock in RCA for transferring their radio patents. Westinghouse didn't want to be a passive observer and gave all its radio patents and licenses to RCA. In return, Westinghouse got 40 percent of RCA's receiver manufacturing for RCA and General Electric received 60 percent. The company soon owned the radio patents of General Electric, AT&T, Westinghouse, and United Fruit Company. By March 1921, General Electric owned 30.1 percent of RCA, Westinghouse 20.6 percent, AT&T 10.3 percent, and United Fruit 4.1 percent, with the remainder in investors' hands. AT&T was to concentrate on radio-telephone systems and toll customers while making some equipment, GE and Westinghouse on making radio receivers, and RCA's Marconi unit on wireless spark technology. RCA would also be the marketing outlet for radio receivers but was forbidden to manufacture them.

David Sarnoff in 1921 became general manager of Radio Corporation of America at a salary of $15,000. He became president in 1930 and chief executive officer in 1947. Throughout this period, the company expanded and became a dominant force in the communications world.

RCA made money from the sale of patent rights and technology. More than 75 percent of the radios built in 1922 and 1923 were from competitors, and some of them seemed to be infringing on RCA's patents. RCA did not have the freedom of action of an independent company and was handicapped by its dependency on General Electric and Westinghouse for its manufacturing capability. In 1923, the government accused RCA of a monopoly because of its patent position. Many antitrust actions followed.

In the end, a Justice Department antitrust suit led the company to independence. The Federal Trade Commission accused RCA, AT&T, Westinghouse, and GE with creating a monopoly in the manufacture and sale of radio devices. In 1930, Sarnoff started to negotiate his way out from the manufacturing and financial control of General Electric and Westinghouse. The matter was settled with a consent decree in 1932 calling for RCA's divestiture from GE and license its patents to competitors. RCA was now free to manufacture its own sets and vacuum tubes.

Radio had started as a way of connecting two locations or two people together. As such, it was a natural outgrowth of the telegraph or telephone industries and was of interest to Western Union and AT&T. The customer knew whom he wanted to contact and was prepared to pay for the cost of the message. This business arrangement of two-way communication has been called "narrowcasting."

David Sarnoff and RCA

In 1916, Sarnoff had envisaged radio as "a household utility." Radio music boxes could be used for entertainment as music and voice were transmitted. But this vision required a number of simultaneous developments: radios owned by a large number of people, radio stations to supply signals, and programs to utilize this transmission capability. But who would develop these three aspects of "broadcasting," and who would pay for them? It was a completely new approach to a new business.

David Sarnoff had the capability to foretell new trends in technology. Shrewd, farsighted, and with an excellent memory, he could cut through technical and business jargon to the essence of an issue. Sarnoff saw the future of radio, the merging of the radio with the phonograph in a home entertainment center, network broadcasting, television, and the use of this electronic technology in the movie industry to create sound pictures.

RCA continued in marine radio and radiotelegraphy, where radio was confined mainly to dots and dashes. It maintained leadership in two-way radios, including ham radio, which enabled two people anywhere in the world to talk to one another. There were about 5,000 radio amateurs before World War I, and the number increased significantly afterward. RCA started long-distance communication in 1920. Messages were routinely sent to England, France, Germany, Norway, Hawaii, and Japan. Traffic expanded commercially during the 1920s, as worldwide radio became possible.

But it was the growth in home radio that made possible RCA's major advances. RCA started to market radios in 1922, and the use of radio sets grew rapidly.

Thomas Alva Edison constructed the first talking machine late in 1877, and over the following forty years, many improvements were made to the quality of recorded sound. American Gramophone Company started producing phonograph records in 1889. The National Gramophone Company followed, and both were acquired in 1901 when Eldridge Johnson founded the Victor Talking Machine Company and made the Victrola. In 1905, the success of the Victrola required furniture to house it, resulting in a state-of-the art cabinet factory in Camden, New Jersey. Those over the age of fifty recognize the symbol of the Victor Talking Machine Company of a small dog looking into a phonograph. The name of the dog was Nipper and through the 1950s, the RCA Camden employees' restaurant was called the Nipper Grill.

The 78 rpm record was developed in 1915. By the 1920s, Victor had to either start making its own radio receivers that also produced music and join the twenty-five leading radio manufacturers, or merge with another company. Owen Young supported the integration of Victor into RCA.

In 1929, RCA acquired the Victor Talking Machine Company and its Camden, New Jersey, plants. RCA owned 50 percent of the stock, GE 30 percent, and Westinghouse 20 percent. Someone then came up with the idea of combining radio and phonograph in one cabinet, resulting in the largest and most important piece of furniture in many American homes. The next few years witnessed the expansion of Radio Corporation of America from music boxes to radio network to motion pictures.

David Sarnoff returned to his earlier idea of radio broadcasting, and the company financed a number of experiments. It decided to create national broadcasts by stringing together hundreds of radio stations and to solve broadcasting problems by looking at a national rather than a regional solution. In the spring of 1923, station WJZ in New York City was transferred from Westinghouse to RCA. It had a small 500-watt transmitter and had a limited audience.

The National Broadcasting Company (NBC) was incorporated in 1926 to create a programming service that would increase RCA radio sales. NBC controlled radio stations owned by RCA, General Electric, Westinghouse, and AT&T and was owned 50 percent by RCA, 30 percent by GE, and 20 percent by Westinghouse. NBC originally had a separate board of directors, which included some people from Westinghouse and General Electric. For years, NBC was RCA's most profitable division.

Two RCA networks, the Red and the Blue, debuted on November 15, 1926. NBC soon had twenty-five stations nationwide and provided radio programs to other stations. It dominated broadcasting until the late 1940s. In 1941, the FCC ruled that RCA would have to get rid of one network. The Blue was sold to Edward J. Noble, president of LifeSavers Candy, and James McGraw, president of McGraw-Hill. Eventually, the Blue network became the American Broadcasting Company. In 1932, RCA moved its headquarters into Rockefeller Center, which became known as Radio City. On July 2, 1921, encouraged by Julius Hopp, manager of Madison Square Garden concerts, RCA aired a live boxing match from Jersey City between Jack Dempsey and Georges Carpentier, the first major sporting event in American radio history. It had hundreds of thousands of listeners. That year, the first World Series games were also broadcast. In 1926, John McCormack and Lucrezia Bori, stars of the Metropolitan Opera, made their debut on WBZ. In most cases, original performers were not paid and did programs for the prestige. The first Rose Bowl was covered nationally in 1927. In 1937, Arturo Toscanini came to the United States and performed exclusively for RCA. He led the NBC Symphony Orchestra on Christmas night, 1937. This program had one of the highest radio audiences in history.

Meanwhile, RCA was entering the world of motion pictures. In 1926, silent pictures became talkies. Soon thereafter RCA developed talking pictures with General Electric and Westinghouse. Joseph Kennedy (father of John Kennedy) owned Keith-Albee-Orpheum, a string of 200 theaters nationwide. David Sarnoff and Kennedy formed RKO (Radio-Keith-Orpheum) to introduce sound motion picture technology to movie audiences.

In 1930, David Sarnoff was made president of RCA. In May 1933, Owen D. Young retired as chairman and a director of RCA, which by then had become an independent company. General Electric no longer had a board role at RCA. It is worth adding here some information from the Radio Corporation of America's 1933 *Annual Report*.

> *From its beginning as a small communication company aiming in particular at the development of marine and transoceanic radio, the Radio Corporation of America has extended its activities into manufacturing enterprises, broadcasting, sound motion pictures, and other fields, associated with communications, electrical entertainment, and radio progress. ... Ever since its early development, radio has been an indispensable agency of communications. During recent years, it has advanced in the home field from a novelty and entertainment luxury to a household requirement. Because of the type and variety of its services, its independent status and its attention to future requirements, the Corporation occupies an important position among the nation's essential industries.* [1]

The 1933 *Annual Report* declared gross revenues of $62.3 million and reported 19,934 employees working in the manufacture and sales of radio and phonograph equipment, radiotelegraph operations, NBC, and other activities. It also described partial ownership of the Radio-Keith-Orpheum Company as well as research in a new area—television.

By 1923, Sarnoff believed television would be next big step in communications. Television, like radio, is a systems concept, requiring construction of transmitters, television stations, mobile equipment, studios, TV cameras, home receivers, networks, program development and production, and a way of paying for it all through television sales, advertising, and subsidies. Television also needed standards for broadcasting and for equipment manufacture. Every manufacture had to scan visual images in the same way and every television set had to decode the information to re-create visual images.

In 1927, AT&T mounted the first public display of television, sending pictures of Herbert Hoover, then secretary of commerce, from Washington, D.C., to New York City. The fifty-line picture, transmitted at eighteen frames per second, was received on a two-by-three-inch screen. In 1928, radio telephone became operational between London and New York City. That year, both GE and AT&T sent images in motion across significant distances. General Electric offered its first television set, the Octagon, in 1928.

This new television technology not only had commercial applications, it had military potential. David Sarnoff, at the Army War College on January 31, 1927, said

Perhaps it would be too fantastic to consider the part that may be played by direct television in the war of the future, but it is not too early to consider the direction which laboratories should take in its application to military uses.[2]

Sarnoff had made a long-term commitment to television. That year, a young Westinghouse engineer, Vladimir Zworykin, another Russian emigrant who came to the country in 1919, visited Sarnoff. Zworykin joined the research group in Camden and began looking at electronic alternatives to a mechanical spinning disc. He became director of RCA's television research operations. Vladimir Zworykin created the iconoscope camera, an important development for television.

In 1930, RCA had experimental television broadcasting stations in New York City and Camden and Bound Brook, New Jersey. Philco, Dumont, Zenith, GE, and AT&T were also developing equipment, and by the late 1930s, Dumont, GE, and RCA all were selling television sets with very small screens—at a very high price.

The depression cut off money to support the rapid development of early television. In the 1930s, RCA acquired De Forest Radio and Charles Francis Jenkins television receivers and studios. In 1932, RCA demonstrated an all-electronic television system from its Camden plant by sending signals a distance of a few miles. In 1937, the first mobile television van appeared in New York City with cameras plus transmitter. The 1936 Berlin Olympics were televised by Telefunken using RCA equipment. The 1937 coronation of King George VI was televised in England. Commercial television was now on the horizon.

By 1939, RCA's revenue had reached $110 million, or almost three times that of IBM. It had almost 23,000 employees and was a leader in radio and phonograph equipment; vacuum tubes; motion picture sound equipment; network broadcasting, serving the 45 million radios in homes and automobiles; radio communication to forty-five countries and 1,000 ships worldwide; and technical training. It was well positioned for the new field of television.

RCA, with Sarnoff's leadership, invested millions in television development. In 1939, RCA produced a major public demonstration of television at the New York World's Fair. NBC began limited commercial broadcasting in 1939 and 1940 in New York City, with baseball games, boxing matches, variety shows, and dramas. Their model TRK television set sold for $600 at a time when an automobile cost $750, a house $6,400, and an average annual salary was $1,850.

David Sarnoff had been commissioned a lieutenant colonel in the army signal corps reserves in 1924. He was called to active duty in 1944, leaving RCA and working as a communications consultant to General Dwight Eisenhower. He became a brigadier general and insisted thereafter on being called General.

By the early 1950s, television was responsible for half of RCA's revenue. Television advertising quickly grew from 10 percent of that spent in radio to 250 percent, increasing NBC's profits.

Sarnoff channeled vast amounts of RCA capital into research and development of color television. To focus on color television took self-confidence, a vision, and lots of both time and money. Again his vision paid off with sales and profits.

In 1947, Sarnoff became RCA's chairman of the board; the company now led the world in television broadcasting. RCA had television stations in New York City, Hollywood, Chicago, and Cleveland, and became a leader in the manufacture of television sets, transmitters, and vacuum tubes, and creating broadcast facilities and programs.

Beginning early in his career, David Sarnoff realized the value of self-promotion and publicity. He was a visionary who had faith in science and technology. He backed those who worked for him, but he could be a powerful adversary for those who stood in his way. Because Edwin Howard Armstrong and Philo Farnsworth had other approaches to FM radio and television, Sarnoff fought them over patent legislation in court and in the business world, and they paid dearly.

Sarnoff received numerous honors and awards. His early grasp of this new technology and his vast commitment to it put a television set in nearly every home. RCA sold 5 million television sets in 1965. Annual retail sales of color televisions reached $3 billion in 1966. Color television was now part of the American home. Both radio and television changed the way Americans were entertained and received information.

In addition to radio and television, RCA was a leader in many other aspects of the electronics world. Sarnoff had invested in innovation during the depression when most firms were cutting back on engineering staffs. His relentless pursuit of technology continued after the war. In 1940, RCA had done development work on the electron microscope, and by 1962, the company had delivered 1,000 of them.

During World War II, RCA engineers had worked on high frequency tube design, acoustics, radar and radio antennas, infrared sniper scopes, acoustical depth charges, radar jamming, radio systems, shoran navigation (short-range navigation) and blind-bombing systems, airborne radar equipment, electronic fire control, proximity fuses, communications, marine radio equipment, and training of army and navy personnel.

In the 1950s and 1960s, RCA continued the military and defense work that it had started in World War II. In 1958, it became project manager of the Ballistic Missile Early Warning System. It was involved in the early space program and satellite technology. By 1970, military applications accounted for about half of the electronics industry's research-and-development budget, as the country increased spending during the Cold War and RCA received its share of the research dollars.

For RCA, commercial innovation followed scientific innovation: in vacuum tubes at Harrison, New Jersey, where most manufacturing took place; in transistor and radio telephones; in records, with RCA producing 50 million 45 rpm records in 1950; in UHF television; clock radios; color TV; industrial television; larger color tubes; TV magnetic tape recording; electron light amplifiers; electronic music synthesizers; high fidelity; satellite communications; portable TV; and transistor radios. RCA was the world's technical electronics leader.

Sarnoff had supported his engineers and scientists, and in 1951, the RCA Laboratories in Princeton, New Jersey, were rededicated as the David Sarnoff Research Center. David Sarnoff retired in 1970 and died on December 12, 1971. Praise came from all around the world: "He was not an inventor, nor was he a scientist. But he was a man of astounding vision who was able to see with remarkable clarity the possibility of harnessing the electron."[3]

> *He was tenacious of purpose and unlimited in his energetic support and promotion of any idea or plans which he judged worthy of support. He had an extraordinary sense of values and of the public reaction to new services or devices.*[4]

On Management

David Sarnoff was interested in the world and in technology's impact on it. Like Henry Ford and Ken Olsen, he was engineering-driven, whereas Andrew Carnegie and Thomas Watson Sr. were sales-and-marketing-driven. Products flowed from labs to manufacturing to markets, sometimes independent of what the customers might want. But Sarnoff's vision, especially in radio and television, was better than that of his potential customers. David Sarnoff, through his ideas and their implementation, changed America.

At RCA, Sarnoff made all-important decisions himself, which helped when bringing forward all aspects of radio and television. He would not delegate decisions, decentralize management, and never faced management succession. In that regard, he was like Henry Ford.

David Sarnoff wrote much about his views on technology, business, and life, and some of his ideas are worth repeating. A more complete listing of his speeches is included in his book *Looking Ahead: The Papers of David Sarnoff* (1968).

On technology:

> *In my years of association with scientists and engineers I have acquired a deep respect for their creative faculties, their constant search for knowledge and facts and for their integrity of purpose. I have tried in my small way to stimulate and encourage them in their work, to share with them their dreams and disappointments, and to rejoice with them in their triumphs.*[5]

He also observed: "Without creativity, the world would be lost. Whether that be in science, politics, psychology, business or anything else. The world depends not only on creative ideas, but on a constant flow of them."[6] And: "No man has a monopoly on brains. No organization has all the knowledge required in a continuously changing and developing art and industry."[7] He continued: "The more I have lived in the world of science and technology, the more I have become convinced that the really practical men in this field are the dreamers."[8] "With the advent of television a new force is being given to the world. Who can tell what the power to extend vision will mean eventually in the stream of human life?"[9]

On management and business:

> *When bankers look upon the balance sheet of a business in which they are interested, they must remember that the assets and liabilities and the records of earnings of the past five, ten, fifteen or twenty years no longer are sufficient to assure the success of the enterprise for the future. The health of an enterprise may depend more on the imagination, courage, adaptability and wisdom of its management than upon the record of its past earnings.*[10]

> *There is no satisfaction that can come to the head of an organization greater than to be able to sit back and watch the results achieved by men under his direction without him having to give them orders to tell them what to do. Give them the mission and let them perform. Let them make their mistakes, too, because no one is perfect. There is only one way to learn and that is by the mistakes you make as you go along.*[11]

Perhaps because of his early training as a religious scholar, David Sarnoff also had much to say about life: *"Knowledge is not enough, unless it leads you to understanding, and, in turn, to wisdom."*[12] And: *"Whatever course you have chosen for yourself, it will not be a chore but an adventure if you bring to it a sense of the glory of striving—if your sights are set far above the merely secure and mediocre."*[13] He reflected that *"man cannot go someplace and not take himself along. ... Change—don't retire. Change from a position to something else where you may try to express your forces in another line. To retire to achieve self-indulgence doesn't mean anything."*[14]

> *Thinking is a most important and neglected art. One of the criticisms I would suggest against our present system of education is the lack of training in the art of thinking. I think it can be developed by spending more time on the interpretation of knowledge rather than in the mere acquisition of facts.*[15]

Let us not lose the sense of the awe and mystery of life. Our very triumphs in penetrating nature have disclosed our mortal limitations. The more we learn, the more remains to be learned. Science, far from making us arrogant, teaches us to be humble. In this universe of endless wonders, the most wondrous is the human mind capable of delving so deeply, and the human heart aware of depths it can never plumb.[16]

And finally: *"We must face the fact that man has shown greater ability to explore the secrets of nature than to explore his own heart and mind. We have been able to harness the forces of nature better than we have been able to master ourselves."[17]*

The Legacy of David Sarnoff

"Accept the fact that the only certainty in your lives will be change."[18]

In the late 1950s and 1960s, RCA was a leader in many growing industries—communications, entertainment, space, and many aspects of the electronics industry. It had achieved this position because of David Sarnoff's leadership. Yet it managed to lose its position in each of these fields.

As was stated in chapter 1, growth or decline of a business enterprise is largely the long shadow of management. Nowhere is that more apparent than with the Radio Corporation of America, under the leadership of both David Sarnoff and his successors.

In December 1955, Robert Sarnoff was appointed president of NBC, replacing Pat Weaver. He did a good job at NBC. He became president of RCA in 1966 and chairman in 1969, succeeding his father. He practiced decision making by consensus versus his father's one-man rule, and began to decentralize management. During the 1960s, Robert Sarnoff tried to find an area with the growth potential of radio and television. He settled on computers, and that story is told in chapter 9.

But most of management's energy went into diversification at a time when the electronics industry was growing significantly. RCA wanted a portfolio of operating companies, perhaps to fund investments in computers and electronics. In May 1966, the company acquired Random House. It then bought Arnold Palmer Enterprises, Hertz, Alaska Communications Systems, Banquet Foods, Gibson Greeting Cards, Coronet Carpets, the real estate enterprise of Cushman and Wakefield, and two British frozen-food producers—Oriel Foods and Morris James Jones.

In November 1975, Robert Sarnoff was removed as chairman of RCA based on diversifications that didn't work, the computer investments, and NBC losing market position to CBS and ABC in the television broadcasting world.

His successor, Edward Griffith, also believed in the conglomerate model. He divested many subsidiaries, sold off divisions, and bought CIT Financial Corporation, another conglomerate, which owned savings and loan associations, an insurance company, an office-furniture maker, and a greeting card company. RCA now bore little resemblance to the company David Sarnoff had built.

Often a business school will teach that a good manager can manage anything. But is that actually true? There is little in the story of RCA or most conglomerates to indicate that the answer to that question is in the affirmative. Perhaps Andrew Carnegie's philosophy about learning the business still applies today.

Meanwhile, the electronics and communications industries were growing rapidly. New companies (including many of those listed in chapters 1, 7, and 9) were founded and they took market share as RCA declined. By 1975, consumer electronics accounted for less than 25 percent of RCA's earnings at a time when Sony, Matsushita, Hitachi, and others were growing significantly. Until the 1970s, the United States led the world in consumer electronics, but growth in Japanese and European consumer firms affected RCA's position in radio and television.

Satellite communications, in which RCA had an early lead, affected radio and television distribution. Ted Turner started a "superstation" and then founded CNN, with worldwide distribution. NBC's dominant position began to slip as new forms of news and entertainment were developed.

In June 1986, General Electric bought RCA and NBC for $6.3 billion. General Electric had 1984 revenues of $28.9 billion, and RCA had 1984 revenues of $10.1 billion, including $4.9 billion in electronics and $3 billion in entertainment. GE retained the brand name RCA and made NBC an autonomous division. Quickly, RCA was pulled apart and many of its operations either integrated with existing GE divisions or closed down. Hertz was sold, and then the consumer electronics division was sold to France's Thomson. The company of David Sarnoff was no more.

Earlier questions were raised about the fact that large companies often cannot deal with change and entrepreneurs build new companies and industries. Two of David Sarnoff's ideas are worth quoting to that effect: "The greatest menace to the life of an industry is industrial self-complacency."[19] And: "The will to preserve is often the difference between failure and success."[20]

David Sarnoff, as well as others described in this book, was never satisfied and kept after his long-term objectives. He built RCA, while his successors destroyed it. David Sarnoff was a practical dreamer.

CHAPTER 9

Computers
The Information Age (1945–2000)

Human history is in essence a history of ideas.
    —Herbert George (H. G.) Wells

I agree with you that there is a natural aristocracy among men.
The grounds of this are virtue and talents.
    —Thomas Jefferson in a letter
    to John Adams

It is as difficult to imagine a world without computers today as it would have been to imagine a world without automobiles in the 1930s or without television in the 1960s. Yet, in each case, they went from a prototype device to a standard part of life within in a few decades.

Today, a person runs into computers everywhere—at the market, the bank, in restaurants, when paying bills or making reservations, and on the job. A significant number of American workers use computers in their employment or sit next to people who do. How did this growth in and dependency on the digital computer happen?

The Early Days (1450–1945)

Some people assume that the current state of the computer industry, with personal computers, software by Microsoft, and a World Wide Web, is the way it always was. In fact, some personal Web sites describe the history of the computer industry in terms of the professional life of the writer. This is similar to writing "The History of the World since I Was Born."

Industrial computers are perhaps sixty years old, yet the roots go far back in time. Like the automobile, the computer industry had a long genesis and history of innovation. Many people and many inventions helped create the technology and the industry.

223

For centuries, people have been interested in calculation, in communication, and in control. For a business to analyze payroll, pricing, and profitability, calculations must be performed. To control a machine or to communicate with someone miles away requires mathematical analysis. To determine the position and orbit of the planets, to push the limits of understanding of the skies, to determine how to build on earth—buildings, bridges, and tunnels—to move beyond the simple addition and subtraction calculations easily figured with a pencil and a paper—all these require new tools.

This chapter will describe the first computers during and just after World War II, the first UNIVAC and IBM computers, the IBM 360, the minicomputer industry with the PDP-8 and PDP-11, the microcomputer with the Apple II and IBM PC, and technical innovations in input/output, computer storage, software, and communications. Then the story of the industry will be brought up to the present day with a discussion of networks, windows, application programs, and personal computers.

What building blocks were required before the modern computer was possible? In answer to this question, three areas are described: mathematics, systems, and technology.

This is not the place for a history of mathematics, but certain concepts can be introduced here. For millennia, humans had to be able to refer to the quantity of an item in order to count animals or crops or goods. For this, they needed numbers. The ability to add, subtract, multiply, and divide were necessary in everyday life.

Any symbols can be used to express numbers, but how many different symbols would be used before the symbols repeated themselves? People are accustomed to the decimal system (base 10), which means that the symbols repeat themselves every ten times. This is logical, since people have ten fingers. But base 10 is not automatic. Some civilizations have used other bases, 5 (the fingers on one hand), 20 (by the Mayans), or 70 (by the Greeks).

Around 3500 B.C., the Babylonians began using a sexagesimal system in which numbers repeated themselves every 60 times, and they developed a complete system of arithmetic using the base 60. Before ignoring this as an obscure fact of history, it is worth noting that the Babylonian system of arithmetic continues today, with 60 minutes in an hour, 60 seconds in a minute, and 360 degrees in a circle.

Another important mathematical concept is the idea of zero, that is, both nothing and place. The use of zero allows numbers to have significance. The Romans, for example, had no concept of zero. The numbers I, X, C, and M all meant 1, in other words, 1, 10, 100, and 1,000. But since there was no zero, different symbols had to be used. To understand the importance of the concept of zero, try to add or multiply roman numerals. Zero was used in India in the ninth century, and the idea spread to the Islamic world and then on to Europe. The symbol 1 can be used as 1, 10, 100, or 1,000, all having different meanings, depending on the position of 1 and the number of 0s.

In 1848, George Boole proposed the use of the base 2 for a number system and developed Boolean algebra. Although a decimal system works nicely in the mechanical world, where it is easy to develop a switch with ten positions, a binary system is far better in an electronic world, where circuits and memory devices can be designed to either be on or off, high or low. All modern computers owe a debt to George Boole.

Two other mathematical developments are worth mentioning. In 1615, the Scottish inventor John Napier invented logarithms, another way of describing numbers. Logarithmic tables allowed the process of multiplication and division to be replaced by addition and subtraction. And in 1622, William Oughtred developed the slide rule, a linear measuring tool based on logarithms. Every engineer over the age of sixty used slide rules for calculating solutions to problems. Most engineers under the age of forty have no idea what slide rules are used for.

Turning to some of the systems that helped with the development of calculation, the first would have to be the abacus. The abacus was invented more than 2,500 years ago and was used in China, Babylon, Egypt, Japan, and Rome. The abacus is a wooden rack of two horizontal wires with beads strung on them that make simple arithmetic very easy and fast, and it continues to be widely used around the world. In the seventeenth, eighteenth, and nineteenth centuries, many mechanical devices were developed to assist in calculations, including Blaise Pascal's mechanical calculator of 1642; Gottfried Wilhelm von Leibniz's stepped reckoner of 1671, which performed addition, subtraction, division, and multiplication of numbers up to twelve digits; Earl Stanhope's multiplying calculator; and Charles Xavier Thomas's mechanical calculator that could add, subtract, multiply, and divide. Charles Babbage realized that many of the calculations needed to perform arithmetic were a series of repeatable operations.

His difference engine, capable of computing navigational tables, and his analytical engine, built to perform any calculation, were both financed in part by the British government. Babbage's inventions, which used brass, steel, and pewter clockwork and punched cards for instructions, never were completed due to the mechanical tolerances required. But his ideas of programmable devices did influence future inventors. And his analytical engine is called by some the first general-purpose computer.

In 1855, Georg and Edvard Scheutz of Sweden built a mechanical computer based on Babbage's work. By the late nineteenth century, desktop calculators were in production. In 1886, William Seward Burroughs developed the first commercially successful mechanical adding machine.

The other system advance that should be mentioned is electricity and its applications in the telegraph, telephone, and telephone exchanges. The ability to send a controlled electric signal down a wire was essential to the development of the computer.

The papers of Alan Turing on the mathematical theory of computing, Claude Shannon in 1948 on using relays to implement Boolean algebra, John Von Neumann on mathematical organization, and other scientists provided the ideas and prepared the theoretical foundations for the development of the computer.

Finally, it is useful to review a number of technologies and inventions that paved the way for the rapid advances in computers after World War II. Paper was invented in China in the first century, and by the Middle Ages, its production was widespread in Europe. Movable type was used to print on paper, first in China and then, in the mid-fifteenth century, by Johann Gutenberg in Germany. The volume of paper, books, and other printed material increased sharply, with about 18 million volumes and 30,000 titles printed in the first forty-two years after Gutenberg's printing press.

Henry Mill in England received the first patent for a typewriter in 1714. The first U.S. patent for the typewriter was issued in 1829 to William Burt. Remington started manufacturing typewriters in 1874, based on a design by Christopher Sholes. In the nineteenth and early twentieth centuries, printing technology was substantially improved. In the 1880s, Ottmar Merganthaler invented the monotype, which used a keyboard to cast individual letters, and the linotype machine, which produced complete lines of metal type. In 1935, IBM began to market an electric typewriter.

Joseph-Marie Jacquard used punched cards to set up an automatic loom in 1805, and they were widely used in the textile mills of England and America. The use of punched cards to mechanize census-data processing was proposed by Herman Hollerith and John Shaw Billings. The 1880 census had taken 1,500 people seven years to complete. Moreover, delays in completing a census affected the ability to assign the correct number of seats in the House of Representatives as specified by the U.S. Constitution. In 1884, Herman Hollerith obtained the first of more than thirty patents for punched-card keyboards and readers. They were used in 1890 to record census data and enabled the Census Bureau to record results in three months rather than the planned two to four years. The Census Bureau could then recheck the cards to analyze birthplace, ages and number of children in a family, number of people who spoke English, and other data.

Hollerith helped form the Tabulating Machine Company in 1896, making punched-card machines for railroad accounting. The International Time Recording Company was formed in 1900 and the Computing Scale Company of America, which made scales and clocks, in 1901. In 1911, Computer-Tabulating-Recording Company was formed through a merger of these three companies. Thomas Watson, formerly of National Cash Register, joined the company in 1914 as general manager and became president the next year. In 1924, the company changed its name to International Business Machines (IBM) Corporation. The company supplied tabulators, punched cards, typewriters, and accounting machines, and by 1920, its revenue reached $9 million. In 1928, IBM standardized the eighty-column punched card and in 1935 marketed the IBM 601—a punched-card machine with an arithmetic unit based on relays and capable of doing multiplication. In 1935, IBM won a contract to administer the new Social Security Act employment records of 26 million people.

In 1857, Sir Charles Wheatstone used paper tape to store data by punching holes in a long tape. Paper tape was widely used thereafter, especially in the telegraph industry. In 1844, Samuel Morse's telegraph connected Washington and Baltimore, and the concept of the Morse code, in which letters and numbers are represented by coded electrical signals, also had future applications. Morse in 1840 designed a "read only memory" to assist people in sending Morse code. In 1870, the stock ticker was first used on Wall Street. A similar concept existed for wire photo, developed in 1882, in which a picture could be sent from one location to another or from a central news office to many newspapers. A picture was scanned line by line and transmitted a series of numbers relative to the amount of black or white at each point. In 1921, Western Union began wire photo service.

Advances in magnetic technology were made for the entertainment industry. In 1899, magnetic sound recording was invented, and in 1904, it produced the first double-sided phonographic disk. Gustav Tauschek of Austria patented in 1928 an electromagnetic drum storage unit with an optical reading device. As the twentieth century advanced, more and more information could be stored magnetically.

There were continual advances in electronic technology, as described in chapter 7. The generation and distribution of electric power was an essential step toward the invention of the computer. Vacuum tubes were developed in 1906 with Lee De Forest's three-element vacuum tube, the triode, which enabled electronic signals to be amplified. In 1919, W. H. Eccles and F. W. Jordan developed the flip-flop, an electronic circuit that had two states: on or off, high or low. This advance allowed George Boole's binary logic to be implemented. In 1875, William Crookes invented the cathode-ray tube. For the next seventy years, advances in cathode-ray technology continued as early television was developed. In 1939, the first vacuum tube machines that could calculate were introduced.

By 1940, the hardware building blocks were in place for an electronic computer. Vacuum tube circuitry had been designed. Magnetic storage media had been improved, including magnetic tapes, discs, and drums. Input devices for entering data were available, such as punched cards or paper tape; output printing devices were available, and cathode-ray tubes and typewriters could be provided for the operator, enabling him or her to provide instructions to the computer.

Most mechanical machines did the same activity over and over again. Jacquard had developed the punched card, which enabled the operator to relatively easily change the operation of a loom. Cards had to be replaced or wires moved to change the machine's performance. This design was acceptable if the operation required changes in the machine's performance in minutes or hours, but not if changes had to be made in fractions of a second. John Von Neumann of Princeton in 1945 proposed that the computer itself be able to change its instructions without any change in hardware. This concept, the stored program, allowed the computer's performance to be changed when needed based on instructions stored in a memory. Subroutines could be stored in the memory unit and then brought out as needed. Electronic storage of programming information eliminated the slower methods of programming and changing instructions using punched cards and paper tape. With a stored-program machine, the computer could make the decisions itself.

Thus the ideas and technologies were in place for the computer industry to develop.

> *Before computers were available, mechanical aids for computing and managing data existed. These products represented a broad range of mechanisms that supported data input, calculation, communication, and dozens of other devices to increase the ability of office and manufacturing personnel to manage their firms more effectively, to increase control over their jobs, and to improve their ability to make better decisions.[1]*

There were also companies in place to help start the computer industry. Burroughs, founded in 1886 by William Seward Burroughs, was the leading supplier of adding machines, calculators, and bookkeeping equipment. IBM, the successor to Herman Hollerith's company, was the leading supplier of punched-card and tabulating equipment. National Cash Register (NCR), bought by John Henry Patterson in 1884, dominated the cash register business and provided written point of sales information. Remington was a leading manufacturer of arms during the Civil War. Afterward, it looked for other areas where it could use its mass-production capability and took a leading position in typewriters, punched-card products, and accounting machines. In 1927, Remington Rand was formed by James Henry Rand to offer equipment to all sectors of the office industry—typewriters, adding machines, tabulating equipment, and card punch and sorting equipment.

By 1940, these four companies were the leading suppliers of office equipment, but none had annual revenues in excess of $50 million. RCA, as discussed in chapters 7 and 8, was the leading designer of electronic technology. Also on the scene and ready to participate in the computer industry were Bendix,

General Electric, Honeywell, Philco, Raytheon, Royal McBee, and many others. In 1938, Hewlett-Packard was founded to make electronic instruments, and there would be many more companies to come.

By the early 1940s, not only the hardware—the things that the computer was made of—but also some of the software—the ideas and instructions that could make a computer run—were in place. And there were companies ready to expand. But first there was a world war to fight, and most of the technical people were needed for that war.

It is worth pointing out here that there are many aspects of the computer industry. With the auto industry, in addition to the design of the automobile, there were questions regarding the type of engine power, petroleum versus electricity or steam, roads, tires, services to support the automobile, and many other aspects that made the modern automobile possible. The same process applied to computers. There was the question of how information entered into and received from the computer was to be stored. Paper tape and cards were fine and permanent, except that a hole punched into a tape or card cannot be changed. There were questions of how to store and process information in the computer. Thus, a discussion of the industry has to deal with magnetic material, magnetic tapes, discs, drums and cores, electronic advances in performing addition, analysis, and control, and finally, how the computer was to be told what to do. The following sections will deal with these issues. An early history of the industry will be followed by a section on memories and input/output, the software to tell the computer what to do, and the use of communications to enter data and instructions from afar.

For illustration, following is a computer block diagram showing the organization of a computer. It is from a book the author wrote in 1967 and will be referred to in future sections to define changes and evolution in the design of hardware.[2]

Figure 9.1. Computer block diagram

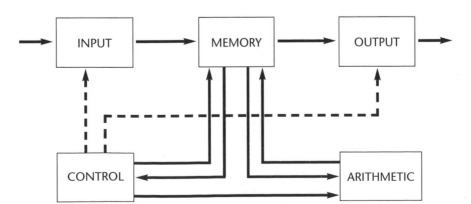

From an Idea to a Business:
The Computer as a Clerk (1945–1970)

There is significant disagreement about who developed the first computer, but in the years during and after World War II, there were a number of people who were responsible for major innovations. Just as with automobiles, there were a number of inventors and companies with claims to first place.

In the 1930s, there was work done on analog equipment. An analog signal is continuous and can take on any one of an infinite number of possible values. In contrast to an analog signal, digital has a discrete, discontinuous, numerical value. You may have an analog watch on your wrist, or you may have a digital watch. One shows the continuous positions of hands, the other discrete numbers. Vannevar Bush of MIT developed an analog differential engine in 1930, which could perform many kinds of scientific calculations. Analog computers were developed to establish gun direction and aiming during World War II as well as controls for airplane simulators in early flight training.

During World War II, there were electronic digital computer systems in Britain and the United States used for message gathering and analysis, including the 1943 Colossus code breaker designed by Thomas Flowers in Britain, the Harvard Mark I sequence-controlled ballistic computer by Howard Aiken in 1943, and the ENIAC from the University of Pennsylvania in the 1940s.

One early computer was a vacuum tube device proposed by Professor John Vincent Atanasoff and graduate student Clifford Berry at the University of Iowa. Partially built between 1939 and 1942, the system had a binary system 16-bit adder, a special purpose calculator with sixty words of regenerative condensers for memory, and did parallel processing. It weighed 700 pounds, had 300 vacuum tubes, and could calculate in about fifteen seconds. In a 1973 patent suit, a judge ruled that this was the first automatic digital computer.

Konrad Zuse, a Berlin engineer, developed the Z1, a mechanical floating-point calculator in 1938. The Z1 could perform floating-point arithmetic, had high-capacity memory, and stored information. In 1941, Zuse built the Z3 computer in Germany, the first programmable calculator with automatic control of its operations. At the end of the war, Zuse moved to Zurich and developed the Z4 control computer in 1949. It was in operation until 1955 at Zurich's Federal Polytechnical Institute and led to a series of machines built by the Siemens Corporation.

During World War II, it was essential for Britain to be able to break the secret codes used by the Germans. In December 1943, British intelligence at Bletchley Park placed in operation a fixed-program, electronic computer. Thomas Flowers and associates designed the Colossus vacuum tube computer, and ten were built to assist in code analysis.

Starting in 1938 and finishing in 1944, Howard Aiken designed the Mark series of computers at Harvard University, cosponsored by IBM. The Mark I

Automatic Sequence Controlled Calculator was used by the U.S. Navy for gunnery and ballistic calculations. It was an electromechanical-relay-based machine and took six seconds for multiplication and division. It weighed about five tons, was fifty-five feet long and eight feet high, and had 760,000 separate parts. The computer was controlled, that is, programmed, by prepunched paper tape, with an electric typewriter for output. It carried out math functions, could reference previous results, and had special routines for logarithms and trigonometric functions.

IBM introduced the 404 Alphanumeric Accounting Machine in 1941, the 604 Electronic Calculator in 1948, and the Card Programmed Electronic Calculator the following year. Each of these machines allowed punched cards to be handled more effectively and calculations to be performed more quickly.

The first all-electronic digital computer was the Electronic Numerical Integrator and Computer (ENIAC), which John Presper Eckert and John William Mauchly developed at the University of Pennsylvania. It was designed for the Ballistic Research Laboratory and the Aberdeen Proving Grounds in Maryland for ballistic computations of the performance of shells and bombs. The design was completed in 1946, and the system was one thousand times faster than any calculating machine to date and could perform 5,000 additions per second. Previously, a skilled person could compute a sixty-second ballistic trajectory in about twenty hours. ENIAC took thirty seconds. However, it was not easy to reprogram the machine, and programming changes could take technicians days or weeks to rewire the system. But the system demonstrated that high-speed digital computing was possible using vacuum tube technology.

For comparison with modern computers, ENIAC used 18,000 vacuum tubes, 1,500 relays, hundreds of thousands of resistors, capacitors, and inductors, weighed thirty tons, and had dimensions of thirty feet by fifty feet. It had punched-card input/output, and instructions to make up a program were established by separate plug-in modules to determine the flow of information. ENIAC used thousands of watts of power and, because of heat buildup, could only run an hour at a time.

Other early computers included the 1948 Manchester University Mark I, with 1,300 vacuum tubes and magnetic drum storage; the Cambridge University EDSAC developed in 1949, the first stored-program computer with a series of programming subroutines stored on punched paper tape; and the Whirlwind I designed at MIT between 1947 and 1952. The Whirlwind was designed by Jay Forrester and used 4,500 vacuum tubes, magnetic drum memory, paper-tape input, magnetic tape, and a cathode-ray tube. It eventually had a magnetic iron core memory—for which a patent was issued in 1956—and this improved its performance and memory capacity.

Most computers were special purpose and made one at a time. According to one source, in 1951, ten computers systems were installed with an average sales price of $3,000,000.[3] This was at a time when a new car could be purchased for about $1,200 and a new home for $6,000. There were 3,000 computers installed in 1959 and 82,000 computers installed in 1971. Prices dropped from an average of slightly more than $1 million in 1959 to about $375,000 in 1971. How was that accomplished?

Computers initially did what an adding machine did, but faster. In data processing, computers took raw data, performed calculations, and organized it into information. These were accounting computers that performed simple calculations, with lots of input and output. Processing might include classifying and sorting of input data, calculating, recording, and summarizing. The first financial computers were used for recordkeeping, payroll, production scheduling, customer billing, general accounting, purchasing and order writing, and customer analysis.

In addition to the data-processing machines, which had simple calculations and lots of input and output, some computers helped scientists in their analyses with large amounts of calculation and required little output. In short, some applications were limited by the speed of getting data into and out of the computer and others by the speed of calculation of the computer.

In order to understand the history of computers, it is worth reviewing the history and contributions of some of the key companies. For the computer industry to grow, input and output speed had to be increased, the machines had to have more memory capacity, and the mainframe had to be faster and have greater accuracy. In short, all of the hardware parts shown in Figure 9.1 had to increase in performance. In addition, it was necessary to instruct the machines on what to do, and this led to the growth of programming. Each of these issues will be addressed.

In chapter 1, it was stated that the creation of jobs has largely been the product of good leadership. The decline and destruction of established companies has largely been the product of poor leadership. Entrepreneurs control the use of market, technology, and economic factors in all stages of business. All of this has been very well demonstrated in the computer industry.

In 1945, the computer industry had several million dollars in revenue. By 1970, it was in excess of $20 billion. There were many companies that could have been the leaders—Burroughs, National Cash Register, Remington, or IBM because of their product position in typewriters, adding machines, tabulating equipment, cash registers, and bookkeeping equipment; RCA and GE because of their leadership in electrical equipment and the fact that they were both significantly larger than the preceding four companies; Honeywell because of its position in control equipment; and others. Why did the computer industry develop the way it did? Was it because of good and bad leadership or was it an accident of history? Does management bear any role in the success or failure of their enterprises? Clearly, the author believes that they do and will amplify on this point in this and the concluding chapter.

It is helpful to start by looking at the first quarter century of the computer industry and examining some companies. Then, the last three decades of the industry will be reviewed. Keep in mind the lessons learned about leadership in the steel, auto, and electronics industries.

Remington Rand had revenue of $43 million in 1940 and $108 million at the end of World War II. A major supplier of typewriters, adding machines, and calculators, the company was well positioned to enter a new business arena and become the first commercial computer company.

Because of disagreements with the University of Pennsylvania over patent ownership, in March 1946 John Presper Eckert and John Mauchly left the university and started the Electronic Controls Company in downtown Philadelphia. In 1950, Remington Rand bought the company and its name was changed to Universal Automatic Computer (UNIVAC). The UNIVAC computer had an add time of 120 microseconds and could print output information at 600 lines per minute. The first customer was the U.S. Census Bureau, which wanted high speed and more complete data analysis. In 1951, the UNIVAC I was installed at the Census Bureau, using an input/output printer, magnetic tape, typewriter, delay lines, 5,200 vacuum tubes for logic, and a magnetic tape unit as a buffer memory. In 1952, the UNIVAC computer was used to predict the results of the Eisenhower-Stevenson presidential race. The computer accurately predicted the results based on early voting patterns, and UNIVAC became a household name.

Forty-six UNIVAC computers were sold at an average price of $1 million, and Remington Rand became the first American manufacturer of commercial computer systems. Early customers included General Electric, Metropolitan Life, DuPont, U.S. Steel, and the U.S. government. In addition, UNIVAC was in direct competition with IBM's punched-card technology.

In 1952, Remington Rand acquired another computer company, Engineering Research Associates of Saint Paul, Minnesota, an early supplier of special-purpose data-processing equipment. The leader of that group was William Norris. In 1950, Remington Rand had 29,909 employees, slightly more than IBM. In 1955, Sperry merged with the Remington Rand Corporation to form Sperry Rand, and retired general Douglas MacArthur became its chairman.

The company had a three-year head start on competitors and was the leading computer supplier in the early 1950s. Among its early products were UNIVAC III, 1107, 9000, and 1050. In 1953, Remington Rand developed the first high-speed printer for the UNIVAC.

Remington had three research facilities—in Philadelphia (Eckert-Mauchly), Saint Paul (Engineering Research Associates), and Norwalk (Sperry). There was little attempt to integrate their work; James Rand preferred to purchase new operations rather than manage in detail what they did. The company also preferred to focus on government contracts. The sales department sold all products, including computers, and had little interaction with engineering. UNIVAC soon lost its early lead to IBM. Between 1956 and 1967, the UNIVAC division of Sperry Rand lost $250 million.[4] In 1986, the company merged with Burroughs to become Unisys.

In 1957, Control Data Corporation (CDC) was formed by William Norris and eleven others. They had left Remington Rand because of differences with management over the required level of support for the development of computer equipment. Their strategy was to develop machines for government agencies at the high end of both the price and performance range and then spin them off for commercial customers. In 1958, Control Data built the CDC 1604 for scientific and engineering applications. In 1963, Control Data acquired the Bendix Computer Division and two years later, Control Precision's Librascope Division. In 1964, Seymour Cray designed the first supercomputer, the CDC 6600. It had one central processor and ten peripheral processors and, at the time, was the most powerful computer ever designed. When Control Data introduced the CDC 7600, which used 60-bit words and parallel processing, it completely owned the high end of the computer market. In 1972, Seymour Cray left to start his own company, Cray Research. Meanwhile Control Data, believing that small companies were far more innovative than large ones, acquired almost ninety companies between 1960 and 1980 in order to acquire engineering talent.

Burroughs had a long history of supplying office equipment and had 7,000 employees in 1930. The depression hit the company hard, and it was the smallest and least profitable of the four office suppliers during the 1930s and early 1940s. After the war, management got aggressive, changing executives and trying new marketing and product programs. John Coleman became president, and between 1946 and 1956 revenues grew from $46 million to $273 million and profits from $2 million to $14 million. The company plowed earnings back into the business, financing its growth.

Burroughs had a strong position in the banking business and in 1959 pioneered the use of magnetic ink character recognition on checks. Burroughs took a long time to strongly enter the general computer business and was not a viable computer supplier until the 1960s. Early Burroughs machines included the E101 magnetic drum computer; the 204, 205, and 220 in the 1950s; and the B160, B170, B5000, and B5500 in the 1960s. Burroughs focused on small computers for the business market and was a leader in software development. Its emphasis on software was validated as the cost of programming went up and computer memory costs decreased. Burroughs had a very loyal customer base, served by its accounting machine and computer sales force.

National Cash Register was the leading supplier of cash registers for more than three-quarters of a century. These devices, called "point of sale terminals," had by the 1970s put the company in a good position to dominate the computer industry. Its position with accounting machines gave it the customer base and economic strength to compete. It took a long time to do so, however, because the company stuck with the old proven path.

In the nineteenth and early twentieth centuries, John Patterson at NCR built one of the best technical and sales organizations in America. He established the system of trained salesmen in assigned territories with assigned sales goals. Among those who worked at NCR was Charles Kettering, who developed an electric cash register and then went on to join General Motors, and Thomas Watson, who was trained as a cash register salesman and went on to head IBM. When John Patterson died in 1922, the company was turned over to his son, a very ineffective leader. He was replaced, and the company's revenue reached $38 million in 1940 and $77 million by the end of the World War II.

NCR's cash registers were in most retail outlets, including department stores and supermarkets, but untrained clerks often had difficulty operating complex systems. The amount of data analysis necessary to make a complete system was significant, and NCR seemed unwilling to make the software and systems investment for this to occur. It held back from changing from electro-mechanical devices to electronics. In 1953, NCR established an electronics division to pursue applications for business machines and acquired the Computer Research Company of Torrance, California, a start-up from Northrop Aircraft. NCR's first computers were the 303 and 304, then the 315 and 390, all of which were small computers built for the business market.

The NCR sales force were compensated well for selling adding machines and many of its members did not want to learn about or sell computers. Management did not force the issue. NCR finally moved strongly into computers in 1971, when it introduced the Century 50. But by then, competition in the computer industry was well ahead of NCR. NCR was sold to AT&T in 1991.

RCA, because of its strength in electronics, was in an excellent position to become a major competitor in the computer world. In 1952, RCA started developing Bizmac, the first computer with a commercial magnetic core memory and a magnetic drum supporting a database. The first Bizmacs were shipped in 1956, followed by the RCA 501 and 301. The company did well through the mid-1960s.

In 1970, RCA planned a major expansion with the Spectra 70, which would compete directly with IBM and was able to run software developed for the IBM 360. With the Spectra 70, RCA hoped to capture 10 percent of the computer market by 1975. The company brought in an IBM executive, Ed Donegan, to provide leadership, and built an extensive facility in Marlboro, Massachusetts. But the Computer Systems division lost money in 1971 and showed little sign of becoming profitable through 1975. At this point, RCA had to decide whether to invest heavily in computers as it had in radio and television.

David Sarnoff had retired, and his son Robert was now president of RCA. RCA had become a conglomerate, having purchased Random House, Hertz, Banquet Foods, and Coronet Industries, and was no longer purely an electronics firm with a strong chief executive officer. Management decided to cut its losses. After trying to sell the computer business, RCA announced that it was closing the division and taking an extraordinary loss of $490 million.

General Electric had been a leading producer of electrical equipment since the 1890s, and it had the technical talent and financial resources to dominate the computer industry. In the 1950s, it pioneered banking and time-sharing applications. GE offered the 200 computer series, the 400 series, and the 600 series, including the GE 645 with Multics. In 1964, GE acquired Compagnie des Machines Bull (France) and Olivetti Computers (Italy), giving it a major position in the fast-growing European market.

In 1969, GE developed a plan for a family of 32-bit computers to compete with the IBM 360 and put the company in a leading position in the 1970s. This plan would require a major corporate investment. At the same time, GE's management was also evaluating its position in nuclear power and jet engines. Ultimately, they recommended investing in these and shutting down the computer division, selling it to Honeywell.

Honeywell had gotten into the computer industry through the back door. In 1957, the Datamatic 1000 was built by Raytheon and Minneapolis Honeywell. Because the unit performed less than optimally, Raytheon sold its 40 percent stake in the enterprise and Honeywell was in the computer business.

Under the leadership of Walter Finke, Honeywell prospered and focused on small computers for the business market. IBM had developed the 1401, a small computer used for billing and payroll processing. As IBM moved forward, Honeywell in 1964 introduced the H-200, attacking IBM's installed base of 1400 systems with its own machine, which could run the IBM software. The Honeywell Model 800, a transistorized system similar to the IBM 1400 punched-card equipment, and the Honeywell 296 and 610, sold to industrial plants and the chemical industry, soon followed. Finke had built the computer business into a sizable operation, with more than $500 million of installed base. But in 1967 he left to become chairman of the Dictaphone Corporation.

In 1966, Honeywell acquired Computer Control Company, the number-two company in the minicomputer industry. Honeywell also built on its excellent position in process control, and, in 1970, Honeywell acquired General Electric's computer line. In addition, Honeywell bought Scientific Data System's business from Xerox in 1975. With a significant position in both large mainframes and minicomputers, with marketing outlets in Europe through Bull and

Olivetti as well as throughout North America, Honeywell was in a strong position. Despite these advantages, however, the company fell behind the competition in both large mainframes and in minicomputers. By 1986, Honeywell was out of the computer business altogether. The management in Minneapolis had proved to be better at buying companies than running them.

Throughout the 1960s, seven companies—Burroughs, Control Data, General Electric, Honeywell, NCR, RCA, and Remington UNIVAC—were called the seven dwarfs to IBM. Yet any one of them, with their strengths, could have become an industry leader.

International Business Machines

To describe the history of IBM in the early years of the computer industry, it is best to start with its president, Thomas J. Watson Sr. Watson was in charge of the company from 1915 until 1956. He was, first and foremost, a salesman's salesman. The customer was very important, and the sales force was very well compensated. Trained at National Cash Register under John Patterson, Watson brought the management skills he learned there to IBM. NCR had the Hundred Point Club, and IBM the Hundred Percent Club, in which salespeople who had achieved their sales quota were greatly honored. Watson convinced customers to trust their bookkeeping to the primitive accounting machines of IBM.

But Watson was more than a salesman. In the 1920s and 1930s, he simplified IBM's product lines, getting rid of items that did not meet his goals, including industrial scales, meat slicers, and time clocks. He also made a decision to lease rather than sell most of his products. Although this had a short-term negative impact on earnings, it enabled the sales force to keep in continual touch with customers. And when the depression hit the United States in the 1930s, IBM's revenue decreased far less than many of its competitors that relied on new sales for income. Watson expanded IBM's sales force during the 1930s. The company survived the depression, entered World War II a $40 million company, and left it a $140 million business. It was, however, a mechanical tabulating company, with most of its business card-based, rather than an electronics company.

Watson ran IBM as a family as well as a business. He placed a major emphasis on instilling company pride in every worker, having dress codes and family outings, and even created a company songbook. There was guaranteed employment, and IBM very early offered a range of benefits, including life insurance, paid vacations, and health insurance. Watson could be very inspiring, but he also was paternalistic, strong willed, and sometimes arbitrary.

But as the world changed and the computer industry grew, Watson made his son, Thomas Watson Jr., president in 1952, and the younger Watson became chief executive officer when his father died in June 1956 at the age of eighty-two. The younger Watson had started in the 1930s as a field salesman and was a pilot during the war, where he was exposed to the world of electronics. Thomas Watson Jr. moved the company into computers because he saw the field's great opportunities. He hired tens of thousands of new employees. After suffering a heart attack, he retired at age fifty-seven and went into public service. The son may have been an even better leader than his father.

> *I believe the real difference between success and failure in a corporation can often be traced to the question of how well the organization brings out the great energies and talents of its people. What does it do to help these people find common cause with each other? How does it keep them pointed in the right direction despite the many rivalries and difference between them? And how can it sustain this common cause and sense of direction, which take place from one generation to another?*[5]

After the war, IBM's revenue grew each year, from $116 million in 1946 to $266 million in 1950, $570 million in 1954, $1.2 billion in 1957, $1.8 billion in 1960, $3.57 billion in 1965, and $7.19 billion in 1969. IBM was highly profitable, with net earnings more than 10 percent of sales each year from 1946 until 1970. Since much of its business was leased, income was spread over many years, and this required cash to finance the company's growth. IBM financed this growth through earnings, increased bank debt, and public stock offerings in 1957 and 1966.

Whereas some other computer companies focused on special systems for government agencies, IBM tried to develop standard systems for commercial customers where it could obtain orders in sufficient quantities to lower manufacturing costs and increase profits. At first, this strategy was for electromechanical systems. IBM had cooperated with the design of the Mark I Automatic Sequence Controlled Calculator at Harvard. But this was a mechanical system and left the company behind as UNIVAC took the lead in electronic computers. IBM followed into electronics and soon caught up. Whereas some competitors built one of a kind large machine, IBM attempted to find applications and equipment that met multiple customers' needs.

In 1948, IBM introduced the Selective Sequence Electronic Calculator, which computed scientific data and was put on public display at the company's Manhattan headquarters. The system had 12,500 vacuum tubes, 20,000 electromechanical relays, and could perform fifty multiplications per second. In 1952, IBM introduced the 701, its first electronic stored-program computer, which was designed for government and scientific applications. It was vacuum tube based, had electrostatic storage tube memory, and used two magnetic tape units to store information. The 701 was IBM's first large-scale electronic computer and started the transition from punched-card machines to electronic computers. Over the next two years, IBM introduced the 702 for commercial use and the 650 magnetic drum calculator. Almost 2,000 of the IBM 650s were sold, making it the most popular computer of the 1950s. Other early first-generation computers (based on vacuum tube technology) included the IBM 604 electronic calculating punch and the 704 and the 705 random-access method of accounting and control (RAMAC) bulk memory with faster access to stored material.

By the mid-1950s, transistors were replacing vacuum tubes in most designs; memory, printers, and other peripherals were improving in performance; and more powerful software was being developed. Those subjects will be covered shortly.

Between 1955 and 1964, IBM increased its product line significantly. In 1959, the company introduced the 1401, its first transistor based computer, replacing the vacuum tubes of earlier systems, the 1620, 1790, and the 7000 Series mainframes. There were more than 10,000 1401s shipped during its lifetime. New products included the 709 computer; the IBM 7040, 7044, 7070, 7080, and 7090 systems; the Series 50 basic accounting machines; the 1410 data-processing system; the 1600 and 1620 scientific computers; the 7094 at the high end of the 7000 Series; and the IBM 1130. All of these systems used transistors and core memories for faster operation.

According to a variety of estimates, IBM had the dominant share of the computer market in 1961, the year it introduced the 1400 and through the 1960s, with the remainder of the market split between its many competitors.[6] There was no question of who was leading the industry.

But this growth, product breadth, and market domination came at a price. Every computer line required its own hardware, peripherals, and software design, and even many of the cables were not compatible. The sales force and field service personnel had to be able to support many products, and the customer at some point might have additional requirements that could not be satisfied by the models of a particular IBM family. In that case, the customer would have to change systems, which meant a high cost of system migration, and the computer he or she chose might be from another vendor.

By 1960, the computer's role in business had been established. Companies had customers in banking, airlines, insurance, manufacturing, mail order, automotive suppliers, engineering, universities, and many other fields. In 1961, IBM prepared a plan for their computer line through 1970. The plan dealt with the wide variety of IBM systems in both the domestic and international marketplace, the required software and applications programs required to support them, projected changes in both semiconductor and communication technology, and planning for the growth of the computer business while preserving the installed base of leased equipment.

In April 1964, IBM introduced the System/360, a family of small to large computers with interchangeable software and peripheral equipment. Initially, five processors with various combinations of speed, power, and memory were announced: the 360 Models 30, 40, 50, 65, and 91. They were all 32-bit machines, with four 8-bit words. Other models introduced later included the Model 25 as a new entry-level machine, the Model 44 for scientific applications, Models 75, 85, and 95, which increased power at the high end, and the Model 67 for time-sharing.

Whereas the first generation of computers had used vacuum tubes and the second individual transistors wired into circuits, these were third-generation computers, IBM's first integrated circuit computers. The company developed Solid Logic Technology microelectronics, which were denser, faster, and more reliable than transistor circuits, with most components interconnected on a chip.

These systems also used core memories. The 360 Model 25 came with 4,000 to 49,000 bytes of main memory, and the mid-list Model 50 came with 65,000 to 524,000 bytes of main memory. The size of the available memory affected the software design, a subject that will be returned to later. All the machines had the same instruction set, although smaller units performed many instructions in software (microcode) rather than hardware. Because of memory limitations, there were slightly different operating systems—the DOS 360 for smaller machines, OS 360 for the mid-range and high end, and TSS/360 for time-sharing applications. The smaller machines had instructions loaded from punched cards and were used for specialized applications.

The IBM 360 was introduced with about forty peripherals, including card readers and punches, paper-tape readers, optical readers, magnetic character readers, printers, cathode display terminals, core memories, magnetic drum storage, disc storage, tape drives, audio response units, and communication units.

There were major problems in designing and manufacturing this family of machines, software, and peripherals, and some schedules were missed. *Fortune* magazine called the 360 "IBM's $5 billion gamble."[7] The Model 40 was the first to ship in 1965 and was followed during that decade with the other machines and most of the promised software. Orders soon climbed to 1,000 per month. In the summer of 1970, IBM announced a new family of machines, called the System/370. Rather than commit to a new computer, a future customer could simply upgrade parts of their IBM hardware. And with the System/360, electronic computer systems replaced punched-card systems. By 1980, the 360 and its descendants had generated more than $100 billion in revenue for IBM, and much more since then.

Customers using the IBM 1400 Series, 7070 Series, and 7090 IBM Series had to be converted to the System/360. Some customers were upset because IBM was not enhancing their existing systems and left the company to become customers of Honeywell, UNIVAC, Burroughs, GE, and Control Data, each of which made the transition easier with supporting software. IBM did have software emulators, but some customers nevertheless decided to move to another vendor.

The market grew substantially, and IBM's revenue increased. With the introduction of the System/360, IBM had become the undisputed leader in the computer business. But there were complaints from competitors and the federal government. On January 17, 1969, the government sued IBM under the Sherman Antitrust Law for attempting to monopolize the general-purpose electronic digital computer market. Charges against IBM included devising business strategies that appeared to hinder competition, announcing machines that could not be built to the specified schedule in order to stop the sale of competitors' machines, hindering the development of service and peripheral competition by maintaining a unified pricing policy combining hardware, software, technical assistance, training, and maintenance with the monthly lease, and many other charges. The trial began on May 19, 1975, and lasted six years. There were more than 950 witnesses and the submission of tens of thousands of exhibits. Finally, in 1982, before the judge could rule on the evidence, the government attorney withdrew the case.

IBM appeared to have won outright, although it did agree to sell computers rather than only lease them, to allow non-IBM equipment to be connected to IBM machines, and perhaps to restrict some of the overly extravagant claims of some salespeople relative to the advantages of IBM equipment and the dangers of using competitors' products. But technology often moves in different directions and faster than the law. And developments in the 1970s through the end of the century made this suit and the tremendous time and money spent on lawyers moot.

New competitors entered the marketplace, in software, plug-compatible peripherals, IBM compatible mainframes, systems support, and most important, in technical advances in semiconductors and communications. These competitors made the second twenty-five years of the commercial computer industry quite different from the first.

Out of the Fishbowl: Data Processing, Communications, and Control (1960–1980)

When IBM introduced its System/360, a number of changes were occurring in the computer industry. Not only was the technology changing from vacuum tubes to transistors to integrated circuits, customers were becoming more knowledgeable about how to use a computer. Some companies noticed that IBM's profit margins were significantly higher than their own and wondered if it was appropriate to give all hardware, software, system support, and training contracts to one vendor. The first IBM plug-compatible peripherals, systems, and application software were being developed by new companies and are discussed in the next sections.

By 1962, new companies began to provide computer services, including Automatic Data Processing, with payroll and personnel services; Electronic Data Systems, which purchased time on others' computers to run applications and provided computer facility management; and Computer Sciences, with software development, technical services, and facility management. All of these companies went on to become billion-dollar enterprises. Gene Amdahl, formerly of IBM, started a company in 1970 to develop compatible mainframes for the 360, financed in part by Japanese computer companies. There was competition at the high end of the market. In 1976, Seymour Cray introduced the Cray 1—the first commercially developed supercomputer. It had 200,000 integrated circuits and was used for weather forecasting, physics problems, and animation.

But the most important change may have been in the development of the minicomputer industry. It was the forerunner of the microcomputer and personal computer industry and led to the vast expansion in the numbers of computers and customers.

In the 1950s, most computers were leased to administration and financial departments where they were used for accounting, payroll, inventory control, ordering supplies, and billing, and they were kept in special air-conditioned rooms to do financial calculations more effectively. Some computers were used in science applications for large-scale computation. If engineers or scientists had a problem that they wanted the computer to solve, they had to write a program and prepare it on punched cards that were then given to the computer operators to run the program in a batch with others programs. The users were removed from the computer and were buffered by people whose job was to keep the expensive computer fully loaded.

Starting in the early 1960s, two companies decided to get the computer out of the fishbowl and into the hands of the user and thereby created the minicomputer industry. One of these companies was Digital Equipment Company (DEC) of Maynard, Massachusetts, under the leadership of Ken Olsen. (For the detailed story of Ken Olsen and DEC, see chapter 10.) The second company was Computer Control Company of Framingham, Massachusetts, under the leadership of Ben Kessel.

The minicomputer industry did not exist in 1959. By 1975, it had $5 billion in annual revenue. Following is an examination of the applications, the companies in this market, and the reason for the industry's rapid growth.

One study prepared in the early 1970s divided the minicomputer market into the following categories: engineering, including industrial automation; laboratory computation and specialized data acquisition and control; support for larger machines; business data processing; communications; and other applications. As one who was in the business for twenty-five years, this author never ceased to be surprised at how large the miscellaneous category of the minicomputer industry was. As prices for computers declined, applications increased from flight simulators to typesetting to weighing trucks and even to animation applications at Disneyland.

The market for industrial and manufacturing control was obvious. The use of sensors, transmitters, instruments, displays, valves, and other equipment for various industries (chemicals, power, pulp, paper, etc.) had existed for a long time. Using a special computer in place of electronics or an operator for controlling the process made economic sense. Raw material and energy costs were increasing; certain manufacturing processes required accurate control of the temperature, pressure, and flow of the process; labor costs were increasing; and government pressures existed regarding pollution abatement and occupational safety. A computer, properly priced, could assist in these areas.

It also made sense to use computers in the laboratory to assist engineers and scientists. Previously, numbers from instruments had to be written down, keypunched, and brought to a centralized computer, where the calculations were performed on a batch basis. The results were then brought back to the laboratory, sometimes days later. As the cost of personnel increased and the cost of computers decreased, it became appropriate to do things differently.

What was not so obvious was why the minicomputer entered the world of data processing. To understand this phenomenon, it is necessary to look at the way larger machines were marketed. First, for many companies, customers were finance or administration departments. Engineering, manufacturing, and sales departments wanted their own tools for analysis and did not want to depend on some "bean counter" telling them how they were doing. But equally important, IBM and other companies leased rather than sold their machines. And to manage a lease base, companies had to think of what equipment was installed and on lease—that is, what technical decisions did they make years ago? A supplier could not use the latest technology if introducing it would cause a larger amount of older equipment to be returned for newer equipment.

In short, leasing slowed down technical innovation. IBM and the other mainframe companies ignored the minicomputer industry, betting on large mainframes and centralized financial management. Leasing its computers had the potential of creating long-term relationships with customers and hence greater revenue to IBM. The minicomputer manufacturers sold their equipment because they didn't have an installed customer base to protect and couldn't raise the cash necessary to build one. And because the 1970s were a time of great technical innovation, the minicomputer manufacturers each year could bring out newer and faster machines at lower prices, as advances were made in the semiconductor, magnetic memory, printer, communications, and systems arenas. That is why minicomputers moved into the world of data processing through the back door.

Costs came down—from the multimillion-dollar price tags of the big computers to $100,000 and eventually to below $10,000. No longer was the computer a special system; it became a tool. Computers were sold directly to engineers and scientists who used them to solve their problems. And because these computers used the latest electronic technology, costs decreased every year. The person and the application became more important than the computer. The typical early minicomputer was 8 to 16 bits in word length, with 8,000 to 64,000 bytes of main memory, a Teletype, and a paper-tape reader. During this period, minicomputers improved significantly in performance, available memory, and software. The minicomputer industry flourished with DEC, Computer Control, Data General, Wang, Prime Computer, and others, showing that as costs came down, as the individual not the machine became the center of the world, applications expanded. This trend continued with Apple Computer, Compaq, Dell, RadioShack, Gateway, and other personal computer manufacturers driving the prices down and the market continuing to grow.

There were a number of important and successful minicomputer companies. First was Digital Equipment Corporation. Founded in 1957 by Ken Olsen, who left MIT's Lincoln Lab, it introduced the PDP-1, with a price tag of $100,000, in 1960. With the DEC PDP-8, priced below $10,000, the PDP-11, and the other machines described in chapter 10, Digital became the industry leader. In 1974, it became a Fortune 500 leading American industrial company.

A second early innovator was Computer Control Company, founded in 1953. It introduced the DDP-116, a transistorized 16-bit computer, and then the DDP-416, 516, and 716, integrated circuit versions that developed a significant market position. The company was a leader in systems for NASA, in typesetting, in industrial and process control, and in communications, and developed some of the first integrated circuits used in computers. When Honeywell purchased the company in 1966 and in 1970 acquired General Electric's computer line, talent left the company, and Computer Control Company lost its number-two position in the minicomputer industry.

In 1969, Data General was started by people who had left DEC and introduced the Nova series of 16-bit computers. It built a strong position at the low end of the minicomputer industry as an alternative to Digital Equipment.

In 1971, Prime Computer was founded by engineers and salespeople from Honeywell, including the author. Prime built a major presence at the high end of the minicomputer business, the so-called megaminis, positioning itself between IBM and DEC. It offered semiconductor memory, extensive software, and powerful systems at substantially lower prices than IBM. It also may have been the first computer company with the motto "software first," designing computers with the needs of the programmers as the major consideration. Prior to that, hardware engineers designed a computer and programmers were then brought in to make it work.

Another important company was Wang Laboratories, founded in 1951 by An Wang. It started making electronic calculators and soon developed excellent computer products. By 1976, Wang had announced a word processing system and began to dominate that part of the business. All three of these companies, Data General, Prime Computer, and Wang, became Fortune 500 companies, each with annual sales in excess of $1 billion.

Another interesting industry leader was Scientific Data Systems (SDS) of Los Angeles, which in 1966 introduced the Sigma 7 and then the SDS 92, both of which were used by NASA and other government agencies. In 1969, Xerox bought SDS for nearly $1 billion. There were management and technical differences between the California and upstate–New York people. Xerox in 1975 closed the division, ceased to manufacture the equipment, and sold the remains to Honeywell.

Hewlett-Packard was started in 1939, and by 1947, sales reached $850,000. It was a dominant manufacturer of scientific instrumentation, and in 1970, sales reached $365 million. In 1966, Hewlett-Packard introduced its first computer, the H-2115, which supported BASIC, ALGOL, and FORTRAN computer languages. In 1974, Hewlett-Packard introduced the first desktop portable electronic calculator, and in 1984, the inkjet printer and laser jet printer. The company became a major force in the industry.

Other minicomputer manufacturers included Computer Automation, Datapoint, General Electric, IBM, Interdata, Microdata, Modular Computer, Silicon Graphics, Tandem, Texas Instruments, Varian, Wang, and Xerox Data Systems.

In 1959, there were perhaps 3,000 computers in the United States. By 1978, the total number exceeded half a million and two years later, a million.

Initially, scientists and engineers used the minicomputer. But in the 1970s and 1980s, the minicomputer entered the world of finance and data processing. Intelligent terminals were introduced, followed by word processing systems, workstations, personal computers, and computer networks. Semiconductor manufacturers were not only providing faster and lower cost transistors, they were supplying integrated circuits with more and more electronic capability. New applications required system and application software. Some competitors changed their product and marketing strategy, some competitors dropped out, and others entered the field, some to become major corporations. New channels of distribution, including original equipment manufacturers (OEMs) and computer stores, developed.

Some Related Technologies:
Main Memories, Mass Storage, and Input/Output

A computer's speed is not only dependent on the performance of the electronics within the central processor, but also on the size and performance of the main memory, on the amount of mass storage available to hold data, and on the methods of getting data in and out of the computer. Each of the boxes shown in Figure 9.1 had to improve, or the computer industry was going to remain limited.

This section describes advances made from 1950 to 2000 in main memory, mass storage magnetic tapes and discs, and input/output devices, including paper tape, cards, printers, terminals and keyboards, optical and magnetic character readers, scanners, plotters and displays, automatic teller machines (ATMs), and other special terminals. Obviously, these subjects will be covered only in brief, but they are intended to show that the performance and cost of a computer and the software that could run on it were dependent on many factors that improved during this half century.

The first computers were hardwired, which meant that if one wanted the computer to perform other functions, it had to be rewired. This could take hours or even weeks. Sometimes, the operations of computers were changed with punched cards or paper tape. This also took time. After sitting at a keypunch, scientists quickly realized that they could not erase a hole. Many scientists became good typists.

Very early in the computer industry, the idea of a stored-program machine was developed. If instructions could be stored in the computer, then the performance of the machine and what it did could be modified. This internal storage needed to be comparable in speed to the speed of the machine itself. Early systems used magnetic drum memory, electrostatic memory, and mercury delay lines to store the instructions.

This development led to the invention of the magnetic core memory, which was first used in the early 1950s on the MIT Whirlwind computer. A magnetic core memory was a more compact and reliable technology than punched cards or paper tape. The names of some of the pioneers of core memory are familiar ones—Jay Forrester, Ken Olsen, and An Wang.

A core memory consisted of thousands of iron or ferrite rings—imagine Cheerios strung together on a matrix of fine wires. Electrical currents through the wires could cause a core to be magnetized either clockwise or counterclockwise. Thus each core stored a 1 or a 0 and a series of cores can store words of data.

Each core had at least three wires strung through it, two to select the core in the x and y direction and one to serve as a sense wire. In some designs, a fourth or fifth wire was used to control operation. To read a core, a signal was sent on the x and y lines and the sense wire determined if the core's magnetic properties changed. This is a destructive read memory, i.e. a read cycle destroys the contents of a memory location and the core receives a second signal to return it to its original state.

A core memory had some advantages. Each core was magnetized in one direction or the other, and it kept its magnetization when the current was removed. Core memories did not lose contents when the system power was turned off. They were fast enough for vacuum tube and transistorized computers but not for those designed around integrated circuits. Early core memory systems were about six microseconds (millionth of a second) in speed. Later, they improved to about one microsecond. And the cost of core memories, high at first, came down with time and volume.

Think about the manufacturing process. Start with small ferrite cores where someone had to hand wire each core with three or more wires strung through each one. A core stack is made up of a matrix of core planes each for one bit. An 8-bit word would have eight core planes stacked on top of each other. The system had to be tested and the bad cores replaced and rewired.

An early UNIVAC computer ganged eight planes into a stack. Each plane was hand assembled and cost $6,000 ($48,000 total). The IBM 2361 core storage was about the size of a telephone booth or two. The Digital Equipment Corporation PDP-8 offered as its largest memory 16,000 12-bit words, or 192,000 cores strung together. If the manufacturing cost was 2 cents per core, the memory cost was $3,840, and the memory system had to be priced at several times that amount. Next to IBM, DEC soon became the largest consumer of cores. It built its own magnetic core manufacturing business, and by the mid-1970s, Digital was producing 30 billion cores per year for its own requirements.

If one wanted to double the memory size, the cost doubled. Furthermore, the small memory size affected software design. Many early computers had between 4,000 and 16,000 words of main memory. (The effect and limitation of this on programming will be discussed in the next section.) Yet for twenty years, from the 1950s to the 1970s, core memories were the main memory system used in almost all computers.

There were attempts to find better and faster memories, and IBM did much work in this area. The semiconductor lab and memory design group at Honeywell's Computer Control Division, as well as other computer companies, also worked on semiconductor alternatives to core memories.

In 1970, Intel released the 1103, the first dynamic random-access memory. By 1972, it was the best-selling memory chip in the world and had started to replace core memories. With its Prime 200 in 1972, Prime Computer was the first computer company to commit exclusively to semiconductor memory. The Hewlett-Packard 9800 soon followed. By the late 1970s, semiconductor memories had become less expensive than core memories, and all-new machines were developed using them. Early semiconductor memories were volatile; they lost their content when power was turned off, and engineers had to work around this limitation. But the decrease in cost and increase in performance of semiconductor memories made the modern computer industry possible.

Today, a typical personal computer might have 256 million bytes of main memory (versus the 8,000 bytes of earlier computers), run at .004 microseconds (versus the one microsecond of an earlier core memory), and cost about .0000001 cent per bit (versus the 2 cent per bit of the earlier core memories). Almost all performance improvement and cost decrease in computers can be traced to the switch from core memories to semiconductor memories and the improvement over time in semiconductor memory performance and cost.

As main memory performance increased and costs came down, ancillary storage costs also decreased. Since the early days of the computer industry, it has been true that fast memories have been more expensive than slower memories, and there has been a need for a hierarchy of storage elements. Computers needed ever-increasing amounts of data, with high-speed, low-cost, random-access bulk memory. Magnetic drums, disc packs, or tapes were used to store data in the computer and store output information.

Realizing that both punched cards and paper tape were too slow, IBM pioneered the use of magnetic tape in 1952 with the 726 half-inch tape drive, a 2,400-foot tape reel. In 1956, IBM delivered the first disc file, the RAMAC 305—fifty magnetically coated metal platters with a total of 5 million bytes of data. In 1963, IBM introduced its first storage unit with removable discs, the IBM 1311.

For half a century, there were improvements in memory capacity, access time, data-transfer rate, and cost per bit of storage. These were accomplished with both magnetic tape and disc systems, whose performance continued to improve over the years. For the past half century, the general rule was that if the speed of the main memory was X, a moving head disc was 10 percent to 1 percent as fast, and tapes were 0.1 percent to 0.01 percent as fast. But discs and tapes had more capacity and were significantly less expensive per byte of storage than main memory.

In 1960, at a time when computer main memories might be 8,000 bytes, bulk memories contained about 6 million bytes of storage. They were very large devices, with an access time of about one-third of a second, and a cost of about 0.1 cents per bit. By 1962, disc drives had as much storage as 25,000 punched cards. The IBM 3340 had a storage of 70 million bytes, with twenty-five-millisecond access time. The price was about $25,000 per storage unit plus $39,000 for the disc controller. And as the cost of computers and main memories decreased, so did that of mass storage.

In 1971, IBM developed the eight-inch floppy diskette with a magnetic iron oxide surface. The floppy disc allowed data portability from one machine to another and made desktop computing possible. In 1976, the first 5-1/4 inch discs were introduced by Shugart Associates for Wang Laboratories. In 1980, Seagate provided five megabytes of data on a hard disc. Sony introduced the 3-1/2 inch floppy discs for Hewlett-Packard, and they became the next industry standard. The three-inch floppy was followed by the Zip disc and CDs, the current standards for smaller, low-cost storage.

Meanwhile, there were many advances at the high storage end. In 1973, IBM introduced the Winchester multiplatter disc drive. The drive had two spindles, each containing 30 million bytes of data, hence the "thirty-thirty" was called the Winchester. This unit had sealed discs that could not be removed. The IBM 3310 was introduced in 1979. The IBM 3330 was a 100 million–byte storage device. In 1984, IBM introduced the 3840 half-inch tape cartridge, with a 3-million-bytes-per-second transfer rate, and in 1991, 1 gigabyte (billion bytes) on a three-and-a-half-inch hard disc. Other advances were in optical disc memories and automated tape libraries.

The performance of a magnetic memory or tape is dependent on the design of the magnetic head used to read and write the magnetic signal, the distance of the head from the surface, the magnetic density of the material, and the size of the media. By 1980, thin film technology allowed 12 million bits per square inch. During the next twenty years, costs came down and disc density and performance went up.

Today, 40 billion bytes (40 gigabytes) of mass storage for a personal computer cost about $100. This is more data storage than was available in all of the computers manufactured in the 1950s.

The first computer printers were typewriters. Then, in 1953, Remington Rand developed the first high-speed printer. With the introduction of the 360, IBM introduced enhancements to the 1403 printer, a chain printer that could print at rates up to 1,100 lines per minute. In 1957, IBM came out with the first dot matrix printer, followed a year later by the Epson EP-101 dot matrix printer. Epson, a subsidiary of Seiko, soon was manufacturing about 100,000 printers each month.

Chester Carlson in 1938 discovered a dry printing process and sold it to Halloid Corporation of Rochester, New York, in 1949. The company was later renamed Xerox and grew to become a very large company. In 1978, Xerox invented a laser printer, the 9700. It was very fast—120 pages per minute—but expensive. In 1976, IBM offered the 3800, their first laser printer. Hewlett-Packard in 1984 introduced its LaserJet printer (eight pages per minute) at $1,000 and in 1988, its DeskJet inkjet printer.

There were also advances in other input/output devices. In 1962, Teletype shipped the Model 33 keyboard and punched-tape terminal used in many early computers. It quickly became obsolete, however, as terminals, keyboards, and cathode-ray-tube displays increased in performance and did much of the input control. Small computers were soon used as intelligent terminals and workstations. In the minicomputer field, electrical signals from instruments and processes were fed directly into the computer and, upon analysis, corrective signals fed back into the manufacturing process. The use of optical and magnetic readers became widespread. For example, at the bottom of every check you write is a series of magnetic characters that are read directly by computers. When you check out of a supermarket, the bar code on items are scanned, prices read directly, and the inventory of items in the store adjusted. Many people use ATMs for all their banking. Credit cards are scanned and the information fed electronically into the computer. The spread of the computer throughout society is due in large part to the availability of specialized methods of entering and handling information without manual intervention.

In 1968, Stanford Research Institute demonstrated the first system with keyboard, mouse, and windows graphic interface, and in 1974, Xerox designed the Alto, the first workstation with windows and a built-in mouse. The use of icons and a mouse to point to desired operations has made the computer useful to a much greater number of people. No longer did users have to understand programming, they just has to point and click.

There were a number of independent suppliers of magnetic storage devices, printers, and other devices that should be mentioned. They all contributed to the growth of the industry and, in turn, became major companies themselves: Ampex, Canon, Connor Peripherals, EMC, Hewlett-Packard, Lexmark, Memorex, Quantum, Seagate Technology, Shugart, Storage Technology, Telex, Western Digital, and many others.

Today, entering data into a computer and manipulating the data once entered continues to affect business. For instance, music can be sent down a communication line, and this new method of distribution is impacting the record and entertainment industries. Using computers to inquire about airline and hotel availability and costs has changed the travel industry in fundamental ways. Digital cameras and computers are challenging Eastman Kodak and Polaroid. Polaroid was in the instant photography, not the instant film business, and with-out the leadership of Ed Land, digital cameras have put the company in major trouble. None of these changes would have occurred if computer data entry, output, and main memory had remained at 1950s and 1960s technology levels.

Software: Making the Computer Do Something

All computers are used to solve problems. The word *problem* here describes scientific, engineering, marketing, manufacturing, financial, management, and personal areas in which calculations must be performed or information processed, analyzed, reduced, or compared, followed by some sort of output activity—from printing checks to sending electronic signals to a manufacturing process.

The circuits, memories, peripheral equipment, wires, and physical things within a computer are called hardware. Software or programs are the sets of instructions that tell the computer what to do. Computers can only operate on digitally formatted binary data—a series of ones and zeros. Once data has been converted to binary form, a software program has to tell the computer what to do with this data. The computer sequentially executes the instructions and comes up with the answers.

During the last fifty years, there have been major advances in software, just as there have been in hardware. Early machines had very small memories, sometimes 4,000 to 16,000 bytes of memory, making it impossible to develop large programs that would occupy a significant portion of the computer's memory. Moreover, during the 1950s, new computers were being designed, and they were all different and produced in small quantities, each with its own software. New computers made older ones and their software obsolete. Since computers were expensive and the cost of personnel was low, the goal was to keep the computer running. Programmers had to submit their jobs on punched cards to people whose responsibility it was to keep the computer loaded in a batch mode. It could take hours or even days for the programmer to receive results from the computer.

But gradually, memory and computer costs decreased and memory capacity increased. Advances in computer design, especially with the IBM System/360, produced machines that were built in larger quantities. The IBM 360 offered both binary and decimal arithmetic for both scientific and business applications, and had one major operating system. The 360 was the largest software project to date, and much was learned in the 1960s about managing, creating, and testing software. Programmers now could spend more time developing software that could be used on more than one application or one computer.

The computer itself only recognizes ones and zeros, and the early programs had their instructions written in binary code (machine code). In 1963, the American Standard Code for Information Interchange (ASCII) was proposed. ASCII allowed machines from different manufacturers to exchange data in 128 unique set of ones and zeros, which were used to represent both alphabetic and numeric information. Later, other industry standards for hardware and software made computer compatibility easier.

The first generation of computer software used machine code. Programmers had to write a series of ones and zeros. The second developed assembly language by using alphanumeric symbols instead of ones and zeros. However, each computer had its own assembly language, which translated these symbols into appropriate signals the machine could understand. This usually prevented one machine's programs from running on another. Third-generation systems with higher level languages allowed programmers to work on more than one machine without learning another assembly language, and made many programs portable from one machine to another. The fourth-generation languages, called very high level languages, used interpreters and relied on reusable and portable code.

During the early days of the computer, software was simple and written to fit within the available small main memory. It consisted of assemblers, debugging tools, and ways of loading a batch of programs into the computer. By then advances were made in system software, programming languages, operating systems, and utility software. Languages and advanced software were developed to make writing programs easier as new applications for the computer developed and as more main memory became available

An operating system is a computer program that acts as an interface between the user and the bare machine. An operating system controls input, output, and peripherals, and it acts as the interface between the operator, the hardware, and the software running on the computer. It mediates all interactions between users, application programs, and computer hardware.

There are differences in operating systems based on many factors. They can differ based on the application—serial batch, multiprogramming, multiprocessing, time-sharing, and real time—or based on the number of users, programs, and machines that can use it, ranging from a single user on a single machine with a single application to multiple users, machines, and/or applications.

Software was developed that began to solve other computer performance issues, including job scheduling, memory management programs to control access and manage memory hierarchy, file management, loading system software, compilers, assemblers, user resident application programs and system data, diagnostics, file conversion, automatic program restarting, scheduling input and output devices, remote terminal support, security, performance statistics, and a comprehensive group of routines that contributes to the efficient and convenient running of programs on a computer. Programmers needed larger memories to develop advanced software.

As computers became more powerful and memories became larger, software advances made the computer more useful and opened up new markets for the industry. They also provided opportunities for many companies to enter the market.

In the 1960s, IBM bundled all software and support with its hardware, and it was included in the monthly lease. In 1969, IBM introduced the System 3, a minicomputer line with separate prices for hardware and software. The company then began to charge a separate fee for all its software and allowed independent programmers to develop and sell software for IBM computers. By 1975, computer software sales approached $800 million and grew rapidly after that.

Computers can only process binary code. An assembler is a program used to translate from the symbolic language of assembly-level programming into binary machine instructions. Soon higher level languages, more like English, were developed to express programming code. Each language has to be converted back to binary code through a compiler, a program-translating source code within a higher language, to machine code, a series of binary instructions that can be processed by a computer.

In 1945, Grace Murray Hopper, a naval officer and computer scientist, became the first programmer for the Mark I. She later worked with Eckert-Mauchly Computer Corporation, where she helped design the first high level language compiler, invented the language APT, and worked on the development of COBOL, a language that operates on machines made by different manufacturers.

When she retired from the navy at age eighty in 1986, Rear Admiral Grace Murray Hopper told the Voice of America:

> *Up until this time, computer programs had to be written in assembly code, machine code, or there was one compiled for mathematical problems. But I felt that more people should be able to use the computer and that they should be able to talk to it in plain English. And that was the beginning of COBOL.*

In that same interview she also said something that might be a motto for most entrepreneurs: "It is much easier to apologize than to get permission."[8]

There have been more than 200 languages created to make writing computer programs easier by allowing statements written by the user to express in a high level of symbolism the desired action by the machine. They included, in the early days, COBOL (common business oriented language); RPG (report program generator, another early business language); FORTRAN (formula translation), developed in 1954 at the Applied Science Division of IBM; and BASIC (Beginners All-purpose Symbolic Instruction Code), developed at Dartmouth in 1964 to run on time-sharing machines and teach programming to beginners. These higher level languages were developed to make it easier to write computer code and to reuse the computer code developed for older machines.

For a while, programmers were identified by which of these languages they understood. But soon other languages entered the scene. They included ALGOL (algorithmic language), a structured procedural language created in 1960; APL (a programming language), developed by Harvard University and IBM in 1962; C programming language, developed at Bell Labs in 1972; Java; JOVIAL; LISP (list processing), developed at MIT for artificial intelligence applications; PASCAL;

PL-1, released by IBM in 1964 with the 360; PostScript; SimScript; UNIX; developed in the 1970s at Bell Labs; and many others.

It is also possible to examine the history of software through its suppliers. IBM initially offered a turnkey system in which hardware, software, and support were supplied together in one monthly lease price. This approach changed with time. The minicomputer manufacturers, led by Digital Equipment Corporation, did not have the resources to solve all of their customer's programming needs. Instead, they sold hardware with a certain level of system software and then relied on their customers or OEMs to develop the customized application software. Capabilities in software design spread and were no longer only the domain of the large computer manufacturers. By 1967, there were more than 2,500 software firms in the United States.

This trend in software development continued with the growth of personal computers. That part of the industry will be discussed later, but a commentary on software development is appropriate here. Personal computers are dependent on the availability of application software since the customer does not want to write code to make the computer perform. Initially, small, independent companies developed almost all of the software for personal computers.

There are three application programs that, in the beginning, made the personal computer industry grow: word processing software, spreadsheets, and database management. In addition, operating systems and software for communications were essential.

A word processor is like a typewriter with certain additional features, including the ability to delete, insert, and move text; spell-check the material; and choose easily among typefaces and page designs. Perhaps the first word processing software package was WordStar in 1979. Over the next decade, a variety of other word processing software was made available, including Magic Wand, WordPerfect, and Write. In 1983, Microsoft introduced Word and in 1990, an improved version, Word 3.0. In 1985, Aldus introduced PageMaker for the Macintosh, significantly improving the quality of word processing output and allowing text and graphics information to be mixed.

An accounting spreadsheet is a large sheet of paper with a number of rows and columns. Relationship of any cell or location (address) to others can be specified by formulas. In 1979, Dan Bricklin and Bob Frankston developed VisiCalc, the first computer spreadsheet program, for the Apple II E. With VisiCalc, one could change any number and the entire spreadsheet would be recalculated. One could enter numerical data and immediately see how it affected other numbers, something that a large mainframe could not do. This software made the Apple II E useful in business and helped build an industry. Bricklin and Frankston's company, Personal Software, also introduced a version of VisiCalc for the Tandy TRS-80, Commodore Pet, and Atari 800. In 1982,

Lotus 1-2-3 added charting, plotting, and database capabilities to the spreadsheet concept. It interfaced with the IBM video capability and ran faster. Later, Microsoft developed the Excel spreadsheet.

Databases are collections of organized information. For instance, your list of people and addresses for Christmas cards or your favorite restaurants with phone numbers is a small database. There are large databases as well. Airline reservation systems can store data on all planes and all passenger reservations on all flights for several months out. A computerized checkout system in a supermarket must track the entire product line in the store. In the 1980s, database software was developed for personal computers, and one of the first was dBase II by Ashton-Tate. The Lotus Database management system was a collection of data with a sophisticated program to retrieve and process the data.

The other major system issues relate to disk operating systems (DOS) and windows, with its mouse. Many people and organizations were involved in this area, including Xerox, Seattle Computer Products, and Digital Research.

In 1972, Bill Gates and Paul Allen formed the Traf-O-Data Corporation, which made car counters for highway departments. It was renamed Microsoft in 1975, when the company developed a form of BASIC for the MITS Altair personal computer. In 1977, the company shipped FORTRAN for personal computers using the CP/M-operating system. In 1981, the company bought all rights to DOS from Seattle Computer Products, and MS-DOS was introduced. Microsoft was asked by IBM to write the operating system for the IBM Personal Computer (PC) in 1980 and started work on the Intel 8086 version of AT&T UNIX operating system. Meanwhile, IBM was working on its own product called Top View. It was released in February 1985 but was discontinued two years later. Microsoft Windows was announced in 1983; in 1985, Microsoft shipped Windows 1.0, and in 1990, Windows 3.0.

Bill Gates turned out to be one of the best computer leaders, combining knowledge of technology, great skill as an entrepreneur, and imagination. He built the first pure software organization to become a major company and convinced larger companies such as IBM and Apple to do things his way. Like Henry Ford with the Model T, Gates brought a product, the computer, to the masses, and his software became the industry standard. By 1990, Microsoft had revenue in excess of $1 billion and by 2002, revenue had reached $30 billion.

There are similarities between Microsoft today and IBM during its great growth years. First, and least important, they have both been sued by the Justice Department on antitrust grounds. Microsoft today dominates its industry, just as IBM did in the 1960s and early 1970s. Both are full-service turnkey companies that do not easily allow others to interface with their products. And both bundled their systems in pricing. There are obvious differences, however—especially in the number of customers, the growth in standard features, and the price per unit.

From 1950 to 1990, there were many advances in software design. Because there was more memory in computers, new software features could be added. As computer costs came down and communication advances occurred, programmers no longer had to stand in line to use a computer. Every programmer could have his or her own machine or be online to a very large machine. Major companies developed to provide software services or manage large databases, including Computer Associates, IBM, Systems Development Corporation, and many others. Software companies included Adobe, Affiliated Computer Sciences, American Management Systems, Automatic Data Processing, Borland, Computer Associates, Computer Sciences, Electronic Data Systems, First Data, Informix, Lotus, Microsoft, Novell, Oracle, PeopleSoft, Sybase, and Veritas Software.

In 1996 there were many thousand active software publishers, selling about 20,000 software titles. Software revenue reached $80 billion in 1999. The field has grown since Grace Hopper was a programmer for the Mark I. In 1961, the number of programmers had reached about 60,000. According to the U.S. Department of Labor, about 1 million people were employed as computer programmers and software developers in 2002.[9] Perhaps 4 million people are employed in the information technology industry in the United States, and the number of people who use computers in their daily work is substantially higher than that.

At this point, the story of computers becomes both one of an increasingly smaller world and of an increasingly larger world, for in the last quarter of the twentieth century, computers became smaller and smaller, while their reach became enormous—almost universal. How did this happen? The next two sections will describe two major developments.

The Priesthood: Can You Trust a User with a Computer? (1980–2000)

Early computers cost millions of dollars and took up hundreds of cubic feet. With the development of the IBM 360, with technical advances from many people and companies, and with the growth of the minicomputer industry, costs came down and sizes decreased. Today, a personal computer can cost less than $1,000 and takes up a small place on your desk or in your briefcase.

In the 1960s, computers were very expensive, and it was vital that their usage be optimized. Engineers, scientists, and trained computer operators could use computers—not just the finance and administration departments. What was next? Were computers the province of technically trained personnel, or could anyone operate them? Could people be trusted with a machine? And what would they do with it if they had one? For twenty years, there were questions about the applicability of computers for people in their homes, and there were also questions about data integrity, security, and customer education.

In 1972, Nolan Bushnell of Atari developed Pong, the first computer game. In 1975, Ed Roberts of Micro Instrumentation and Telemetry Company (MITS) introduced the Altair personal computer, a 256-byte computer kit that cost $397. Its input and output consisted of switches and lights. A number of people bought one—mostly "computer nerds."

In April 1976, Steve Wozniak and Steve Jobs released the Apple I computer. It was the first single circuit board computer, and had 8,000 bytes of memory, a keyboard, and a video interface to a television set. The Apple I was sold in kit form for $666.66 to hobbyists. In 1977, Apple Computer was founded and the Apple II was released. It sold for $1,298, came with an audiocassette drive for storage, and 4,000 bytes of main memory. Later, its memory was expanded to 48,000 bytes, and a floppy disc drive replaced the cassette drive. The Apple II E was a very successful machine, and by 1981, more than 120,000 customers had purchased one and Apple had captured half of the personal computer market. By 1982, Apple had achieved sales of $583 million.

In 1975, the Commodore Personal Electronic Transactor (PET) was introduced, with 4,000 bytes of main memory, graphics, and an audiocassette drive. It sold for $795, about half of the price of the Apple II. Microsoft developed its first BASIC for the PET and then offered a version for the Apple II.

In 1977, RadioShack announced the TRS-80, a microcomputer with 4,000 bytes of memory. In its first month of production, 10,000 were sold; 55,000 were sold in the first year. The TRS-80 Model II came with an eight-inch disc drive, and was followed by Models III and IV. In 1983, the company introduced the Tandy 2000, which ran MS-DOS, and the next year introduced the Tandy 1000, which was IBM compatible. By 1986, RadioShack, owned by Tandy, had more than 7,300 retail outlets and soon became an industry leader.

In 1976, Wang Laboratories announced a word processing system built around its minicomputer line. In 1978, Atari announced the Atari 400 and 800 personal computers, and the following year, Clive Sinclair started Sinclair Research and announced the ZX80. This was followed by the ZX81 and the Spectrum.

The growth of personal computers was extraordinary. In 1979, 150,000 home computers were sold. In 1980, the leading suppliers were RadioShack, Apple, Hewlett-Packard, Zenith, IBM, and Commodore. Others included Altos, Atari, Kaypro, Mattel, NEC, North Star, Osborne, Sinclair, Sony, Texas Instruments, Timex, and Xerox. By 1983, 1 million Apple II computers had been sold. And this was just the beginning.

A factor that contributed to this growth was the movement away from text-based computers and into graphics. In 1973, the design of an Altos workstation computer had been started at the Xerox Palo Alto Research Center. Windows, icons (pictures), menus, and pointing devices (WIMP) were integral to the Xerox 8010 Star System in 1981. The technology was used by Apple in 1984, as the company developed the Apple Macintosh with a Microsoft Windows operating system, and later by Microsoft for MS-DOS, and then with the IBM PC as Windows 3.0 became popular. With a windows system, users did not have to remember computer codes or know programming—they just had to point at the screen and click.

The Macintosh was a personal computer based on the Motorola 68000 processor, with 128,000 words of main memory, had one floppy disc, Mac OS 1.0 software, and sold for $2,495. Sales of the new system started slowly but got a boost when Aldus PageMaker software and the Laser Writer printer became available. The Macintosh was the first successful graphic interface machine and had major applications in desktop publishing with the creation of the PostScript software. People who did graphic design loved this computer.

Another major factor in the growth of personal computers was the development of the IBM PC in 1981. IBM's product made this part of the computer industry something to be taken seriously. IBM's personal computer introduction was a low-key event since the company did not have great expectations, but sales took off and grew to $5 billion in the next four years. The IBM PC used the Intel 8088 chip, floppy disc drives, ran Microsoft MS-DOS and two other operating systems, and had VisiCalc and other supporting software, including BASIC. It cost $1,600 to $6,000, depending on system configuration.

Microsoft had an agreement with IBM to develop their operating system and then to be able to sell it separately from the IBM product. Microsoft soon sold it to a variety of new IBM PC-compatible suppliers. There was a burst of creative energy by many companies in both hardware and software, and independent vendors at a rapid rate developed application software for the computer. By 1983, the IBM PC and its equivalents had market dominance.

In 1978, the total number of computers used in the United States exceeded half a million, and by 1980, that number had grown to 1 million. The sale of home computers reached 2 million in 1982. In 1986, the number of computers in the United States exceeded 30 million, and in 1989, 50 million. In 1982, *Time* magazine named the computer its "Man of the Year."

New competitors entered the marketplace, and others left. In 1983, Compaq shipped 53,000 computers in its first year and by 1986, had shipped 500,000 machines. In 1984, Michael Dell started his own company, and Dell Computer soon becomes a major leader. Gateway was started and grew rapidly. Meanwhile, Packard Bell/NEC left the U.S. market, and RadioShack, Zenith, Commodore, Osborne, Sinclair, Texas Instruments, and Xerox were no longer major players. Today, the leading suppliers are Apple, Compaq, Dell, Gateway, Hewlett-Packard, and IBM, but that may change tomorrow. In 1996, IBM and clones had achieved an 83 percent share of the personal computer market.

Why has this part of the computer industry grown so fast and prices dropped so much? It is because the computer industry, and especially the low-cost segment, is affected by the major advances in the semiconductor industry described in chapter 7. The computer industry is dependent on improvements in computer memory performance and advances in semiconductor microprocessors—the Intel 4004 introduced in the late 1970s; the 6502; the Intel 8080 chip; the Motorola 6800, 8086, 8087, and 8088; the Motorola 88000 and 68040; the Intel 80486 and 486; and the Intel Pentium chip.

In the 1960s, a computer manufacturer had to have capability in circuit design, logic design, system design, packaging, and manufacturing. Now those skills are obsolete as the logic circuitry is on a chip, designed and constructed by Intel, Motorola, National Semiconductor, or others. Everyone's personal computer is compatible with the IBM PC (except for Apple's), and the only supplier difference may be price, customer support, and advertising.

Computers are now available as desktop computers, notebook PCs, word processors, office workstations, and handheld/wireless machines. As prices continue to drop, many manufacturers are moving into the office market, providing additional software and support and finding ways of increasing average revenue. But, at the same time, current suppliers, including Compaq, Dell, Gateway, Hewlett-Packard, IBM, Sony, and Toshiba, are fighting for market share with products that all use the same or similar integrated circuits and memories.

Computers and Communications: Time Sharing, E-mail, and the Web

As personal computers were getting smaller, they had an increasingly global reach. This trend was due to improved communications, networks, and the World Wide Web.

In the very earliest computers, all equipment was in the same room, wired together. But beginning in those earliest days, there were issues about what problems should be solved in a central computer, with all inputs entered locally, and what should have data entered or be solved in remote locations. Some problems, such as airline reservations, require that people around the country, and even around the world, be able to look at information and enter data. Other problems, such as payroll, may require that information be far more confidential and centralized. Over the last fifty years, limitations in hardware and software, as well as the state of the communications industry, have affected the trade-off between centralized and decentralized information handling.

The first major system that had decentralized inputs may have been the SABRE (Semiautomatic Business Related Environment) Airline Reservation System built by IBM in 1964. Up until then, reservation requests for airlines were phoned in by a travel agent to the airline, and someone checked to see if there was space available. If so, the agent was told by phone and could write a ticket for a particular flight. Typically, seats were assigned when a ticket holder showed up at the airport. The ability of travel agents and airline offices to make reservations online was a major step forward. SABRE linked 2,000 terminals through several thousand miles of leased telephone lines to a pair of IBM 7090 computers, giving information on any flight in a few seconds. But the amount of data that was sent from remote locations to the centralized computer was small and could be handled by the computers and telephone systems available at that time. This was a special application with dedicated hardware and software.

In 1954, IBM introduced remote job entry, in which the data entry device did not have to be physically in the same room as the computer. In 1960, AT&T designed its Dataphone, its first commercial modem to convert digital computer data to analog signals for transmission across a long-distance network and then back to digital data at a remote location. In 1963, MCI, under the leadership of William McGowan, applied to the FCC to provide communication services and it received permission six years later. AT&T now had its first serious telephone industry competitor in almost a century.

In 1973, Ethernet was developed as a standard of how various terminals, computers, peripherals, and other equipment could be wired within a building using a single cable. This design program was supported by DEC, Xerox, and Intel, and made possible local area networks. In 1974, IBM announced the Systems Network Architecture—a planned, evolutionary approach to communications, and provided a stable environment within the IBM world.

Many users, such as insurance companies, banks, hotel chains, transportation companies, and the Defense Department, were developing their own networks. The National Science Foundation supported private research networks as did other government agencies. Minicomputers were beginning to be used as mainframe front ends, taking some of the communication load off of the big computers.

It is worth noting the types of equipment that might have to be interconnected. In 1977, one estimate was that the following types of terminals existed in the United States: 680,000 typewriters and Teletypes, 390,000 alphanumeric displays, 85,000 intelligent terminals, 50,000 remote data stations, 210,000 point of sale devices, 65,000 bank teller machines, and 180,000 low-cost portable terminals.[10] Many of these devices would increase significantly in number during the next ten years. Meanwhile, for comparison, that year there were 20 million touch-tone phones and 175 million rotary phones in the United States.

Time-sharing was one of the advances in the 1960s. Time-sharing divides computer power cyclically between users. Several users could share a computer, each believing they were the only user. Users would be billed based on the amount of computer resources required. An early time-sharing system ran at MIT on IBM 709 and 7090 computers. Project MAC (Man and Computer) started at MIT in 1963 and soon connected twenty-four terminals around the campus. It also used DEC's new PDP-1. Soon, 160 terminals were connected on the campus, and 30 could be used at the same time. Multics (multiplexed information and computing service) was developed by MIT, GE, and Bell Labs starting in 1963 and supported 1,000 terminals, 300 of which could be in use at one time. As the number of users increased, the cost of computing per user decreased significantly.

There were many types of telecommunication applications, including data entry, data inquiry, record update, remote batch entry, and remote job entry. Progress in computer design had to be made for bank funds transfer, for remote data collection, and to minimize corporate paper shuffling. But networking was difficult because of incompatible or nonstandard hardware, incompatible data formats, different software, and because few users saw advantages in sharing data or computer processing power. Also, there were difficulties in the development of remote systems because of the types of communication services costs offered by AT&T and the associated costs.

In the 1970s, a system might have consisted of a wide range of devices: terminals, both dumb and intelligent (remote terminals that could do some work independent of the remote computer), buffered and online interfaces, modems, multiplexers, concentrators, front ends, message processors, and computers. There were 3.6 million terminals and computers installed by 1983, and these might have had different protocols and standards and might have been stand-alone, in clusters, or in local area networks.

Problems arose when digital data was sent through the phone system. There were more than 70 million American homes wired into the phone network, and every business had phones. But, because of their available bandpass, that is the speed of information that could be sent through telephone wires, the standard phone system lines were limited for computer communication capability. The phone system was analog, and some of AT&T's switching networks had been installed before World War II. A home or office might be able to operate at speeds no faster than 2,400 or 4,800 baud (bits per second), which could support a very slow typist, but the transfer of significant amounts of digital data was impossible without dedicated higher speed lines. These could operate at greater speeds, up to 19,200 baud, but at higher cost.

Starting in 1974, there was a slow but relentless merging of computer and communications technology. As of 1974, only 3 percent of AT&T's revenue was from data communication. There were a number of small companies, however, that developed modems to connect digital computers into the phone system. They included Codex, Paradyne, Intertel, Universal Data Systems, and in 1981, Hayes Microcomputer, which announced the Smartmodem 300 that became the standard for personal computers. With the breakup of AT&T and the entrance into the communications field of new companies, including MCI, IT&T, GTE, and many cable companies, and then in the 1990s, with the development of fiber-optic lines, communication speeds increased significantly. Facsimile machines, data transmission, distribution of information processing, integrated voice-data-video systems, networks, and communication servers became feasible. Communication satellite systems, including Telstar, and fiber-optic cables developed by Corning Glass increased the speed of data that could be transmitted.

Dr. J.C.R Licklider in 1962 forecast globally connected computers. He went to the Department of Defense to set up research-and-development programs in time-sharing in networks. The ARPAnet (Advanced Research Projects Agency network) of the U.S. Department of Defense was started in 1969 to allow sharing of software resources and remote databases among several large computers around the country. The system used packet switching, cutting up data into discrete units and sending them over high-speed telephone lines by various routes and putting messages back together. ARPAnet soon expanded among universities and other research centers. Starting with four host computers in 1970, by 1974 the first international connections were in England and Norway, with sixty-two total host computers. The federal government and universities funded most early development of the Internet.

The commercialization of the Internet concept began in 1975 when Telenet, the first commercial private packet switching network, was started by Bolt, Beraneck and Newman, which believed that there would be many independent networks rather than one international organized network.

Widespread development of personal computers, workstations, and local area networks allowed the Internet to develop with many local and international networks. But, there were questions of how to interconnect many networks and what the internetworking architecture should be.

In 1990, the World Wide Web was born at CERN in Geneva, Switzerland. It started with a common way of addressing any information on the Internet. The Internet is similar to an internal mail service and the U.S. Postal Service, or to an internal phone directory with local extensions and an international phone system with country, area code, and local number required. Addresses have to be more complete if users are geographically or technically diverse.

There is no reason to have a phone if you have no one to talk to or no way of getting a phone number. The same thing applied to the early Internet, which took time to expand. There was a significant growth in the number of host computers, starting with 4 in 1969, 35 in 1973, 111 in 1977, 562 in 1983, 2,300 in 1986, 80,000 in 1989, 727,000 in 1992, 5,846,000 in 1995, 29,670,000 in 1998, and 93,047,000 in 2000.[11]

There was an equivalent growth in users. By 1994, more than 30 million people had access to the Internet; by 2000, 90 million Americans had access, and 327 million people around the globe used the Internet in 2000 to obtain information and contribute new data.[12] Electronic mail now outnumbers regular mail more than ten to one. People use the Internet for everything from getting travel information and shopping to checking the weather and looking for potential dates.

In the last quarter of the twentieth century, new companies were founded to develop the hardware and software required to connect private networks to public networks or to operate networks and provide network services. That process was similar to the old telephone company, which provided operators and telephone directories so a person could figure how to call someone, and then provided lines and telephone switches to route the calls.

Companies established since the early 1970s and now providing these services include America Online (AOL), Cisco Systems, Earthlink, Google, Microsoft, Netscape, Novell, Oracle, Sun Microsystems, and 3Com. Some provide the technology for local area networks, some develop the router—the switching hardware between public and private networks—some provide workstations and network software, some provide Web services or search engines, and some provide the software to run database management systems. All of these companies, which were not around when the ARPAnet was established in the 1960s, have been founded, developed products and services, and are now major corporations

The Information Society: Promises, Plans, and Problems

From its beginnings as a very small industry in 1950, the computer industry has grown significantly. Companies were started with a few people, and within a decade or so, have become some of the largest companies in America. Some have become specialists in personal computers, peripherals, communications, databases, application software, networks, Web hosting, or facility management. At the same time, other established companies have tried to grow in this field and failed. In the year 2000, the information industry was the second largest industry in the world after food production.

Today, anyone can use any telephone or computer in the world and reserve an airline seat on almost any airline to almost any place in the world. People fly on airplanes designed with the aid of computers, navigated by computer systems, and flown by pilots trained on computer simulators. After a 600-mile-per-hour trip, people arrive at their destination and may wait one hour while baggage is unloaded manually. Or the baggage may have been sent to another city thousands of miles away by a computer.

Not all applications of the computer are equally effective, and some things that have occurred in the last half century may not be user-friendly. But without question, the computer has changed the world positively in many ways.

First, there has been a change in competition and the companies who have become the leading suppliers. Whereas the automobile industry had a period of innovation followed by a long period of consolidation with very few suppliers, in the computer industry, many new companies have been established in every decade, and some of them have become very large companies. Meanwhile, older established companies fell by the wayside. As a rule, it can be said that megamergers in the computer industry generally haven't worked except to provide financial rewards to a few executives and the investment bankers. With that in mind, one could wonder about the future of three large and successful companies in information technology—Digital Equipment Corporation, Compaq, and Hewlett-Packard—as they have merged and have been brought under the same management.

Second, computers and networks have become international in scope. Business and information do not stop at national borders. Anyone, anywhere with a computer and a modem can access all the world's information. In that sense, computers are similar to one of the greatest developments in American history: the beginnings of the free public library a century ago. All of the world's knowledge, experience, and imagination are available to anyone with a library card if they but take the trouble to learn.

Today, most computers have a network connection or modem and can access the World Wide Web. The world for computers and communications is global in nature, and new and major international competitors are in the market. From Europe, Siemens-Nixdorf; from Japan, Fujitsu, Hitachi, NEC, Toshiba, Packard Bell/NEC, Canon, and Matsushita; and in China, India, and elsewhere, many companies and ideas have prospered. Meanwhile, some American companies and institutions have neither understood nor participated in this industry. Many, which have failed, have been named in this chapter.

Some promises of the industry have not come true. There has often been overselling and overpromising to consumers. For more than a quarter century, there have been forecasts about electronic banking, online newspapers, the paperless society, and charging for some network services, and for specific reasons they have not occurred or have been delayed many years. Simply because something can be accomplished technically does not mean that it will be done. Customers decide which services to use and which they are willing to pay for.

In fifty years, the computer grew from an electronic curiosity to a product that is in the businesses and homes of millions of Americans. In that regard, it is not different from the telephone, the lightbulb, the automobile, the radio, or the television. Each of these innovations produced major changes in American society.

But because the computer deals with the world of ideas, there is a very substantial difference between it and other inventions. With ideas, the human mind and creativity may be without limit; certainly its limit has not yet been reached. So the computer may still be in its infancy. But its future growth now is not predominantly in hardware, in making the computer smaller and less expensive.

The computer started as one type of information technology, as numbers and words were processed for computational, productivity, and connectivity purposes. It is moving today toward audio and visual information and entertainment, and there is a large amount of digital content in visual material. For example, the digital image of a book cover may take up more memory than the whole text of the book. Some see the future of the information world as a convergence of digital technology across all media, which raises questions of entertainment versus content, of one-way or two-way communications, of copyright ownership, and of many other issues not considered fifty years ago.

There has been a growth in business sites, as *cybermarketing* becomes the new buzzword. For many, going online is the way to reach additional customers. In that sense, it is similar to advertising and is beyond the scope of this book. But all users are aware of the problems of advertising, of unwanted messages, of spam, which cause some to give up on the Internet and e-mail.

In the September 1999 issue of *Fortune* magazine, Jack Welch, then CEO of General Electric, said:

> *Electronic commerce is the biggest revolution in business in our lifetimes. … It will change relationships with customers. Customers will see everything. Nothing will be hidden in paperwork. … It will change relationships with suppliers. All of our suppliers will supply us over the Internet or they won't do business with us.*

Although this may be true in time, it is worth mentioning that Mr. Welch's predecessors at General Electric pulled out of the television, the computer, and the semiconductor industries.

Relative to the computer and networks, there are some issues that should be raised. There is a difference between noise and data, between data and information, and between information and meaning.

Computers cannot develop a skill that is not there. A word processing computer does not make a bad writer into a good writer. It just means that a bad writer can turn out bad material faster. A computer design program does not make someone with no sense of form, design, or presentation into a good designer.

The computer is a tool, and tools are effective only in the hands of craftspeople. My grandfather could take a few hand tools and make a beautiful cabinet. I can take the same tools and only make sawdust. The same thing applies with writing software, designing computer systems, or solving problems. All users are not created equal. Machines—even computers—cannot improve a skill that isn't there.

There is much talk about today's information society, but it may be more properly called the data society, or even the noise society. Much information on the Web is incorrect, as anyone can discover by examining children's school papers prepared using Web sources. Some facts are incorrect, and others are no more than opinions of the writer. Furthermore, getting 125,800 references or hits on a Web inquiry may be worse than getting no information at all. It is difficult if not impossible to find the information you require.

Throughout its short history, the computer industry has progressed rapidly, but it has also seen many promises that did not come true and plans that never reached fruition. In that sense, it is similar to the auto industry or the drug industry, sometimes promising more than it can deliver. One does not automatically get the date of one's dreams by driving a Buick, using Ipana Toothpaste, or getting on a computer dating service. Where has the computer industry exceeded expectations and where is it selling snake oil?

The Way of the World

In every industry there are tradeoffs. The new auto industry of the early twentieth century provided a lot of choices, but most cars had a hand crank, an open frame that let in the weather, and did not use established technology. Now, there are better cars but fewer choices.

One of the outstanding writers in history is Anon., and this author seems even busier in the days of e-mail. This commentary came through the wires in late 1998. It, perhaps, is a way of comparing industries and their status.

At a recent computer expo, Bill Gates reportedly compared the computer industry with the auto industry and stated: "If GM had kept up with technology like the computer industry has, we would all be driving twenty-five dollar cars that got 1,000 miles to the gallon."

In response to Gates's comments, General Motors issued a press release stating the following:

> If GM had developed technology like Microsoft, we would be driving cars with the following characteristics:

1. For no reason whatsoever, your car would crash twice a day.
2. Every time they repainted the lines on the road, you would have to buy a new car.
3. Occasionally, your car would die on the freeway for no reason, and you would accept this, restart, and drive on.
4. Occasionally, executing a maneuver such as a left turn would cause your car to shut down and refuse to restart, in which case you would have to reinstall the engine.
5. Only one person at a time could use the car, unless you bought "Car98" or "CarNT." Then you would have to buy more seats.

6. Macintosh would make a car that was powered by the sun, was more reliable, five times as fast, and twice as easy to drive, but would only run on 5 percent of the roads.
7. The oil, water, temperature, and alternator warning lights would be replaced by a single "general car fault" warning light.
8. The airbag system would say "Are you sure?" before going off.
9. Occasionally, for no reason whatsoever, your car would lock you out and refuse to let you in until you simultaneously lifted the door handle, turned the key, and grabbed hold of the radio antenna.
10. GM would require all car buyers to also purchase a deluxe set of Rand McNally road maps (now a GM subsidiary), even though they neither need them nor want them. Attempting to delete this option would immediately cause the car's performance to diminish by 50 percent or more.
11. Every time GM introduced a new model, car buyers would have to learn how to drive all over again because none of the controls would operate in the same manner as the old car.
12. You'd press the "Start" button to shut off the engine.

Although the above is amusing, it does point out that, for a while, consumers put up with conditions that, as the industry develops, are no longer acceptable. We do not require books for dummies on driving a car, turning on a light, or using a radio. People expect consumer products to work.

What is the status and future of the information society? And where will innovation take us? The question is no longer whether American industry makes computers that work. Rather, it is whether it can make computers easier to use and of more value to the consumer.

CHAPTER 10

Kenneth Olsen (1926–)
The Commonplace Computer

Choose a job you love and you will never have to work a day in your life.
—Confucius

The future belongs to the learners, not the knowers.
—Eric Hoffer

C omputers, like semiconductors, have had major influence on life in the second half of the twentieth century. Although many people, including Blaise Pascal, Charles Babbage, George Boole, Herman Hollerith, Alan Turing, John Eckert, John Mauchly, John Von Neumann, Thomas J. Watson Sr. or Jr., David Packard, Steve Jobs, Michael Dell, or Bill Gates, could represent the computer industry, the person selected is Ken Olsen. Olsen was a computer leader for almost four decades, built a start-up into the world's second largest computer company, and his company changed the way computers were designed, sold, and used. In 1986, *Fortune* magazine described Ken Olsen as "the most successful entrepreneur in the history of American business."[1]

Biography

Kenneth Harry (Ken) Olsen was born in Stratford, Connecticut, in 1926, the second of four children born to Oswald and Elizabeth Svea Olsen, who were children of Norwegian and Swedish immigrants. His brother Stan was two years younger than Ken, and they grew up in a Norwegian working-class community. Their father was a machine tool designer who tinkered with gadgets in his spare time and taught Ken machine shop practices. During World War II, between 1944 and 1946, Olsen served in the navy where he received electronics technician training at Great Lakes Boot Camp. After training, Olsen was sent to the

Pacific. After the war was over, Olsen ended up in China on an admiral's staff, where he helped maintain communications equipment.

The war demonstrated the importance of electronics in communications, radar, radio, sonar, navigation, and countermeasures. Olsen, like many military veterans, believed that the machine tool of the future was electronics. In 1950, Olsen received his BS in electrical engineering from MIT, and in 1952, his MS. After MIT, he worked on the Whirlwind computer that the university was building for the Office of Naval Research. Jay Forrester's design of an air defense system used 10,000 vacuum tubes. The vacuum tubes had an average design life of 500 hours each, and in order to prolong tube life, were never turned off. Two hundred fifty volts of AC power drove each vacuum tube, with huge transformers needed for power distribution. Jay Forrester and others invented a core memory system, with a method of selecting magnetic cores in three dimensions by specifying an x, y, and z coordinate. Their design became the foundation of early computer memory design.

In 1951 at MIT's Lincoln Labs, Olsen designed the TX-O, a small transistorized computer to test the memory device of the Whirlwind computer used for the Semi-Automatic Ground Environment (SAGE) early warning system. IBM won the contract to manufacture SAGE, and Olsen was sent to Poughkeepsie for thirteen months to work at IBM and oversee the system's production. IBM was secretive about every part of the project. "It was like going to a communist state. They knew nothing about the rest of the world and the world knew nothing about what went inside."[2] It was a change going from the freewheeling engineers at MIT and Lincoln Labs to IBM's bureaucracy.

While at MIT, a neighbor of Olsen's parents had a college student from Finland, Eeva-Lisa Aulikki Valve, visit them for the summer. She returned to Finland, and Olsen soon followed her and got a job in a ball bearing factory in Goteborg, Sweden. In two weeks they were engaged, and the couple bicycled around Finland. The couple was married in Lahti, Finland, on December 12, 1950. Like Henry Ford's wife, Clara, Olsen's wife, Aulikki, brought stability and meaning to his life.

Olsen founded Digital Equipment Corporation in 1957. After looking for backing to create a small interactive computer, he and associate Harlan Anderson received an investment of $70,000 from American Research and Development (ARD) for 70 percent of the company. They were told that no one in their right mind would think of competing with IBM, GE, Burroughs, and RCA, so they kept their plans for computer manufacture quiet.

> *We made our proposal to American Research and Development. They gave us three bits of advice. First was, don't use the word computer because Fortune magazine said no one had made any money in computers, and no*

one was about to. So we took that out. We said we would make modules, which were the pieces we had to make first anyway. Second, they suggested that five percent profit wasn't enough. You see, when we looked through Moody's, it seemed that all good companies made five percent. I think Dorothy Rowe said, "'If you are going to risk somebody's money, you've got to promise more return than RCA.'" So we promised ten percent. And, of course, the lesson is obvious. If we aimed for five percent, that's all we would have made. So we aimed for ten percent. Lastly, they suggested, promise fast results because most of the board is over eighty. So we promised to make a profit in a year, which we did.

American Research gave us $70,000 to start the company and that lasted us eight years. The nice thing about seventy thousand dollars is that there are so few of them you can watch every one. We found space in the old mill in Maynard, Massachusetts, on the second floor, with a narrow stairway and no elevator. We paid 0.25 a square foot per year with watchman service and heat.[3]

Built in 1845 as a woolen mill on the Assabet River for Amory Maynard, William Knight, and the Assabet Manufacturing Company, the mill where Olsen set up shop originally made blankets and uniforms for the Union Army. Olsen leased 8,650 square feet in the mill. There were initially three employees: Kenneth Olsen, Harlan Anderson, and Ken's brother, Stan. Harlan (Andy) became the administrative person, with Stan in charge of manufacturing and Ken in charge of design. They did everything themselves. At first, the company made only printed circuit logic modules and memory test equipment. Transistorized modules, including flip-flops, gates, power amplifiers, clocks, and adders, were sold to engineers who wanted to build things, and the modules were also used to build computers. Both DEC and neighboring Computer Control Company (3C) used the profits from their module business to finance their entry into computers.

In the 1950s, computers were leased to administration and financial departments and kept in special air-conditioned rooms. If an engineer or scientist had a problem for the computer to solve, he or she had to write a program and prepare it on punched cards. The cards were then given to the computer operators who ran the program along with others in a batch. Only designers, operators, and system programmers could access the computer. The user was remote from the computer and was buffered by people whose job it was to keep the computer fully loaded by supplying sequential batches of jobs. Computers were untouchable. The computer, not the user, was important. Users often had to wait one to three days before their work was performed. Digital Equipment Company, under Ken Olsen's leadership, changed that.

In 1957, the year DEC started, IBM passed $1 billion in revenue and had garnered more than 80 percent of the computer market. IBM focused on large systems that they leased to customers.

Digital Equipment Corporation created the minicomputer industry and changed the nature of the computer business. DEC had profits and revenue grow at a 30 percent compounded annual rate for two decades. The company sold computers directly to engineers and scientists, who used them to solve problems. Because these computers used the latest electronic technology, costs came down every year. The person and the application became more important than the computer. Uses opened in manufacturing, communications, data acquisition, process control, health care, machine tool control, and dozens of other fields. An expensive centralized computer, which had to be kept loaded, was replaced by many inexpensive computers each doing its own job.

In the early years, Olsen was dependent on General Georges Doriot, professor at the Harvard Business School and head of American Research and Development.

> *Doriot had a strong following, his ideas being very practical, integrity, quality, honesty, doing the right thing. His contribution to us was to encourage us, give us support, and show patience. They wouldn't buy and sell companies at the first opportunity. They would stick with and work with the company until they were successful or until they failed.*[4]

Doriot also believed in taking chances. "If failure can be explained, and it's not based on a lack of morality, then to me failure is acceptable."[5] From the beginning, Digital Equipment Corporation took chances.

In 1959, the year it introduced its first computer, Digital Equipment Corporation's revenue exceeded $1 million. Throughout its early years, DEC created a series of minicomputers that brought computer technology to the mass market. The company introduced the Programmed Data Processor, or PDP-1, in 1959. It was called a PDP rather than a computer because many organizations, including the government, had policies specifying how computers were to be bought and who had control of them. A computer cost more than $1 million and was typically managed by financial organizations. This new device for engineers cost far less and was used differently than the big mainframes, so it needed a new name to get through corporate management and the purchasing departments of some companies and facilities.

The PDP-1 was about the size of a refrigerator and was simple and easy to use. It was an 18-bit machine, built of transistor modules with a typewriter and paper-tape input, had a cathode-ray tube and 4,000 words of main core memory, and cost $120,000. Fifty-three of these computers were sold. Influenced by the work of Jay Forrester and his staff at MIT, the company built a computer that individual users could interact with directly through a video or keyboard terminal. "The idea of an interactive computer, where both machinery or people can interact, was one of the key concepts at MIT and was really the basis upon which we built DEC."[6] Also from MIT came the idea of networking, in which many computers were interconnected.

DEC gave one of the first PDP-1's to MIT for students to use. Over the next thirty years, many university students wrote their first programs on Digital Equipment machines, as the company made them available to the leading engineering colleges.

"We demonstrated all the ideas of high speed transistor computers, and we thought the world would waiting in open arms for this. Nobody cared. And it turns out that it takes more than ideas. You've got to sell your idea."[7]

The PDP-1 was followed by a series of innovative computers—smaller and more powerful, cheaper and faster. Transistors became less expensive and circuit design better, so one could put more on a printed circuit module. The PDP-2, a 24-bit computer, and the PDP-3, a 36-bit computer, were designed but not extensively marketed. The 18-bit PDP-4, introduced in 1962, was a successor to the PDP-1. Fewer than fifty of these machines were sold. The PDP-4 was followed by other 18-bit machines, the PDP-7, PDP-9, and the PDP-15.

The PDP-5 was the first of the small general-purpose 12-bit computers and had a sales price of $27,000. To get its cost down, a Teletype printer was used in place of a regular printer. The PDP-5 eventually sold almost 1,000 computers, making it very popular for its time. The year of its introduction, 1963, Digital's revenue reached $10 million. The company had been profitable each year since its founding.

The PDP 6, a 36-bit computer, was designed for time-sharing applications in which one computer had many terminals and each person thought he had a computer to himself. It was introduced in 1964, but priced at $300,000, was too big and expensive a machine for the company to build and market. Only twenty-three were sold.

In 1965, the PDP-8 was introduced. It was the first true minicomputer. The PDP-8 revolutionized the way industries conducted business, and sales sky-rocketed. It was a 12-bit computer used for applications for which the precision of calculations could be kept low. It had 4,000 to 32,000 words of core memory and interfaced with a Teletype. When the computer received an interrupt command, the computer shut down and worked on the interrupt command until the requirement was satisfied. It was initially priced at $18,000, but costs came down. The PDP-8A was priced at $7,900, and later, the Decmate—a

PDP-8-based word processing system was introduced. Speed, size, and price made the PDP-8 a winner. Priced below $10,000, a company could provide computers to many people. Over its fifteen-year life span, 50,000 of the PDP-8 machines were sold. The success of the PDP-8 drove revenue upward, from $15 million in 1965 to $23 million in 1966.

In 1967, DEC launched the PDP-10, a successor to the PDP-6. A $300,000 to $400,000 computer, the PDP-10 was designed for time-sharing applications in universities and research labs, and for attacking the IBM dominated mainframe market. The PDP-10 family of computers was in production for fifteen years and had a loyal following.

The IBM System/360, introduced in 1964, changed mainframe design by making an 8-bit word (one byte) and its multiples the industry standard. DEC's 12- and 18-bit computers were no longer leaders. Future computers would be multiples of 8 bits: 16 bits (a word equals two bytes), 24 bits, 32 bits, and 64 bits. Digital Equipment Company started work on the PDP-X, a 16-bit computer, and had a preliminary design in 1967. However, a complicated design and internal reservations caused the project to be killed. Disagreeing with this decision, Edson de Castro, who had designed the PDP-8 and the PDP-X, left DEC in April 1968 to found Data General.

DEC introduced the PDP-11, a 16-bit machine, on January 5, 1970, at a price ranging from $10,800 to $20,000. The PDP-11 recaptured DEC's minicomputer industry lead from Computer Control Company, which had produced the industry's first 16-bit computers—the DDP 116, 316, 416, and 516. New companies, including Data General, Varian, and Wang, entered the minicomputer market and grew. DEC once again became the leading minicomputer manufacturer in the world. The PDP-11 and subsequent machines 11/05 through 11/94 sold a quarter million units.

IBM and the other mainframe companies ignored the minicomputer industry, believing in large mainframes and centralized management. Meanwhile, each year, the minicomputer manufacturers introduced newer and faster machines at lower prices as advances were made in the semiconductor, magnetic memory, printer, communications, and systems fields.

Original Equipment Manufacturers (OEMs) bought computers from DEC, did their own programming, and sold them as their own products. This arrangement saved DEC the cost of writing application software and providing systems engineering, as it built relationships with small and fast-growing systems companies.

Digital Equipment Corporation had a reputation as a company that built excellent computers and provided good technical support to keep products relatively trouble free. The sales force was made up of engineers on a straight salary, with no commissions.

Olsen emphasized engineering for the marketplace. There were informal networks within the technical organizations, and Olsen was considered an engineer's engineer. There was no government funding for research, no mergers or acquisitions, and no dividends to shareholders—profits were plowed back into financing growth, as they had been with Henry Ford. "My history has always been to solve problems. We rarely had the fastest computer. We did take the best care of customers."[8]

As the company grew, Olsen changed the management to make it more responsible to the increasingly complex computer market. Many semi-autonomous operations with product-line managers were created, each of whom had to develop, market, and financially control a product line, becoming entre-preneurs within DEC. Matrix management was good for handling explosive growth, speed of response in an unstable market, and encouraged corporate democracy. Everyone had two bosses, reporting to one boss in a business unit, another in a specialty unit. Conflict was built into the matrix. This decentral-ized system of management produced nineteen years of significant annual revenue growth but put pressure on Olsen. In 1966, twenty-seven people reported directly to Ken Olsen.

DEC and IBM shared one trait in their early years: guaranteed employ-ment. An employee worked at DEC for life. There were no layoffs, and employees were members of the family. There were no frills, no special perks for managers, and there was an open, informal environment. New jobs were posted, and any employee in the company could apply. Olsen wanted to control but did not claim to have all the answers. The best ideas from anyone in the organiza-tion were supposed to come to the surface and be implemented.

As the company grew, Hewlett-Packard, Control Data, Singer, Xerox, and Harris all tried to buy DEC. Olsen said no.

In August 1966, the company went public at $22 per share. ARD's $70,000 investment was now worth $38.5 million. The company continued to grow and in 1967, revenue hit $39 million.

Computer Control Company was a highflier until it was acquired by Honeywell in 1966 and lost its technical edge with post-acquisition bureaucracy. The same applied to Scientific Data Systems after it was acquired by Xerox. Many others entered the minicomputer industry, and some disappeared as competitors.

In 1970, DEC revenue reached $136 million, a twelvefold increase since 1963. By this time, the company was structured around product lines, each with separate profit and loss responsibility. A matrix management was in place for taking the company through its next growth phase.

During the company's first phase, it grew from a start-up with three people to a major company with thousands of employees and revenue in excess of $100 million. The next period was one of continued growth, with a hundredfold revenue increase and an expanded customer base. These fifteen years would also see changes—in technology, in applications of computers, and in competition. Throughout this period, Digital Equipment Corporation handled the opportunities as well as anyone.

Data General and others brought out low-cost machines to compete with the PDP-8 and PDP-11. Prime Computer in 1974 introduced the megaminis, computers positioned between the minicomputers and the large machines built by IBM. The IBM Series 1, introduced in 1976, was IBM's attempt to enter the $5 billion minicomputer industry. For a short time, DEC fell behind competitors technically.

The Computerization of America

In June 1972, DEC had 7,800 employees and nearly $200 million in revenue. In 1974, DEC introduced the Virtual Address Extension, or VAX, technology, which was as powerful as the IBM 370 at a quarter of the price. DEC was a market leader in the 1970s and 1980s and began linking computers so they could talk to each other in distributed data-processing systems. In October 1977, DEC introduced the VAX 11/780 superminicomputer. Memories were expanded from the few thousand bytes of the early computers to 1 million bytes, making the computer more versatile and allowing programmers to develop more powerful software. For the next two decades, there was a stream of new VAX models in all price categories. By 1990, 200,000 VAX systems had been installed.

The VT 100, an intelligent computer terminal that was introduced in 1978, became the industry standard. In 1983, MicroVAX brought the VAX concept down to a workstation level. DEC, which had always built most of its own components, entered the semiconductor component business with the LSI-11, a downsizing of the PDP-11.

In the 1970s, Wang took the lead in the word processing business. In the early 1980's, DEC was taken by surprise by the proliferation of microcomputers, or personal computers, that threatened to isolate the company in the minicomputer market. Companies such as Apple Computer had been established and were producing lower cost computers. In 1983, DEC's earnings were off 32 percent, the first decrease in years, and the company saw lower profits in 1984 as well. DEC's low-end products were not selling, and there were delays at the high end with VAX enhancements. There were high expenses in marketing as well. In 1986, *Business Week* reported that DEC's profitability still lagged behind its competitors. According to the article, the five-year average return on equity was as follows: IBM, 24 percent; Prime Computer, 20 percent; Hewlett-Packard, 17 percent; Wang, 14 percent; and DEC, 12 percent. But DEC was investing in its future.

It is in the domain of personal computers that professional hindsight is most critical of Olsen. At MIT, Olsen had designed one of the first personal computers, and interactive computers were the hallmark of the early days. However, he had doubts about people wanting computers in their homes. He had said, "The personal computer will fall flat on its face in business."[9] He believed in smart, or intelligent, terminals instead. A few have called Olsen's belief a major mistake, similar to Henry Ford's failure to block General Motor's high-end flanking movement in the 1920s.

Yet at the company's 1983 annual meeting, Olsen stated:

Personal computers are very important to us. We claim that the personal computer market, as it is known today, is an offshoot that we introduced 26 years ago and that have been at the heart of our company. As I have emphasized before, we are not in the home computer business. We have decided to sell only through channels that serve professional, commercial and industrial users. We design our products to satisfy the more critical needs of industrial, office, scientific, educational and engineering markets.[10]

This appears to be a very reasonable position, and it is doubtful if Digital Equipment Corporation, with its high internal expenses, could ever have competed with Apple, Dell, Compaq, and other personal computer companies.

In the early 1980s, the personal computer business was growing. In August 1981, IBM introduced its PC and was amazed by the response. Because the company had purchased 80 percent of the electronic components for its PC from outside vendors, it was able to quickly increase production.

At Digital Equipment, no one was responsible for countering this part of the market, and the company had a poor personal computer strategy. Different product managers introduced different and incompatible products: Professional Personal Computer Models 325 and 350, the Rainbow 100, and the Decmate 11. Lateness to market and dearth of application software caused the machines to sell below expectations.

The designers of the first spreadsheet program were rebuffed at DEC and their product, VisiCalc, was then written for the Apple II, and not for a DEC machine. The Lotus 1-2-3 software integrated spreadsheet, word processing, and graphics capability and made the IBM machine the industry standard for personal computers. Lotus was subsequently purchased by IBM.

IBM launched a massive ad campaign. DEC sold 300,000 units, IBM 1 million. Copies of the IBM machine turned the personal computer into a commodity business. Customers cared about two things: price and application software. Digital was not the leader in either, and gradually the IBM Personal

Computer and its compatible machines took over from both DEC and Apple. DEC introduced the VAXmate in 1986, a machine with IBM PC compatibility, but again, sales were disappointing.

At the other end of the market, Digital had a much stronger strategy. It had worked with Xerox and others on Ethernet, a way to interconnect computers, terminals, and personal computers. This was a simplified and efficient interconnection scheme that significantly speeded up data transmission in offices.

IBM, always known as the safe buy among users, had boxed-in thousands of customers with incompatible architectures, operating systems, application software, and machines. Many IBM product lines could not talk together. Large corporations needed to link computers so that they could distribute mainframe data to office workers. By 1985, Digital linked 173,000 computers and peripherals together and thereby gained entry into many IBM accounts.

DEC marketed the VAX 8600 superminicomputer, a small but mighty mainframe. In DEC's 1986 *Annual Report,* Olsen said:

> *Our goal is to connect all parts of an organization—the office, the factory floor, the laboratory, engineering department—from the desktop to the data center. We can connect everything in a building; we can connect a group of buildings on the same site or at remote sites; we can connect an entire organization around the world. We propose to connect a company from top to bottom with a network that includes the shipping clerk, the secretary, the manager, even the president.*[11]

Ted Johnson joined DEC as the company's first salesman in 1958 and soon became head of worldwide sales and service. The company offered excellent support to its customers. By 1983, the sales force had grown to 5,500, and the field service team 16,000. There were 5,100 software and software support specialists for customized software development, call-in software support centers, guaranteed uptime for critical applications, remote diagnosis facilities, 170 carry-in repair centers worldwide, and 340 training courses in seventeen languages around the world. In 1984, there were three geographic sales divisions, each with profit and loss responsibility. Much was invested in sales. Sales and administration costs climbed from 21 percent of revenue in 1984 to 33 percent in 1992. DEC continued to invest in growth at the expense of maximizing short-term profitability.

The company's revenue reached $265 million in 1973, $533 million in 1975, $1.06 billion in 1977, $2.3 billion in 1980, and $4.2 billion in 1983, when its worldwide employment had climbed to 73,000 people. The company had been profitable every year since its founding. About half of all revenue came from outside the United States, most from western Europe. By 1986, DEC had invaded some of IBM's old markets, and DEC's annual revenue had grown to $7.6 billion. The company emerged as the leading installer of computer networks within office buildings.

AT&T tried to acquire Digital in 1983 and again in 1985. Both purchases fell through. AT&T then acquired 25 percent of Olivetti, and DEC continued as an independent company. As *Fortune* magazine pointed out, DEC's share of the computer market in 1987 ranked second only to IBM and was bigger than Ford Motor Company's market share when death claimed Henry Ford or Carnegie Steel when Andrew Carnegie retired.

In 1988, Digital Equipment Company became an $11 billion company, the thirty-eighth largest industrial company in the Fortune 500, and with profits of $1.6 billion, the thirteenth most profitable. It employed 120,000 people worldwide. After an increase in revenue from $100 million in 1970 to $11 billion in 1988, the company was now definitely number two in the computer industry.

IBM had problems. Its net income dropped in 1986, and it trimmed its workforce, its first major layoff. Still, IBM had $51 billion in revenue that year. DEC was one-fifth the size of IBM and growing stronger. By 1989, Digital Equipment was ready to go head to head with IBM in the business world.

Digital had a reputation for quality and a variety of good products, from large mainframes to minicomputers to personal computers. It had intelligent terminals, workstations, word processing systems, and was a leader in computer networks. Both the company and its value-added partners had excellent software.

These were two companies with different philosophies. IBM often treated customers as technology neophytes and said, "We'll take care of you." DEC treated them as partners. IBM provided heavy support and service for products they leased, whereas DEC let customers do more for themselves with equipment they purchased. DEC's customers did not always need the systems engineers, software packages, and training programs that were always supplied with IBM computers. When they did, they paid for them. It was marketing versus engineering leadership, a sales force on commission versus one on salary. But soon, DEC was providing bonus systems for its best sales performers, and they were competitively compensated. Moreover, it was increasing its support team.

But in the 1980s while DEC was chasing IBM, others were chasing both DEC and IBM. Personal computer manufacturers now included Apple, Compaq, Dell, and Gateway. New companies were entering the communication market, including Cisco Systems, America OnLine (AOL), Sun Microsystems, and Oracle Systems. Microsoft had been rebuffed by Digital Equipment and was growing in the IBM personal computer and networking world, and Intel and other semiconductor manufacturers were supplying integrated circuits with more and more electronic capability as well as larger semiconductor memories. The manufacturing and assembling capabilities of Digital Equipment were no longer of such great value since many interconnections were now being made on the chip. The company that had started with three people had eventually grown to 125,900 employees, but now it needed fewer people in view of the changing electronic technology.

DEC planned its attack against IBM with the introduction of its most powerful computer, the VAX 9000, in 1990. That same year, there were takeover rumors that included interested companies such as AT&T, Ford, Mitsubishi, and Matsushita. But for the time, Digital Equipment remained independent.

The company's revenue increased slightly in 1990, but its profits dropped substantially. DEC's revenue continued to grow, reaching a peak of $14 billion in 1993. In 1991, DEC suffered its first ever loss of $588 million due to major restructuring charges. In 1992 and 1993, Digital Equipment's revenue was approximately $14 billion, but the company had losses of $2.1 billion in 1992 and $237 million in 1993. It is worth pointing out that in the same three years, IBM had operating losses of $2.86 billion, $4.9 billion, and $8.1 billion— including restructuring charges—the largest loss of any U.S. company up to that time. Clearly, something was changing in the computer industry.

During these few years, DEC had problems due to the rapid growth of personal computers and changes in the marketplace and technology. Critics charged that Olsen had let engineers reign supreme and had neglected customers. Digital was behind rivals in cutting costs, and posted operating losses for four years. Changes in the market demanded a leaner, meaner operation, and new management at DEC executed drastic cost-cutting measures, including laying off people for the first time in the company's history. There had always been very low turnover at DEC, with loyalty up and down the organization, but that had changed.

In 1992, Ken Olsen resigned as president of Digital Equipment after thirty-five years of heading the company. But Olsen had built a large and very successful company, created a large number of jobs, satisfied the needs of many customers, and led the computer industry into important and new directions. Not bad for a man who had ignored the advice of the Boston financial experts who had told him not to enter the computer industry against IBM.

On Management

DEC had grown without changing its culture or buying other companies. Olsen, a patriarch, was a role model for work habits and casual dress. He spent long hours at the company and never forgot the job. He worked Saturdays and nights and often called people at home. Olsen sat on the Ford Motor Company's board of directors and drove a Ford Pinto and then a Ford van. Throughout his company's growth, he maintained loyalty among his subordinates. But some senior people left because of job pressure and the perceived lack of backing from Olsen.

Unlike Andrew Carnegie and Henry Ford, Ken Olsen never wrote a book and discouraged others to write about him. Unlike David Sarnoff, who gave hundreds of speeches, Ken Olsen kept his thoughts inside the corporation. Most of his ideas were expressed at stockholder meetings and in annual reports, internal memoranda, company policy manuals, and a few interviews. But along with the other three pioneers featured in this book, Ken Olsen had ideas that can help all in the world of business.

On customers and business objectives: "We must be honest and straightforward with our customers and be sure they are not only told the facts, but that they understand the facts."[12] "When dealing with a customer, vendor or an employee, do what is 'right' in each situation."[13] In addition, he said: "Don't be dishonest in the slightest way. Don't mislead, don't oversell, don't avoid facts or data. Individuals will never trust you even though they will not publicly raise the issue."[14]

> *One of the exciting things about this business is that you have an interesting, diverse set of customers with very interesting problems. Each one is different. Most of them are quite exciting, all the way from physics to telephone controls ... education to medicine. Working with them is important. Through our history, many of the ideas come from our customers.*[15]

On business and personal objectives:

> *Don't ever become lazy. Remember that you only have fun in life and you only can stay ahead if you keep learning. Calculators are not an excuse for not learning how to do arithmetic. As for the things that computers do, you've always got to be sure that you can do a certain number of things by hand and know something and learn something. Always learn and don't ever let computers fool you into thinking you don't have to. I tell our people when I'm asked to lecture, look at the old people you want to be like. I can tell you ahead of time that some people continue to think, are excited about things and learn about things and the ones who are boring are those who stop learning and don't think about things.*[16]

Like Henry Ford, Olsen had questions about the role of government. On the difference between working in a defense business and a commercial business, he said:

> *The government business ... the way Congress sets it up and the way people want to run things, worries about you making a profit. They worry less*

*about what they get. That's absolutely contrary to the commercial activity.
Most commercial customers want to do business with you only if you make
a profit, and like you more if you make a good profit because it shows you're
doing things wisely and you'll be around for a while. The commercial companies always want to buy the best product and they have learned, those
that are successful, to trust their suppliers. The way government business is
set up, it's always distrust. The supplier is always the enemy.[17]*

Some of Olsen's other ideas also had similarities with Henry Ford's. "Success
is measured by profit. With success comes the opportunity to grow, the ability
to hire good people and the satisfaction that comes from meeting your goals."[18]
He also said: "The wise thing is to get people to make decisions themselves and
hold them responsible for it. They work much harder if they make the decisions,
because they've got to make them work."[19] And: "You've got nothing to offer
society if you only follow."[20] And: "You learn to manage by managing."[21]
"Remember that ideas that make us unique can give us a unique position more
easily than ideas that say we should do what IBM did two or three years ago."[22]
And finally: "Above all, remember that our future is dependent on good ideas,
original ideas, unique ideas, and people who think them out so that we can be
successful with them."[23]

And having watched many of his competitors sell their companies and then
have them disappear, he recognized the danger of doing things just for money.
Olsen valued independence. "Success is probably the worst problem for an
entrepreneur. As people get successful, they tend to stop learning."[24]

The Legacy of Ken Olsen

In the late 1980s, Ken Olsen had said: "The final picture of success, is how well
the company does after you're gone."[25]

Robert Palmer was Olsen's handpicked successor and took over from Ken
Olsen in 1992. He acted boldly to turn the company around.

Digital Equipment Company lost almost $5 billion between 1991 and
1994, including more than $4 billion in restructuring charges because of slower
sales in workstations and new mainframes as well as technological changes.
Digital was cut from a peak of 125,000 employees to 65,000 by July 1995. The
company reduced manufacturing space by one-third, and there were major
plant closings. It moved 60 percent of all company sales to third-party resellers.
The remaining sales force dropped all customers who bought less than
$500,000 per year and focused on the 1,000 largest customers. Digital stream-
lined management, eliminating Olsen's favorite matrix management structure.
In order to raise cash, it sold most of its storage business to Quantum

Corporation for $360 million. From 1995 to 1997, Digital Equipment had 65 percent of its sales outside the United States. But during the 1990s, Europe, where DEC had 50 percent of its sales, went through a recession, and many orders were delayed or cancelled.

DEC's chief financial officer described the company's downsizing: "We cannot profitably pursue the high growth sector of the economy, the small and mid-size enterprises, here or elsewhere in the world with our traditional selling model (geography based units) offering all products to business customers large and small."

With these changes, DEC was able to post a small profit in 1995. Some on Wall Street were impressed. By May 1996, *Financial World* said DEC has turned the corner.

Yet questions arose about what DEC's strategy was. It had always been clear under Olsen. For more than thirty years, he and his engineers were able to design new products, and his marketing group could find new customers during times of major change in the computer technology. How was the company to deal with the computer world of the 1990s? What was special about Digital Equipment Corporation in the mid-1990s?

Robert Palmer, who had come from the semiconductor division, continued the investment in Alpha, the company's very fast, 64-bit reduced-instruction-set computing semiconductor chip. But Intel and others were working on their own 64-bit chips. Did it make sense to invest in the semiconductor business and one's own chips instead of buying standard chips from established semiconductor companies? Although the Alpha series was successful, much of the company's resources were devoted to semiconductor development rather than systems work.

One of DEC's major goals at this point was to streamline the sales force and get rid of salespeople. In 1994, Digital turned sales for about 7,000 to 8,000 of its customers over to distributors and value-added resellers in order to reduce operating losses. The remaining salespeople focused on high margin customers. It was a great idea in theory, but which products would become the next PDP-11 or VAX, and which new customers would, in time, become major ones? DEC was now selling to old customers. Hewlett-Packard and others were finding new ones.

Palmer also focused on personal computers, and sales in this area increased from $160 million in 1991 to almost $2 billion in 1995. But then they turned down. Meanwhile, there were lots of "experts" from the investment community ready to suggest what Digital Equipment should do next. Olsen had never listened to them and had charted his own course. Now these people became louder. Some on Wall Street wanted the company to focus on the high end, high margin products à la IBM. Others suggested workstations, networks, or other special areas.

Digital Equipment Corporation had been a company built on brainpower, teamwork, and consensus, with many ideas flowing upward through the organization. It was now driven from the top, with a major objective of reducing costs and getting rid of people. Some of the best and most creative people left to join new and growing companies.

The company missed the change in technologies that make up the Web. It ignored the actions required to become a leader in the personal computer market. Although it had the technology, it became less of a factor in client server networks. In workstations, DEC fell behind Sun Microsystems, Hewlett-Packard, and IBM, with Silicon Graphics closing in fast.

Digital was caught in the switch to more powerful integrated circuits and the need for fewer employees. The company was almost profitable in those four years, except for the cost of getting rid of people. And without an Olsen at the helm, Digital Equipment did not have a strong plan of what it was. It needed the creative leadership of Harlan Anderson, Gordon Bell, Ed de Castro, Win Hindle, Ted Johnson, Pete Kaufmann, Andy Knowles, John Leng, Nick Mazzarese, Stan Olsen, Jack Shields, Jack Smith, and hundreds of other engineers and salespeople. But they were gone, and now management focused on reducing head count. Wall Street ran the company. The company lost money in 1996 and then was profitable in 1997. But it seemed to have lost its way.

In June 1998, Digital Equipment Corporation ceased to exist as an independent corporation when it was purchased and absorbed by Compaq Computer of Houston, Texas, for $9 billion. The history of these two companies could not be more different.

Compaq was founded in February 1982 and financed by a high-tech venture-capital firm. Within twenty months, Compaq had an initial public offering and raised $67 million. This compares with the $70,000 that Ken Olsen had originally received from ARD and which lasted him for eight years. In a sense, it was the conservatism of New England versus the freewheeling spending of Texas. It was also one leader and his vision for thirty-five years versus a series of hired managers.

Compaq's objectives were to grow as fast as possible by investing in marketing and technology, either by building or buying it. They purchased Thomas-Conrad, Networth, Tandem Computer, and Wang's facility in Scotland, before acquiring Digital Equipment Corporation. Compaq set up joint agreements with RadioShack, Microsoft, Disney, and Starbucks. In both 1990 and 2000, when the stock market did not properly appreciate their value, Compaq started to repurchase significant blocks of their shares. Finally, in 2001, Compaq and Hewlett-Packard announced plans to merge. After significant objections to the merger by members of the Hewlett and Packard families and many employees, the merger went through in May 2002, forming a $87 billion company.

Through all of these mergers, acquisitions, and stock repurchases, operations were consolidated and downsized and employees were terminated. In 1992, the total number of employees for DEC, Compaq, and Hewlett-Packard was 220,000. Ten years later, it stood at 141,000 and was declining. Eighty thousand people, or more than 35 percent of all employees, have lost their jobs. Today, the Digital Equipment Corporation established by Ken Olsen in Maynard, Massachusetts, is but a shadow of its former self.

One wonders what might have happened if Olsen and his successors had been given a chance to continue their innovation. Is a company at $87 billion more innovative than one at $8 billion or $800 million or even $8 million? Are the customers or the employees or the vendors or even the stockholders better off because of this merger mania? And does that mean that things will be better with further mergers and additional layoffs? Or is there a limit to growth, stock trading, and remote management?

Companies are measured by the service they provide to customers, growth in employment, and return to shareholders. For thirty-five years, under the leadership of Ken Olsen, Digital Equipment had been a success. Since its acquisition by Compaq and then Compaq's acquisition by Hewlett-Packard, the company has been a failure in all three areas.

In chapter 1, it was pointed out that large organizations, with all their resources, seldom lead in innovation. Ken Olsen addressed that issue:

> *The place of entrepreneurship in our society is obvious. The traditional enterprises do not or are reluctant to try new ideas and new approaches, and to gamble, to risk, to pay the price for competition. It is the place of the entrepreneur to introduce new ideas, new products and new approaches. Few entrepreneurs survive very long, either because of success or because of failure. But out of many approaches comes good; as with evolution, improvements come with many attempts, better things arrive.*[26]

CHAPTER 11

The Nature of Professional
and Personal Change

*Whatever you dream you can do, begin it. Boldness has genius,
power and magic in it. Begin it now.*
                                    —*Johann Wolfgang von Goethe*

*Never be afraid to try something new. Remember that amateurs
built the Ark. Professionals built the Titanic.*
                                    —*Dave Barry*

The previous ten chapters have described the history of American business, new technologies, and the role of the entrepreneur in building industries and creating jobs. For those who only wish to look at the past, the book is now over. For others, this chapter, which deals with the nature of professional and personal change and has some observations on American business, may be of interest.

Management, Companies, and Technology

This chapter contains a number of conclusions and observations. Even though some of these ideas may be controversial, the author believes that these points are worth bringing to the attention of the reader for thoughtful consideration and discussion.

What can be learned from a review of American business history? Several ideas come to mind. One has to do with the development of technology and the role that entrepreneurs have played in this area. There are several observations that can be made about the four entrepreneurs in this book as well as others, including Walt Disney, DeWitt and Lila Wallace, David Packard, Ray Kroc, Sam Walton, William Norris, Ed Land, An Wang, Bob Noyce, Steve Jobs, Ted Turner, and Bill Gates.

As has been shown throughout this book, small companies employ most people in this country. New industries and new companies create jobs. Of these small companies, some grow into larger operations and a few into very large organizations. Older companies and industries may have a large number of employees, but they are often in the process of reducing their total employment due to changes in markets and technology and a desire to optimize short-term profits, especially after they have acquired existing companies. Sometimes the leaders of large corporations are concerned with preserving the status quo and sometimes they are buffered from reality by too many layers of management and bureaucracies, and are unable to provide leadership. But meanwhile, the world changes.

To start a company and build it, you have to have a purpose, a dream, a feeling that what you are trying to do is important and that you and your associates can make your dream happen as you move toward an uncertain future. Entrepreneurs are basically optimists, and although they face problems, these are essentially short-term setbacks and do not get in the way of long-term objectives. These business leaders differ in background, in training, in age, and in personal characteristics. But they share one trait: optimism. They are positive in personality and believers in the future. They also share another, which can be called self-confidence, determination, or stubbornness. Heart and desire matter as much in business as in sports. Entrepreneurs will get where they want to go, no matter what the obstacles.

They also know that a business leader has responsibility to many groups—customers, employees, stockholders, vendors, and the community. They do not let one set of responsibilities dominate at the expense of all others. And certainly short-term reaction to the needs of one group cannot take precedence and ruin entrepreneurs' dreams, plans, and the future of the company. Perhaps entrepreneurs' greatest responsibility is to themselves, their vision, to integrity, and to independence. To abandon that is to recognize that one is at best a "hired gun." That is a price that some leaders will not pay, no matter how much they are offered. Ford, Sarnoff, Olsen, and many others turned down repeated offers to sell their companies. To them, there was more to life than money. There was freedom and independence.

As stated in chapter 1, businesspeople, like politicians, are dependent on the economic, social, and cultural environment in which they live. But, as with all leaders, they are eventually measured by what they do with these resources. The creation of jobs has largely been the product of good leadership. The decline and destruction of established companies has largely been the product of poor and shortsighted leadership. And business leaders, like baseball players, are not measured by how much they are paid, but whether over the long run, their teams win or lose, grow or shrink, live or die. Corporate performance through the years is the measuring stick by which business leaders must be judged.

The four entrepreneurs discussed in this book—Carnegie, Ford, Sarnoff, and Olsen—at times had problems in implementing their dreams. But they were believers in the importance of what they were doing and did not let outsiders—bankers, lawyers, analysts, competitors, critics, or the press—influence where they were going with their companies. They built companies and industries and did it one customer at a time, one employee at a time, one product at a time. There are few shortcuts to business success.

There is another type of business leader. These leaders are usually better educated and better trained to run companies. They come in and look for short-term performance, trying to satisfy the stock market and the analysts' expectations for the next quarter or the next year. They often cut large numbers of employees in order to make certain that quarterly earnings meet forecast. They may have the long-term vision of a mole and sometimes do not know what products their companies make, who their customers are, or many of their employees by name. They are paid well, perhaps too well, but they don't create; they, in time, destroy.

They may be pessimists, not believing in their company or its future. They want to get what they can, while they can, because things could get worse in the long term. Their only management skill may be in convincing the board of directors to overpay them. They are eager to get substantial salaries and bonuses, to obtain company stock at bargain prices, and to sell it at high prices. Ten years later, or often sooner, they are gone, and few remember their names—only what was and what might have been.

Anybody can lay off 15,000 people. It takes a different set of skills to grow a company, to build a customer base, and to create 15,000 jobs. Or 5,000. Or 50. Some business people have loyalty and value it in their employees. For others, anything can be bought or sold—products, executives, employees, and customers.

There is a difference between being a business leader and being an individual investor. One can buy shares of stock in General Motors or General Electric or Bank of America today and sell them tomorrow if the stock price has gone up or if personal goals change. There is no commitment to the company, only to the stock price.

Being responsible for creating or running General Motors or General Electric or Bank of America or Digital Equipment or XYZ Company is different. Here, one's career and dream are invested in the company, and there cannot be any short-term trading. One is in it for the long term.

In the important parts of life, that is the way it is. No one does a quarterly review of one's spouse or a break-even analysis on one's children. One cannot describe anything with a few numbers—not a mate, a child, or a company. One does not or should not listen to the opinions of outsiders on how to choose a spouse or raise a child or where to live or how to spend one's leisure time. These are personal decisions, made for the long term.

There should be differences between a general view of "the markets" and of one's company, just as there should be between a view of "the younger generation" and of one's own family. You pay special attention to the people and things you care about most.

Perhaps that is why there is loyalty, admiration, and even love toward one kind of business leader—one who is an optimist, has a dream, knows that people are important, does not bow to the current fashion, and builds something of lasting value. Usually these people share the credit and the rewards with their colleagues, recognizing that in business, like sports, you win or lose as a team. People who worked for Andrew Carnegie, Henry Ford, David Sarnoff, Ken Olsen, Gordon Moore, Donald Douglas, Sam Walton, Ed Land, Walt Disney, and others admired them and look back on their experiences as the high point of their professional career.

Perhaps that is why some other business leaders receive no loyalty, are not admired, and often are disliked by their associates. They sometimes want to prove how tough they are, want to be feared, want to show who is boss. They fire people at will, obtain huge compensations, and are in it just for themselves. If there is no loyalty to those below, there is no loyalty to those above, especially when they are vastly overpaid and may be gone tomorrow.

The Training of Leaders

The business schools of America are partially to blame for this view of leadership. They often teach that a good manager can manage anything, an idea with which many entrepreneurs would disagree. Like many oversimplifications, this statement has enough truth in it to be appealing, enough falsehood to be dangerous. It is analogous to saying that a good athlete can play any sport well. It may be true that some children can be stars in many sports. By college, a few athletes will win letters in more than one sport. But almost never does an athlete compete successfully as a professional in more than one sport. And in managing successful businesses, one competes against professionals.

Unless one understands the business, its rules, its trade-offs, its customers, and the competition, one is less likely to succeed. Few engineers can design both computers and bridges, few salespeople can sell automobiles and medical equipment, and few financial people can assist businesses unless they understand them. That is why conglomerates seldom work in the long run, why Xerox failed with Scientific Data System, AT&T with National Cash Register, and why Time Warner failed with AOL. General Electric, which rotated managers from light-bulbs to the missile division, eventually failed to provide leadership in its computer, television, and semiconductor divisions. The managers were there for only a short time and did not understand the business.

A good manager can manage anything better than a bad manager can, but a good manager who understands the business will manage better than a good manager who is just passing through. The statement by Andrew Carnegie on page 4 may not be completely true, but it does contain enough truth to cause a business school professor to pause and think.

Business schools charge very high amounts for education, often promising that the student can quickly earn it back in the "real world." But these schools often do not teach creativity, business ethics, or interpersonal relationships. It may be no accident that most of the twentieth century's successful entrepreneurs got their training in business and not in business schools.

This is not to minimize the value of education. It is to say that business leaders have to deal with people and provide leadership in much the same way that the manager or coach of a sports team has to select, organize, and motivate athletes. Imagination, leadership, and people skills are not typically taught in universities. Perhaps it is too difficult to teach, or the professors have no experience in the subject. It is easier to teach accounting and financial analysis, case studies on the history of established companies, advertising techniques, and the use of computers, rather than the art of leadership, imagination, and the management of creative people. This may, in part, be due to the Alfred P. Sloan's business philosophy, in which organization and financial management skills matter more than technical, production, and marketing skills. Yet all of the entrepreneurs featured in this book had these skills and completely understood their businesses.

In the 1960s and 1970s, the business leaders in America were generally unknown except to their colleagues. In the 1990s, some of them became superstars, with their pictures on magazines, their wealth trumpeted throughout the press, and their salaries and bonuses in the stratosphere. Now those days may be behind us, as a few of these superstars are facing investigations and possible prison terms for creative accounting, while others have retired or been forced out of their companies, although sometimes with golden parachutes.

These people no more represent American business than those featured in *People* magazine represent American society. There is a substantial difference between image and reality. Many—no, most—business people have their goals, are decent people, and are building their companies. And the small and growing companies and entrepreneurs are what have made the United States the leading economic power in the world.

History and a Sense of Time

Some business leaders tend to look at things from a longer-term perspective. They recognize that things take time and that there will be short- and long-term implications for much of what they do.

Why do things take time? Sometimes it is because potential customers have to be educated about the value of a new product or service. Technologies can be ahead of themselves. Sometimes it is because the product or service is not valuable until many buy it. The first people to buy telephones had no one to talk to. The same phenomenon occurred three-quarters of a century later with computer networks and e-mail. So, paradoxically, you may need many customers before you can attract any. Sometimes an industry's growth is dependent on external factors. The growth in automobiles was dependent on the growth of the gasoline and rubber industries, the development of roads, the availability of filling stations and places to eat and stay, and the ability to finance car purchases. The U.S. steel industry could not have grown in the eighteenth and early nineteenth centuries. It required new customers, new applications, and a good transportation system to bring the raw materials to the mills and the finished steel to the customers. A similar delay in market development applied to the radio, television, semiconductor, and computer industries, as described earlier. Many consumers are followers, and many companies do not want to change to new technologies and leave the old and comfortable way of doing things. Old and new technologies may coexist for a long time, as customers work within their own product life cycles and stick with proven technologies. Sometimes the investors in a business are in too much of a rush and demand instant results. The entrepreneur has to be strong and not react to external pressures. Patience and a long-term view are required to build successful companies.

Some business people and investors have no sense of business history. They assume that the dot-com stock market of the 1990s is typical of the investment climate in general, ignoring the 1950s, 1970s, and 1980s, which may be more typical of American financial history. They assume that networks started in the 1990s, ignoring the work at Bolt, Beranek and Newman in 1969, and that computers started with Dell and Microsoft, ignoring the prior half-century of computer innovation at IBM, UNIVAC, Burroughs, DEC, and Apple.

Inventions and their applications typically have a long history of development. The more one understands that history, the more one can deal with the present and plan for the future. It is worth reading the history of science, technology, and business, including reading a selection of the books listed in this book's bibliography. At universities, there are courses on technical and business history as well as organizations devoted to the history of technology and science.[1] There are lectures that you can hear in your home or car.[2] The good leader is always learning and dependent on the knowledge of others. In remarks prepared for delivery at the Trade Mart in Dallas on the day he was killed, November 22, 1963, John Kennedy was to say, "Leadership and learning are indispensable to each other."[3]

Things take time. As shown in the book, every industry has many antecedents in both technology and business. And then, it can take between ten and twenty-five years between an innovation and its evolution to a point that customers accept it. Then after a longer time, innovation may give way to standardization.

As an example, the start of the American automobile industry could be considered as 1893, the year that Charles and Frank Duryea built their first automobile. In 1900, 4,000 cars were sold; in 1908, the industry built 65,000 cars, and in 1915, 1 million cars were built.

A similar growth occurred in radios. The inaugural year might be 1898. It was 1922 before 40,000 radios were sold and 1927 before 6 million were sold. The following chart shows the growth in six industries described in this book. The figures are approximate since several sources disagree slightly in the manufacturing numbers. Also, the year that the industry started is subject to discussion, as shown throughout the book. Finally there is a difference in a buyer's commitment to buying an automobile compared to having a phone installed, and agreeing to pay a small monthly fee for using it.

The figures present an interesting picture and indicate that things take time.

Figure 11-1. Approximate time for market penetration[4]

Product	Telephone	Auto	Radio	TV	Computer	Network
Invented	1876	1893	1898	1927	1945	1969
Years to reach:						
10,000 customers	3	10	18	19	16	18
100,000 customers	5	15	24	21	26	21
1,000,000 customers	24	22	26	22	35	24
5,000,000 customers	30	55	29	23	38	26
10,000,000 customers	53	63	34	24	41	29

Both a company's and an industry's success are not only dependent on their marketing, technical, and manufacturing capabilities, but also in the growth and success of their customers. Steel makers grew in the nineteenth and early twentieth centuries not only because they could make better steel at lower prices, but also because other people were developing railroads, bridges, buildings, ships, munitions, automobiles, roads, and other items that required steel. The steel industry stopped growing because their customers did not expand, their needs were satisfied, there were fewer things being built that required steel, or because their customers found other ways of satisfying their requirements, including plastics, aluminum, and other metals. Steelmakers today can make better steel than they could in the late nineteenth century; there is just not a growing market for their product.

Yet even here management matters. A company that was founded in 1908 by Ransom Olds, developer of the Oldsmobile and REO motorcars, went bankrupt in the 1930s and 1950s. It then became Nuclear Corporation and in 1964, facing further problems, hired Kenneth Iverson as CEO. It became profitable and was renamed Nucor Steel. The company has been innovative in the applications of technology, employee relations, and management. Nucor became one of the leading American steel manufacturers and grew revenues at a compounded rate of 17 percent per year for the thirty years Iverson ran the company, with excellent return on equity. Meanwhile, Bethlehem Steel, founded by Charles Schwab, fell on hard times and is currently in bankruptcy. Leadership matters.

The semiconductor industry has grown in the last few decades because companies could make better semiconductors, put more on a chip, and offer them at lower prices. But the industry also has grown because there have been entrepreneurs in a variety of new industries who were able to start and build companies that required semiconductors—mainframe computers, minicomputers, personal computers, cell phones, televisions, home entertainment, communication networks, satellites, the Internet, instrumentation, and electronic games and toys. And what of the future of these industries? Their success and growth is of major importance to those in the semiconductor industry. Both the steel and semiconductors have turned into businesses requiring large-volume production to justify their high capital investment. To be successful, they need their customers to grow.

Understanding that things take time, that there is a prior history of technology and business, knowing customers and their needs, having a dream and a plan to achieve it, and possessing the patience to look at things on a long-term basis—all of these factors increase the chances for the success of a business.

Investors, Administrators, and Builders

Bankers, lawyers, stockbrokers, analysts, and business writers do not make companies successful. They are spectators on the sidelines as the game is played. The people who work in the enterprise, their customers, and their vendors build companies.

If a chief executive officer's objectives are long term, he or she wants investors and owners in for the long pull. If the company is successful, they will be amply rewarded. In the short term, a president has little effect on the company's stock price. Stocks go up and down daily based on a number of factors outside the control of the people running the company. Although most may not go as far as Henry Ford, quoted below and on page 162, they know that every time someone buys a stock, someone sells the stock—and they both can't be right.

> *The stock market as such has nothing to do with business. It has nothing to do with the quality of the article that is manufactured, nothing to do with the output, nothing to do with the marketing, it does not even increase or decrease the amount of capital used in the business. It is just a little show on the side.*[5]

The stock market is a zero sum game; that is, the amount gained by some equals the amount lost by others. In fact, it is a negative sum game, since brokers and mutual funds take a percentage on each transaction. In the short term, the price of a stock can be adversely affected by a number of factors—world events, the economy, consumer confidence, an analyst's negative report on the industry or the company, stock traders short selling because they believe anything can be bought and sold daily, a mutual fund's need to raise cash or to invest cash, and a number of things that have nothing to do with the underlying performance or the future of a business.

The motivation of some venture capitalists and individual investors is often to make the maximum amount of money in the minimum amount of time, sometimes in a year or even a few months. Although this is a fine goal, it is usually in conflict with the goal of building a long-term company. Investing in research and development and in building market position requires time and patience, something that many investors lack.

If the successful entrepreneur is not usually thinking about the daily stock price, he or she is even less influenced by stock analysts and business writers. In the years between 1959 and 1993, Ken Olsen and Digital Equipment were frequently ignored by the analysts, often criticized at a time when the company was investing in its future, and then overly praised when problems were on the horizon. Anyone who looks only at events daily or quarterly is unlikely to understand the longer-term picture, in business as in life.

A number of today's high-technology companies have Web sites that not only describe the history and current products and services of the company but also the current price and price history of the stock. That may be a method of increasing support and promoting the stock, often for the benefit of the management and directors. It is difficult to believe that any of the entrepreneurs described in this book would have permitted such an activity for their company. They were builders, not stock promoters. Money was a tool, not an end in itself.

The chief executive officer needs directors who understand the objectives and help the company focus on its core competency and build on a long-term basis. A director or venture capitalist whose goal is to promote a stock and then unload it on a gullible public is hardly following in the tradition of General Georges Doriot and American Research and Development (see page 271). There is more to supporting a company through its growth phase than touting a stock.

That does not mean that any executive can or should ignore the stock market. It does mean that an entrepreneur realizes that to build something of lasting value, one has to run a company for customers, employees, vendors, the community, and investors, not primarily for stock analysts, chambers of commerce, or business writers. If you succeed, then they will come around, and if you fail, it doesn't matter what they say. Accounting numbers tell what has happened, not what will happen. They are, at best, an inexact measurement of the past, not of the future.

Nothing grows exponentially, except a cancer cell, and it, in time, kills. Although it would be nice to grow a constant 15 percent a year, leaders know that there are ups and downs in the economy, in the needs of customers, and in a company's product and market competitive positions. The effective leader keeps the company moving in the correct direction for long-term success. It is the entrepreneur's company, and success cannot be measured daily or quarterly.

Although it may have been true in a limited number of cases from the 1920s through the 1940s, a review of business history for the last sixty years shows that over the long term *there is no economy of scale in American business.* A company may purchase competitors and grow into a stronger position for a while, but its market share, employment levels, and return to shareholders may be on their way down as new companies enter the marketplace and smaller competitors become more innovative.

Companies do not have to reach a certain size in order to be successful, not in the manufacturing, airlines, retail, publishing, banking, or service industries. Large organizations and their hierarchies don't generally cope well with change or take chances by trying something new. That is why small companies can be established and grow. What seems to matter, independent of the size of the enterprise, is leadership.

Often, the bigger the company, the more the top executives are paid and the higher the fees paid to investment bankers, lawyers, and directors. So these people may want growth at any cost. But if the purpose of a company is measured in terms of service to customers, financial reward to stockholders, and opportunities for employees, larger is not automatically better in the business world anymore than it is in the animal world. Cats and deer seem to do better than dinosaurs and rhinos.

It is worth pointing out that many of the pioneers described in this book— from Andrew Carnegie and Henry Ford to Sam Walton, from Bob Noyce and Ted Turner to Bill Gates—in building something of long-term value, did well financially for themselves and their associates. In time, accomplishments and long-term contributions are very well rewarded.

The lists of successful companies, provided in Table 1.1, were started by entrepreneurs in all decades and under all economic conditions. Whether starting companies was in fashion or not, whether there was too little or too much available capital for new companies, entrepreneurs started companies and industries and succeeded. Some grew, like Digital Equipment Company, with only small amounts of outside capital during the first years. Although some companies had little initial investment to start with and might have benefited from more, there can be a risk of having too much money from venture capitalists and the stock market. If the initial investment in a company is $1 million and the company grows to $10 million in revenue, the investors will have made a good return. If, on the other hand, the early investment in a company is $100 million, then the investors have to demand that management build a very large company quickly and/or merge the company into another institution, trading one kind of paper for another. The history of Digital Equipment and Compaq are worth studying from that vantage point. One company remained independent and grew for almost forty years, providing good returns to the investors. The other had many leaders in its much shorter life, acquired companies, bought and sold its own stock, and was soon sold to Hewlett-Packard.

The concept of the conglomerate, a company whose only value is in having control of other companies in unrelated fields, has come in and out of fashion during the twentieth century. Harold Geneen left Raytheon and made International Telephone and Telegraph a very large company. His successor sold off most of the parts. Among others, LTV under James Ling, Gulf and Western under Charles Bluhdorn, Tyco under Dennis Kozlowski, and Textron under Royal Little tried this process, with mixed financial results and operational success, and eventually some of the pieces were sold. Robert Sarnoff made his father's company, RCA, into a holding company, and this major electronics company lost its lead in a growth industry and eventually its independence. So growth, especially in unrelated fields, does not appear to automatically lead to increased financial performance, the creation of jobs, marketing dominance, or better customer service.

Pioneers and Plodders

The leader's major responsibility is to lead and to lead successfully. As President Harry Truman said: "A leader has to lead, or otherwise he has no business in politics."[6] Or in business.

In World War II, the oldest generals, or those with the best grades at West Point, did not automatically become the most successful. General Omar Bradley and General George Patton are acknowledged as major figures in the war, and these two men had completely different personalities and leadership techniques. But they were both effective leaders. It is a tribute to Generals George Marshall and Dwight Eisenhower that they could identify Bradley and Patton and give the two the opportunity to lead. The best baseball or football players are often not the best managers. There are different sets of skills required for doing something yourself and for planning and motivating others to perform to the peak of their ability. A similar observation also applies to business.

The successful business leader has to have the ability to select and motivate people, decide how to train them and when to bring people from outside the company who may have talent but may not know the industry or its culture.

There is no one way to found and run a company anymore than there is one way to run your life. What works for one, either professionally or personally, may not work or be right for another. Yet there are some observations that may be in order.

Business is ultimately a people business, and this means that management matters. Management is more than administration, it is about selecting and motivating people, as individuals and as members of a team. The best managers can select good people and make them perform better as a group. Communication and information sharing are important. The effective leader wants to hear the ideas of his or her employees and customers. Employees, or at least many of them, need to have a feeling of participation, of belonging to something special. And with a growth company, the best people can grow, try new things, feel they are important, and contribute to the success of the enterprise. That is one reason those who decrease the number of employees for short-term profits often destroy what made the company grow. The best people lose their personal stake in the business.

Some of the characteristics of successful entrepreneurs include vision, clarity of thought, independence, imagination, stubbornness, enthusiasm, inspirational leadership, patience, the ability to select and motivate people, optimism and a positive attitude, high energy levels, good communication and listening skills, and perhaps a touch of luck.

There is something about starting with an idea and a blank sheet of paper, whether one is a writer, an artist, a composer, an engineer, or an entrepreneur. To create is exciting; to do something new is wonderful. How much is an idea worth? What is the value of a blank canvas before a painting is started, a stack of papers before the first word of a novel is written, or a company before the first employee is hired? To start with nothing except a dream and then to build a large and successful company is to create jobs, customers, and wealth. It is no accident that many of the largest fortunes in American history are held by entrepreneurs, their families, and associates. There can be great excitement, personal satisfaction, and financial reward for those who found and build companies.

Selling an established item, whether an art dealer selling an old painting, a used car dealer selling an old automobile, or an investment banker selling a company, is not the same. And someone who trades cars, paintings, or companies requires different skills from those who create them.

Many of the major American entrepreneurs were creative people or people who respected creativity in their scientists, engineers, designers, and manufacturing people. People who come readily to mind include Walt Disney, Donald Douglas of Douglas Aircraft, Henry Ford, Paul Galvin of Motorola, Bill Gates of Microsoft, Joyce Hall of Hallmark, Steve Jobs of Apple, Ed Land of Polaroid, Gordon Moore and Bob Noyce of Intel, Akio Morita of Sony, William Norris of Control Data, Ken Olsen, and David Sarnoff.

Others applied their creativity to the marketing and distribution phases of business. Notable people in this category include Ray Kroc of McDonald's, William McGowan of MCI Communications, John Patterson of National Cash

Register, James Cash Penney of JC Penney, Ross Perot of Electronic Data Systems, Ted Turner of CNN, Frederick Smith of Federal Express, Theodore Vail of AT&T, Sam Walton of Wal-Mart, and Thomas Watson Sr. of IBM.

Being creative and valuing creative people is an essential component in building a growth company. It is difficult for a company to have long-term viability without a history of innovation and product or marketing leadership. "Me too" companies selling a common commodity only on price seldom last.

There is more to establishing a company than building an engineering model or a prototype. Building one of everything and two of nothing does not lead to business success. The successful company has to take that prototype and move it into large-scale production. It also has to identify customers, build sales outlets, and find ways of distributing the product in order to increase production levels.

Each of the entrepreneurs featured in this book also recognized that potential customers are worldwide and not just in the United States. Andrew Carnegie knew the relative production costs of his overseas competitors and favored import tariffs to protect the developing American steel industry. But, as it became the lowest-cost producer, Carnegie Steel was selling surplus steel production around the world against German and British competitors. Ford built his first overseas plant in 1908 and by 1928, he had manufacturing plants in twenty countries and sales outlets in many others. RCA started as an international radio phone company and sold its radios, phonograph records, and television sets across the globe. And from its earliest days, about half of Digital Equipment Company's revenue was from non–U.S. sources, with engineering, manufacturing, sales, and marketing outlets in many countries.

It is worth pointing out that these and many other executives sold their products around the world. They also hired people in many countries to design, build, and sell their products in those countries. That is quite different from some companies today who provide their products or services only in the United States and outsource jobs to lower cost areas in order to increase earnings a few cents per share of the stock. As Henry Ford said when he increased wages as described in chapter 6, "The owners, the employees and the buying public are all one and the same, and unless an industry can so manage itself as to keep wages high and prices low, it destroys itself, for otherwise it limits the number of its customers."

The creation of jobs is one of life's greatest achievements; the destruction of jobs and companies for personal gain is one of life's sins. Anything that can be managed can be mismanaged. Companies can rise or fall, they can grow or shrink, and the cause, in most cases is the quality of management. Can management deal with change and does it encourage innovation? Do employees identify with the company?

Look at who is in charge and their goals. Are they following a dream or the quick buck? Are they a builder or a destroyer of companies? Does the company encourage or discourage innovation? Consider Bethlehem Steel under the leadership of Charles Schwab and today in bankruptcy, RCA in its first forty years and afterward, and Digital Equipment then and now. The company of William Hewlett and David Packard of the 1930s to the 1980s, with their trust in people and open management style, is quite different from the Hewlett-Packard of today. That may be the reason why the founders' children opposed the merger of Hewlett-Packard and Compaq.

What are the objectives and capabilities of management? Examining the airline industry may reinforce the importance of management objectives. From the 1920s to the 1950s, the president of most airlines was a pilot: Eddie Rickenbacker at Eastern, Juan Trippe at Pan American, Robert Six at Continental, Walter T. Varney at United, Howard Hughes and Jack Frye at TWA. Today, presidents are financial people, and they look at the world differently from their predecessors. Pilots consider aircraft performance, instruments, weather conditions, and passenger safety and comfort. Financiers consider cash flow, debt servicing, profit margins, and load factors. The world of aviation has changed, and not necessarily for the better.[7] Did you enjoy flying when you were a customer, and your needs, including schedule, excellent food, and comfort, were met? Do you enjoy flying today when you are part of a load factor and the only airline differentiation, in many cases, is price? Examine the job satisfaction and morale of airline employees then and now. Leadership matters. Pan American, TWA, and Eastern survived and grew during the depression and World War II, and they are now out of the airline business at a time when there are substantially more customers. (Three billion passengers were carried by the world's airlines in 2000.) United, American, Delta, Northwest, and others are in financial hot water. Yet even here there are outstanding successes. At a time when many airline companies are in or near bankruptcy, Southwest Airlines is in its thirtieth consecutive year of profitability.

If load factor, market share, and price are the ultimate judges of success, then the model for the airline industry is the New York subway system. Customers stand up so a great number fit into the vehicle, they don't get fed, and there is a very small crew. The airlines' management forgot that theirs is a service business, and that there is more to an airline than offering the lowest price. There is comfort, adequate seating space, good meals, satisfied employees, a smile, on-time performance, customer loyalty, and airline reputation. Profitability, not market share, are important and customer relations do matter. No other business treats its best customers worse, by charging them substantially more for their tickets than the occasional flier who can deal with the obscure rules and frequent ticket price changes. Leadership in the airline industry may be responsible for its current unsettled status, with many companies in financial difficulty.

Another industry that appears to have lost its purpose is banking. Banking is fundamentally a service business. Where once the tellers and bank officers knew their customers, now some banks charge you to talk to a real teller instead of using an ATM and even ask for your personal identification to deposit money. An effective reaction is to ask for the identification of the teller since you are giving him or her your money. Many in the banking business do not know their individual or business clients. The saying that a banker will lend you an umbrella when it is sunny but not when it is raining seems even more true today. Once upon a time, the name of the bank was chiseled in stone on the building. Now names are transitory and may be attached to the bank by Velcro. An interesting goal today is to have the name of the bank last longer than the checks you order. Is there any real difference between banks today other than service and the knowledge of its customers? Bigger does not mean better unless service and customer knowledge increases or, at the very least, do not deteriorate with mergers. Bank mergers with subsequent laying off of large number of employees of the purchased bank do not seem to have any customer advantages.

Why these two examples? It is to point out that mergers and growth, in and of themselves, may benefit a few executives. But they do not increase customer service, offer new products, or benefit the economy in any way. And they open opportunities for other entrepreneurs to start and build successful companies. The purpose of an existing enterprise is not to achieve maximum market share or pay the officers the most money, but to exist to provide needed products, to grow profitably in their specific markets, to know and serve their customers, to build customer loyalty, to give opportunities to their employees, and to be prepared to deal with the future and its changes.

There is apparently no relationship between the amount of money the senior executive earns and the effect he or she has in dealing with changing technology, creating jobs, or creating something of long-term value. Some presidents of established companies seem only motivated as stock traders, trying to make the maximum amount of money in the minimum amount of time. Although that goal may be important to the individual, it in no sense should be confused with building a company, helping found an industry, or creating jobs. Do not equate current wealth with accomplishment. If they were the same, then the children and grandchildren of successful entrepreneurs would be the ones to admire. And Aspen, Colorado; Greenwich, Connecticut; or Santa Barbara, California, would be more important to a study of business history than Silicon Valley, Route 128, Seattle, Austin, or other places where new things happen.

Science fiction stories occasionally can lead to reality. But money trails and does not lead creativity. The same is true with the press and publicity. Some of the best work by the most important entrepreneurs—Ken Olsen, Steve Jobs, Bill Gates, Sam Walton, Bob Noyce, Ray Kroc, and others—was done early in their company's development. In time, fame and financial reward followed, but it was not their principal motivation. They wanted to follow their dreams.

In his recent book on publishing and education, Hal Miller wrote about the importance of corporate culture, that is, the spirit and character of a company.[8] This culture is often established early by the founder and associates and is passed through the company, often with many leaders and over several generations, each of whom understands the culture and builds on it. In New England, most people knew the culture of Houghton Mifflin, Little Brown, Digital Equipment, Polaroid, State Street Bank, Raytheon, and other institutions. The culture of successful organizations in Chicago, Kansas City, Dallas, Minneapolis, San Francisco, and other cities are known to the residents of those places. Other companies with established cultures would include IBM, Pan American, RCA and CBS, EDS, CNN, Johnson & Johnson, Morgan Bank, Disney, Hewlett-Packard, Wal-Mart, and Southwest Airlines. When the culture is lost through acquisition, significant change in corporate direction, or new and incapable management, more is lost than merely revenue and jobs. The loss also includes what made that company what it was, its customer relationships, its brand name, identification of employees with the company, and, often, their pride in their jobs. Fear of losing one's job is a poor long-term motivator for most people. The best employees move on. Do not confuse firing large numbers of people with building a company, or thick corporate manuals and detailed job descriptions with leadership.

By the time everyone knows something, it is too late to be a pioneer. Pioneers listen to themselves and try to create and build something that will last. They often want to change the world. The names of those who were with Lewis and Clark on their trip west are known. Many farmers later plowed the fields that Lewis and Clark traversed, but their names are forgotten. The same applies to business leaders. Tribute is due to those who did something, made something happen, created something of value, not in terms of only quarterly earnings, but in long-term viability. There are few statues to bankers or accountants or bureaucrats or lawyers or consultants.

Management Succession and Corporate Independence

This book has addressed the issues of establishing and building new companies and industries. Yet a word should be said about corporate succession. What happens as the founder ages? Every business leader, like every other person, grows old and will die. A working career may be between thirty and fifty years, and the company may have been founded late in a career. What will happen to the company the entrepreneur has created? Will it outlast the founder? Will it continue to grow and prosper?

There is nothing wrong and something very right about starting a company and running it for a quarter century, creating jobs, building market position, helping the economy even if, in time, the company goes out of business. In my opinion, it is more admirable than taking an existing company and destroying the business for personal financial gain.

But many companies do last more than a decade or two— some more than a century—which raises the question of management succession and corporate culture. As Walter Lippmann wrote: "The final test of a leader is that he leaves behind him in other men the conviction and the will to carry on."[9]

In some companies, successors have been selected and trained by the founder. These companies have continued as successful independent organizations with the original corporate culture intact, sometimes for a few decades after the founder retired, sometimes for more than a century. Among companies in this category are ADP, Boeing, Citicorp, Colgate-Palmolive, DuPont, Eli Lilly, Emerson Electric, General Electric, IBM, Intel, Johnson & Johnson, Motorola, Proctor & Gamble, Sony, and Wal-Mart.

Board members are often financial people, lawyers, or business leaders from outside the industry who usually lack the vision of the founding entrepreneur. Therefore, it is easier for them to sell a business than to help guide it. Does the company survive the founder or is the board eager to sell the company to the highest bidder and watch it disappear as RCA did with General Electric, Nixdorf with Siemens, or Digital Equipment with Compaq? Although they have other responsibilities, board members may mistakenly believe that their only responsibility is to the stockholders and thus they sell the company quickly for the highest price they can get. Often, this is for stock in another company, and a few years later, the stock is worth significantly less than at the time of the sale. Mergers often destroy the corporate culture and then the company itself.

The major role of a board of directors is to select and monitor the CEO on a long-term basis. Part of that involves deciding on and implementing a management succession plan. Some chief executives may not wish to consider their mortality or possible declining capabilities. William Paley at CBS and Michael Eisner of Disney are but two examples of executives who hired and then forced out their anointed successors. But the board as well as the founder has much at stake in guaranteeing the continuation of the corporation. Although neither the founder's children nor executives are guarantees of continued success, failure to address the succession issue is a potential for corporate failure.

Here, it is appropriate to look at the four companies featured in this book and their leadership succession. Although the stories are told earlier, they will be amplified here.

Andrew Carnegie always had other executives who had operational control of Carnegie Steel. Carnegie once stated, "Mr. (J. P.) Morgan buys his partners. I raise my own."[10] When U.S. Steel was established more than a century ago, Carnegie selected Charles Schwab to run the new company. But the company's board of directors were financial men and not steel people. Schwab soon left to take over Bethlehem and built it to become the second largest steel manufacturer. U.S. Steel under the leadership of Judge Gary provided good returns to its shareholders but started losing market share in 1901 and continued to decline in market share for a century.

Henry Ford named his son, Edsel, as his successor. Edsel Ford was a much better manager than Henry, but he died early at the age of forty-nine, and Henry held on far too long. The company was in major trouble when Henry Ford's grandson, Henry Ford II, finally took over and revitalized the company during and after World War II. Today, Ford Motor Company continues as a major force in the automobile business.

David Sarnoff named his son, Robert, as his successor. Yet at a time of great growth and opportunity, RCA stopped being the leading electronics company. Robert Sarnoff and his successor took the company in another direction, that of a holding company. RCA was soon sold and went out of business.

The most interesting story and the most recent one was that of Ken Olsen and Digital Equipment Corporation. In 1991, Digital Equipment got into major trouble. But everyone lost money in the computer industry that year, a fact that should have been obvious at the time. In 1991 through 1993, DEC lost $2.9 billion; IBM lost $15.9 billion during the same three years. Olsen was sixty-five, the same age as Henry Ford when he designed the Model A with his son Edsel, and Olsen was capable of continuing to run DEC for a few years more. Perhaps Olsen should have trained his successor earlier. Perhaps DEC was in too many markets and had too many employees. Regardless, the board of directors lost confidence, forced Olsen out, and brought in a new team, some of whom were unfamiliar with the industry. The board then sold the company to the wrong buyer, an organization whose financial condition was no stronger than DEC's. The result was a dismantling of Digital Equipment within five years and the loss of its executives, its people, its brand name, and many of its products and customers. It is difficult to believe that things would have been worse with Olsen staying in control and being told by the board of directors to train a successor.

Like DEC, IBM had expanded its employment with its growth. It had 6,346 employees in 1930, 12,656 employees in 1940, and had grown to 22,246 employees after the war when its revenue reached $116 million. From then on employment increased rapidly. Employment was 30,261 in 1950, 104,241 in 1960, 269,291 in 1970, 341,279 in 1980, and reached 373,816 in 1990.[11] The same technological changes that affected DEC and all computer companies in the early 1990s hit IBM hard. The company had major losses in 1991 through 1993. IBM, which had a policy of lifetime employment, shed employees at a rapid rate through early retirement and layoffs. Employment was quickly reduced to 219,839 employees.

But where DEC's board of directors panicked, sold the company, and watched revenue, market position, and employment decline permanently, IBM's board took an active role. IBM changed management; brought in a new CEO, Lou Gerstner, from outside the industry; and built on IBM's strengths. Gerstner made some strategic decisions, put the right people in positions of authority, and returned IBM to its growth days as an independent company. Employment increased and reached 316,303 by the year 2000. Once again, management matters.

Acquisitions

The acquisition of one company by another, larger one generally does not work out for the acquired company, its employees, or its customers. Why does one company acquire another? Historically there are three reasons.

The first is to eliminate a competitor. This may have advantages for the acquiring company's stockholders, but it definitely has disadvantages for the employees of the acquired company as well as its customers and the economy. With fewer choices of suppliers, innovation is reduced, choices are minimized, and in general, prices increase. This has been the result in many fields, from airlines and retail to the computer, newspaper, and communication industries. The fewer competitors there are, the easier it may be for the surviving companies but the worse for their customers and community.

The second reason is for the benefit of the chief executive officer. If a company is acquired, the resulting company is larger, the salary of the chief executive is usually raised, and it becomes difficult for stock analysts to compare year-to-year results. In short, an acquisition gives instant growth and buys time for an executive to perhaps perform someday. As an example, from 1994 to 2001, Tyco acquired 1,000 companies, or about three a week, and spent $63 billion doing so.[12] Is it possible that they were all good choices? Did anyone on the board or in senior management even know what these companies did?

A third reason can have potential advantages. If a company acquires another company in its own or a directly related field, and if management understands the new business, the resultant enterprise may be able to better grow and gain market share, offer more products and services, and compete against larger companies. Combining customer bases, sales forces, product positions, manufacturing capabilities, and good people in management, it should be possible for 2 + 2 to equal more than 4. Why, then, do so many acquisitions fail, and 2 + 2 not even add up to 3?

The answer comes down, as always, to leadership, people, and corporate culture. Often, acquisitions start off with great promises of additional financial support and no changes. The selling chief executive receives a substantial bonus, not for his or her skills but for cooperation, and a few senior executives receive cash payouts, with little given to the remaining employees, the customers, or the long-term investors.

Then, one by one, the senior officers and many creative people leave, and finally the products of the acquired company are eliminated in favor of those of the buyer. Product-line decisions become political battles. The importance of brand identification, whether that of Digital Equipment, UNIVAC, or XYZ, are ignored. Old customers from the acquired company are left high and dry, with the products they selected no longer supported, and these customers begin to look for new suppliers. Sales forces jockey for position, and the losing people, often the best, move to other organizations. New and often arbitrary personnel policies and procedures are forced on the acquired company. If the merger was done with borrowed money, then eventually the lenders have to be paid back. Although it is possible for this to be accomplished through increasing revenues, in almost all cases it is through cutting expenses. And generally, the older employees, being the highest paid, are let go first and replaced with younger and lower-paid employees. The corporate culture disappears along with the people who knew the products, customers, character, and history of the company.

The chief executive of the selling company often cooperates in the sale, either because he or she has been bought off with an overly generous compensation package or, as one former executive of a company that was sold ten years after his tenure said, "because the chief executive officer lacks guts and was not prepared to fight for his company, its employees and customers."

Companies headquartered in various American cities and their executives have been major supporters for local art and science museums, symphonies, hospitals, universities, and other institutions. As companies are acquired by remote and often foreign conglomerates these supports decline or are eliminated. So the community not only suffers economically as jobs are eliminated but also culturally.

Certainly there are successful acquisitions. But those occur when top management makes them work, devoting the time to understand the people and the history of the acquired company, and building on the strength of that company as well as its own. To successfully acquire a company requires leadership and hard work.

In most cases, acquisitions do not work, at least operationally. Some senior people exercise stock options and get paid bonuses when the merger is completed. But if the purpose of a business is measured in terms of products and services to customers, opportunities for employees, growth in the business, and long-term financial rewards to stockholders, acquisitions generally fail. Within a few years, the acquired company may be sold again, as an entity or in parts. Spin-offs, divestitures, and changes in corporate focus are used to justify the sale. When an individual sells his or her stock in a company, it has no effect on the business. But when a corporation buys and then sells a business, in the meantime eliminating many of its senior personnel and destroying the company's corporate culture, it usually destroys the business, stockholder value, and the careers of many people.

Examples are numerous, but in the computer industry alone, failed acquisitions include Xerox's acquisition of Scientific Data Systems, Honeywell's purchase of Computer Control Company and General Electric's computer operations, AT&T's acquisition of National Cash Register, the sale of EDS to General Motors, Burroughs's purchase of UNIVAC, the sale of Digital Equipment to Compaq, and Compaq's subsequent sale to Hewlett-Packard. Why don't mergers and acquisitions work? It is because business is ultimately people, not numbers, and because management matters. There is both good and bad leadership, and special talents are needed to make acquisitions succeed. Companies are born, grow, age, and without effective leadership, die.

Business Leadership and a Career

What does all of this mean for the individual? In the first place, if one enters the workforce at twenty-five and retires at sixty-five, a working career may be longer than that of a company, or even an industry in which one works. In any case, the technology and market competition will change during a career. Change will be a part of almost everyone's professional experience. Some people coast in the workplace, but one can only coast downhill. Earlier it was said that there is a difference between being an investor and an employee. One can trade in a stock quickly, but it is more difficult to change a career or the skills that have been developed. Yet a person may have to, since the world will change during a professional lifetime. The individual also has to grow and change.

In work, as in a personal life, there is no such thing as security. The fact that people have been loyal employees of AT&T, Montgomery Ward, Sears, Roebuck, or Bethlehem Steel does not guarantee employment until they are sixty-five and a good pension and benefits thereafter. Look at what happened to those who worked in the steel industry, railroads, or telephone companies for job security and good benefits. If a company is not well run, if it does not deal with change, if it goes out of business or is outrun by competitors, then the individual will share in its fate. So the performance of management and their loyalty to the organization matter a great deal.

If the officers of the company are making several hundred times what the average worker in the company is making, this may be a sign of poor management objectives. Most of the entrepreneurs listed in this book made reasonable salaries during the founding years. At one time it was called sweat equity, the founder getting stock in a new enterprise but gathering a minimum salary. A person who organizes a company, obtains a huge salary from the beginning, and gets enormous amounts of stock is not an entrepreneur. An entrepreneur is a person who organizes, operates, and assumes the risk of a business venture. If there is no risk and the founder is extremely well compensated from the beginning, then he or she may be called a promoter, a hired gun, or even in some cases in the 1990s, a pillager.

In Japan and Germany, the average CEO makes about eleven times what the typical hourly employee makes, whereas some American executives of large but average performance companies make 500 times or more what the typical worker makes.[13] These executives are obviously more interested in their own well-being than that of their employees. If their golf game, their trips to Aspen, and their own financial success are uppermost in their minds, they probably are not leading the company well.

Being creative, flexible, and independent; trying new things; deciding on alternatives in a changing world—all these give one a better and more fulfilled life. Are employees using their brains, developing new skills, and creating intellectual capital for the company? Can workers make decisions and contribute, or are they merely following orders? Are promotions based on talent, on seniority, or on political considerations? A good leader values people who try things, make some mistakes, and achieve successes because they are alive and striving. An organization or leader that punishes those who make a mistake guarantees that survivors will never try anything new and risky.

Finally, those who acquire so much debt in obtaining their education and in subsequently buying fancy cars, expensive houses, and all kinds of material things decrease their freedom to take chances. For some people it is not how much they own that is important but their freedom. Everyone should have time to chase a dream, be part of new things, travel, go fishing, or spend time with a child. Restricting one's freedom and choices by being too deeply in debt results in the banker and finance company controlling a person's life. As Charles Dickens wrote, "Annual income twenty pounds, annual expenditure nineteen nineteen six, result happiness. Annual income twenty pounds, annual expenditure twenty pounds ought and six, result misery."[14]

Views of the Future

One thing that can be guaranteed about the future is that new companies will be founded, new industries will develop, and established companies will go out of business, either through sale or liquidation. The creative and information, health care and service industries will become more important as manufacturing continues to lose jobs to overseas producers. And entrepreneurs and small companies will continue to lead the country forward.

In the early 1980s, there were a number of newspapers, magazine articles, and books about the future decline of the United States in the world economy. Japan, Germany, Scandinavia, and many of the growing nations of the Pacific Rim, including Taiwan, Singapore, Korea, and Hong Kong, were held up as models for the future. American businesses were believed to be noncompetitive in the global economy; American products and technology were behind those of other parts of the industrialized world. In this world of prognostication, the United States would follow the example of Spain in the eighteenth century or Great Britain and France after World War II, and retreat from center stage, becoming a second-rate economic and technical power.

These predictions by so-called experts, often tired executives and writers, professors, and consultants sitting on the sidelines, were to a very large extent wrong when they were made. Insofar as there was truth in them, the United States roared back. The United States, after all, has a unified market of more than 270 million people, the best capital sources, some of the best business leaders, has been used to world competition for a long time, and leads the world in technology and its applications. American technology is dominant in semiconductors, computers, microprocessors, software, communications, aircraft manufacture, the information highway, genetic engineering, medicine, and other industries. America automobile producers, after relearning the message of W. Edwards Deming, the American reliability and efficiency expert who had advised the postwar Japanese auto industry, became low cost suppliers and started to provide higher quality automobiles. American firms dominate movies, television, music, and other aspects of the entertainment world. American colleges and universities are the leading institutions in the world, and people from across the globe send their children to the United States for an education.

Wherever you travel in Asia, Latin America, or Europe, questions arise regarding America's business dominance. American technology, marketing, and financial clout are felt worldwide, and there are many reasons for this. By and large, the United States has been the home of capitalism. It has also been the place where good ideas and good people have opportunities, with a more upwardly mobile society than other places in the world. It has an excellent university system and has invested in research and development for the last sixty years.

But to a large extent, the United States lead is due to the entrepreneurs who have built the technologies and industries of the nineteenth and twentieth centuries. The United States has been the home of entrepreneurs, far more so than Germany, the United Kingdom, Japan, or the rest of the world. Although many large companies protect their market position, merge with each other to become even bigger, and decrease the size of their workforce by massive layoffs, new companies build businesses. Most job creation in the last fifty years has been among small companies. Some of these small companies become large companies and create new industries, led by the entrepreneurs that founded them. The following industries and companies did not exist in 1950 and were founded by people who had a vision. In minicomputers, Computer Control, Digital Equipment, Data

General, Prime Computer, and Tandem; in personal computers, Apple Computer, Commodore, Compaq, Conner, Dell, Seagate Technology, and Sun Microsystems; in semiconductors, Advanced Micro Devices, Fairchild, Intel, LSI Logic, Motorola, National Semiconductor, and Texas Instruments; in software, Adobe, America Online, Lotus, Microsoft, Netscape, Novell, and Oracle; in genetic engineering, Amgen and Genentech; in freight, Federal Express, UPS, and Ryder; in communications, McCaw, MCI, Turner Broadcasting; in clothing, L.A. Gear, Nike, and Reebok; in computer services, ADP, EDS, and Computer Sciences; in entertainment and television, Blockbuster, CNN, General Cinema, and most of cable television; and in dozens of other industries and thousands of other companies, people have started companies, founded industries, and provided jobs. And most of these companies have competed in a world market from the beginning.

That perhaps is the major reason why the Unites States remains the leader in technology and business as the twenty-first century begins. Americans have faith in the future and a belief that hard work and talent can lead to high rewards. This is the country where the business, financial, and personal environment exists to take risks, to follow dreams, to start new companies and new industries. Two of the entrepreneurs featured in this book were immigrants, and the other two were children or grandchildren of immigrants. Leadership is not dependent on the choice of ancestors, financial inheritance, or an Ivy League education. The American dream was and continues to be available to all who have the ability. Thomas Jefferson in a letter written to John Adams, said: "I agree with you that there is a natural aristocracy among men. The grounds of this are virtue and talents."[15]

At the start of the twenty-first century, America is the most powerful industrial and military country in the world. Throughout the world, capitalism and free trade are ascendant and there has been a worldwide economic boom, although it varies from place to place and region to region. During the past century and certainly since 1940, American technology has been dominant, and the United States the economic colossus of the world. The twentieth century has rightly been called the American Century. Perhaps because of the continued innovation of its entrepreneurs, the twenty-first century may be as well.

Notes

Chapter 1. Technology, Growth, and Employment

1. U.S. Census Bureau, *Historical Statistics of the United States— Colonial Times to 1970* (Washington, D.C.: U.S. Census Bureau, 1975).
2. Ibid.
3. U.S. Census Bureau-School Enrollment, October 1999. The Census Bureau releases an annual report on school enrollment, available through the Web (http://www.census.gov/population/www/socdemo/school.html).
4. Bureau of Labor Statistics, *Handbook of Labor Statistics* (U.S. Department of Labor, Bureau of Labor Statistics, 2000).
5. American Telephone and Telegraph Company, *Annual Report of the Directors* (Boston, Mass.: AT&T, 1904), 5.
6. Ibid., 10.
7. Andrew Carnegie, *The Empire of Business* (New York: Doubleday Page and Co., 1902), 106–108.
8. Bureau of Labor Statistics, 2000 Federal Census (U.S. Department of Labor, Bureau of Labor Statistics).
9. *Newsweek,* October 16, 2000, 74.
10. Richard Henkoff, "Cost Cutting How to Do It," *Fortune* magazine, April 9, 1990.

Chapter 2. Two Hundred Years of American Business

1. J. H. Adams and E. F. Folland, *The Shepherd of the Ocean* (Boston: Gambit, 1964), 123.
2. U.S. Census Bureau, *Historical Statistics of the United States— Colonial Times to 1970* (Washington, D.C.: U.S. Census Bureau, 1975).
3. *Proceeding of the Massachusetts Historical Society,* vol. IV (Boston, 1944), 422–423.
4. Victor S. Clark, *History of Manufacturing in the United States,* 3 vols. (Washington, D.C.: Carnegie Institution, 1929), 9–31, 194–215.
5. Albert S. Bolles, *Industrial History of the United States* (Norwich, Conn.: The Henry Bills Publishing Company, 1879 [reprinted 1966]), 850.
6. U.S. Census Bureau, *Historical Statistics of the United States— Colonial Times to 1970* (Washington, D.C.: U.S. Census Bureau, 1975).
7. United States Department of Agriculture, History of American Agriculture Web site, http://www.usda.gov/history2/back. htm.
8. Robert C. Baron, *The Garden and Farm Books of Thomas Jefferson* (Golden, Colo.: Fulcrum Publishing, 1987), 178.
9. Richard Brookheiser, *Alexander Hamilton, American* (New York: Touchstone, 1999), 24.
10. Ibid., 101.
11. John Steele Gordon, *The Great Game: The Emergence of Wall Street as a Great Power, 1653–2000* (New York: Scribner, 1999), 65.
12. Albert S. Bolles, *Industrial History of the United States* (Norwich, Conn.:

The Henry Bills Publishing Company, 1879 [reprinted 1966]), 54.

13. Robert S. Woodbury, "The Legend of Eli Whitney and Interchangeable Parts." *Technology and Culture*, Summer 1960. Also Peter Boda, "Eli Whitney's Other Talents," *American Heritage*, May 1987.

14. Joseph A. Schumpeter, *Essays on Entrepreneurs, Innovations, Business Cycles and the Evolution of Capitalism* (New Brunswick, N.J.: Transactions Publishers, 1989).

15. Albert S. Bolles, *Industrial History of the United States* (Norwich, Conn.: The Henry Bills Publishing Company, 1879 [reprinted 1966]), 249–250.

16. John Steele Gordon, *The Great Game: The Emergence of Wall Street as a Great Power, 1653–2000* (New York: Scribner, 1999).

17. Robert C. Baron, *The Garden and Farm Books of Thomas Jefferson* (Golden, Colo.: Fulcrum Publishing, 1987), 20.

18. U.S. Census Bureau, *Historical Statistics of the United States—Colonial Times to 1970* (Washington, D.C.: U.S. Census Bureau, 1975).

19. Ibid.

20. Ibid.

21. Mark Sullivan, *Our Times: Vol 1. The Turn of the Century* (New York: Charles Scribner's Sons, 1926), 34.

Chapter 3. Steel: The Basic Material (1860–2000)

1. American Iron and Steel Institute.

2. Albert S. Bolles, *Industrial History of the United States* (Norwich, Conn.: The Henry Bills Publishing Company, 1879 [reprinted 1966]), 635.

3. Irving S. Olds, *Half a Century of United States Steel* (New York: The Newcomen Society, 1951).

4. Irving S. Olds, *Judge Elbert S. Gary* (New York: The Newcomen Society, 1947).

5. United States Steel Corporation, *Annual Report* (Hoboken, New Jersey: United

States Steel Corporation, 1902).

6. Olds, *Judge Elbert S. Gary.*

7. United States Steel Corporation, *Annual Reports* (Hoboken, N. J.: U.S. Steel Corporation, 1901–2000).

8. Ida M. Tarbell, *The Life of Elbert H. Gary* (New York: D. Appleton and Company, 1916).

9. Ibid.

10. Robert Hessen, *Steel Titan: The Life of Charles M. Schwab* (New York: Oxford University Press, 1975), 174.

11. Bethlehem Steel, *Annual Reports* (Newark: N.J.: Bethlehem Steel, 1905–1995).

12. *The Life History of the United States*, vol. 11 (New York: Time Books, 1964), 111.

13. Olds, *Half a Century of United States Steel.*

14. International Iron and Steel Institute, *Annual Statistical Report* (Washington, D.C.: International Iron and Steel Institute, 2000).

15. International Iron and Steel Institute, *Annual Foreign Trade Statistics* (Washington, D.C.: International Iron and Steel Institute, 2000).

16. John P. Hoerr, *And the Wolf Finally Came* (Pittsburgh: University of Pittsburgh Press, 1988), 607–613.

17. International Iron and Steel Institute.

18. Ibid.

Chapter 4. Andrew Carnegie (1835–1919): Partner and Benefactor

1. James Frazier Wall, *Andrew Carnegie* (New York: Oxford University Press, 1970), 46.

2. Andrew Carnegie, *Autobiography* (Boston: Houghton Mifflin, 1920, [reprinted 1986], 3.

3. Ibid., 12.

4. Ibid., 12.

5. Ibid., 60.

6. Andrew Carnegie, *The Empire of Business* (New York: Doubleday, Page & Co. 1902), 291.

7. Ibid., 293–294.

8. Carnegie, *Autobiography*, 60.
9. Carnegie, *The Empire of Business*, 294–295.
10. Letter, December 1868, St. Nicholas Hotel. In James Frazier Wall, *Andrew Carnegie*, 224–225.
11. Carnegie, *Autobiography*, 110.
12. Carnegie, *The Empire of Business*, 17.
13. Carnegie, *Autobiography*, 136.
14. Ibid., 130.
15. Ibid., 218.
16. Carnegie, *The Empire of Business*, 231.
17. Ibid., 241–242.
18. Carnegie, *Autobiography*, 117.
19. Carnegie, *The Empire of Business*, 121.
20. Ibid., 238.
21. Ibid., 221.
22. Andrew Carnegie, *The Gospel of Wealth and Other Timely Essays* (New York: Century, 1900).
23. Ibid.
24. Carnegie, *Autobiography*, 45, 46, 249.

Chapter 5. Automobiles: Everybody Wants at Least One (1860–2000)
1. T. K. Derry and Trevor I. Williams, *A Short History of Technology from the Earliest Times to A.D. 1900* (New York: Oxford University Press, 1961), 601–604.
2. "The Automobiles of 1904," *Frank Leslie's Popular Monthly*, January 1904.
3. Automobile Manufacturing Association, *Automobiles of America* (Detroit: Wayne State University Press, 1968).
4. James J. Flink and Glenn A. Niemeyer, "The General of General Motors," *American Heritage*, August 1965.
5. Alfred P. Sloan Jr., *My Years with General Motors* (Garden City, N.Y.: Doubleday, 1963), 220.
6. Ibid., 150.
7. *Engineering News of 1912*, 227.
8. *Ward's Motor Vehicle Facts and Figures 2001* (Southfield, Mich.: Ward's Communication, 2001).
9. *Forbes* magazine, July 23, 2001.
10. Worldwatch Institute, World Automobile Production and Fleet Web site, http://people.hofstra.edu/geotrans/eng/ch3en/conc3en/carprodfleet.html.
11. Comite des Constructeur France d'Automobiles (CCFA), *Carmakers Annual Report*, available on their Web site, http://www.ccfa.fr.

Chapter 6. Henry Ford (1863–1947): Getting the Costs Down
1. Henry Ford and Samuel Crowther, *My Life and Work* (Garden City, N.Y.: Doubleday, Page & Co., 1923), 23.
2. Ibid., 23–24.
3. Ibid., 29.
4. Ibid., 176.
5. Ibid., 239.
6. Ibid., 234.
7. Ibid., 206.
8. Ibid., 120.
9. Ibid., 86.
10. Ibid., 40.
11. Henry Ford and Samuel Crowther, *Today and Tomorrow* (Garden City, N.Y.: Doubleday, Page & Co., 1926), 23.
12. Ford and Crowther, *My Life and Work*, 86.
13. Ibid., 51.
14. Ford and Crowther, *Today and Tomorrow*, 229–230.
15. Ford and Crowther, *My Life and Work*, 157.
16. Ibid., 137.
17. Ibid., 224.
18. Ibid., 155.
19. Ibid., 247.
20. Ford and Crowther, *My Life and Work*, 91.
21. Ibid., 92.
22. Interview with Charles N. Wheeler of the *Chicago Tribune*, May 25, 1916.

Chapter 7. Electronics: The Basic Material (1880–2000)
1. David Sarnoff, *Edison (1847–1931)* (New York: The Newcomen Society, 1948).
2. *Engineering News* 67 (January–June 1912), 1240–1244.
3. See http://www.earlyradiohistory.us.
4. Daniel Stashower, *The Boy Genius and the Mogul: The Untold Story of*

Television (New York: Broadway
Books, 2002), 5.

5. Alfred Chandler Jr., *Inventing the
Electronic Century: The Epic Story of the
Consumer Electronics and Computer
Industries* (New York: Free Press,
2001).

6. Robert C. Baron, *What Was It Like
Orville: Thoughts on the Early Space
Program* (Golden, Colo.: Fulcrum
Publishing, 2002).

7. *Datamation* (April 1980), 439.

Chapter 8. David Sarnoff (1891–1971): The Practical Dreamer

1. Radio Corporation of America,
Annual Reports (New York: Radio
Corporation of America, 1933).

2. Speech at Army War College, January
31, 1927. Reprinted in David
Sarnoff, *Looking Ahead: The Papers of
David Sarnoff* (New York: McGraw
Hill, 1968), 199.

3. *New York Times* obituary, December
13, 1971.

4. Dr. Alfred Goldsmith, Vice President,
RCA in Carl Dreher, *Sarnoff: An
American Success* (New York:
Quadrangle, 1977), 253.

5. Wisdom Magazine, *The Universe of
David Sarnoff* (Beverly Hills, Calif.:
The Wisdom Society, 1958), 69.

6. Ibid., 69.

7. Ibid., 74.

8. David Sarnoff, *Looking Ahead: The
Papers of David Sarnoff* (New York:
McGraw Hill, 1968).

9. David Sarnoff, *Journal of Applied
Physics* (July 1939), reprinted in
Looking Ahead, 101.

10. Wisdom Magazine, *The Universe of
David Sarnoff*, 72.

11. Ibid., 73.

12. Ibid., 7.

13. Ibid., 71.

14. Ibid., 69.

15. Ibid., 70.

16. Ibid., 72.

17. Ibid., 72.

18. Ibid., 72.

19. Ibid., 69.

20. Ibid., 69.

Chapter 9. Computers: The Information Age (1945–2000)

1. James W. Cortada, *Before the
Computer: IBM, NCR, Burroughs and
Remington Rand and the Industry They
Created 1865–1956* (Princeton, N.J.:
Princeton University Press, 1993), 3.

2. Robert C. Baron and Albert T.
Piccirilli, *Digital Logic and Computer
Operations* (New York: McGraw-Hill,
1967), 6.

3. Elias M. Awad, *Business Data
Processing* (Englewood Cliffs, N.J.:
Prentice Hall, 1975), 24.

4. Katharine Davis Fishman, *The
Computer Establishment* (New York:
Harper & Row, 1981), 44.

5. Thomas J. Watson Jr., *A Business and Its
Beliefs* (New York: McGraw Hill, 1963).

6. There are many estimates about IBM's
share of the computer industry. In
part, they are based on what is
included in the market. In the government anti-trust suit, the government
claimed that IBM's share of the market
ranged between 83 percent and 71
percent between 1961 and 1972. IBM
claimed its share had declined from 78
percent in 1952 to 33 percent in 1972.
Source: Katherine Davis Fishman, *The
Computer Establishment*, 379–387.

7. T. A. Wise, "IBM's $5 Billion Gamble,"
Fortune magazine, September 1966.

8. There is no biography of Grace
Hopper although one is needed.
Anyone who could deal for forty years
with computer entrepreneurs and
programmers and naval brass is very
special. Information is from several
Web sites, including the Computer
Hall of Fame (http://www. computer-
halloffame.org), Grace Hopper
Celebration of Women in Computing
Conferences (http://www.gracehop-
per. org), Software History Center

(http:// www. softwarehistory.org), and
The Wit and Wisdom of Grace
Hopper (http:// www.cs.yale.
edu/homes/tap/Files/ hopper-wit.html.)

9. U.S. Department of Labor, Bureau of
Labor Statistics, *2002 National
Occupational Employment and Wage
Estimates.* The numbers are probably
low since many software people work
in industry, medical, educational, and
other institutions.

10. International Data Corporation.

11. Data is from many industry history
Web sites. Among the best are
Hobbes' Internet Timeline (http://www.
zakon.org/robert/internet/timeline/),
BBN Technologies (http://www.bbn.com),
and History of the Internet by Dave
Kristula (http://www.davesite.com/
webstation/net-history.shtml).

12. Ibid.

Chapter 10. Kenneth Olsen (1926–): The Commonplace Computer

1. *Fortune* magazine, October 27, 1986.

2. Glenn Rifkin and George Harrar, *The
Ultimate Entrepreneur* (Chicago:
Contemporary Books, 1988), 23.

3. Kenneth H. Olsen, *Digital Equipment
Corporation: The First Twenty-five
Years* (New York: The Newcomen
Society, 1983).

4. David Allison, *Oral History Interview
with Ken Olsen* (Washington, D.C.:
National Museum of American
History, September 1988), 19.

5. Tom Peters and Nancy Austin, *A
Passion for Excellence* (New York:
Random House, 1985), 136.

6. Olsen, *Digital Equipment Corporation:
The First Twenty-five Years,* 12.

7. Allison, *Oral History Interview with
Ken Olsen,* 18.

8. Interview, *Network Computing News,*
May 1997.

9. Rifkin and Harrar, *The Ultimate
Entrepreneur,* 194.

10. Digital Equipment Corporation,
*Report of the 1983 Annual Meeting of
Stockholders* (Boston, 1983).

11. Digital Equipment Corporation, *Report
of the 1986 Annual Meeting of
Stockholders* (Boston, 1986).

12. Internal DEC Report, 1974. In
Rifkin and Harrar, *The Ultimate
Entrepreneur,* 133.

13. Ibid.

14. Rifkin and Harrar, *The Ultimate
Entrepreneur,* 276.

15. Allison, *Oral History Interview with
Ken Olsen,* 23.

16. Ibid., 37.

17. Ibid., 24.

18. Rifkin and Harrar, *The Ultimate
Entrepreneur,* 132.

19. Rifkin and Harrar, *The Ultimate
Entrepreneur,* 142.

20. Ibid., 166.

21. Allison. *Oral History Interview with
Ken Olsen,* 20.

22. Rifkin and Harrar, *The Ultimate
Entrepreneur,* 277.

23. Ibid., 277.

24. Ibid., 310.

25. Ibid., 313.

26. Ibid., 308.

Chapter 11. The Nature of Professional and Personal Change

1. The Society for the History of Technology,
http://www.shot@iastate.edu.

2. Lawrence M. Principe, *History of
Science Antiquity to 1700* (Chantilly,
Va.: The Teaching Company, 2002).

3. Entire speech is in John Jenkins,
*Neither the Fanatics Nor the Faint
Hearted* (Austin, Tex.: The Pemberton
Press, 1963).

4. Henry Ford and Samuel Crowther,
Today and Tomorrow (Garden City,
N.Y.: Doubleday, Page & Co., 1926),
229–230.

5. Merle Miller, *Plain Speaking: An Oral
Biography of Harry S. Truman* (New
York: Berkeley Publishing Group,
1974), 422.

6. Robert Baron, *Airplanes and Airlines
in the Twentieth Century* (San Mateo,

Calif.: San Mateo County Historical Society, 2002).

7. Harold Miller, *Publishing: A Leap from Mind to Mind* (Golden, Colo.: Fulcrum Publishing, 2003).

8. Walter Lippman, *Roosevelt Has Gone*, April 14, 1945. This column was reprinted in many newspapers on that date.

9. James Frazier Wall, *Andrew Carnegie* (New York: Oxford University Press, 1970), 665.

10. IBM, *IBM Annual Reports* (Armonk: N.Y.: IBM, 1935–2000).

11. *Time* magazine, February 9, 2004.

12. Several articles including *Business Week*, April 15, 2004; *Forbes*, May 14, 2001.

13. Charles Dickens, *David Copperfield*, quoted in *Barlett's Familiar Quotations*, 470.

14. Thomas Jefferson, letter to John Adams, October 28, 1813 in *Jefferson: Library of America*, 1305.

Bibliography

*The man who does not read good books has no advantage over
the man who can't read them.*
—Mark Twain

The longer you look back, the farther you can look forward.
—Winston Churchill

Chapter 1. Technology, Growth, and Employment

Chandler, Alfred D. Jr. *Strategy and Structure*. Cambridge, Mass.: Harvard University Press, 1962.

———. *The Visible Hand*. Cambridge, Mass.: Harvard University Press, 1977.

Cochran, Thomas C. *Business in American Life: A History*. New York: McGraw-Hill, 1972.

De Bono, Edward. *Eureka: An Illustrated History of Inventions from the Wheel to the Computer*. London: Thames and Hudson, 1974.

Gras, Norman S. B. *Industrial Evolution*. New York: Augutus M. Kelly, 1966.

Hacker, Louis M. *The Course of American Economic Growth and Development*. New York: John Wiley and Sons, 1970.

Kross, Herman and Charles Gilbert. *American Business History*. Englewood Cliffs, N.J.: Prentice Hall, 1972.

Livesay, Harold D. *American Made: Men Who Shaped the American Economy*. Boston: Little, Brown, 1979.

Sobel, Robert. *The Entrepreneurs*. New York: Weybright and Talley, 1974.

U.S. Census Bureau. *Historical Statistics of the United States: Colonial Times to 1970*, bicentennial ed. Washington, D.C.: Bureau of the Census, 1975.

———. *Statistical Abstract of the United States, annual ed*. Washington, D.C.: Government Printing Office, 1990 and 2000.

U.S. Department of Labor. *Handbook of Labor Statistics*. Washington, D.C.: Government Printing Office, December 1980.

———. *Employment Size of the Enterprises for the United States*. Washington, D.C.: Government Printing Office, 2000.

Chapter 2. Two Hundred Years of American Business

Adams, Henry and Charles Francis Adams Jr. *A Chapter of Erie and Other Essays*. Boston: James R. Osgood, 1871.

Adams, J. H. and H. F. Follend. *The Shepherd of the Ocean: An Account of Sir Walter Raleigh and His Times*. Boston: Gambit, 1969.

Allen, Zachariah. *The Science of Mechanics as Applied to the Present Improvements in the Useful Arts in Europe and the United States of America.* Providence, R.I.: Hutchens & Cory, 1829.

Andrist, Ralph K. "The Erie Canal Passed This Way." *American Heritage,* October 1968.

Appleton, Nathan. *Introduction of the Power Loom and Origin of Lowell.* Boston: Eastburn's Press, 1858.

Bagnall, William R. *Samuel Slater and the Early Development of the Cotton Manufacture in the United States.* Middelton, Conn.: J. S. Stewart, 1890.

————. *The Textile Industry of the United States.* Cambridge, Mass.: Harvard University Press, 1893.

Bailey, Chris. *Two Hundred Years of American Clocks and Watches.* Englewood Cliffs, N.J.: Prentice Hall, 1975.

Baron, Robert C. *The Garden and Farm Books of Thomas Jefferson.* Golden, Colo.: Fulcrum Publishing, 1987.

Barry, William David. *A Vignetted History of Portland Business 1632–1982.* New York: The Newcomen Society, 1982.

Berry, Robert E. *Yankee Stargazer: The Life of Nathaniel Bowditch.* New York: McGraw-Hill, 1941.

Bishop, J. Leander. *A History of American Manufactures from 1608–1860,* 2 vols. Philadelphia: Edward Young and Co., 1864.

Blackwell, Frederick S. *Invention and Industry—Cradled in New England.* New York: The Newcomen Society, 1946.

Bolles, Albert S. *Industrial History of the United States.* Norwich, Conn.: The Henry Bills Publishing Company, 1879 (reprint 1966).

Boorstin, Daniel J. *The Americans: The Colonial Experience.* New York: Alfred A. Knopf, 1958.

————. *The Americans: The National Experience.* New York: Random House, 1965.

Bourne, Russell. *Invention in America.* Golden, Colo.: Fulcrum Publishing, 1996.

————. *Rivers of America: Birthplace of Culture, Commerce, and Community.* Golden, Colo.: Fulcrum Publishing, 1998.

Bowditch, Nathaniel. *The New American Practical Navigator.* Newburyport, Mass.: Edward W. Blunt, 1802.

Brookheiser, Richard. *Alexander Hamilton, American.* New York: Touchstone, 1999.

Brown, William H. *History of the First Locomotives in America.* New York: D. Appleton and Co., 1874.

Browne, George W. *The Amoskeag Manufacturing Company.* Manchester, N.H.: J. B. Clark, 1915.

Bruce, Robert V. *The Launching of Modern American Science.* New York: Alfred A. Knopf, 1987.

Bruchey, Stuart. *The Wealth of Nations.* New York: Harper & Row, 1988.

Bruno, Leonard. *The Tradition of Technology.* Washington, D.C.: Library of Congress, 1995.

Buckingham, Earle. *Principles of Interchangeable Manufacturing.* New York: The Industrial Press, 1921.

Burke, James. *Connections.* London: Macmillan, 1978.

Cameron, Edward H. *Samuel Slater: Father of American Manufacturing.* Freeport, Maine: B. Wheelwright, 1960.

Canfield, Cass. *The Incredible Pierpont Morgan.* New York: Harper & Row, 1974.

Carosso, Vincent. *Investment Banking in America: A History.* Cambridge, Mass.: Harvard University Press, 1970.

Chandler, Alfred. *Strategy and Structure: Chapters in the History of the Industrial Enterprise.* Cambridge, Mass.: Harvard University Press, 1962.

————. *The Visible Hand: The Managerial Revolution in American Business.* Cambridge, Mass.: Harvard University Press, 1977.

Chapelle, Howard I. *The History of American Sailing Ships.* New York: W. W. Norton & Company, 1935.

Clark, Victor S. *History of Manufacturing in the United States,* 3 vols. Washington, D.C.: Carnegie Institution, 1929.

Cochran, Thomas C. *Two Hundred Years of American Business.* New York: Basic Books, 1977.

Davis, Donald A. *The Stanley Works.* New York: The Newcomen Society, 1969.

Depew, Chauncey M., ed. *One Hundred Years of American Commerce,* 2 vols. New York: D. O. Haynes and Co., 1895.

Derry J. K. and Trevor J. Williams. *A Short History of Technology from the Earliest Times to A.D. 1900.* New York: Oxford University Press, 1961.

DiBasco, Thomas. *Made in the U.S.A.* New York: Harper & Row, 1987.

Dolan, J. R. *The Yankee Peddlers of Early America.* New York: Bromhill House, 1964.

Dolzell, Robert I. Jr. *Enterprising Elite: The Boston Associates and the World They Made.* Cambridge, Mass.: Harvard University Press, 1987.

Douglas, Elisha P. *The Coming of Age of American Business.* Chapel Hill: University of North Carolina Press, 1971.

Drucker, Peter. *The Concept of the Corporation.* New York: Mentor, 1983.

Dulles, Foster Rhea. *Labor in America.* New York: Thomas Y. Crowell, 1949.

Fiske, John. *The Beginnings of New England.* Boston: Houghton Mifflin, 1889.

Frazer, Cecil E. and George F. Doriot. *Analyzing Our Industries.* New York: McGraw-Hill, 1932.

Gibson, Charles R. *The Romance of Modern Manufacturing.* London: Seeley & Co., 1910.

Gies, Thomas and Frances. *The Ingenious Yankees.* New York: Thomas Y. Cromwell and Company, 1976.

Goldenberg, Joseph A. *Shipbuilding in Colonial America.* Charlottesville: University Press of Virginia, 1976.

Gordon, John Steele. "Technology Transfer." *American Heritage,* February 1990.

———. *The Great Game: The Emergence of Wall Street as a World Power 1653–2000.* New York: Scribner, 1999.

Grant, Ellsworth S. "Gunmaker to the World." *American Heritage,* June 1968.

Gras, Norman Scott. *Industrial Evolution.* Cambridge, Mass.: Harvard University Press, 1930.

———. *A History of Agriculture in Europe and America.* New York: F. S. Crofts, 1940.

Gras, Norman S. B. and Henrietta M. Larson. *Casebook in American Business History.* New York: Crofts, 1939.

Greeley, Horace, et al. *The Great Industries of the United States.* Hartford, Conn.: J. B. Burre Hyde, 1872.

Green, Constance M. *Eli Whitney and the Birth of American Technology.* Boston: Little, Brown, 1956.

Habakkuk, H. J. *American and British Technology in the Nineteenth Century: The Search for Labor Saving Inventions.* Cambridge, Mass. 1962.

Hamilton, Alexander. *Report on the Subject of Manufacturers.* Washington: December 5, 1791. Reprinted *Hamilton.* New York: Library of America, 2001.

Handlin, Oscar and Mary F. Handlin. *Commonwealth: A Study of the Role of Government in the American Economy: Massachusetts 1774–1861.* Cambridge, Mass.: Belknap Press, 1969.

Hawke, David Freeman. *Nuts and Bolts of the Past: A History of American Technology, 1776–1860.* New York: Harper & Row, 1988.

Hindle, Brooke and Steven Lubar. *Engines of Change: The American Industrial Revolution 1790–1860.* Washington, D.C.: Smithsonian Institution, 1986.

Hounshell, David A. *From the American System to Mass Production, 1800–1932.* Baltimore: The John Hopkins Press, 1984.

Howe, Octavius T. and Frederick C. Matthews. *American Clipper Ships 1833–1858.* Salem, Mass.: Marine Research Society, 1926.

Jefferson, Thomas. *Notes on the State of Virginia.* London: John Stockdale, 1787.

Jerome, Chauncey. *History of the American Clock Business.* New Haven, Conn.: F. C. Dayton, Jr., 1860.

Kebabian, Paul B. and Dudley Witney. *American Woodworking Tools.* Boston: New York Graphic Society, 1978.

Keller, Allan. *Colonial America.* New York: Hawthorne Books, 1971.

Kelly, Alfred, Winfred Harbison, and Herman Belz. *The American Constitution: Its Origins and Development,* 6th ed. New York: W. W. Norton & Company, 1983.

Kranzberg, Melvin and Conrad W. Purcell. *Technology in Western Civilization.* New York: Oxford University Press, 1967.

Landes, David S. *Revolution in Time.* Cambridge, Mass.: Harvard University Press, 1983.

Linklater, Andre. *Measuring America.* New York: Walker and Company, 2002.

Lodge, Henry Cabot. *Alexander Hamilton.* Cambridge, Mass.: Riverside Press, 1882.

Mabee, Carlton. *The American Leonardo: A Life of Samuel F. B. Morse.* New York: Alfred A. Knopf, 1943.

Maiken, Peter T. *Night Trains.* Chicago: Lakine Press, 1989.

Mayr, Otto and Robert C. Poston, eds. *Yankee Enterprise: The Rise of the American System of Manufacture.* Washington, D.C.: Smithsonian Institution Press, 1981.

McKay, Richard. *Some Famous Sailing Ships and Their Builders.* New York: G. P. Putnam's Sons, 1928.

McWilliams, James E. "The Kitchen Garden in Early New England." *The New England Quarterly,* March 2004.

Micklethwait, John and Adrian Wooldridge. *The Company: A Short History of a Revolutionary Idea.* New York: Modern Library, 2003.

Miller, William, ed. *Men in Business: Essays in the History of American Business.* Cambridge, Mass.: Harvard University Press, 1952.

Mirsky, Jeanette and Allan Nevins. *The World of Eli Whitney.* New York: Macmillan, 1952.

Morgan, Edmund S. *Benjamin Franklin.* New Haven: Yale University Press, 2002.

Morison, Samuel Eliot. *The Maritime History of Massachusetts 1783–1860.* Boston: Houghton Mifflin, 1921.

———. *Builders of the Bay Colony.* Boston: Houghton Mifflin, 1930 (revised 1964).

———. *The Oxford History of the American People.* New York: Oxford University Press, 1965.

Murphy, John J. "Entrepreneurship in the Establishment of the American Clock Industry." *Journal of Economic History,* 26: 1966.

Olmsted, Denison. *Memoirs of Eli Whitney.* New Haven, Conn.: Durrie and Peak, 1846.

O'Malley, Michael. *Keeping Watch: A History of American Time.* New York: Viking Penguin, 1990.

Pusateri, C. Joseph. *A History of American Business.* Arlington Heights, Ill.: Harlan Davidson, 1988.

Quinn, David B., and Alison M. Quinn, eds. *The English New England Voyages.* London: The Hakluyt Society, 1983.

Ratner, Sidney, James H. Soltow, and Richard Sylla. *The Evolution of the American Economy.* New York: Basic Books, 1968.

Reck, Franklin M. *The Romance of American Transportation.* New York: Thomas Y. Crowell, 1962.

Rolt, L. T. C. *Tools for the Job: A History of Machine Tools to 1950.* London: HMSO, 1965.

Rorabaugh, W. J. *The Craft Apprentice: From Franklin to the Machine Age in America.* New York: Oxford University Press, 1986.

Russell, Howard S. *A Long Deep Furrow: Three Centuries of Farming in New England.* Hanover, N.H.: University Press of New England, 1976.

Schumpeter, Joseph A. *Capitalism, Socialism and Democracy.* New York: Harper & Row, 1950.

Sloan, Eric. *A Museum of Early American Tools.* New York: Ballantine, 1964.

State Street Trust. *Other Industries of New England.* Boston: 1924.

Stearns, Raymond Phineas. *Science in the British Colonies of America.* Urbana-Champaign: University of Illinois Press, 1970.

Steeds, W. A. *A History of Machine Tools, 1700–1910.* New York: Oxford University Press, 1969.

Straw, William Parker. *Amoskeag in New Hampshire.* New York: The Newcomen Society, 1948.

Struik, Dirk J. *Yankee Science in the Making.* Boston: Little, Brown, 1948.

Sullivan, Mark. *Our Times,* 6 vol. New York: Charles Scribner's Sons, 1931–1935.

Taylor, George R. *The Transportation Revolution 1815–1860.* New York: Rinehart, 1951.

Thomas, Isaiah. *The History of Printing in America.* Worcester, Mass.: Isaiah Thomas, 1810 (reprint New York: Weathervane Books, 1970).

Tocqueville, Alexander de. *Democracy in America.* New York: Knopf, 1945.

Tucker, Barbara. *Samuel Slater and the Origins of the American Textile Industry.* Ithaca, N.Y.: Cornell University Press, 1984.

Uglow, Jenny. *The Lunar Men: Five Friends Whose Curiosity Changed the World.* New York: Farrar, Straus and Giroux, 2002.

Weeden, William B. *Economic and Social History of New England 1620–1789.* Boston: Houghton Mifflin, 1891.

Westcott, Thompson. *The Life of John Fitch, the Inventor of the Steamboat.* Philadelphia: J. B. Lippincott & Co., 1857.

Whipple, A. B. C. *The Clipper Ships.* New York: Time-Life Books, 1980.

White, George Savage. *Memoir of Samuel Slater, the Father of American Manufactures.* Philadelphia: 46 Carpenter St., 1836.

Williams, Roy S. *Seven Romances of Bay State Industry.* New York: The Newcomen Society, 1951.

Williamsen, J. A., ed. *The Cabot Voyages and Bristol Discovery under Henry VII.* London: The Hakluyt Society, 1961.

Wilson, Mitchell. *American Science and Invention.* New York: Simon & Schuster, 1954.

Winthrop Papers. Boston: Massachusetts Historical Society, 1929.

Woodbury, Robert S. "The Legend of Eli Whitney and Interchangeable Parts." *Technology and Culture,* Summer 1960.

———. *History of the Lathe.* Cambridge, Mass.: MIT Press, 1961.

Woolsey, Theodore, et al. *The First Century of the Republic: A Century of American Progress.* New York: Harper and Brothers, 1876.

Wright, Irene A., ed. *Further English Voyages to Spanish America 1583–1594.* London: The Hakluyt Society, 1951.

Wyllie, Irwin G. *The Self-Made Man in America.* New York: Free Press, 1954.

Chapter 3. Steel: The Basic Material (1860–2000)

American Iron and Steel Institute. *Steel's Centennial—1957: The First 100 Years of the Steel Industry.* New York: 1957.

———. *Steel at the Crossroads: The American Steel Industry in the 1980s.* New York: 1980.

Ashton, T. S. *Iron and Steel in the American Revolution.* Manchester, England: Manchester University Press, 1963.

Beale, Sir Louis. *The British and American Steel Industry: Their Common Heritage.* New York: The Newcomen Society, 1948.

Bent, Quincy. *Early Days of Iron and Steel in North America.* New York: The Newcomen Society, 1950.

Bethlehem Steel. *Annual Reports.* Newark: N.J.: Bethlehem Steel, 1905–1995.

Blough, Roger M. *Steel in Perspective.* New York: The Newcomen Society, 1958.

Burn, Duncan. *The Steel Industry 1939–1959: A Study in Competition.* New York: Cambridge University Press, 1961.

Butler, Joseph Green. *Fifty Years of Iron and Steel.* Cleveland, Ohio: The Penton Press, 1918.

Casson, Herbert N. *The Romance of Steel.* New York: A. S. Barnes and Company, 1907.

Chandler, Alfred D. *The Railroads: The Nation's First Big Business.* New York: Harcourt, Brace and World, 1965.

Chernow, Ron. *The House of Morgan.* New York: Atlantic Monthly Press, 1990.

Clark, T. C. *The American Railway.* New York: Charles Scribner's Company, 1897.

Cooling, Benjamin Franklin. *Grey Steel and Blue Water Navy.* Hamden, Conn.: Archon Books, 1979.

Crandall, Robert W. *The United States Steel Industry in Recurrent Crisis.* Washington, D.C.: Brookings Institute, 1981.

Cutter, Arundel. *The Authentic History of the United States Steel Corporation.* New York: The Moody Magazine and Book Company, 1916.

———. *United States Steel: A Corporation with a Soul.* New York: Doubleday, Page & Co., 1921.

Dougherty, Carrol R., Melvin G. DeChazeau, and Samuel S. Stratton. *Economics of the Iron and Steel Industry.* New York: McGraw-Hill, 1937.

Fida, Kenichi. *Sources of Differences in Steelmaking Yield between Japan and the United States.* Knoxville: Middle Tennessee State University, 1979.

Fisher, Douglas Alan. *The Epic of Steel.* New York: Harper & Row, 1963.

Forbes, Robert Joseph. *Metallurgy in Antiquity.* London: E. B. Brill, 1950.

Hartley, Edward Neal. *Ironworks on the Saugus.* Norman: University of Oklahoma Press, 1957.

Hendriksen, Eldon S. *Capital Expenditures in the Steel Industry 1900–1953.* New York: Arno Press, 1978.

Hessen, Robert. *Steel Titan: The Life of Charles M. Schwab.* New York: Oxford University Press, 1975.

Higgins, Carter C. and Bradley C. Higgins. *Craftsmanship in Steel.* New York: The Newcomen Society, 1956.

Hoerr, John P. *And the Wolf Finally Came: The Decline of the American Steel Industry.* Pittsburgh: University of Pittsburgh Press, 1988.

Hogan, William T. *Economic History of the Iron and Steel Industry in the United States,* 5 vols. Lexington, Mass.: Lexington Books, 1971.

———. *World Steel in the 1980s.* Lexington, Mass.: Lexington Books, 1983.

Howell, Kenneth T. and Elinar W. Carlson. *Men of Iron: Forbes and Adam.* Lakeville, Conn.: Pocketknife Press, 1980.

Kawahito, Kiyoshi. *Japanese Steel Industry.* New York: Praeger Publishers, 1972.

Kranzberg, Melvin and Carroll W. Pursell Jr. *Technology in Western Civilization.* New York: Oxford University Press, 1967.

Martin, Edmund F. *Promise for the Future.* New York: The Newcomen Society, 1967.

Moriarity, Wilson D. *A Century of Steel Castings.* New York: The Newcomen Society, 1961.

Mountfield, David. *The Railway Barons.* New York: W. W. Norton & Company, 1979.

Olds, Irving S. *Judge Elbert H. Gary.* New York: The Newcomen Society, 1947.

———. *Half a Century of United States Steel.* New York: The Newcomen Society, 1951.

Paskoff, Paul. *The Iron and Steel Industry in the Nineteenth Century.* New York: Facts On File, 1988.

Plowden, David. *Steel.* New York: The Viking Press, 1981.

Robbins, Frederick J. *The Permanence of Change.* New York: The Newcomen Society, 1968.

Schreiner, Samuel A. *Henry Clay Frick.* New York: St. Martin's Press, 1995.

Seely, Bruce E. and William H. Becker. *Iron and Steel in the 20th Century.* New York: Facts On File, 1992.

Steel, Edward M. *The Speeches and Writings of Mother Jones.* Pittsburgh: University of Pittsburgh Press, 1988.

Tarbell, Ida M. *The Life of Elbert H. Gary.* New York: D. Appleton & Company, 1926.

Temin, Peter. *Iron and Steel in 19th Century America: An Economic Inquiry.* Cambridge, Mass.: Harvard University Press, 1964.

United States Steel. *Twenty Fifth Anniversary Report of U.S. Steel.* U.S. Steel, 1925.

———. *Annual Reports.* Hoboken: N.J.: U.S. Steel, 1901–2000.

Walker, John Bernard. *The Story of Steel.* New York: Harper and Brothers, 1926.

Warren, Kenneth. *World Steel.* Devonshire, England: David and Charles, 1975.

———. *American Steel Industry 1850–1970.* Oxford, England: Clarendon Press, 1978.

Wertime, Theodore A. *The Coming of the Age of Steel.* Chicago: University of Chicago Press, 1960.

Chapter 4. Andrew Carnegie (1835–1919): Partner and Benefactor

Alderson, Bernard. *Andrew Carnegie, the Man and His Work.* New York: Doubleday, Page & Co., 1908.

Bobinski, George S. *Carnegie Libraries-Their History and Impact on American Public Library Development.* Chicago: American Library Association, 1969.

Bridge, James Howard. *The Inside History of the Carnegie Steel Company.* New York: The Aldine Book Company, 1903 (reprint Pittsburgh: University of Pittsburgh Press, 1991).

Carnegie, Andrew. *Round the World.* New York: 1879.

———. *Our Coaching Trip.* New York: Private Circulation 1882.

———. "An Employers View of the Labor Question." *Forum,* 1 (April 1886).

———. *Triumphant Democracy.* New York: Scribners, 1886 (reprint 1971).

———. *The Gospel of Wealth and Other Timely Essays.* New York: Century, 1900.

———. *The Empire of Business.* New York: Doubleday, Page & Co., 1902.

———. *Problems of Today: Wealth, Labor, Socialism.* New York: Doubleday, Page, 1908.

———. *Autobiography of Andrew Carnegie,* ed. John C. Van Dyke. Boston: Houghton Mifflin, 1920.

Hacker, Louis M. *The World of Andrew Carnegie.* Philadelphia: J. B. Lippincott, 1968.

Hendrick, Burton J. *The Life of Andrew Carnegie.* Garden City: Doubleday, Doran, 1932.

Krause, Paul. *The Battle for Homestead, 1880–1892.* Pittsburgh: University of Pittsburgh Press, 1992.

Livesay, Harold. *Andrew Carnegie and the Rise of American Business.* Boston: Little, Brown, 1975.

———. *American Made.* Boston: Little, Brown, 1977.

Wall, Joseph Frazier. *Andrew Carnegie.* New York: Oxford University Press, 1970.

———. "The Rich Man's Burden and How Andrew Carnegie Unloaded It." *American Heritage,* October 1970.

Chapter 5. Automobiles: Everybody Wants at Least One (1860–2000)

Abernathy, William J. *The Productivity Dilemma.* Baltimore: The John Hopkins Press, 1978.

Anderson, Rudolph E. *The Story of the American Automobile.* Washington, D.C.: Public Affairs Press, 1950.

Automobile Manufacturers Association. *100 Million Motor Vehicles.* Detroit: Wayne State University Press, 1948.

———. *Automobiles of America.* Detroit: Wayne State University Press, 1968.

Bacon, John H. *American Steam Car Pioneers.* Exton, Penn.: Newcomen Society of the United States, 1984.

Bailey, L. Scott. "GM: The First 75 Years of Transportation Products." *Automobile Quarterly Magazine,* 1983.

Barber, H. L. *Story of the Automobile: Its History and Development from 1760 to 1917.* Chicago: A. J. Munson & Co., 1917.

Bentley, John. *Great American Automobiles.* New York: Bonanza Books, 1957.

Bhaskar, Krish. *The Future of the World Motor Industry.* London: Kogan Page, 1980.

Bourne, Russell. *Americans on the Move.* Golden, Colo.: Fulcrum Publishing, 1995.

Brooks, John. *The Autobiography of American Business.* Garden City: Doubleday & Co., 1974.

Chandler, Alfred Dupont. *Strategy and Structures: Chapters in the History of the American Industrial Enterprise.* Cambridge, Mass.: The MIT Press, 1962.

———. *Giant Enterprise: Ford, General Motors and the Automobile Industry.* New York: Harcourt, Brace and World, 1964.

Chow, Gregory C. *Demand for Automobiles in the United States.* Amsterdam: North Holland Publishers, 1957.

Chrysler, Walter P. and Boyden Sparks. *Life of an American Workman.* Philadelphia: Curtis Publishing Company, 1938.

Cleveland, Reginald McIntosh and S. J. Williamson. *The Road Is Yours.* New York: Greystone Press, 1951.

Codrington, George W. *Shadow of Two Great Leaders: Rudolph Diesel and Alexander Winton.* New York: The Newcomen Society, 1945.

Cusumano, Michael A. *The Japanese Automobile Industry.* Cambridge, Mass.: Harvard University Press, 1985.

Davis, Susan S. *The Stanleys: Renaissance Yankees.* New York: The Newcomen Society, 1997.

Doolittle, James Rood. *The Romance of the Automobile Industry.* New York: The Klebold Press, 1916.

Dunn, Robert Williams. *Labor and Automobiles.* New York: International Publishers, 1929.

Engineering News. New York: Hill Publishing Company, January–June 1912.

Flink, James J. *The Car Culture.* Cambridge, Mass.: MIT Press, 1975.

Flink, James J. and Glenn A. Niemeyer. "The General of General Motors." *American Heritage,* August 1973.

Forbes, Bertie Charles. *Automotive Giants in America.* New York: B. C. Forbes Publishing Company, 1926.

"The Automobiles of 1904." *Frank Leslie's Popular Monthly,* January 1904.

General Motors Corporation. *General Motors Annual Reports.* Detroit: General Motors Corporation, 1920–2000.

Georgano, Nick. *The American Automobile: A Centenary 1893–1993.* New York: Smithmark, 1992.

Ginsburg, Douglas H. and William Abernathy. *Government, Technology and the Future of the Automobile.* New York: McGraw-Hill, 1980.

Glasscock, Carl Burgess. *The Gasoline Age.* Indianapolis, Ind.: Bobbs-Merrill, 1937.

Greenleaf, William. *Monopoly on Wheels.* Detroit: Wayne State University Press, 1961.

Groner, Alex. *The American Heritage History of American Business and Industry.* New York: American Heritage Publishing Company, 1972.

Gunnell, John. *One Hundred Years of American Cars.* Iola, Wisc.: Krause Publications, 1993.

Hornung, Clarence P. *Portrait Gallery of Early Automobiles.* New York: Harry N. Abrams, 1968.

Howe, Irving and B. J. Widick. *The UAW and Walter Reuther.* New York: Random House, 1949.

Jerome, John. *The Death of the Automobile.* New York: W. W. Norton & Company, 1972.

Kettering, Charles Franklin, and Allen Orth. *American Battle for Abundance.* Detroit: General Motors, 1947.

King, Clyde L. *The Automobile: Its Promise and Its Problems.* Philadelphia: American Society of Political and Social Sciences, 1904.

Lohr, Lenox R. *Fifty Years of Motor Cars, 1895–1945.* New York: The Newcomen Society, 1946.

Martin, Albro. *Railroads Triumphant.* New York: Oxford University Press, 1992.

Matteucci, Marco. *History of the Motor Car.* New York: Crown, 1970.

May, George S. *Automobile Industry, 1920–1980.* New York: Facts On File, 1989.

McCarthy, Joe. "The Lincoln Highway." New York: *American Heritage Magazine,* June 1974.

McCraw, Thomas K. *American Business 1920–2000: How It Works.* Wheeling, Ill.: Harlan Davidson, 2000.

Nader, Ralph. *Unsafe at Any Speed.* New York: Grossman, 1965.

Norbye, Jan P. *The 100 Greatest American Cars.* Blue Ridge Summit, Penn.: Tab Books, 1981.

Ogburn, Charleton. "The Motorcar versus America." *American Heritage,* June 1970.

Oppel, Frank, ed. *Motoring in America: The Early Years.* Secaucus, N. J.: Castle Books, 1903 (reprint 1989).

Presbrey, Frank. *Motoring Abroad.* Deposit, N. Y.: The Outing Press, 1908.

Rae, John Bell. *American Automobile Manufacturers: The First Forty Years.* Philadelphia: The Clinton Company, 1959.

———. *The American Automobile.* Chicago: University of Chicago Press, 1965.

———. *The American Automobile Industry.* Boston: Twayne Publishers, 1984.

Roberts, Peter. *Veteran and Vintage Cars.* New York: Crescent Books, 1982.

———. *The History of the Automobile.* New York: Exeter Books, 1984.

Rothchild, Emma. *Paradise Lost.* New York: Random House, 1973.

Scharchburg, Richard P. *Carriages without Horses: J. Frank Duryea and the Birth of the American Automobile Industry.* Warrendale, Penn.: Society of Automotive Engineers, 1993.

Schroeder, Joseph J. *The Wonderful World of Automobiles 1895–1930.* Chicago: Follett, 1971.

Seltzer, Lawrence Howard. *A Financial History of the American Auto Industry.* Boston: Houghton Mifflin, 1928.

Shimokawa, Koichi S. *The Japanese Automobile Industry: A Business History.* Atlantic Highlands: Humanities Press International, 1994.

Sloan, Alfred P. Jr. *My Years with General Motors.* Garden City, N.Y.: Doubleday, 1963.

Smith, Philip Hillyer. *Wheels within Wheels.* New York: Funk and Wagnalls, 1968.

Smith, Roger B. *Building on 75 Years of Excellence: The General Motors Story.* New York: The Newcomen Society, 1984.

Sogo, Shinsaku. *From Foe to Friend: One Man's Experience in Japanese American Trade.* Golden, Colo.: Fulcrum Publishing, 2002.

Stein, Ralph. *The Treasury of the Automobile.* New York: The Ridge Press, 1961.

Stover, John. *The Life and Decline of the American Railroad.* New York: Oxford University Press, 1970.

Taylor, Frederick W. *The Principles of Scientific Management.* New York: Harper and Brothers, 1911.

Tunis, Edwin. *Wheels: A Pictorial History.* Cleveland, Ohio: The World Publishing Company, 1955.

Ware, Michael E. *Veteran Motor Cars.* Aylesbury, England: Shire Publications, 1983.

Weisberger, Bernard A. *The Dream Maker: William C. Durant.* Boston: Little, Brown, 1979.

Womack, James, Daniel Jones, and Daniel Roos. *The Machine That Changed the World.* New York: HarperCollins, 1991.

Wyatt, Horace Mathew. *The Motor Vehicle.* London: Pitman and Son, 1918.

Yates, Brock. *The Decline and Fall of the American Automobile Industry.* New York: Empire Books, 1983.

———. "The Greatest American Cars." *American Heritage,* March 1986.

———. "Dussenberg: The Most Magnificent American Car." *American Heritage,* July 1994.

Chapter 6. Henry Ford (1863–1947): Getting the Costs Down

Brinkley, Douglas. *Wheels for the World: Henry Ford, His Company and a Century of Progress.* New York: Viking, 2003.

Burlingame, Roger. *Henry Ford.* New York: Alfred A. Knopf, 1961.

Clancy, Louise B. and Florence Davies. *The Believer: The Life Story of Mrs. Henry Ford.* New York: Coward-McCann, 1960.

Ford, Henry, and Samuel Crowther. *My Life and Work.* Garden City, N.Y.: Doubleday, Page & Co., 1923.

———. *Today and Tomorrow.* Garden City, N.Y.: Doubleday, Page & Co., 1926.

———. *Moving Forward.* Garden City, N.Y.: Doubleday, Doran, 1930.

Ford Motor Company. *The Ford Industries.* Detroit: Ford Motor Company, 1924.

———. *Thirty Years of Progress 1903–1973.* Dearborn, Mich.: 1933.

———. *Ford at Fifty: 1903–1953.* New York: Simon & Schuster, 1953.

Gelderman, Carol W. *Henry Ford: The Wayward Capitalist.* New York: Dial Press, 1981.

Graves, Ralph Henry. *The Triumph of an Idea.* New York: Doubleday, Doran, 1934.

Guther, John. *Inside U. S. A.* Philadelphia: Curtis Publishing Company, 1947.

Halberstam, David. "Citizen Ford." *American Heritage,* October 1986.

Jardim, Anne. *The First Henry Ford.* Cambridge, Mass.: MIT Press, 1970.

Lacy, Robert. *Ford: The Man and the Machine.* Boston: Little, Brown, 1986.

Leonard, Jonathan Norton. *The Tragedy of Henry Ford.* New York: G. P. Putnam's Sons, 1932.

Lewis, David L. *The Public Image of Henry Ford.* Detroit: Wayne State University Press, 1976.

Lohr, Lenox R. *Fifty Years of Motor Cars, 1895–1945.* New York: The Newcomen Society, 1946.

Merz, Charles. *And Then Came Ford.* Garden City, N.Y.: Doubleday, Doran, 1929.

Nevins, Allan. *Ford: The Times, the Man, the Company.* New York: C. Scribner's Sons, 1954.

Nevins, Allan and Frank Ernest Hill. *Ford: Expansion and Challenge 1915–1933.* New York: C. Scribner's Sons, 1957.

———. *Ford: Decline and Rebirth 1933–1962.* New York: C. Scribner's Sons, 1963.

Olsen, Sidney. *Young Henry Ford.* Detroit: Wayne State University Press, 1963.

Sorensen, Charles E. and Samuel T. Williamson. *My Forty Years with Ford.* New York: W. W. Norton & Company, 1956.

Stephenson, Albert T. "Secrets of the Model T." *American Heritage,* July 1989.

Sward, Keith Theodore. *The Legend of Henry Ford.* New York: Rinehart, 1948.

Taylor, Frederick W. *The Principles of Scientific Management.* New York: Harper and Brothers, 1911.

White, E. B. *Farewell to Model T.* New York: G. P. Putnam's Sons, 1936.

Wik, Reynold M. *Henry Ford and Grass Roots America.* Ann Arbor: University of Michigan Press, 1972.

Chapter 7. Electronics: The Basic Material (1880–2000)

Aitken, Hugh G. J. *The Continuous Wave: Technology and American Radio, 1900–1932.* Princeton, N.J.: Princeton University Press, 1985.

American Telephone and Telegraph Company. *1904 Annual Report of the Directors.* Boston: Alfred Mudge and Son, 1905.

Archer, G. L. *History of Radio to 1926.* New York: The American Historical Society, 1938.

Atherton, W. A. *From Compass to Computer: A History of Electrical and Electronics Engineering.* San Francisco: San Francisco Press, 1983.

Balderston, William. *Philco: Autobiography of Progress.* New York: The Newcomen Society, 1954.

Barnett, Lincoln. "The Voice Heard Round the World." *American Heritage,* April 1965.

Baron, Robert C. *A High Speed Transistorized Analog to Digital Computer.* Philadelphia: Eastern Joint Computer Conference, 1959.

———. *Designing Minimum Power Digital Circuits for Mariner II and Other Spacecrafts.* (NATO) Scientific Symposium on Micropower Electronics held in France, England, Germany, and Italy, June 1963. Published in *Micropower Electronics.* London: Pergamon Press, 1964.

———. *Semiconductor Memories.* Munich: Third International Conference on Microelectronics, 1968.

Bazerman, Charles. *The Language of Edison's Light.* Cambridge, Mass.: MIT Press, 2002.

Bendz, W. I. *Electronics for Industry.* New York: John Wiley and Sons, 1947.

Boda, Peter. "Breaking the Connection: A Short History of AT&T." *American Heritage,* June 1985.

Brandt, Nat. "Nikola Tesla." *American Heritage,* August 1977.

Braun, Ernest and Stuart Macdonald. *Revolution in Miniature: The History and Impact of Semiconductor Electronics Re-Explored.* New York: Cambridge University Press, 1982.

Briggs, Asa. *The BBC: The First Fifty Years.* New York: Oxford University Press, 1985.

Brooks, John. *Telephone: The First Hundred Years.* New York: Harper & Row, 1975.

Brown, Les. *Television: The Business Behind the Box*. New York: Harcourt Brace Jovanovich, 1971.

Buderi, Robert. *The Invention That Changed the World: The Story of Radar from War to Peace*. Boston: Little, Brown, 1996.

Casson, Herbert Newton. *The History of the Telephone*. Chicago: A. C. McClurg, 1910.

Caverly, Don P. *A Primer of Electronics*. New York: McGraw-Hill, 1943.

Chandler, Alfred. *Inventing the Electronic Century: The Epic Story of the Consumer Electronics and Computer Industries*. New York: Free Press, 2001.

Chapuis, R. J. and A. E. Joes. *Electronics, Computers and Telephone Switching: A Book of Technological History*. Barking, England: Elsevier Science, 1990.

Cheney, Margaret. *Tesla, Man Out of Time*. New York: Dell, 1988.

Chew, V. K. *Talking Machines*. London: Her Majesty's Stationery Office, 1967.

Clark, Ronald W. *Edison: The Man Who Made the Future*. New York: G. P. Putnam's Sons, 1977.

Coleman, John S. *The Business Machine*. New York: The Newcomen Society, 1949.

DeForest, Lee. *Father of Radio*. Chicago: Wilcon and Follett, 1950.

D'Humy, Fernand E. *The Birth of the Vacuum Tube: The Edison Effect*. New York: The Newcomen Society, 1949.

Dorfman, Nancy. *Innovation and Market Structure: Lessons from the Computer and Semiconductor Industries*. Cambridge, England: Ballinger, 1987.

Douglas, Susan. *Inventing American Broadcasting, 1899–1920*. Baltimore: John Hopkins Press, 1987.

Dummer, Geoffrey W. *Electronic Inventions and Discoveries*. London: Pergamon Press, 1983.

Dunlap, Orin Elmer. *Marconi: The Man and His Wireless*. New York: Macmillan, 1937.

———. *Radio and Television Almanac*. New York: Harper, 1951.

Dunnine, John. *On the Air: The Encyclopedia of Old Time Radio*. New York: Oxford University Press, 1998.

Everson, George. *The Story of Television*. New York: W. W. Norton & Company, 1949.

Fisher, David E. *Tube: The Invention of Television*. New York: Harcourt, 1997.

Fisher, David E. and Marshall Jon Fisher. "The Color War." *Invention and Technology*, Winter 1997.

Gorman, Paul A. *Century One … A Prologue*. New York: The Newcomen Society, 1969.

Gould, Jack. *All about Radio and Television*. New York: Random House, 1958.

Gregory, Gene. *Japanese Electronics Technology: Enterprise and Innovation*. New York: John Wiley and Sons, 1986.

Gupta, A., and M. D. Toong. "Microprocessors: The First Twelve Years." *Proceedings of the IEEE*, 1983.

Hammond, John W. *Men and Volts: The Story of General Electric*. Philadelphia: J. B. Lippincott, 1941.

Harborrd, General James G. *The 40 Year March of Radio*. New York: The Newcomen Society, 1943.

Harmon, Jim. *The Great Radio Comedians*. Garden City, N.Y.: Doubleday, 1970.

Hoddeson, Lillian, and Michael Riordan. *Crystal Fire: The Birth of the Information Age*. New York: W. W. Norton & Company, 1997.

Hong, Sungook. *Wireless: From Marconi's Black Box to the Audion*. Cambridge, Mass.: MIT Press, 2001.

Hurdeman, Anton A. *The Worldwide History of Telecommunications*. Hoboken, N. J.: John Wiley and Sons, 2003.

Institute of Radio Engineers. *Proceeding of the IRE, 1912–1962, Fiftieth Anniversary*. New York: Institute of Radio Engineers, 1962.

Ives, H. E. "Television." *Bell Systems Technical Journal*, 6 (October 1927).

Jackson, Tim. *Inside Intel: Andy Grove and the Rise of the World's Most Powerful Chip Company*. New York: Dutton, 1997.

Jakle, John A. *City Lights: Illuminating the American Night.* Baltimore: John Hopkins University Press, 2001.

Johnstone, Robert. *We Were Burning: Japanese Entrepreneurs and the Forging of the Electronic Age.* New York: Basic Books, 1999.

Josephsen, Matthew. *Edison. A Biography.* New York: McGraw-Hill, 1959.

Keonjian, Edward, ed. *Micropower Electronics.* Oxford, England: Pergamon Press, 1964.

Lessing, Lawrence. *Men of High Fidelity.* New York: Lippincott, 1956.

Lewis, Thomas. *Empire of the Air: The Men Who Made Radio.* New York: Edward Burlingame Books, 1991.

Macauley, David. *The Way Things Work.* Boston: Houghton Mifflin, 1988.

MacKenzie, Catherine. *Alexander Graham Bell: The Man Who Contracted Space.* Boston: Houghton Mifflin, 1928.

MacLaurin, W. Rupert. *Invention and Innovation in the Radio Industry.* New York: Macmillan, 1949.

Marquis, Alice Goldfarb. "Radio Grows Up." *American Heritage,* August 1983.

McCraw, Thomas K., ed. *America versus Japan: A Study in Business/ Government Relations.* Boston, Mass.: Harvard University Press, 1986.

Millard, Andre. *Edison and the Business of Invention.* Baltimore: Johns Hopkins Press, 1990.

Mitchell, Don G. *Sylvania During Fifty Years 1901–1951.* New York: The Newcomen Society, 1951.

Moore, Gordon. "Intel: Memories and Microprocessors." In *Power of Boldness: Ten Master Builders of American Industry Tell Their Success Stories.* Washington, D.C.: Joseph Henry Press, 1996.

Morgan, Jane. *Electronics in the West: The First Fifty Years.* Palo Alto, Calif.: National Press Books, 1967.

Morita, Akio. *Made in Japan.* New York: Dutton, 1986.

Newsome, Iris. *Wonderful Inventions: Motion Pictures, Broadcasting and Recorded Sounds at the Library of Congress.* Washington, D.C.: Library of Congress, 1985.

Noyce, Robert N. "From Relays to MPU's." *Computer,* December 1976.
———. "Hardware Prospects and Limitations." *In the Computer Age: A Twenty Year View.* Cambridge: MIT Press, 1980.

Page, Arthur Wilson. *The Bell Telephone System.* New York: Harper and Brothers, 1941.

Paper, Lewis J. *Empire: William S. Paley and the Making of CBS.* New York: St. Martin's Press, 1987.

Passer, Harold C. *The Electrical Manufacturers, 1875–1900.* Cambridge, Mass.: Harvard University Press, 1953.

Petrakas, Harry Mark. *The Founders Touch: The Life of Paul Galvin of Motorola.* New York: McGraw-Hill, 1965.

Probst, George, E. *The Indispensable Man: The Story of Thomas Alva Edison.* New York: Shorewood Publishers, 1962.

Reed, Philip D. *Facets of a Diamond Anniversary in America* (General Electric Company). New York: The Newcomen Society, 1953.

Ritchie, Michael. *Please Stand By: The Prehistory of Television.* New York: Overlook Books, 1996.

Romano, Frank. "The Phototypsetting Era." *Printing History,* vol. 13, #2.

Saxenian, Anna Lee. *Regional Advantage: Culture and Competition in Silicon Valley and Route 128.* Cambridge, Mass.: Harvard University Press, 1994.

Schlesinger, Carl. *The Biography of Ottmar Mergenthaler.* New Castle, Del.: Oak Knoll, 1989.

Schwartz, Evan I. *The Last Lone Inventory.* New York: HarperCollins, 2000.

Settel, Irving. *A Pictorial History of Radio.* New York: Grosset and Dunlap, 1960.

Sigismund, Charles G. *Champions of Silicon Valley: Visionary Thinking from Today's Technology Pioneers.* New York: John Wiley and Sons, 2000.

Staples, Philip C. *Patent No. 174,465.* New York: The Newcomen Society, 1947.

Stashower, Daniel. *The Boy Genius and the Mogul: The Untold Story of Television.* New York: Broadway Books, 2002.

Susskind, Charles. *The Early History of Electronics,* 6 parts. New York: IEEE Spectrum, 1968–1970.

Todd, Daniel. *The World Electronics Industry.* New York: Routledge Chapman, & Hall, 1990.

Wachhorst, Wyn. *Thomas Alva Edison.* Cambridge, Mass.: MIT Press, 1981.

Williams, Christian. *Lead, Follow or Get Out of the Way: The Story of Ted Turner.* New York: New York Times Books, 1981.

Zworykin, V. K. and G. A. Morton *Television.* New York: John Wiley and Sons, 1940.

Chapter 8. David Sarnoff (1891–1971): The Practical Dreamer

Bilby, Kenneth. *The General: David Sarnoff and the Rise of the Communication Industry.* New York: Harper & Row, 1986.

Dembling, Merwin. *Scientists on Science.* New York: Dutton, 1965.

Douglas, Alan. *Radio Manufacturers of the 1920s.* Vestal, N.Y.: Vestal Press, 1988.

Dreher, Carl. *Sarnoff: An American Success.* New York: Quadrangle, 1977.

Graham, Margaret. *R.C.A. and the Video Disc: The Business of Research.* New York: Cambridge University Press, 1986.

Lavine, Sigmund A. *Famous Industrialists.* New York: Dodd, Mead, 1961.

Lyons, Eugene. *David Sarnoff: A Biography.* New York: Harper & Row, 1966.

MacLaurin, William Rupert. *Invention and Innovation in the Radio Industry.* New York: Macmillan, 1949.

McCaw, Thomas K. *American Business and How It Works.* Wheeling, Ill.: Harlan Davidson, 2000.

Myers, Elizabeth. *David Sarnoff: Radio and TV Boy.* Indianapolis, Ind.: Bobbs-Merrill, 1972.

Radio Corporation of America. *Annual Reports.* New York: Radio Corporation of America, 1933–1960.

Sarnoff, David. *Edison (1847–1931).* New York: The Newcomen Society, 1948.

———. *Looking Ahead: The Papers of David Sarnoff.* New York: McGraw-Hill, 1968.

Sobel, Robert. *R. C. A.* New York: Stein and Day, 1986.

Sterling, Christopher H. *The Radio Industry.* Introduction by David Sarnoff. New York, 1928 (reprint 1974).

Wisdom Magazine. *The Universe of David Sarnoff.* Beverly Hills, Calif.: The Wisdom Society, 1958.

Chapter 9. Computers: The Information Age (1945–2000)

Angel, Karen. *Inside Yahoo.* New York: John Wiley and Sons, 2002.

Aspray, William. *John Von Neumann and the Origins of Modern Computing.* Cambridge, Mass.: MIT Press, 1990.

———. *Computer: A History of the Information Machine.* New York: Basic Books, 1996.

Awad, Elias M. *Business Data Processing.* Englewood Cliffs, N.J.: Prentice-Hall, 1975.

Baron, Robert C. *A Universal Circuit and Packaging Approach to the Design of Integrated Circuit Modules, Memories, Systems and Computers.* Munich: Second International Symposium on Microelectronics, 1965.

———. *The Computer Manufacturer.* Washington, D.C.: Industrial College of the Armed Forces, 1974.

———. *What Was It Like Orville: Memories from the Early Space Program.* Golden, Colo.: Fulcrum Publishing, 2002.

Baron, Robert C., and Albert T. Piccirilli. *Digital Logic and Computer Operation.* New York: McGraw-Hill, 1967.

Bashe, Charles, L. R. Johnson, J. H. Pugh, and Emerson W. Pugh. *IBM's Early Computers.* Cambridge, Mass.: MIT Press, 1984.

Belden, Thomas and Marva Thomas. *The Lengthening Shadow: The Life of Thomas J. Watson.* Boston: Little, Brown, 1962.

Berkeley, E. C. *Giant Brains or Machines That Think.* New York: John Wiley and Sons, 1949.

Bernstein, Jeremy. *The Analytical Engine.* New York: Vintage Books, 1966.

Bourne, Charles P. and Trudi Bellardo Hahn. *A History of Online Information Services, 1963–1976.* Cambridge, Mass.: MIT Press, 2003.

Butcher, Lee. *Accidental Millionaire. The Rise and Fall of Steve Jobs at Apple Computer.* New York: Paragon House, 1988.

Butter, Andrea and David Pogue. *Plotting Palm.* New York: John Wiley and Sons, 2002.

Ceruzzi, Paul E. *A History of Modern Computing.* Cambridge, Mass.: MIT Press, 1998.

Chandler, Alfred. *Inventing the Electronic Century: The Epic Story of the Consumer Electronics and Computer Industries.* New York: Free Press, 2001.

Clark, Jim and Owen Edward. *Netscape Time.* New York: St. Martin's Press, 1998.

Coleman, John S. *The Business Machine.* New York: The Newcomen Society, 1949.

Cortada, James W. *Before the Computer: IBM, NCR, Burroughs and Remington Rand and the Industry They Created 1865–1956.* Princeton, N.J.: Princeton University Press, 1993.

Dertouzos, Michael L. and Joel Moses, eds. *The Computer Age: A Twenty-Year View.* Cambridge, Mass.: MIT Press, 1979.

Diebold, John. *Automation.* New York: Van Nostrand, 1953.

Diehr, George. *Business Programming with Basic.* New York: John Wiley and Sons, 1972.

Eckert, J. Presper. "Thoughts on the History of Computing." *Computer,* December 1976.

Elbourn, R. D., and W. H. Ware. "The Evolution of Concepts and Languages of Computing." *Proceedings of the IRE, 1912–1962.* New York: Institute of Radio Engineers, May 1962.

Ferguson, Charles H. *Computer Wars: How the West Can Win in a Post-IBM World.* New York: Random House, 1993.

Fisher, Franklin M., et al. *IBM and the U.S. Data Processing Industry.* New York: Praeger Publishers, 1983.

Fishman, Katharine Davis. *The Computer Establishment.* New York: Harper & Row, 1981.

Flores, Ivan. *Computer Organization.* Englewood Cliffs, N.J.: Prentice-Hall, 1969.

Freiberger, Paul. *Fire in the Valley: The Making of the Personal Computer.* Berkeley, Calif.: Osborne/McGraw-Hill, 1984.

Gear, C. W. *Computer Organization and Programming.* New York: McGraw-Hill, 1969.

Goldstine, Herman Heine. *The Computer from Pascal to von Neumann.* Princeton, N.J.: Princeton University Press, 1972.

Goldstine, H. H. and John von Neumann. *Planning and Coding Problems for an Electronic Computing Instrument.* New York: Van Nostrand Reinhold, 1947.

Greenia, Mark W. *History of Computing: An Encyclopedia of the People and Machines That Made Computer History.* Sacramento, Calif.: Lexikon Services, 1994.

Gruenberger, Fred and David Babcock. *Computing with Minicomputers.* New York: John Wiley and Sons, 1973.

Halberstram, David. *The Fifties.* New York: Villard Books, 1993.

Hodges, Alan. *Alan Turing: The Enigma.* New York: Simon & Schuster, 1983.

Hopper, Grace W., and J. W. Mauchly. "Influences of Programming Techniques on the Design of Computers." *Proceedings of the Institute of Radio Engineers* 41 (October 1953).

IBM. *IBM Annual Reports.* Armonk: N.Y.: IBM, 1935–2002.

Jager, Rama Dev, and Ortiz Rafael. *In the Company of Giants: Candid Conversations with the Visionaries of the Digital World.* New York: McGraw-Hill, 1998.

Kidder, Tracy. *The Soul of a New Machine.* Boston: Little, Brown, 1981.

Lindgren, Michael. *Glory and Failure: The Difference Engine of Johann Muller, Charles Babbage and Georg and Edvard Scheutz.* Cambridge, Mass.: MIT Press, 1990.

Lo, Arthur W. "Development in High Speed Switching Elements." *Proceedings of the IRE, 1912–1962.* New York: Institute of Radio Engineers, 1962.

Lundstrom, David E. *A Few Good Men from Univac.* Cambridge, Mass.: MIT Press, 1987.

Macdonald, Ray W. *Strategy for Growth: The Story of the Burroughs Corporation.* New York: The Newcomen Society, 1977.

Macrae, Norman. *John von Neumann.* New York: Pantheon, 1992.

Martin, James. *Future Developments in Telecommunications.* Englewood Cliffs, N.J.: Prentice Hall, 1977.

McCarthy, Scott. *Eniac: The Triumphs and Tragedies of the World's First Computer.* New York: Walker, 1990.

Mindell, David A. *Between Human and Machine: Feedback, Control and Computing.* Baltimore: John Hopkins University Press, 2002.

Moschovitis, Christos and Hillary Poole. *History of the Internet: A Chronology 1843 to the Present.* New York: ABC-CLIO, 1999.

Myers, Ware. "Key Developments in Computer Technology: A Survey." *Computer,* November 1976.

Nash, Stephen G., ed. *A History of Scientific Computing.* Reading, Mass.: Addison-Wesley, 1990.

Norberg, Arthur L. "The History of Computing." *IEEE Transactions on Education,* November 1984.

Packard, David. *The H-P Way: How Bill Hewlett and I Built Our Company.* New York: HarperCollins, 1995.

Popps, John R. "New Univac Solid State Computer." Cincinnati, Ohio: Spring Technical Conference on Data Processing, 1959.

Pugh, Emerson W. *Memories That Shaped an Industry: Decisions Leading to the IBM 360.* Cambridge, Mass.: MIT Press, 1984.

———. *Building IBM: Shaping an Industry.* Cambridge, Mass.: MIT Press, 1995.

Ritchie, David. *The Computer Pioneers: The Making of the Modern Computer.* New York: Simon & Schuster, 1986.

Rodgers, William. *Think: A Biography of the Watsons and IBM.* New York: Stein and Day, 1961.

Rosenberg, Jerry Martin. *The Computer Prophets.* New York: Macmillan, 1965.

Serrell, R., M. M. Astrahan, G. W. Patterson, and I. B. Pyne. "The Evolution of Computing Machines and Systems." *Proceedings of the IRE, 1912–1962.* New York: Institute of Radio Engineers, 1962.

Shurkin, Joel N. *Engines of the Mind: A History of the Computer.* New York: W. W. Norton & Company, 1984.

Sobel, Robert. *IBM: Colossus in Transition.* New York: Times Books, 1981.

"The State of Computing." IEEE Centennial. *Computer* 17 (10), October 1984.

Sutherland, Ivan E. "Computer Displays." *Scientific American,* June 1970.

Von Neumann, John. *The Computer and the Brain.* New Haven, Conn.: Yale University Press, 1950.

Wallace, James. *Hard Drive: Bill Gates and the Making of Microsoft.* New York: John Wiley and Sons, 1992.

Wang, An and Eugene Lindis. *Lessons: An Autobiography.* New York: Addison-Wesley, 1986.

Watson, Thomas J. *Exploring Life: The Autobiography of Thomas J. Watson.* New York: Appleton, 1926.

Watson, Thomas J. Jr. *A Business and Its Beliefs.* New York: McGraw-Hill, 1963.

Watson, Thomas J. Jr. and Peter Petre. *Father, Son and Co.: My Life at IBM and Beyond.* New York: Bantam, 1990.

Wiener, Norbert. *Cybernetics.* New York: John Wiley and Sons, 1948.

Williams, Michael R. *A History of Computing Technology.* Englewood Cliffs, N.J.: Prentice Hall, 1985.

Worthy, James C. *William C. Norris: Portrait of a Maverick.* Cambridge, Mass.: Ballegher Publishing, 1987.

Wulforst, Harry. *Breakthrough to the Computer Age.* New York: Scribner's, 1982.

Zellers, John A. *The Typewriter.* New York: The Newcomen Society, 1948.

Zuboff, Shosana. *In the Age of the Smart Machine.* New York: Basic Books, 1988.

Chapter 10. Kenneth Olsen (1926–): The Commonplace Computer

Allison, David. *Oral History Interview with Ken Olsen.* Washington, D.C.: National Museum of American History, 1988.

Digital Equipment Corporation. *Annual Reports.* Maynard, Mass.: Digital Equipment Corporation, 1967–1995.

———. *Report of the 1983 Annual Meeting of Stockholders.* Boston: Digital Equipment Corporation, 1983.

———. *Report of the 1986 Annual Meeting of Stockholders.* Boston: Digital Equipment Corporation, 1986.

"Digital Equipment: A Step Ahead in Linking Computers." *Business Week* April 21, 1986.

Jones-D'Agostino, Steven. "It's Better to Work with People." *Worcester Business Journal,* May 24, 1999.

Olsen, Kenneth H. *Digital Equipment Corporation: The First Twenty-five Years.* New York: The Newcomen Society, 1983.

———. *Digital from the Beginning.* Maynard, Mass.: DEC Video, 1992.

Osterland, Andrew. "Hitting the DEC." *Financial World,* May 20, 1996.

Pearson, Jamie Parker, ed. *Digital at Work: Snapshots from the First 35 Years.* Burlington, Mass.: Digital Press, 1992.

Rifkin, Glen, and George Harrar. *The Ultimate Entrepreneur: The Story of Ken Olsen and DEC.* Chicago: Contemporary Books, 1988.

Chapter 11. The Nature of Professional and Personal Change

Abernathy, William J., Kim B. Clark, and Alan M. Kantrow. *Industrial Renaissance.* New York: Basic Books, 1983.

Baron, Robert. *High Technology and America in the Twenty-First Century.* Concord, Mass.: Meeting of Latin American Fulbright Scholars, 1988.

———. *Twentieth Century America: Key Events in History.* Golden, Colo.: Fulcrum Publishing, 1996.

———. *An Overview of the Twentieth Century: Longer, Wider but Shallower.* Cambridge, Mass.: American Academy of Arts and Sciences, 1997.

———. *Airplanes and Airlines in the Twentieth Century.* San Mateo, Calif.: San Mateo County Historical Society, 2002.

Blackford, Mansel G. *A History of Small Business in America.* New York: Macmillan, 1992.

Boorstin, Daniel J. *The Discoverers.* New York: Random House, 1983.

Bowser, Hal. "We Get the Technology We Deserve." *American Heritage,* November 1985.

Bradley, Omar N. *A Soldier's Story.* New York: Henry Holt, 1951.

Brooks, John. *The Go Go Years.* New York: Weybright and Talley, 1973.

———. *The Autobiography of American Business.* Garden City, N.Y.: Doubleday and Company, 1974.

Burke, James. *Connections.* London: Macmillan, 1978.

Burns, James MacGregor. *Leadership.* New York: Harper & Row, 1979.

Carlson, Richard, and Bruce Goldman. *Fast Forward: Where Technology, Demographics and History Will Take America.* New York: HarperBusiness, 1994.

Chandler, Alfred D. and Herman Daems. *Managerial Hierarchies.* Cambridge, Mass.: Harvard University Press, 1980.

Clark, Ronald W. *Works of Man.* New York: Viking Penguin, 1985.

Cohen, Eliot A. *Supreme Command: Soldiers, Statesmen and Leadership.* New York: The Free Press, 2002.

Cowan, Ruth Schwartz. *A Social History of American Technology.* New York: Oxford University Press, 1997.

Cyert, Richard M. and David C. Mowery. *The Impact of Technological Change on Employment and Economic Growth.* New York: HarperBusiness, 1988.

DiBacco, Thomas. *Made in the U.S.A.* New York: Harper & Row, 1987.

Drucker, Peter F. *The Practice of Management*. New York: Harper & Row, 1954.

Gardner, John William. *Self Renewal: The Individual and the Innovative Society*. New York: Harper & Row, 1965.

———. *On Leadership*. New York: Free Press, 1990.

Graham, Benjamin. *The Intelligent Investor*. New York: Harper & Row, 1973.

Iverson, Kenneth F. *Plain Talk: Lessons from a Business Maverick*. New York: John Wiley and Sons, 1998.

Kennedy, Paul. *Preparing for the Twenty First Century*. New York: Random House, 1993.

Lamoreaux, Naomi R., Daniel Raff, and Peter Tamin. "Beyond Markets and Hierarchies: Toward a New Synthesis of American Business History." *American Historical Review*, April 2003.

Levitt, Theodore. *The Marketing Mode*. New York: McGraw-Hill, 1969.

Lewis, Hunter, and Donald Allison. *The Real World War*. New York: Coward, McCann & Geoghegan, 1982.

Lynch, Peter, and John Rothchild. *Beating the Street*. New York: Simon & Schuster, 1993.

MacGregor, Douglas. *The Human Side of Enterprise*. New York: McGraw-Hill, 1960.

McCullough, David. *John Adams*. New York: Simon & Schuster, 2001.

Miller, Harold. *Publishing: A Leap from Mind to Mind*. Golden, Colo.: Fulcrum Publishing, 2003.

Naisbett, John. *Megatrends*. New York: Warner Books, 1982.

Peters, Tom. *The Circle of Innovation: You Can't Shrink Your Way to Greatness*. New York: Alfred A. Knopf, 1997.

Peters, Tom and Nancy Austin. *A Passion for Excellence*. New York: Random House, 1985.

Principe, Lawrence M. *History of Science: Antiquity to 1700*. Video and Audio, Chantilly, Va.: The Teaching Company, 2002.

Scharkenbach, William W. *Deming's Road to Continual Improvement*. New York: Simon & Schuster, 1991.

Smithsonian Institution. *The Smithsonian Book of Invention*. Washington, D.C.: Smithsonian Exposition Books, 1978.

Index

AT&T (American Telephone and Telegraph), 175–176, 177, 181, 190, 203, 213, 215, 216, 217, 235, 260, 261, 278, 279, 288, 297, 305

Atwater Kent, 5, 181

Auburn Automobile Company, 133

Auburn Bobtail Speedster, 133

Audion tube, 177

Audio power transistors, 197

Austin, 130, 143

Automatic Data Processing, 12, 242, 256

Automobile electronics, 207

Automobile industry, 60–61, 76, 229, 263–264

Automobiles, 10, 104–147, 207, 290; early days of, 105–111; electric, 106, 108, 116, 130, 147, 207; engineering and production phase, 116–124; entrepreneurs and, 111–116; foreign challenges, 76, 141–145; government and, 139–141; marketing, styling, and financial phases, 124–130; radios in, 183; road improvements and, 136–139; safety of, 140

Auto Nation, 12

Auto Show, 115

AutoZone, 12

Avco, 183

Babbage, Charles, 225, 268

Backward integration, 64

Baird, John Logic, 188

Baker, 111

Baldwin Locomotive, 5

Ballistic Missile Early Warning System, 218

Ballistic Research Laboratory, 231

Balloon tires, 138

Baltimore, Lord, 14

Baltimore and Ohio Railroad, 37

Banking, 38, 206, 299

Bank of America, 287

Bank of New York, 38

Banquet Foods, 221, 236

Bardeen, John, 195

Barry, Dave, 285

Bartering, 38

BASIC, 245, 253, 255, 257

Basic oxygen process, 75

Bath Iron Works, 67

Bay State Lighting Company, 178

Bay State Works, 55

BBC, 188

Beckman, Arnold, 197

Beckman Instruments, 197

Bell, Alexander Graham, 40, 169, 173–174, 175, 196

Bell, Gordon, 283

Bell Company, 174–175

Bell Labs, 194–195, 197, 253, 261

Belmont, 183

Bench, Martha, 150

Bendix, 6, 228–229, 234

Bennett, Harry, 134

Benny, Jack, 183

Bentley, 142

Benz, Karl, 106

Benz & Cie, 106

Bergen, Edgar, 183

Berlin Olympics, 189

Berry, Clifford, 230

Berwick Electric, 130

Bessemer, Henry, 53, 54, 74

Bessemer process, 54, 55, 95

Bessemer Steel, 97

Bethlehem Iron, 53, 58, 66

Bethlehem Steel, 5, 62, 64, 66–69, 70, 72, 84, 292, 298, 302, 305

Beverly, 111

Bicycles, 41, 106

Billings, John Shaw, 226

Binary code, 253

Binary data, 251

Bizmac, 235

Black, Clarence A., 151

Blacksmiths, 16, 49

Blackstone River, 30

Blanc, Honore, 26

Blanchard, Thomas, 27, 31, 106

Blind-bombing systems, 218

Blockbuster, 12, 308

Block making, 18

Blue network, 181, 215

Bluhdorn, Charles, 295

BMW, 142, 207

Board of Trade, 15

Boeing, 301

Bolt, Beraneck and Newman, 262

Bonus plans, 68

Boole, George, 225, 227, 268

Boolean algebra, 225, 226

Bori, Lucrezia, 215

Borland, 256

Boston, Massachusetts, 18, 38

Boston and Lowell Railroad, 37

Boston Manufacturing Company, 28

Boston Worcester, 37

Bowditch, Nathaniel, 33

Bradley, Omar, 295

Braintree, Massachusetts, 50–51

Brakes, 114

Brattain, Walter Houser, 195

Braun, Karl Ferdinand, 187, 195

Brice, Fanny, 183

Bricklin, Dan, 254

Bridges, 52, 60, 95

Bridgeton, 145

Brier Hill Steel Company, 69

Briscoe, 130

Britain, industrialization in, 24–25

British Broadcasting Company (BBC), 180

British Law (1750), 18

British Marconi, 212

British National Physical Laboratory, 185

British Petroleum, 145

Broadcom, 12

Bronze, 46

Brooklyn Bridge, 41–42

Brooks, David, 90

Brown, David, 34

Brown, Joseph R., 31

Brown, Moses, 25

Brown and Sharpe, 151

Bryan, William Jennings, 157

Bryant, Clara Jane, 150

Bryant, John, 150

Bryant, Melvin, 150

Buffalo Electric, 111

Bugatti, 142

Buick, David, 107

Buick Motor Company, 118, 125, 127, 128, 130, 131, 133

Bull, 236

Burdett, Winston, 184

Burger King, 12

Burroughs, John, 157, 158

Burroughs, William Seward, 225, 228

Burroughs (company), 6, 228, 232, 234, 237, 241, 269, 290, 305

Burt, William, 226

Bush, George W., 83–84

Bush, Vannevar, 230

Bushnell, Nolan, 257

Busicom, 202

Cable television, 12, 193–194

Cabot, George, 21

Cadillac, 112, 115, 118, 121, 125, 127, 128, 129, 130, 131, 151

Calculators, 7, 196, 225, 231, 233

Cambra Iron Works, 53, 96

Canals, 22, 34, 36–37, 41

Cannonballs, 51

Cannons, 31

Canon, 250, 264

Cantor, Eddie, 183

Capehart, 190

Capital, business need for, 38

Capital investments, 22–23, 70

Carbon, 47

Cardinal Health, 12

Caremark, 12

Carey, G. R., 176